P   R   A   C   T   I   C   A   L

Business Math

Michael D. Tuttle

P R A C T I C A L

Business Math

A P E R F O R M A N C E A P P R O A C H

Michael D. Tuttle

F O U R T H E D I T I O N

wcb

Wm. C. Brown Publishers
Dubuque, Iowa

Book Team

Editor **Brenda Fleming Roesch**
Developmental Editor **Raphael Kadushin**
Production Editor **David A. Welsh**
Designer **Kay Dolby**
Permissions Editor **Vicki Krug**
Product Manager **Linda Gorchels**

wcb group
Wm. C. Brown Chairman of the Board
Mark C. Falb President and Chief Executive Officer

wcb
Wm. C. Brown Publishers, College Division

G. Franklin Lewis Executive Vice-President, General Manager
E. F. Jogerst Vice-President, Cost Analyst
George Wm. Bergquist Editor in Chief
John Stout Executive Editor
Beverly Kolz Director of Production
Chris C. Guzzardo Vice-President, Director of Sales and Marketing
Bob McLaughlin National Sales Manager
Craig S. Marty Manager, Marketing Research
Colleen A. Yonda Production Editorial Manager
Marilyn A. Phelps Manager of Design
Faye M. Schilling Photo Research Manager

Cover designed by Michael Warrell

Chapter opening illustrations by Joe Kohl

Printed in the United States of America
10 9 8 7 6 5 4 3 2 1

Contents

Preface xi
To the Student xv

Section **1** ## Rebuilding the Fundamentals 1

1 Working with Whole Numbers 3

Performance Objectives 3
Reading and Writing Whole Numbers 3
Rounding Off 6
   Rounding Rules 7
Addition 8
   Horizontal Addition 8
Subtraction 9
   Checking Addition Answers by Subtraction 10
   Checking Subtraction Answers by Addition 10
Multiplication 11
   Multiplying by 10, 100, 1,000, etc. 12
Division 13
   Long Division 14
   Dividing by 10, 100, 1,000, etc. 14
   Checking Answers 15
Assignment 17
Mastery Test 23

2 Working with Fractions 27

Performance Objectives 27
Description and Types 27
Interchanging Fraction Types 29
Reducing Fractions 31
   Trial-and-Error Approach 31
Addition and Subtraction 32
   Common Denominator 33
   Mixed Numbers 36
Multiplication and Division 38
   Common Fractions 38
   Mixed Numbers 42
   Increases and Decreases 44
Ratios 44
Assignment 47
Mastery Test 53

3 Working with Decimal Numbers 57

Performance Objectives 57
Reading and Writing Decimal Numbers 57
Rounding Off 60
Addition 62
Subtraction 64
Multiplication 64
Division 65
Changing Fractions to Decimal Numbers 66
Assignment 67
Mastery Test 73

Section 2 — Getting Started—Business Application 75

4 Banking Records 77

Performance Objectives 77
Deposits and Payments 78
Types of Endorsements 79
   Industry Changes 79
Reconciliation of Bank Statement 80
Assignment 83
Mastery Test 91

5 Payroll 95

Performance Objectives 95
Determining Gross Earnings 95
   Overtime 96
Determining Net Pay 97
   Mandatory Deductions 98
   Voluntary Deductions 102
Employer's Payroll Taxes 104
Assignment 105
Mastery Test 111

6 Measurements 115

Performance Objectives 115
Linear Measure 116
Surface Measure 118
Volume Measure 119
The Metric System 120
   Factors 121
Assignment 125
Mastery Test 129

Section 3 — Percent and Its Application to Business 131

7 Percentage 133

Performance Objectives 133
What Percent Means 133
   Percent to a Fraction 134
   Percent to a Decimal 134
   Decimal to a Fraction 134
   Decimal to a Percent 134
Fractional Percent 135
Percentage 136
Four-Step Process 138
Increases and Decreases 139
Assignment 143
Mastery Test 149

8 Insurance 153

Performance Objectives 153
Property Insurance 154
   Fire Insurance 154
Life Insurance 156
   Term Life 156
   Straight Life 156
   Limited Pay Life 156
   Endowment Life 157
Auto Insurance 158
   Comprehensive Insurance 158
   Property Damage Insurance 158
   Collision Insurance 159
Assignment 163
Mastery Test 169

9 Simple Interest 173

Performance Objectives 173
What Interest Means 173
The Calendar 174
The Formula: $I = P \times R \times T$ 178
Assignment 181
Mastery Test 187

10 Promissory Notes 191

Performance Objectives 191
Legal Environment 191
Discounting 193
   Computing Discount 193
   Computing Proceeds 193
Other Interest Problems 197
   Computing Principal 198
   Computing Rate 198
   Computing Time 198
Assignment 201
Mastery Test 207

11 Consumer Credit and Installment Loans 211

Performance Objectives 211
Credit Purchases 211
  Credit Cards 212
  Installment Loans 217
Legal Environment 217
  Use of Payment Tables 224
Computing the Principal Balance 225
Home Mortgages 227
  Maximum Monthly Cost 227
  Advantages 227
  Effect of Interest Rate Difference 227
  Effect of Term Difference 228

Fixed Rate 229
Variable Rate 229
Fixed Payment Amount 229
Variable Payment Amount 229
Balloon Payment 229
Points 229
Closing Costs 230
Escrow Account 230
Early Payoff Penalties 231
Rule of 78s 232
Computer Applications 233
Estimating the Total Interest on an
  Installment Contract 233
Assignment 237
Mastery Test 243

12 Compound Interest and Present Value 247

Performance Objectives 247
Compound Interest 247
  Savings Accounts 249
  Use of Tables 249
Present Value 252
Annuities 256
  Ordinary Annuity 257
  Growth of an Annuity 257
  Annuity Due 260
Sinking Funds 262
Assignment 267
Mastery Test 273

Section

4 Math of Merchandising 275

13 Discounts 277

Performance Objectives 277
Trade Discounts 277
  Finding the Selling Price 277
Direct Method 279
Cash Discounts 281
  Finding the Net Price 282
  End of Month (E.O.M) 284
  Receipt of Goods (R.O.G.) 285
Combination of Cash and Trade Discounts 286
Transportation Charges 287
F.O.B. 287
  F.O.B. Destination 287
  F.O.B. Shipping Point 289
C.O.D. 291
Assignment 293
Mastery Test 299

14 Commission Sales 303

Performance Objectives 303
Determining Net Sales 303
Determining Gross Earnings 305
  Straight Commission 305
  Commission Formula 306
Assignment 309
Mastery Test 315

15 Markup 319

Performance Objectives 319
Markup on Cost 320
Markup on Sales 321
Finding Cost, Sales, Markup, or Markdown 322
  Markdown or Loss 326
Conversion of Markup Rate 327
Catalog Pricing 329
  Additional Trade Discounts 331
Assignment 333
Mastery Test 339

Section **5** **Math of Accounting 341**

16 **Inventory and Turnover 343**

Performance Objectives 343
Inventory Methods 343
Inventory Valuation 345
    L.I.F.O. 345
    F.I.F.O. 349
    Average Cost 352
    Retail Inventory Estimating
    Method 354
    Specific Identification Method 355
Turnover 356
Assignment 357
Mastery Test 363

17 **Depreciation 367**

Performance Objectives 367
Straight-Line Method 368
Units-of-Production Method 371
Sum-of-Years'-Digits (S.O.Y.D.)
Method 372
Declining-Balance Method 375

Accelerated Cost Recovery System
(A.C.R.S.) Method 377
Depletion 378
Partial Year 379
Assignment 385
Mastery Test 391

18 **Taxes 395**

Performance Objectives 395
Property Taxes 395
    Tax Amount 395
    Determining the Tax Rate 397
Customs Duty 398
    Ad Valorem 398
    Specific 398
    Compound Rate 401
Sales Tax 402
Federal Income Tax 403
    Dependents 403
    Deductions 404
    Determining the Tax 409

Assignment 411
Mastery Test 417

19 **Investments 421**

Performance Objectives 421
Risk, Liquidity, and Cost of
Investment 421
Rate of Return 422
The Effect of Inflation 422
Stocks 422
    Common Stock 422
    Preferred Stock 422
    Dividends 422
    Participating 424
    Cumulative 425
Bonds 426
    Commercial Bonds 427
    Government and Municipal
    Bonds 428
Assignment 431
Mastery Test 437

Section **6** **Measuring Business Performance 439**

20 **Financial Statement Analysis 441**

Performance Objectives 441
Balance Sheet 441
Income Statement 445
    Service Firm 446
    Merchandising Firm 448
Ratios 449
    Current Ratio 449
    Acid-Test Ratio 449
    Net Income to Net Sales Ratio 450
    Accounts Receivable to Net Sales
    Ratio 450
    Accounts Payable to Net
    Purchases Ratio 450
Assignment 453
Mastery Test 457

21 **Statistics 461**

Performance Objectives 461
Finding the Mean 462
Finding the Median 462
Finding the Mode 463
Assignment 467
Mastery Test 471

22 **Charts and Graphs 475**

Performance Objectives 475
Circle Graph 475
Bar Graph 476

Section **7** **Measuring Your Success 493**

23 Review 495

Appendix A *Mini Calculator*
Selection and Operation 505
Selection 505
Operation 505
Memory 507
Appendix B *Math Shortcuts* 508
Interest-Time Shortcuts 508

Aliquot Parts 510
Appendix C *Math of Computers*
511
Appendix D *Employment Math Test*
513
Arithmetic Progression 513
A Sample Employment Math Test 514
Appendix E *Reading Market*
Quotations 517

Glossary *519*
Answers to the Student Edition *522*
Index *539*
Record of Performance on Mastery
Tests on the inside back cover.

Preface

Practical Business Math: A Performance Approach, Fourth Edition, has been thoroughly updated and revised to provide the most complete text-workbook available. The step-by-step non-algebraic approach established in earlier editions has been continued with the emphasis on performance objectives, mastery learning, problem solving, and practical applications.

This text-workbook begins with the fundamentals of arithmetic and progresses to applied material of immediate interest to students in business programs. The student will deal with real business problems beginning with the first chapter and continuing with every chapter thereafter. Clear explanations, worked examples, a variety of problems arranged in order of difficulty, and a self-administered mastery test make this text-workbook an enjoyable, practical, and effective learning tool.

The instructor will also enjoy the variety of problems that are available in this text-workbook, wherein various assignment selections can be made in each level of difficulty without exhausting student material.

New in This Edition

Additional Business Application Problems

Reviewers indicated that they would prefer more word-type problems in a new edition. The discovery of lower performance levels in the areas of basic reading, writing, and math skills over recent years has brought attention to the need for materials that give the student more opportunities in which to practice those skills. To that end, this edition has 30 percent more Business Application Problems than the previous edition.

Accelerated Cost Recovery System Coverage

Full coverage of the A.C.R.S. topic has been included in this edition. Textual coverage, examples, exercises, and problems concerning this topic are included in chapter 17, Depreciation.

Home Mortgage Coverage Expanded

A major topic in most consumers' minds, home mortgages are the largest single expenditure in the family budget. This edition has an expanded coverage of the terminology and explanations of this vital area. The student is given a complete orientation to the area, with several worked examples to firm up the understanding of the material. The assignment section contains practical problems in determining the amount of the monthly payment, the escrow amount, and the principal balance.

Markdown is Expanded

The markdown area has been revised and expanded to include more examples and exercises. This area of the text-workbook has many examples that show the student the variety of situations that may develop and therefore require the complete understanding of the markup area. The additional markdown coverage fits very well in the Markup chapter.

How This Book Works

This text uses a performance approach, applying math principles to business problems. Unlike other texts that dwell on theory, this text is of a more practical nature, using actual business situations, business forms, and papers.

It begins with a review of the fundamentals of math. This review may be used to brush up on the basics or to assure confidence; or it may be eliminated if so desired.

What You Can Look for in Each Chapter

* *Performance Objectives*—These objectives guide the student in identifying the important points of the material to be presented.
* *Exercises Follow Each Concept*—As the student reads through the chapter he or she will be required to respond to a number of exercises following numerous examples.
* *Sets of Worked Examples*—The examples along with the exercises actively involve the student throughout the entire book.
* *Progressive Chapter Assignments*—To further enhance this learning process, chapter assignments measure three levels of progress.
* *Level One*—This basic level consists of numerical skill problems that tie concepts together, providing a mixture of the previously developed material.
* *Level Two, Business Application Problems*—This level presents word problems that motivate the student to analyze the material, sort out the facts, use actual business forms and business papers, and develop a solution. These word problems add the dimension of reading and comprehension.
* *Level Three, the Challenge Problem*—This problem is designed to stimulate the student to perform at his or her peak problem-solving level. This progressive problem solving enables both the student and the instructor to better identify the level where each student needs additional help.
* *Mastery Tests*—Student self-tests are found at the end of every chapter. If the student can pass the test successfully, the performance objectives of this chapter have been achieved. Should the student fail to satisfactorily complete the Mastery Test, the student is then directed back to the section that caused the difficulty. Mastery Tests in chapters 1 through 3 have a problem-by-problem diagnostic analysis. This will direct the student back to the area of the text where the concept is presented.

How the Book Is Organized

Chapters are organized into logical, related topic areas. Recognizing that many students have been away from school for some time, the first section, "Rebuilding the Fundamentals" presents a review of fundamental arithmetic processes.

Section 2, "Getting Started—Business Applications" puts Banking Records, Payroll, and Measurements "up front" in the book to provide practical, interesting business material for assignments.

Section 3, "Percent and its Application to Business" provides six chapters on this vital topic—from Simple Interest to Installment Loans.

Section 4, "Math of Merchandising" covers chapters on Markup, Commission Sales and Discounts.

Section 5, "Math of Accounting" includes Inventory, Depreciation, Taxes, and Investments.

Section 6, "Measuring Business Performance" offers three chapters—Financial Statement Analysis, Statistics, and Charts and Graphs.

"Measuring Your Success" reviews the twenty-two chapters and prepares the student for the final examination. This organizational arrangement provides depth of coverage while allowing the instructor flexibility.

Appendixes Five separate appendixes offer students additional interest-enhancing and skill-building information.

Mini Calculator Selection and Operation, appendix A, introduces students to the mini calculator and shows them not only how to select a calculator, but also how to skillfully operate one.

Math Shortcuts, appendix B, offers students tested methods used in reducing calculation steps.

Math of Computers, appendix C, introduces students to the binary code.

Employment Math Text, appendix D, provides students with a sample mathematical screening device commonly used by business firms.

Reading Stock Market Quotations, appendix E, shows students how to read stock and bond quotations commonly printed in the business section of most newspapers.

The *Glossary* provides definitions of commonly used business terms; an *Index* is also provided.

Answers to the Student Edition appear at the end of the text, and provide students with a workable study guide.

Acknowledgements

The fourth edition has included a great deal of input from many people. I am grateful for the critiques and helpful suggestions of the students who used the book, the reviewers who suggested improvements, and instructors who have volunteered valuable comments and feedback. I would also like to extend special thanks to Nona Groome for her proofreading assistance.

The revision process is a lengthy one. Input from many sources is gathered, analyzed, and considered before making the recommendations part of the text. More Business Application Problems, the A.C.R.S. topic, and home mortgages are three major topics that were a direct result of reviewer comments. For those suggestions and many others that help make this edition a more useful product, I would like to thank all of the reviewers.

Let me take this opportunity to specifically thank Larry D. Barchett, Vincennes University; Sally Preissig, College of Lake County; Robert Pommerich, Loras College; James Border, Berkshire Community College; Cheryl Shearer, Oxnard College; Elizabeth Domenico, Gaston College; Dave Fellows, Allan Hancock College; and Corrine Blagbrough, Middlesex Community College.

To the Student

This text/workbook uses a performance approach specifically to help you achieve a better understanding of the material covered in your business math course. Through the performance approach, which is simply a logical, learn-by-doing method, you will develop a competence in applying business math principles to solving business problems.

Performance Objectives Start Each Chapter

Each chapter begins with a list of performance objectives (the concepts in the chapter that you must learn.) Don't skip these performance objectives because they will provide an outline of what you will be expected to know after completing the chapter. Read the performance objectives and the text material before attending class; you will find that you have a greater understanding of your instructor's explanations.

While reading the text material, notice that key terms are identified in the margin and are also shown in **bold-face type** where they are explained. To further aid you with these terms, a glossary and an index are included at the back of the book.

A review of any chapter will show that after each explanation of a topic there is one or more worked out example. After the worked examples there are exercises; following the sets of exercises you will find an assignment section consisting of skill problems, business application problems (word problems), and a challenge problem.

The skill problems are very similar to the exercises. If you have difficulty with the skill problems, refer back to the appropriate exercise to relearn the correct approach.

The business application problems require an ability to determine what information provided in the problem is really vital to the solution and answer. These word problems will tend to be more difficult.

The last type of problem, the challenge problem, is designed to give you a mental workout after you thoroughly understand the chapter material. It is not an easy problem!

In working problems, you should find that an outline (an organized approach to recording the solution) will aid you in finding errors in incorrect problems. Using an outline will also help when reviewing for quizzes and tests.

To aid you in learning concepts and evaluating your competence, answers to all the exercises and the odd-numbered skill and business application problems are given at the back of the book. Check your progress regularly, as it will enable you to measure your performance.

Mastery Test Sums Up Each Chapter

After completing a chapter you may wonder "Do I *really* know this material?" If you would like to determine your mastery of the material in the chapter, first review the performance objectives at the beginning of the chapter. Do you understand *them*? If you do, at the back of each chapter you will find a Mastery Test. This test measures your mastery of the performance objectives outlined at the beginning of the chapter. Answers to all the problems in the Mastery Tests are at the back of the book. Record your scores for each chapter on the "Record of Progress" page on the inside of the back cover. If you follow this procedure for each chapter, your performance level is sure to be high.

Chaper 23 Aides in Review for Final

Worried about your final exam? Chapter 23 provides fifty review problems to prepare you for the ordeal! Each problem has a chapter page reference to aid you in your review.

Appendixes

Have you thought about the use of a hand-held calculator? Appendix A covers the selection and operation of hand-held calculators; appendix B covers Math Short-Cuts and Aliquot Parts; appendix C covers Computer Math; appendix D covers Employment Test Math; and appendix E concerns the Reading of Market Quotations.

You will find that the material covered in the book includes problems using various careers in business, actual business forms, and business situations to provide a practical approach. A good understanding of the material in the text will prepare you for courses in Business Math, other more advanced business and business-related courses, your career, and your personal finances.

Good luck in business math!

Section **1** # Rebuilding the Fundamentals

1 Working with Whole Numbers
2 Working with Fractions
3 Working with Decimal Numbers

1 Working with Whole Numbers

After mastering the material in this chapter, you will be able to:

1. Read and write whole numbers.
2. Round off whole numbers.
3. Perform the four fundamental arithmetic operations (addition, subtraction, multiplication, and division) of whole numbers with more accuracy and speed.
4. Work word problems using the four fundamental arithmetic operations.
5. Understand and use the following terms:

Place Values	Subtrahend	Multiplier	Divisor
Sum	Borrowing	Product	Quotient
Difference	Multiplicand	Dividend	Remainder
Minuend			

This chapter is concerned with improving your skill in the four fundamental arithmetic operations. These fundamentals will be the building blocks for a better understanding of material to be presented.

Reading and Writing Whole Numbers

Place values

Business communications often include numerical information that must be read. To be able to read and write numbers, you must be able to use place values. Each digit in a number, because of its position, has a place value. Once mastered, these **place values** will aid you in reading numbers. The following illustration gives a number with all of its place values labeled.

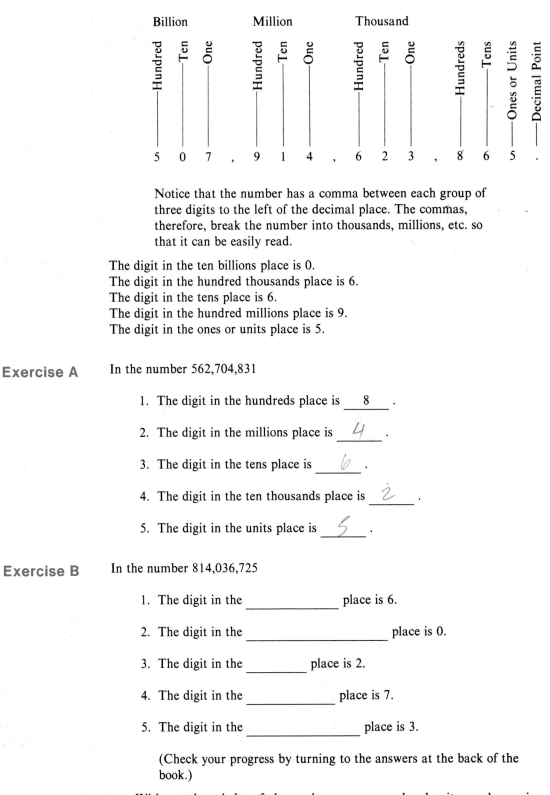

Notice that the number has a comma between each group of three digits to the left of the decimal place. The commas, therefore, break the number into thousands, millions, etc. so that it can be easily read.

The digit in the ten billions place is 0.
The digit in the hundred thousands place is 6.
The digit in the tens place is 6.
The digit in the hundred millions place is 9.
The digit in the ones or units place is 5.

Exercise A   In the number 562,704,831

1. The digit in the hundreds place is ___8___.

2. The digit in the millions place is ___4___.

3. The digit in the tens place is ___6___.

4. The digit in the ten thousands place is ___2___.

5. The digit in the units place is ___5___.

Exercise B   In the number 814,036,725

1. The digit in the _____ place is 6.

2. The digit in the _____ place is 0.

3. The digit in the _____ place is 2.

4. The digit in the _____ place is 7.

5. The digit in the _____ place is 3.

(Check your progress by turning to the answers at the back of the book.)

With your knowledge of place values you can read and write numbers using the word description. In the preceding illustration, each group of three digits to the left of the decimal point has a name (i.e., thousands, millions, billions, etc.). To read a number, first read the digit in the leftmost group followed by that group name and continue with this process until all of the digits are read.

The ability to read numbers will enable you to communicate with others more successfully. It will also improve your image as a competent student, employee, or manager.

Example 1

The number 46,002 is read: 46 thousand, two *or* forty-six thousand, two. Notice that there are no "ands" used in reading the number.

Example 2

The number 693,924,806 is read: Six hundred ninety-three million, nine hundred twenty-four thousand, eight hundred six.

Read the following numbers to yourself.

123,066,231	960,012
7,839,850	3,140
7,016	90,008

When reading numbers that are in dollars, simply add the word "dollars" after the last digit is read.

Example 3

The amount $33,108 is read: 33 thousand, 108 dollars *or* thirty-three thousand, one hundred eight dollars.

Read the following dollar amounts to yourself.

$3,509	$7,750,000
$3,602	$19,436,502,500
$987,503	$51,437

Now that you are able to read whole numbers it will be easier for you to write numbers with words. This knowledge will be useful when writing checks. The check form has a place for the amount to be written with words as well as with numbers.

When writing the number, a *comma* is placed between each written portion corresponding to each group of numbers (i.e., thousands, millions, etc.). Values twenty-one through ninety-nine are *hyphenated*.

Exercise C   Write in the dollar amounts in the following checks using the value in the upper-right corner of each check. Follow the procedure shown in Example 4.

Example 4

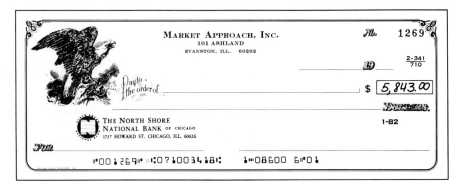

Courtesy of Market Approach, Inc., Evanston, IL.

Rounding Off   Accuracy in arithmetic operations is essential and must be a goal of every business student. There are occasions, however, when the answer may need to be rounded off in order for it to be a more useful figure. The rounding off process does not eliminate the need for accurate arithmetic, but relies on accuracy in order that the answer may be accurately rounded off. Directions for rounding off usually ask you to round off to the nearest ten, hundred, etc. (See Example 5.)

Example 5

"Round off your answer to the nearest ten thousand."

Rounding Rules

If the instructions are to "round off to the nearest ten thousand," then you must be concerned with the digit in the ten thousand's place and the digit immediately to the right of it, that is, the thousand's place. In the number 627,584, the digit 2 is in the ten thousand's place. The 2 will be changed to a 3 if the digit immediately to the right of it is a 5 or larger. In this case the digit is a 7, therefore the answer is 630,000. Notice that all of the digits to the right of the number are dropped and zeros substituted. When the digit immediately to the right is a 4 or smaller, the digit in question remains the same and the value of the digits to the right are changed to zeros.

Example 6

Digit in question (to be rounded)

Decision-making digit (5 or larger ?)

627,584 = 630,000

If the same number would have been rounded off to the nearest hundred thousand, then the answer would be 600,000.

Digit in question (to be rounded)

Decision-making digit (5 or larger ?)

627,584 = 600,000

Rounding rules also apply to values on the other side of the decimal point and will be discussed in chapter 3, Working with Decimal Numbers.

Exercise D Round off the following numbers to the place value indicated.

1. 97,806 to the nearest thousand   98,000   .

2. 2,637 to the nearest ten _____ .

3. 278,901 to the nearest hundred _____ .

Exercise E

1. $1,927,853 rounded to the nearest hundred thousand dollars is
   $1,900,000   .

2. $627,557 rounded to the nearest ten thousand dollars is

   _____ .

3. $323,306,902 rounded to the nearest ten million dollars is

   _____ .

When adding numbers that have more than one column, you must start with the column farthest to the right, then proceed to the left.

Example 7

57	Add the 7 and 4; the sum is 11. Write the 1 under	1
+ 94	the right column and carry the 10 to the left	57
	column. Then add 1 plus 5 plus 9 to a total of 15	+ 94
	for a **sum** or an answer of 151.	151

Sum

Exercise F

Complete the following problems.

A.

1. 46	2. 36	3. 38	4. 163	5. 19	6. 65	7. 82
+ 78	+ 17	+ 74	+ 56	+ 71	+ 41	+ 17
124						

B.

1. 673	2. 45,895	3. 51,920	4. 90,635	5. 10,427
+ 3,671	+ 69,564	+ 23,761	+ 792	+ 7,826

C.

1. $5,432	2. $86,756	3. $ 9,874	4. $62,747	5. $76,344
+ 2,684	+ 5,375	+ 6,543	+ 14,154	+ 12,796

D.

1. $3,798	2. $1,699	3. $450	4. $14,750	5. $9,950
6,500	184	7,699	6,390	1,795
47,950	4,050	995	2,795	4,350
+ 56,387	+ 5,632	+ 75,600	+ 4,000	+ 7,885

Horizontal Addition

Occasionally records are kept in such a way that the information can be totaled horizontally as well as vertically. This approach allows for an analysis of the sum totals for several uses.

Exercise G

The Milton Manufacturing Company of Capital City, Ohio, pays its employees by the number of operations that they complete. It is the responsibility of the shop clerk to maintain a record of the number of operations that each employee completes. From this record the shop foreman is able to determine the success of his department. Total the operations for each employee and the operations for the department for each day.

Employee	Mon.	Tues.	Wed.	Thur.	Fri.	Total Operations Per 5-day Week
J. Patterson	427	506	468	683	492	_____
P. R. Atkins	68	92	49	91	84	_____
A. L. Larson	127	104	106	121	114	_____
P. B. Willis	653	602	608	801	590	_____
K. N. Swix	371	360	346	294	361	_____
L. B. Smith	92	91	86	49	47	_____
N. R. Bowersox	742	955	256	365	513	_____
B. J. Johnson	436	484	427	559	562	_____
L. K. Sommers	328	379	258	382	432	_____
R. R. Kreger	867	549	927	639	528	_____

Total Operations Per Day	_____	_____	_____	_____	_____	_____

Subtraction

Difference
Minuend
Subtrahend

Even though addition is undoubtedly the most frequently used arithmetic process, in business we must also be concerned with our skill in other fundamental processes. Subtraction is the process of finding the **difference** between two numbers. The larger of the two numbers is termed the **minuend** and the smaller number is termed the **subtrahend.** The subtrahend is subtracted from the minuend to find the difference.

Example 8

9	Minuend
− 5	Subtrahend
4	Difference

Borrowing

The subtraction of larger numbers requires an additional operation, namely **borrowing.** Borrowing is required when the subtrahend is larger than the minuend in the place value considered. When this occurs, it is necessary to borrow a unit from the place value to the left, adding the unit or ten to the minuend, and subtracting a unit from the value from which it is borrowed. Subtraction then can proceed as in the previous example. An example will help clarify the terms.

Example 9

		2 1	2 1
34	Minuend	34	34
− 18	Subtrahend	− 18	− 18
	Difference		16

$$\begin{array}{r} 642 \\ +\ 927 \\ \hline 1,569 \\ -\ 927 \\ \hline 642 \end{array}$$

In order to be sure of your accuracy, it is best to check your answers before proceeding with another problem. The best way to check your answer is by subtraction. After you have found the sum or total of two addends, subtract one addend from the sum or total. Your answer should be the remaining addend.

Checking Subtraction Answers by Addition

	854	Minuend
	− 687	Subtrahend
+	+ 167	Difference
	854	Minuend (check)

The accuracy of your subtraction can be improved by checking your answers by the use of addition. Although this method is not foolproof, it will help to detect most of the simple errors. This method requires only one step. After you have found the difference between the minuend and the subtrahend, add the difference to the subtrahend. The result should be the minuend.

Exercise H

Find the difference in the problems below.

A.
1. $\begin{array}{r} 65 \\ -46 \\ \hline 19 \end{array}$
2. $\begin{array}{r} 95 \\ -27 \end{array}$
3. $\begin{array}{r} 83 \\ -59 \end{array}$
4. $\begin{array}{r} 71 \\ -29 \end{array}$
5. $\begin{array}{r} 97 \\ -69 \end{array}$
6. $\begin{array}{r} 61 \\ -45 \end{array}$
7. $\begin{array}{r} 98 \\ -36 \end{array}$

B.
1. $\begin{array}{r} \$114 \\ -\ 97 \end{array}$
2. $\begin{array}{r} \$53 \\ -17 \end{array}$
3. $\begin{array}{r} \$219 \\ -\ 59 \end{array}$
4. $\begin{array}{r} \$321 \\ -183 \end{array}$
5. $\begin{array}{r} \$172 \\ -\ 86 \end{array}$
6. $\begin{array}{r} \$144 \\ -\ 97 \end{array}$

C.
1. $\begin{array}{r} \$653 \\ -479 \end{array}$
2. $\begin{array}{r} \$247 \\ -149 \end{array}$
3. $\begin{array}{r} \$1,420 \\ -983 \end{array}$
4. $\begin{array}{r} \$630 \\ -475 \end{array}$
5. $\begin{array}{r} \$1,051 \\ -\ 987 \end{array}$
6. $\begin{array}{r} \$731 \\ -187 \end{array}$

Exercise I

The Gilton Agency recently fired its accounts payable clerk because she kept poor records in the check register. You are asked, as the new employee, to bring some of the records that are not in order up to date. The former employee recorded the amount of the checks, but failed to keep a running balance.

Your supervisor explains that the amount of the deposit must be added to the previous balance and that the amount of each check is to be subtracted from the previous balance. The check stubs through check number 1273 are in order. Bring the checkbook up to date by following the example shown on check stub number 1268.

Courtesy of Market Approach, Inc., Evanston, IL.

Multiplication

Multiplication is used in business to price stock, compute payroll, determine the interest due, taxes due, depreciation, markup amount, and a variety of other applications. It is really a shortcut approach to addition. Instead of adding a series of values that are all alike, we can multiply the value by the number of repetitions.

Multiplicand
Multiplier
Product

The two numbers used in multiplying are called the **multiplicand** (the number on top) and the **multiplier** (the number on the bottom). The result of this process is called the **product.**

Example 10

427	Multiplicand
× 53	Multiplier
1,281	Partial product (3 × 427)
21 35	Partial product (5 × 427)
22,631	Product (53 × 427)

Multiplying by 10, 100, 1,000, etc.

Frequently the multiplier or the multiplicand is a 10, 100, or 1,000. The problem can be set up and the product found by the normal multiplication process. It is much easier and faster to use the following technique.

Example 11

```
    645    Multiplicand
  × 100    Multiplier
 64,500    Product (645 × 100)
```

Notice in the example that the product has the same number of zeros in it as the multiplier does.

Example 12

$462 \times 1,000 = 462,000$

Example 13

$9,853 \times 100 = 985,300$

Exercise J

Complete the following problems using the methods described above.

A.
1.	2.	3.	4.	5.
673	892	546	891	894
× 100	× 100	× 10	× 1,000	× 10
67,300				

B.
1.	2.	3.	4.	5.
819	961	570	469	162
× 10	× 100	× 10	× 100	× 1,000

C.
1.	2.	3.	4.
$2,871	$4,712	$6,534	$1,927
× 648	× 902	× 751	× 842

D.
1.	2.	3.	4.
$8,965	$83,935	$29,171	$4,782
× 261	× 35	× 69	× 29

Exercise K

The Wortz Hardware Store took inventory on June 30 and found the following merchandise on hand in the paint department. Find the total cost of merchandise on hand in the paint department.

Item Description	Quantity	Cost	Total Cost
Paint			
Pint Cans	47	$ 2	$ 94
Quart Cans	93	3	
Gallon Cans	89	6	
Stain			
Pint Cans	23	2	
Quart Cans	36	3	
Brushes			
$\frac{1}{2}$ Inch	27	1	
1 Inch	51	2	
2 Inch	40	3	
3 Inch	36	4	
4 Inch	32	6	
Thinner			
Quart Cans	41	2	
Gallon Cans	26	4	
Rollers			
9 Inch	42	1	
11 Inch	50	2	
Drop Cloths			
9′ × 9′ Plastic	35	2	
12′ × 12′ Plastic	20	3	
12′ × 12′ Cloth	4	16	
12′ × 16′ Cloth	7	18	
Can Holders	25	2	
Cheesecloth	20	1	
Handles	12	1	
Brush Cleaners	16	3	
Wallpapering Tools	12	3	
Paste	17	4	

Total Value of Merchandise on Hand in Paint Department _____

Division

Dividend
Divisor
Quotient

Division is the fourth and last of the fundamental operations in arithmetic. Like multiplication is to addition, division is a time-saving approach for subtraction. The number to be divided is called the **dividend,** the number that is used to divide by is called the **divisor,** and the answer or result is the **quotient.**

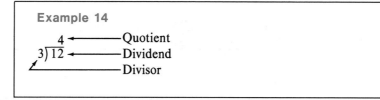

Example 14

```
    4 ←――――Quotient
3)‾12 ←――――Dividend
 ↙ ―――――Divisor
```

The symbol)‾ signifies division. 3)‾12 is read as "3 divided into 12." The division sign (÷) can also be used in the same problem that would be written 12 ÷ 3 or read "12 divided by 3." Notice the key words "divided into" and "divided by." This will become even more important in chapter 3, Working with Decimal Numbers.

Long Division

The problem 5,301 ÷ 57 requires that 57 be first divided into the group of digits farthest to the left of the decimal point. Fifty-seven cannot be divided into 5 or 53, but 57 will divide into 530. Fifty-seven will divide into 530 nine times. The nine is written directly over the last digit to the right in the group.

Example 15

$$\begin{array}{r} 9 \\ 57\overline{)5{,}301} \\ \underline{5\ 13} \\ 17 \end{array}$$

Remainder

Seventeen is leftover or is a **remainder** from dividing 57 into 530. The 1 is brought down as the next digit in the dividend. Now 57 can be divided into 171. We find that 57 divides into 171 three times.

$$\begin{array}{r} 93 \\ 57\overline{)5{,}301} \\ \underline{513} \\ 171 \\ \underline{171} \end{array}$$

This time the remainder is zero. If there had been a remainder of, say, 14, the answer would have been stated as the quotient "93 with a remainder of 14."

Example 16

$$\begin{array}{r} 3{,}076 \\ 18\overline{)55{,}385} \\ \underline{54} \\ 138 \\ \underline{126} \\ 125 \\ \underline{108} \\ 17 \end{array}$$

Answer: 3,076 remainder 17

Dividing by 10, 100, 1,000, etc.

When the divisor is a 10, 100, or 1,000 the technique of multiplication by 10, 100, or 1,000 may be used. The example of 9,853 × 100 was used to show that the zeros are added to the multiplicand in order to find the product 985,300. If the problem were changed to read 985,300 ÷ 100, then the answer could be found by removing the two zeros from the divisor 100 and writing the quotient 9,853.

Example 17

64,820,400 ÷ 10 = 6,482,040

Exercise L   Complete the following problems.

1. $627 \overline{)98,439}$ with quotient 157   2. $49 \overline{)65,366}$ 3. $801 \overline{)94,518}$ 4. $183 \overline{)638,519}$

5. $867 \overline{)365,007}$ 6. $37 \overline{)75,254}$ 7. $389 \overline{)87,500}$ 8. $34 \overline{)657}$

Exercise M   Complete the following problems by the shortcut method. A check can always be made by dividing in the normal manner.

1. $793,000 \div 100 = \underline{\quad 7,930 \quad}$

2. $8,000,630,000 \div 100 = \underline{\qquad\qquad}$

3. $90,600 \div 100 = \underline{\qquad}$

4. $891,000 \div 1,000 = \underline{\qquad}$

5. $5,372,050 \div 10 = \underline{\qquad}$

Checking Answers   Division and multiplication problems can be checked easily by using the opposite process to find the answer.

To check a divisor of 7, a dividend of 58, a quotient of 8, and a remainder of 2:

$$
\begin{array}{r}
8 \\
7 \overline{)58} \\
56 \\
\hline
2
\end{array}
$$

Multiply the divisor by the quotient and add the remainder to the product.

$$
\begin{array}{r}
7 \\
\times\ 8 \\
\hline
56 \\
+\ 2 \\
\hline
58
\end{array}
$$

Example 20

```
      6,054 remainder 7
8) 48,439


      6,054
 ×       8
     48,432
 +        7
     48,439
```

Multiplication can be checked by dividing the product by the multiplier or the multiplicand. The quotient will be the multiplier or multiplicand depending on which was used as a divisor.

```
              602                        9
   602    9) 5,418      OR      602) 5,418
 ×   9       54                     5,418
 5,418       18
             18
```

Use of this check method will help you find errors. Accuracy is important!

Name _____   Date _____   Score _____

Skill Problems   Complete the following problems.

1. 6,603
    560
    1,450
    935
    + 451

2. 847 ÷ 62

3. $634
    ✕   42

4. 695,380
    − 527,592

5. 26)‾465

6. $43,940
    ✕   691

7. $ 568
    3,904
    + 257

8. $ 82,564
   − 12,593

9. $3,549,560 ÷ 25

10. Round off your answer to the
    nearest ten.
    34,962
    ✕   471

11. Round off your answer to the
    nearest hundred.
    5,680
    427
    11,473
    + 1,865

12. Find the difference between sixty-two thousand, eight hundred fifty-seven
     and twenty-nine thousand, six hundred eight.

13. 472,800 ÷ 10

14. $6,547
    −   898

15. $7,980
    ✕   7,643

16. 76)‾34,656

17. $693
    ✕   47

18. Round off your answer to the
    nearest hundred dollars.
    $875
    ✕   37

19. Write the answers to this
    problem in words.
    $860
    ✕   562

20.   9,862
    ✕   567

Complete the following problems using the appropriate fundamental operation.

1. The income from a design studio must be split evenly among seven partners. The income was $115,486 for the year. What was the share for Patsy Lard, a partner?

2. An estate of $46,821 is to be divided evenly among the five surviving children. Before it can be divided, the administrator's fee of $166 must be deducted. How much will each of the children receive?

3. The ABC Party Store had $723 in the cash register at the end of a day's business. When they opened for business that morning, there was $437 in the register. Mr. Lee said that $43 of the money was sales tax they had collected. How much did they sell during the day?

4. Fay bought a blouse on sale for $43. She also purchased a pair of shoes for $10. To pay for the purchase she used her $81 paycheck. How much did she receive in change?

5. At the beginning of the month, Mr. Harold's business car had 15,975 miles on it. At the end of the month, the odometer read 17,193 miles. He estimated that 147 miles were for personal use. How many miles did he travel on business during the month?

6. An employee produced 616 parts in an eleven-hour day. How many parts were produced each hour?

7. Janie decides to purchase her books for the fall semester. At the College Book Store she finds the prices as follows: math, $16; English, $5; history, $8; and accounting, $12. She decides that the prices are too high and goes across the street to the Campus Book Store. She finds the prices there as follows: math, $14; English, $6; history, $7; and accounting, $15. At which store should she buy all her books to get the lowest total price?

8. The production schedule for the Seldon Manufacturing Corporation calls for 1,645 units to be produced on each shift. The company has a three-shift operation. How many units will be produced in five days of production?

9. You are given the task of determining the cost of a banquet for ninty-seven community leaders. The hall will cost $90. The meal will consist of a steak at an estimated cost of $5; a baked potato at $1; vegetable, relish dish, beverage, and roll at $2. Determine the total cost of the banquet rounded off to the nearest hundred dollars.

10. John McKay received $480 per acre for his eighty-seven-acre farm. He also sold a house for $62,500. What was the total value of the real estate he sold?

11. The Municipal Transportation Department bought seven new minibuses at a cost of $9,746 each. They also bought eleven cars for $8,117 each. What was the total expenditure?

12. The Retail Trade Association has decided to create a package to be used by managers for the training of their employees. The cost will be shared equally by each of the 42 members of the association. Each package will consist of 7 cassette tapes @ $14 each; a set of 5 booklets @ $10 each set; stationery supplies @ $1; a hardbound container @ $4; and a set of 14 practice formats @ $42 each set. The association has requested that twenty training packages be assembled for each association member. What will be the total cost for a set of twenty training packages?

13. A salesperson must travel a route of 611 miles in order to cover the sale's territory. There are twenty-eight stops to make on the route; each stop takes about one hour. Traveling time for the complete route is about eleven hours. If the salesperson wishes to work only eight hours a day, how many days will it take to complete the route?

14. The Stuben Oil Company read the meter on the gasoline storage tank. On Monday, the meter read 4,736,902 gallons; on Wednesday, it read 4,019,456. On Thursday morning a delivery of 550,000 gallons was added to the tank. On Saturday at the closing time, the meter read 3,457,995. How many gallons of gas were sold during the week?

15. The town of Norden had a population of 47,867 people on January 1 of last year. During the year 427 babies were born; 381 residents died; 188 people, composing 62 families, moved in; and 73 people moved out. What was the population of Norden at the end of the year?

16. The inventory of Spectrum, Inc. totaled 842 parts of item J926. The cost of the inventory was $13,472. What was the cost per unit?

17. Of the total of 520 staff members of the Programming Department of the City of Belland, 65 have a masters degree and 128 have a bachelors degree. How many do not have a degree?

18. There are seventy-three businesses in the town of Tipin and thirty-one in the city of St. Clair. How many businesses are there in the two towns combined?

19. New lounge chairs for a pool area will cost $127 each. The Recreation Department has decided on a purchase of twenty-three chairs. What will be the cost of the purchase?

20. The Food Mart has decided to add 42 items to their existing inventory of 1,219 items. At the same time, they will discontinue 81 items. What will be the new inventory item amount?

Challenge Problem

At the beginning of the month, the E. L. Robinson Company had 422 units of a product, "Talson," on hand. The company purchased another 960 pieces during the month at a cost of $1.40 per unit. Forty pieces of the new shipment were found to be defective and were returned to the seller. During the month, the company sold 865 units after having 14 returned by customers because of poor packing. If the company made a profit of $1.23 on each unit sold, (1) how much will be made on the units already sold and (2) how much would be made if all of the acceptable units remaining were sold?

Name _____   Date _____   Score _____

1. Find the product of the following numbers: 64 and 850. _____

2. $ 1,457
    5,800
    3,575
 +   41

3. $ 42,803
 + 787,276

4. 18)$\overline{75,859}$

5. The profit of the Edrunton Company must be evenly distributed between the six department managers. The profit for the quarter was $64,638. What will each department manager receive as his or her share of the profits?

6. 549 × 187 =

7. 768 ÷ 40 =

8. The Sales Department of the Wolton Corporation reported the following figures for May: marine equipment—$6,185,005; automotive equipment—$54,980; service repair parts—$7,681; and miscellaneous—$1,822. What were the total sales for the month?

9. Jay Moore produced 891 parts on his machine for the week. One hundred forty-seven of those were determined to be oversize and, therefore, not part of the acceptable lot. Another 63 failed a strength test set up by the Quality Control Department. How many of the parts were acceptable (to the nearest ten)?

10. The answering service tape has recorded a message from the Western Sales Region Manager, A. F. Litona. His statement indicates that sales of the "Aferton" product were "eighty-five thousand, six hundred five dollars," the "Virmonon" product to be "two hundred thousand, thirty-eight dollars," and the "Olsand" product to be "forty-one thousand, eighty dollars." What were the total sales for the period?

11. Find the total difference between the following: 651 units at $387 each and 120 units at $456 each.

12. Write the following value using words: $43,679.

13. Subtract and round off your answer to the nearest ten thousand dollars.

$459,073
−   91,752

14. Mrs. Jesop knows that the salespeople in her group will be successful on one out of every two sales calls that they make. If each call takes two hours and each successful call develops a $98 order, what will be the volume of sales from a sales force of twelve people, each working forty hours a week?

15. Round off 685,224 to the nearest hundred.

(If you missed problems 2, 3, or 8, you need to review Addition; problems 9, 11, or 13, you need to review Subtraction; problems 1, 6, or 14, you need to review Multiplication; problems 4, 5, or 7, you need to review Division; problems 10 or 12, you need to review Reading and Writing Whole Numbers; and if you missed problems 13 or 15, you need to review Rounding Off.) Record your score on the inside back cover for future reference.

2 Working with Fractions

After mastering the material in this chapter, you will be able to:

1. Identify a fraction type.
2. Change mixed numbers to improper fractions and improper fractions to mixed numbers.
3. Reduce fractions to their lowest terms.
4. Perform the basic fundamental processes (addition, subtraction, multiplication, and division) with accuracy in problems dealing with fractions.
5. Develop a ratio from data provided.
6. Understand and use the following:

Denominator	Mixed Number
Numerator	Prime Numbers
Common Fraction	Common Denominator
Improper Fraction	Lowest Common Denominator (LCD)
	Ratio

Description and Types

A fraction can be described as a part of a whole. This description fits many business situations. Mastery of fractions and their applications are therefore required.

Example 1

The fraction $\frac{3}{4}$ states that the whole is divided into four equal parts.

Three of the four parts make up the portion that the fraction is describing. The fraction can be presented graphically in a variety of forms, each describing the same part of a whole: $\frac{3}{4}$.

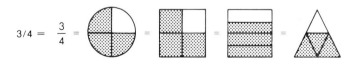

$3/4 = \frac{3}{4} =$

Denominator
Numerator

The bottom portion of the fraction that describes the number of equal parts is called the **denominator.** The top portion that specifies the number of equal parts that the fraction is describing is called the **numerator.**

A fraction can be read in two different ways. The fraction $\frac{7}{8}$ can be read as "seven eighths" or as "seven divided by eight," since the line between the numerator and the denominator signifies division. Either a diagonal line / or a horizontal line — can be used to separate the numerator and denominator.

Example 2

$\frac{72}{146}$ can be read as "seventy-two one hundred forty-sixths" or as "seventy-two divided by one hundred forty-six."

A third way to read a fraction is to describe how it looks (i.e., "seventy-two over one hundred forty-six"). This method is also acceptable.

Read the following fractions to yourself.

$\frac{9}{16}$	$\frac{41}{90}$	$\frac{5}{8}$	$\frac{4}{7}$	$\frac{16}{21}$	$\frac{193}{216}$
$\frac{17}{20}$	$\frac{1}{4}$	$\frac{10}{17}$	$\frac{1}{3}$	$\frac{3}{4}$	$\frac{7}{16}$
$\frac{17}{651}$	$\frac{5}{16}$	$\frac{5}{55}$	$\frac{3}{8}$	$\frac{21}{109}$	$\frac{7}{21}$

Common fraction
Improper fraction

There are three types of fractions. The type that we have been working with is called a **common fraction.** This type has a denominator (bottom number) larger than the numerator (top number). An **improper fraction** has a numerator larger than or equal to the denominator.

Example 3

$$\frac{19}{6} \qquad \frac{40}{10} \qquad \frac{93}{16} \qquad \frac{4}{3} \qquad \frac{19}{9} \qquad \frac{8}{4} \qquad \frac{6}{5}$$

Mixed numbers

Mixed numbers contain a whole number as well as a common fraction.

Example 4

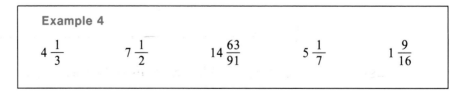

$$4\frac{1}{3} \qquad 7\frac{1}{2} \qquad 14\frac{63}{91} \qquad 5\frac{1}{7} \qquad 1\frac{9}{16}$$

In most instances fractions will be presented as common fractions or as mixed numbers. Improper fractions are found in arithmetic operations and as temporary answers. They are not acceptable as final answers.

Identify the following by type of fraction: common, mixed, or improper.

1. $\dfrac{9}{32}$ _____ common _____

2. $\dfrac{46}{17}$ _____

3. $\dfrac{1,107}{1,000}$ _____

4. $\dfrac{41}{35}$ _____

5. $16\dfrac{2}{9}$ _____

6. $\dfrac{4}{7}$ _____

7. $\dfrac{11}{9}$ _____

8. $\dfrac{76}{81}$ _____

9. $\dfrac{1}{4}$ _____

10. $\dfrac{4}{5}$ _____

11. $4\dfrac{1}{10}$ _____

12. $16\dfrac{2}{3}$ _____

Interchanging Fraction Types

It is sometimes necessary to interchange fraction types in order to perform the fundamental processes or to find the correct answer. All answers in the improper fraction form should be changed to a mixed number or a whole number.

Example 5

$$4\overline{\smash{)}9}$$
$$\underline{8}$$
$$1$$

The improper fraction $\dfrac{9}{4}$ can be changed to a mixed number by dividing nine by four, just as the fraction is read. The result is that there are two whole units in $\dfrac{9}{4}$ and one fourth left over. The answer is then written $2\dfrac{1}{4}$.

Example 6

$$\dfrac{197}{9} = \quad 9\overline{\smash{)}197} \quad = 21\dfrac{8}{9}$$
$$\underline{18}$$
$$17$$
$$\underline{9}$$
$$8$$

Exercise B

Change the following improper fractions to mixed numbers.

1. $\dfrac{13}{8} = \quad 1\dfrac{5}{8}$

2. $\dfrac{67}{12} = \quad$ _____

3. $\dfrac{14}{5} = \quad$ _____

4. $\dfrac{47}{14} = \quad$ _____

5. $\dfrac{19}{6} = \quad$ _____

6. $\dfrac{5}{2} = \quad$ _____

7. $\dfrac{19}{9} =$ _____ 8. $\dfrac{93}{10} =$ _____ 9. $\dfrac{43}{10} =$ _____

10. $\dfrac{9}{8} =$ _____ 11. $\dfrac{16}{4} =$ _____ 12. $\dfrac{57}{8} =$ _____

If an improper fraction can be changed to a mixed number, then we should be able to do the reverse process (i.e., change a mixed number to an improper fraction).

Example 7

The mixed number $4\frac{3}{5}$ can be changed to an improper fraction by multiplying the whole number (4) by the number of equal parts in each unit (the denominator 5) and adding the numerator to the product.

$$4\frac{3}{5} = \frac{(5 \times 4) + 3}{5} = \frac{23}{5}$$

Example 8

$$7\frac{4}{10} = \frac{(7 \times 10) + 4}{10} = \frac{74}{10}$$

Exercise C Change the following mixed numbers to improper fractions.

1. $6\frac{3}{4} = \dfrac{27}{4}$ _____ 7. $18\frac{3}{8} = \dfrac{174}{8}$ _____

2. $9\frac{5}{6} = \dfrac{59}{6}$ _____ 8. $6\frac{2}{3} = \dfrac{20}{3}$ _____

3. $7\frac{4}{5} = \dfrac{39}{5}$ _____ 9. $4\frac{3}{4} = \dfrac{19}{4}$ _____

4. $1\frac{7}{8} = \dfrac{15}{8}$ _____ 10. $1\frac{1}{2} = \dfrac{3}{2}$ _____

5. $110\frac{1}{5} = \dfrac{551}{5}$ _____ 11. $5\frac{7}{16} = \dfrac{87}{16}$ _____

6. $3\frac{1}{2} = \dfrac{7}{2}$ _____ 12. $10\frac{1}{2} = \dfrac{22}{2}$ _____

Reducing Fractions

Answers to problems in fractions are correct only if they are reduced to lowest terms. The part of a whole $\frac{3}{4}$ can also be described as $\frac{6}{8}, \frac{12}{16}, \frac{24}{32}$, etc. In each of the previous examples the numerator had the same relationship to the denominator as the fraction $\frac{3}{4}$. The fraction $\frac{3}{4}$ can be changed to $\frac{6}{8}$ by doubling both the numerator and the denominator. The fraction $\frac{6}{8}$ can be changed to $\frac{12}{16}$ by again following the same process.

In each case the numerator and denominator are being multiplied by an equal amount (2). Any fraction can be changed in this manner. The fraction $\frac{3}{7}$ can be changed to $\frac{15}{35}$ by multiplying both the numerator and denominator by five.

You should also be able to do the opposite operation (i.e., divide both the numerator and denominator by the same number). When both the numerator and denominator are divided by 5 $\left(\frac{15}{35}\right)$ it equals $\frac{3}{7}$. When the numerator and denominator no longer can be divided by a whole number, other than one, the fraction has been reduced to lowest terms.

How do you know when the fraction has been reduced to lowest terms? The best approach is to use **prime numbers** as divisors. When the prime numbers cannot be evenly divided into the numerator and denominator, the fraction is fully reduced. A prime number is divisible only by itself and by one (1). The smaller prime numbers are: 2, 3, 5, 7, 11, and 13.

Prime numbers

Trial-and-Error Approach

A trial-and-error approach can be used to reduce fractions. This method states that the prime numbers are used to find a number that will divide into both the numerator and denominator. It is helpful to use a system that will make this approach easy to follow. Start with the smallest prime number and divide it into both the numerator and the denominator. The first prime number that divides evenly is a common divisor. If you are unsuccessful with the first prime number, go to the next highest prime number until you find one that works. Repeat this process until no prime number will divide evenly. The fraction will then be reduced to its lowest terms.

Example 9

$\frac{12}{45}$ must be reduced.

Try prime number 2. $12 \div 2 = 6$ $45 \div 2 = 22$ r 1
2 does not divide evenly and therefore is not a common divisor.
Try prime number 3. $12 \div 3 = 4$ $45 \div 3 = 15$
3 is a prime number that evenly divides into 12 and 45 and
therefore is a common divisor. The fraction is reduced to $\frac{4}{15}$.

Reduce the following fractions to their lowest terms.

1. $\dfrac{5}{10} =$ _____ $\dfrac{1}{2}$ _____

2. $\dfrac{9}{12} =$ _____ $\dfrac{3}{4}$ _____

3. $\dfrac{14}{20} =$ _____ $\dfrac{7}{10}$ _____

4. $\dfrac{40}{100} =$ _____ $\dfrac{2}{5}$ _____

5. $\dfrac{18}{36} =$ _____ $\dfrac{3}{6} = \dfrac{1}{2}$ _____

6. $\dfrac{14}{16} =$ _____ $\dfrac{7}{8}$ _____

7. $\dfrac{22}{50} =$ _____ $\dfrac{11}{25}$ _____

8. $\dfrac{3}{6} =$ _____ $\dfrac{1}{2}$ _____

9. $\dfrac{6}{8} =$ _____ $\dfrac{3}{4}$ _____

10. $\dfrac{9}{15} =$ _____ $\dfrac{3}{5}$ _____

11. $\dfrac{16}{22} =$ _____ $\dfrac{8}{11}$ _____

12. $\dfrac{6}{16} =$ _____ $\dfrac{3}{8}$ _____

Exercise E

Change the following fractions to fractions of equal value using the denominator indicated.

1. $\dfrac{3}{4} = \dfrac{15}{20}$

2. $\dfrac{3}{5} = \dfrac{33}{55}$

3. $\dfrac{9}{11} = \dfrac{90}{110}$

4. $\dfrac{7}{20} = \dfrac{21}{80}$

5. $\dfrac{3}{7} = \dfrac{15}{35}$

6. $\dfrac{9}{10} = \dfrac{27}{30}$

7. $\dfrac{4}{5} = \dfrac{16}{20}$

8. $\dfrac{1}{2} = \dfrac{5}{10}$

9. $\dfrac{41}{100} = \dfrac{410}{1,000}$

10. $\dfrac{6}{7} = \dfrac{12}{14}$

11. $\dfrac{5}{12} = \dfrac{15}{36}$

12. $\dfrac{1}{4} = \dfrac{5}{20}$

Addition and Subtraction

Fractions, like whole numbers, can be added in order to find the sum or total.

Example 10

$$\frac{5}{13} + \frac{3}{13} = \frac{8}{13}$$

Only the numerators are added. The denominator describes the size of the equal parts and, therefore, is not added.

Common Denominator

In the previous example the addends have had **common denominators** (both denominators were 13s in the example given). When the denominators of a fraction to be added are not the same, they must be made alike before the addition can begin.

Product Approach

A common denominator can always be found by multiplying the denominators. The product, or common denominator, is therefore divisible by each of the existing denominators. The next step is to change the fractions to equal values using the common denominator.

Example 11

$$\frac{3}{4} + \frac{1}{5} =$$

$$\frac{3}{4} = \frac{}{20} + \frac{1}{5} = \frac{}{20} = \underline{\hspace{2cm}}$$

To find the numerator, divide the old denominator into the common denominator and multiply the quotient by the numerator for each fraction.

$$\frac{3}{4} = \frac{(3 \times 5)}{20} + \frac{1}{5} = \frac{(1 \times 4)}{20} = \frac{15}{20} + \frac{4}{20} = \frac{19}{20}$$

Note: Remember to reduce the fraction to lowest terms.

Lowest common denominator (LCD)

Another way to determine a common denominator is to find the **lowest common denominator (LCD).** This will reduce the need for dealing with unnecessarily large fractions when performing additional functions. To use this approach, select the largest denominator and test multiples of it against the other denominators until the other denominators divide equally into the multiple of the first denominator.

Example 12

Find the lowest common denominator for the following fractions.

$$\frac{5}{6} + \frac{3}{8} =$$

The largest denominator is 8. Six will not divide equally into 8, therefore 8 is added to the original 8 to make 16. Six will not divide equally into 16, therefore 8 is added to 16 to make 24. Six will evenly divide into 24, therefore 24 is the lowest common denominator.

$$\frac{20}{24} + \frac{9}{24} = \frac{29}{24} = 1\frac{5}{24}$$

The same approach is used when more than two fractions are to be added.

Example 13

$$\frac{2}{3} + \frac{1}{2} + \frac{3}{5} =$$

$$30 \text{ (common denominator)}$$

$$\frac{2}{3} = \frac{(2 \times 10)}{30} + \frac{1}{2} = \frac{(1 \times 15)}{30} + \frac{3}{5} = \frac{(3 \times 6)}{30} =$$

$$\frac{20}{30} + \frac{15}{30} + \frac{18}{30} = \frac{53}{30}$$

$\frac{53}{30}$ reduces to $1\frac{23}{30}$

that is, $30\overline{)53}$
$$\frac{30}{23} \text{ or } \frac{23}{30}$$

Exercise F   Find the sum in the following problems.

1. $\frac{1}{6} + \frac{2}{3} + \frac{1}{4} =$

  $\frac{13}{12} = 1\frac{1}{12}$

6. $\frac{9}{10} + \frac{3}{8} = \frac{36}{40} + \frac{15}{40} = \frac{51}{40} \, 1\frac{11}{40}$

$\frac{7}{8} + \frac{4}{8} + \frac{6}{8} = \frac{17}{8} = 2\frac{1}{8}$

2. $\frac{7}{8} + \frac{1}{2} + \frac{3}{4} = 2\frac{1}{8}$

7. $\frac{7}{20} + \frac{1}{3} + \frac{1}{2} = \frac{21}{60} + \frac{20}{60} \, \frac{30}{60} = \frac{71}{60}$

$1\frac{11}{60}$

$\frac{30}{105} + \frac{21}{105} + \frac{70}{105} = \frac{121}{105}$

3. $\frac{2}{7} + \frac{1}{5} + \frac{2}{3} = 1\frac{16}{105}$

8. $\frac{2}{5} + \frac{5}{16} + \frac{3}{4} = \frac{32}{80} + \frac{25}{80} + \frac{60}{80} = \frac{117}{40}$

$1\frac{37}{80}$

$\frac{7}{8} + \frac{6}{8} + \frac{6}{8} = \frac{19}{8} = 2\frac{3}{8}$

4. $\frac{7}{8} + \frac{3}{4} + \frac{3}{4} = 2\frac{3}{8}$

9. $\frac{7}{16} + \frac{3}{8} + \frac{1}{4} = \frac{7+6+4}{16} = \frac{17}{16} \, 1\frac{1}{16}$

$\frac{7}{70} + \frac{35}{70} \, \frac{30}{70} = \frac{72}{70} = 1\frac{2}{70} = 1\frac{1}{35}$

5. $\frac{1}{10} + \frac{1}{2} + \frac{3}{7} = 1\frac{1}{35}$

10. $\frac{3}{7} + \frac{5}{6} + \frac{2}{3} = \frac{54 + 105 \, 84}{126} = \frac{243}{126}$

$1\frac{117}{126}$

$= 1\frac{13}{14}$

The subtraction of common fractions is similar to addition, because both require common denominators. Subtraction requires finding the difference of the numerators.

Example 14

$\dfrac{3}{4} - \dfrac{1}{4} = \dfrac{2}{4}$, which reduces to $\dfrac{1}{2}$

Example 15

$\dfrac{1}{3} - \dfrac{2}{9} =$

$\dfrac{1}{3} = \dfrac{(1 \times 3)}{9} - \dfrac{2}{9} =$

$\dfrac{3}{9} - \dfrac{2}{9} = \dfrac{1}{9}$

Example 16

$\dfrac{3}{4} - \dfrac{1}{5} =$

$\dfrac{3}{4} = \dfrac{(3 \times 5)}{20} - \dfrac{1}{5} = \dfrac{(1 \times 4)}{20} =$

$\dfrac{15}{20} - \dfrac{4}{20} = \dfrac{11}{20}$

Exercise G   Find the differences in the following problems.

1. $\dfrac{3}{4} - \dfrac{1}{8} =$

   $\dfrac{6}{8} - \dfrac{1}{8} = \dfrac{5}{8}$

2. $\dfrac{5}{8} - \dfrac{1}{4} = \dfrac{5-2}{8} = \dfrac{3}{8}$

$\dfrac{27-20}{30} = \dfrac{7}{30}$

3. $\dfrac{9}{10} - \dfrac{2}{3} = \dfrac{7}{30}$

4. $\dfrac{1}{4} - \dfrac{1}{5} = \dfrac{5-4}{20} = \dfrac{1}{20}$

$\dfrac{153-40}{180} = \dfrac{113}{180}$

5. $\dfrac{17}{20} - \dfrac{2}{9} = \dfrac{113}{180}$

6. $\dfrac{7}{8} - \dfrac{5}{12} = \dfrac{21-10}{24} = \dfrac{11}{24}$

$\dfrac{16-9}{36}$

7. $\dfrac{4}{9} - \dfrac{1}{4} = \dfrac{7}{36}$

8. $\dfrac{2}{3} - \dfrac{1}{4} = \dfrac{8-3}{12} = \dfrac{5}{12}$

9. $\dfrac{7}{10} - \dfrac{1}{16} = \dfrac{56-5}{80} = \dfrac{51}{80}$

10. $\dfrac{1}{2} - \dfrac{3}{16} = \dfrac{8-3}{16} = \dfrac{5}{16}$

Mixed Numbers

Mixed numbers, like common fractions, can be added to find the sum. This process consists of three steps.

Example 17

In the fractions $8\dfrac{3}{8} + 2\dfrac{1}{8}$, (1) the whole numbers are added,
(2) then the fractions are added, and as a last step, (3) the mixed number answer is reduced.

$$8\dfrac{3}{8}$$
$$+\ 2\dfrac{1}{8}$$
$$\overline{\qquad}$$
$$10\dfrac{4}{8} = 10\dfrac{1}{2}$$

This three-step process is lengthened when the fractions of the mixed numbers have different denominators.

Example 18

$$4\dfrac{1}{3} + 6\dfrac{5}{8} =$$

A common denominator must be found as in adding common fractions.

$$4\dfrac{2}{3} = \qquad 4\dfrac{16}{24}$$
$$+6\dfrac{5}{8} = \qquad +\ 6\dfrac{15}{24}$$
$$\overline{\qquad\qquad}$$
$$10\dfrac{31}{24} = 11\dfrac{7}{24}$$

Exercise H

Find the sum in the following problems. Remember to reduce your answers to lowest terms.

1. $6\dfrac{3}{4} + 8\dfrac{1}{2} =$ $15\dfrac{1}{4}$

$6\dfrac{3}{4} + 8\dfrac{2}{4} = 14\dfrac{5}{4}$

$= 15\dfrac{1}{4}$

3. $3\dfrac{5}{16} + 1\dfrac{3}{4} =$ $3\dfrac{5}{16} + 1\dfrac{12}{16} = 4\dfrac{17}{16} = 5\dfrac{1}{16}$

2. $9\dfrac{2}{3} + 4\dfrac{5}{8} =$

$9\dfrac{16}{24} + 4\dfrac{15}{24} = 13\dfrac{31}{24} = 14\dfrac{7}{24}$

4. $8\dfrac{1}{3} + 2\dfrac{5}{8} =$

$8\dfrac{8}{24} + 2\dfrac{15}{24} = 10\dfrac{23}{24}$

$7\frac{5}{10} + 4\frac{3}{10} = 11\frac{8}{10} = 11\frac{4}{5}$

5. $7\frac{1}{2} + 4\frac{3}{10} =$

8. $1\frac{7}{8} + 6\frac{5}{6} =$ $1\frac{42}{48} + 6\frac{40}{48} = 7\frac{82}{48} =$ $8\frac{12}{24}$

$5\frac{27}{72} + 3\frac{40}{72} = 8\frac{67}{72}$

6. $5\frac{3}{8} + 3\frac{5}{9} =$

9. $2\frac{3}{4} + 8\frac{1}{2} + 4\frac{2}{3} =$

$2\frac{9}{12} + 8\frac{6}{12} + 4\frac{8}{12} = 14\frac{23}{12} = 15\frac{11}{12}$

$17\frac{6}{100} + 7\frac{75}{100} = 24\frac{81}{100}$

7. $17\frac{3}{50} + 7\frac{3}{4} =$

10. $9\frac{1}{6} + 5\frac{3}{8} + 3\frac{1}{4} =$

$9\frac{4}{24} + 5\frac{9}{24} + 3\frac{6}{24} = 17\frac{19}{24}$

The subtraction of mixed numbers uses a similar process.

Example 19

$$
\begin{array}{rcl}
9\frac{5}{6} & = & 9\frac{5}{6} \\[2mm]
-1\frac{1}{3} & = & -1\frac{2}{6} \\[2mm]
\hline
 & & 8\frac{3}{6} \quad = 8\frac{1}{2} \text{ reduced}
\end{array}
$$

Example 20

$$
\begin{array}{l}
19\frac{1}{10} \\[2mm]
-16\frac{7}{10} \\[2mm]
\hline
\end{array}
$$

In this case, a unit of tenths must be borrowed from the 19 in order to complete the subtraction.

$$
\begin{array}{ll}
18\frac{11}{10} & \left(18 + \frac{10}{10} + \frac{1}{10}\right) \\[2mm]
-16\frac{7}{10} & \\[2mm]
\hline
2\frac{4}{10} & = 2\frac{2}{5} \text{ reduced}
\end{array}
$$

Complete the following subtraction problems. Reduce your answers to lowest terms.

1. $14\frac{2}{3} - 7\frac{1}{3} = 7\frac{1}{3}$

6. $6\frac{1}{8} - 1\frac{1}{10} = 6\frac{10}{80} - 1\frac{8}{80} = 5\frac{2}{80} = 5\frac{1}{40}$

2. $3\frac{3}{8} - 1\frac{1}{8} =$

$2\frac{2}{8} = 2\frac{1}{4}$

7. $7\frac{3}{4} - 1\frac{1}{6} = 7\frac{9}{12} - 1\frac{2}{12} = 6\frac{7}{12}$

3. $6\frac{3}{8} - 1\frac{1}{10} =$

$6\frac{15}{40} - 1\frac{4}{40} = 5\frac{11}{40}$

8. $173\frac{1}{2} - \frac{1}{3} = 173\frac{3}{6} - \frac{2}{6} = 173\frac{1}{6}$

4. $59\frac{1}{3} - 6\frac{3}{8} =$

$59\frac{8}{24} - 6\frac{9}{24} = 58\frac{32}{24} - 6\frac{9}{24} =$

$52\frac{23}{24}$

9. $9\frac{3}{4} - 6\frac{2}{3} = 9\frac{9}{12} - 6\frac{8}{12} = 3\frac{1}{12}$

5. $5\frac{7}{10} - 3\frac{1}{3} =$

$5\frac{21}{30} - 3\frac{10}{30} = 2\frac{11}{30}$

10. $8\frac{1}{9} - 1\frac{1}{2} = 8\frac{2}{18} - 1\frac{9}{18} =$

$7\frac{20}{18} - 1\frac{9}{18} = 6\frac{11}{18}$

Multiplication and Division

The multiplication of common fractions is more simple than addition or subtraction. There is no need for a common denominator.

Common Fractions

The denominators are multiplied and the numerators are multiplied. The product should be reduced as in the previous fraction problems.

Example 21

$$\frac{5}{6} \times \frac{4}{7} = \frac{20}{42} = \frac{10}{21} \text{ reduced}$$

Example 22

$$\frac{9}{10} \times \frac{4}{11} = \frac{36}{110} = \frac{18}{55}$$

A shortcut or work-saving step can be used to reduce the amount of multiplication. By reducing the fractions before the multiplication begins, the factors are made smaller and the product is also much smaller.

Example 23

$$\frac{9}{\overset{}{\underset{5}{\cancel{10}}}} \times \frac{\overset{1}{\cancel{2}}}{5} = \frac{9}{25}$$

Reducing can take place anytime you can divide any numerator and any denominator by the same number.

Example 24

$$\frac{3}{4} \times \frac{4}{9} = \frac{\overset{1}{\cancel{3}}}{4} \times \frac{4}{\underset{3}{\cancel{9}}} = \frac{1}{\underset{1}{\cancel{4}}} \times \frac{\overset{1}{\cancel{4}}}{3} = \frac{1}{3}$$

Example 25

$$\frac{6}{11} \times \frac{1}{42} = \frac{\overset{1}{\cancel{6}}}{11} \times \frac{1}{\underset{7}{\cancel{42}}} = \frac{1}{77}$$

A series of fractions may be multiplied just as in the two previous examples. Reducing before multiplication is still advisable.

Example 26

$$\frac{3}{4} \times \frac{7}{8} \times \frac{1}{9} = \frac{\overset{1}{\cancel{3}}}{4} \times \frac{7}{8} \times \frac{1}{\underset{3}{\cancel{9}}} = \frac{7}{96}$$

Example 27

$$\frac{9}{10} \times \frac{3}{4} \times \frac{8}{9} = \frac{\cancel{9}^{1}}{\cancel{10}_{5}} \times \frac{3}{\cancel{4}_{1}} \times \frac{\cancel{8}^{\cancel{2}^{1}}}{\cancel{9}_{1}} = \frac{3}{5}$$

A whole number can be made into a fraction by placing a denominator of one (1) under the whole number. After all, the whole number is only an expression of so many units or ones.

This point may be useful when multiplying fractions and whole numbers.

Example 28

$$\frac{3}{4} \times 8 \times \frac{1}{3} =$$

$$\frac{\cancel{3}^{1}}{\cancel{4}_{1}} \times \frac{\cancel{8}^{2}}{1} \times \frac{1}{\cancel{3}_{1}} = \frac{2}{1} = 2$$

Exercise J Find the product in the following problems. Reduce your answers.

1. $\frac{3}{16} \times \frac{8}{9} =$

$\frac{\cancel{3}^{1}}{\cancel{16}_{2}} \times \frac{\cancel{8}^{1}}{\cancel{9}_{3}} = \frac{1}{6}$

4. $\frac{5}{7} \times \frac{1}{6} = \frac{5}{42}$

2. $\frac{7}{16} \times 2\frac{1}{5} =$

$\frac{7}{16} \times \frac{11}{5} = \frac{77}{80}$

5. $\frac{2}{3} \times \frac{3}{4} = \frac{2}{1} \times \frac{1}{4} = \frac{2}{4} = \frac{1}{2}$

3. $\frac{7}{8} \times \frac{5}{7} =$

$\frac{1}{8} \times \frac{5}{1} = \frac{5}{8}$

6. $\frac{5}{9} \times \frac{7}{10} = \frac{1}{9} \times \frac{7}{2} = \frac{7}{18}$

7. $\dfrac{7}{16} \times 8 \times \dfrac{13}{14} =$ *(handwritten: $\dfrac{13}{4}$ $3\frac{1}{4}$)*

9. $\dfrac{5}{8} \times \dfrac{5}{9} \times \dfrac{6}{7} =$ *(handwritten: $\dfrac{50}{168} = \dfrac{25}{84}$)*

8. $4\dfrac{3}{4} \times 5 \times \dfrac{5}{6} =$ *(handwritten: 475)*

(handwritten: $\dfrac{19}{4} \times \dfrac{5}{1} \times \dfrac{5}{6} = \dfrac{475}{24}$ $19.\dfrac{19}{24}$)

10. $\dfrac{13}{21} \times \dfrac{3}{10} \times \dfrac{5}{16} =$ *(handwritten: $\dfrac{13}{224}$)*

Division

Division of common fractions requires a few additional instructions. The first step is to review the way in which a division problem is read. In chapter 1 on whole numbers, you found that a problem such as 18 ÷ 6 is read "eighteen divided by six" or "six divided into eighteen." Eighteen is the dividend and six is the divisor. In the problem $\dfrac{3}{5} \div \dfrac{1}{2}$, $\dfrac{3}{5}$ is the dividend and $\dfrac{1}{2}$ is the divisor. You must be able to identify the divisor in order to be able to do the additional steps required in the division of fractions.

In the example $\dfrac{3}{5} \div \dfrac{1}{2}$, the divisor $\dfrac{1}{2}$ must be inverted (i.e., tipped upside down) and the (÷) sign changed to a (×) sign. You then continue as you did in the multiplication problems.

Example 29

$\dfrac{3}{5} \div \dfrac{1}{2} =$

$\dfrac{3}{5} \times \dfrac{2}{1} = \dfrac{6}{5} = 1\dfrac{1}{5}$

Example 30

$\dfrac{9}{10} \div \dfrac{2}{5} =$

$\dfrac{9}{10} \times \dfrac{5}{2} = \dfrac{9}{4} = 2\dfrac{1}{4}$

Exercise K

Find the quotient in the following problems. Reduce your answers.

1. $\dfrac{6}{7} \div \dfrac{1}{2} =$

$\dfrac{6}{7} \times \dfrac{2}{1} = \dfrac{12}{7}$

$= 1\dfrac{5}{7}$

2. $\dfrac{9}{10} \div \dfrac{3}{5} =$

$\frac{3}{4} \times \frac{16}{7} = (\frac{12}{7}) 1\frac{5}{7}$

3. $\frac{3}{4} \div \frac{7}{16} =$

7. $\frac{7}{10} \div \frac{1}{5} =$ $\frac{35}{10} = 3\frac{1}{2}$

$\frac{5}{8} \times \frac{4}{1} = \frac{5}{2} \; 2\frac{1}{2}$

4. $\frac{5}{8} \div \frac{1}{4} =$

8. $\frac{3}{4} \div \frac{1}{8} = \frac{24}{4} = 6$

$\frac{3}{8} \times \frac{9}{2} = \frac{27}{16} \; 1\frac{11}{16}$

5. $\frac{3}{8} \div \frac{2}{9} =$

9. $\frac{5}{7} \div \frac{1}{6} = \frac{5 \times 6}{7} = \frac{30}{7} = 4\frac{2}{7}$

$\frac{6}{7} \times \frac{3}{2} = \frac{18}{14} \; \frac{4}{14} = 1\frac{2}{7}$

6. $\frac{6}{7} \div \frac{2}{3} =$

10. $\frac{5}{6} \div \frac{2}{3} = \frac{5}{6} \times \frac{3}{2} = \frac{5}{4} = 1\frac{1}{4}$

Mixed Numbers

The multiplication of mixed numbers requires an additional step (i.e., changing the mixed numbers to improper fractions).

Example 31

$1\frac{1}{6} \times 3\frac{1}{2} =$

$\frac{7}{6} \times \frac{7}{2} = \frac{49}{12} = 4\frac{1}{12}$

Example 32

$2\frac{9}{10} \times 5\frac{1}{6} =$

$\frac{29}{10} \times \frac{31}{6} = \frac{899}{60} = 14\frac{59}{60}$

The division of mixed numbers requires the same step (i.e., changing the mixed numbers to improper fractions).

Example 33

$$4\frac{1}{2} \div 3\frac{3}{8} =$$

$$\frac{9}{2} \div \frac{27}{8} =$$

$$\frac{9}{2} \times \frac{8}{27} = \frac{4}{3} = 1\frac{1}{3}$$

Exercise L   Find the product or quotient in the following problems. Reduce your answers to lowest terms.

1. $6\frac{1}{2} \times 3\frac{3}{16} \times 5\frac{1}{8} =$

$$\frac{13}{2} \times \frac{51}{16} \times \frac{41}{8} =$$

$$\frac{27{,}183}{256} = 106\frac{47}{256}$$

5. $5\frac{1}{6} \div 2\frac{4}{5} =$

$$\frac{31}{6} \div \frac{14}{5} = \frac{31}{6} \times \frac{5}{14} = \frac{155}{84} \quad 1\frac{71}{84}$$

2. $8\frac{1}{4} \div 1\frac{3}{4} = 4\frac{5}{7}$

$$\frac{33}{4} \div \frac{7}{4} = \frac{33}{4} \times \frac{4^1}{7} = \frac{33}{7} = 4\frac{5}{7}$$

6. $10\frac{1}{4} \div 3\frac{4}{5} =$

$$\frac{41}{4} \div \frac{19}{5} = \frac{41}{4} \times \frac{5}{19} = \frac{205}{76} \quad 2\frac{53}{76}$$

3. $6\frac{3}{4} \div 1\frac{5}{8} =$

$$\frac{27}{4} \div \frac{13}{8} = \frac{27}{4} \times \frac{8^2}{13} = \frac{54}{13} = 4\frac{2}{13}$$

7. $5\frac{6}{7} \div \frac{5}{9} =$

$$\frac{41}{7} \div \frac{5}{9} = \frac{41}{7} \times \frac{9}{5} = \frac{369}{35} \quad 10\frac{19}{35}$$

4. $4\frac{2}{3} \div 1\frac{1}{6} = 4$

$$\frac{14}{3} \div \frac{7}{6} = \frac{14}{3} \times \frac{6^2}{7} = \frac{28}{7} = 4$$

8. $5\frac{4}{9} \div 3\frac{3}{5} =$

$$\frac{49}{9} \div \frac{18}{5} = \frac{49}{9} \times \frac{5}{18} = \frac{245}{162} \quad 1\frac{83}{162}$$

Increases and Decreases

Business and government leaders frequently make comparisons of sales, revenue, employees, etc. The way in which the comparison is made is very important. The wording is the key to understanding the change.

Example 34

The sales of the Wallace Company were $4,000,000 in 1985. In 1986 the sales were $5,000,000. This could be expressed as "an increase of $\frac{1}{4}$" or "to $1\frac{1}{4}$ of last years sales." Both mean that sales increased by $1,000,000. Be careful to watch the wording in problems that mention increase or decrease.

Example 35

If the sales of the Wallace Company were to go from $5,000,000 in 1986 to $4,000,000 in 1987, the information could be communicated by stating that sales decreased "by $\frac{1}{5}$" or "to $\frac{4}{5}$'s of last year's sales." Again, in either method of stating the information, the sales decreased by $1,000,000.

Ratios

A **ratio** is the comparison of one value to another. This may be expressed as a fraction such as $\frac{5}{1}$. In this case, 5 is being compared to 1. The number on the bottom is the value that is being compared to; it is the basis of comparison. The ratio may also be written as 5:1. The colon replaces the — sign. The ratio is still read as "5 to 1."

This ability to compare one value to another is useful in many business situations. A comparison can be made of the number of male to female employees in a firm, the amount of profits to sales over a period, and the number of hours of machine time to the number of hours of labor to perform a task.

Example 36

The Giant Food Store had the following items in stock at the point of inventory on July 31, 1983.

Packaged goods $34,000
Produce   8,000
Meat   18,000
Non-food items   20,000

What was the ratio of food items to non-food items in the store?
Total of food items = $60,000
Total of non-food items = $20,000
Ratio of 3:1 (Reduced)

Example 37

There are eighty employees in the Accounting Department. Ten of the employees are in managerial positions. What is the ratio of non-managerial employees to managerial employees?

$80 - 10 = 70$

Ratio of 7 to 1

Exercise M

Use the following data to develop the ratios in this exercise.

Number of employees in firm = 400

Number of employees 40 years old or older = 60

Number of males = 240

Number of employees with 10 or more years of experience = 320

Number of employees that are in clerical positions = 80

Number of non-clerical employees in the firm = 320

Number of employees 50 years old or older = 20

1. Ratio of males to females = __3:2__ .

2. Ratio of those between 40 and 50 years old to the total = _____ .

3. Ratio of non-clerical to clerical employees = _____ .

4. Ratio of all employees to male employees = _____ .

5. Ratio of all employees to female employees = _____ .

6. Ratio of employees who have 10 or less years to those who have 10 or more years of experience = _____ .

Name _____ Date _____ Score _____

Skill Problems Complete the following problems. Reduce your answers to lowest terms.

$\frac{7}{8} + \frac{6}{8} = \frac{14}{8} = 1\frac{5}{8}$

1. $\frac{7}{8} + \frac{3}{4} =$

2. $\frac{7}{16} - \frac{3}{16} = \frac{4}{16} = \frac{1}{4}$

$\frac{1}{6} + \frac{2}{6} = \frac{3}{6} = \frac{1}{2}$

3. $\frac{1}{6} + \frac{1}{3} =$

4. $\frac{3}{4} + \frac{7}{8} + \frac{1}{3} = \frac{18}{24} + \frac{21}{24} + \frac{8}{24} =$
$\frac{47}{24} = 1\frac{23}{24}$

$\frac{21}{30} - \frac{20}{30} = \frac{1}{30}$

5. $\frac{7}{10} - \frac{2}{3} =$

6. $\frac{7}{8} - \frac{1}{2} = \frac{7}{8} - \frac{4}{8} = \frac{3}{8}$

$\frac{21}{8} - \frac{2}{5} = \frac{105}{40} - \frac{16}{40} = \frac{89}{40} =$
$2\frac{9}{40}$

7. $2\frac{5}{8} - \frac{2}{5} =$

8. $\frac{7}{8} + \frac{1}{4} + 1\frac{3}{5} = \frac{7}{8} + \frac{1}{4} + \frac{8}{5}$
$\frac{35}{40} + \frac{10}{40} + \frac{64}{40} = \frac{115}{40} \, 2\frac{35}{40}$

$\frac{5}{t} - \frac{19}{8} = \frac{70}{8} - \frac{19}{8} = \frac{51}{8} = 6\frac{3}{8}$

9. $8\frac{3}{4} - 2\frac{3}{8} =$

10. $6\frac{1}{3} + 5 + 3\frac{3}{8} =$

$\frac{61}{8} - \frac{3}{4} \, \frac{61}{8} - \frac{6}{8} = \frac{55}{8} \, 6\frac{7}{8}$

11. $7\frac{5}{8} - \frac{3}{4} =$

12. $\frac{4}{5} + \frac{3}{8} + \frac{1}{2} + \frac{3}{5} =$

$\frac{7}{24}$

13. $\frac{7}{8} \times \frac{1}{3} = \frac{7}{24}$

14. $2\frac{5}{6} \div \frac{1}{3} =$

$\frac{5}{4} \div \frac{1}{6} = \frac{5}{4} \times \frac{6}{1}$ $\frac{30}{4} 7\frac{2}{4} = 7\frac{1}{2}$ 15. $1\frac{1}{4} \div \frac{1}{6} =$

16. $\frac{4}{5} \times \frac{3}{8} \times \frac{1}{2} =$ $\frac{12}{80} = \frac{3}{20}$

$\frac{6}{28} = \frac{3}{14}$ 17. $\frac{6}{7} \times \frac{1}{4} =$

18. $6\frac{1}{2} \times \frac{5}{6} =$ $\frac{13}{2} \times \frac{5}{6} = \frac{65}{12} = 5\frac{5}{12}$

$\frac{3}{4} \times \frac{3}{1} = \frac{9}{4} = 2\frac{1}{4}$ 19. $\frac{3}{4} \div \frac{1}{3} =$

20. $\frac{3}{8} \times \frac{5}{6} \times \frac{3}{4} = \frac{45}{192}$

$\frac{96}{900} = \frac{32}{300} = \frac{8}{75}$ 21. $\frac{1}{5} \times \frac{3}{4} \times \frac{8}{9} \times \frac{4}{5} =$

22. $4\frac{1}{2} + 3\frac{2}{5} + \frac{7}{8} =$ $\frac{9}{2} + \frac{17}{5} + \frac{7}{8}$ $\frac{180}{40} + \frac{136}{40} + \frac{35}{40}$ $\frac{351}{40} =$ $8\frac{31}{40}$

$\frac{7}{4} \div \frac{5}{8} = \frac{14}{8} \div \frac{5}{8} = \frac{9}{8} = 1\frac{1}{8}$ 23. $1\frac{3}{4} - \frac{5}{8} =$

24. $\frac{1}{2} + \frac{3}{8} + 4 =$ $\frac{4}{8} + \frac{3}{8} + 4 = 4\frac{7}{8}$

Business Application Problems

1. An airline has offered $\frac{1}{4}$ off of the regular fare of all the flights to California. What will the sale price be if the regular fare was \$280?

2. Pat Hough, a sales clerk at Harold's upholstery shop, increased her sales by $\frac{1}{10}$ over last month. Sales last month were \$14,630. How much was the increase?

3. Lillian McTole found that she should devote $\frac{1}{4}$ of her available time to studying her business courses. She has three business courses that she feels deserve equal attention. Lillian has twenty-four hours of free time over the weekend. How much time should she spend on each business course?

4. Andy Coulter worked the following hours during last week: Monday, $6\frac{3}{10}$ hours; Tuesday, $8\frac{3}{10}$ hours; Wednesday, 9 hours; Thursday, $8\frac{1}{10}$ hours; and Friday, $9\frac{1}{10}$ hours. How many hours did he work in total?

5. A display rack and accessories sold for $2,700 five years ago. A replacement would cost $13,500 today. What is the ratio of today's price to the price of five years ago?

6. A man's coat was priced at $188. The proprietor of Jule and Justin's Men's Store decided to have a $\frac{1}{4}$ -off sale of all the merchandise in the store for the month. What would be the sale price on the coat?

7. Sales of the Ampster Corporation increased to $1\frac{1}{2}$ of last year's level. Last year the sales were $543,670. What is the amount of the increase?

8. Jim worked $2\frac{3}{10}$ hours in the morning and later returned to work $5\frac{1}{2}$ hours. How many total hours did he work for the day?

9. There are 628 employees in the Wixom Company of Bedford. Of the total, 157 are over 50 years old. What is the ratio of all employees to those who are over 50?

10. The price of a commodity increased to five times its price of three years ago. The current price is $465. To the nearest ten dollars, what was the price three years ago?

11. Judi earns $4 per hour. When she works overtime she is paid at $1\frac{1}{2}$ times her regular rate. What is her overtime rate?

12. The delivery truck for Chuck's Tuxedo Shop ran the following route Tuesday morning: to the cleaners, $\frac{4}{10}$ miles; to the Post Office, $7\frac{1}{10}$ miles; to the trucking company, $5\frac{3}{10}$ miles; to the store, $6\frac{9}{10}$ miles; to the gas station, $\frac{1}{10}$ mile; to the coffee shop, 2 miles; back to the shop, $1\frac{1}{10}$ miles. What was the total mileage for the delivery truck that morning?

13. A piece of land has increased in value by $\frac{1}{4}$ over the past four years. What was the average increase for each year?

14. A piece of yard goods must be cut into lengths of $2\frac{1}{4}$ feet each. The bolt of material is 500 feet long. How many whole pieces can be cut from the bolt?

15. One-fifth of the college's enrollment is made up of upperclassmen (juniors and seniors). How many are underclassmen if the total enrollment is 38,110?

16. According to U.S. Census data, a city's population has grown to $1\frac{2}{7}$ of its previous size. At the previous census, the population was 187,684. What is the present size?

17. The hours worked by employees in the shipping department were as follows:

A. Rimshaw $\qquad$ $39\frac{1}{10}$

P. Borgstun $\qquad$ $36\frac{3}{10}$

W. Billings $\qquad$ $38\frac{3}{10}$

F. Stalworth $\qquad$ $37\frac{7}{10}$

B. Feller $\qquad$ $39\frac{9}{10}$

H. Tolunmar $\qquad$ $36\frac{4}{10}$

Total the hours for the department.

18. The manufacture of a gelatin substance used in the food industry is made up of $\frac{1}{4}$ labor cost and $\frac{3}{4}$ material cost. The gelatin in its finished form sells for $180 per ton. What is the dollar amount of the labor factor in the production of 81 tons of the gelatin substance?

19. Of the 650 units of a condominium project, four out of five are "pre-sold" prior to the start of construction. How many remain to be sold?

20. The turnover rate of employees at C.D.C. is 9 out of 10 over a period of one year. If the year began with 450 employees, how many will still be employed at the end of the year?

Challenge Problem   The sales of Bilkton Marketing Corporation are three times the sales of a year ago. The increase in sales, one-half of which is due to more effective advertising, was welcome. The Board of Directors indicated that $\frac{1}{4}$ of the increase will be paid out in dividends. The dividend would amount to $2.20 a share for each of the 1,630,000 shares. What was the amount of sales last year?

Name _____   Date _____   Score _____

1. Label the fraction parts below.

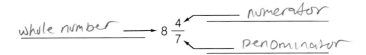

whole number ———→ $8\frac{4}{7}$ ← numerator ← Denominator

2. Match the following.

_____B_____ 1. $6\frac{1}{3}$

_____A_____ 2. $\frac{3}{4}$

_____C_____ 3. $\frac{5}{4}$

_____A_____ 4. $\frac{7}{8}$

_____B_____ 5. $4\frac{2}{3}$

_____C_____ 6. $\frac{15}{10}$

A. Common Fraction
B. Mixed Number
C. Improper Fraction

3. Add $\frac{3}{4} + \frac{4}{5}$

$\frac{15}{20} + \frac{16}{20}$ $\frac{31}{20} = 1\frac{11}{20}$

4. Subtract $\frac{2}{3}$ from $1\frac{1}{2}$

$\frac{3}{2} - \frac{2}{3} = \frac{9}{6} - \frac{4}{6} = \frac{5}{6}$ $\frac{9}{6} = \frac{1}{6}$

5. Multiply $15 \times 3\frac{1}{3}$ $\frac{150}{3} = 50$

$\frac{15}{1} \times \frac{10}{3} = \frac{150}{3} = 50$

6. Divide $\frac{7}{8}$ by $\frac{1}{5}$

$\frac{7}{8} \div \frac{1}{5} = \frac{7}{8} \times \frac{5}{1} = \frac{35}{8} 4\frac{3}{8}$

7. Reduce $\frac{16}{3} = 5\frac{1}{3}$

8. Sales for Campbell & Associates have increased by $\frac{1}{2}$ over last quarter's sales of $98,480. What are the sales for this quarter?

9. Nine hundred eighty-six citizens of a small city are over sixty-two years old. The city's population is 8,874. What is the ratio of all of the citizens to those over sixty-two?

10. James Roberts worked $8\frac{1}{2}$ hours on Wednesday. During the day he spent $3\frac{1}{10}$ hours on the phone following up on orders that he had placed earlier in the month. How many hours did he spend off of the phone?

11. Half of the inventory of the Cason Company is more than one month old. The total inventory value is $57,960. What is the value of the inventory that is dated more than one month old?

12. Ted and Kay each worked $6\frac{1}{2}$ hours on Thursday. They were paid $6 per hour. What was their combined total earnings?

13. There are 800 employees in the accounting department of a life insurance company. One-half of these people will be retrained due to the automation of their jobs. Of the remainder, $\frac{1}{4}$ are women, and $\frac{1}{10}$ of the men are to retire within the next year. How many men will there be in the accounting department a year from now?

(If you missed problems 1 or 2, you need to review Description and Types; problems 3, 4, or 10, you need to review Addition and Subtraction; problems 5, 6, 8, 11, 12, or 13, you need to review Multiplication and Division; problem 7, you need to review Reducing Fractions; and problem 9, you need to review Ratios.) Record your score on the inside back cover for future reference.

3

Working with Decimal Numbers

Performance Objectives

After mastering the material in this chapter, you will be able to:

1. Read and write decimal numbers.
2. Round off decimal numbers accurately.
3. Perform all the fundamental processes on decimal numbers.
4. Change fractions to decimal numbers.
5. Work word problems that require the use of decimal numbers.
6. Understand and use the following:
   Place Values   Decimal Point Placement Rule
   Rounding Rule

Reading and Writing Decimal Numbers

A decimal number is another way of expressing a fraction or portion of a whole unit. The figure below shows the representation of a decimal number as part of a whole. Note that this decimal number can be shown in a way similar to the fraction $\frac{3}{4}$ in the previous chapter. The decimal value .3 can be shown as follows:

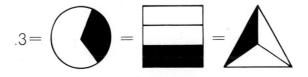

Additional information will be covered in this chapter that will allow you to adapt your knowledge of the fundamental processes to decimal numbers.

Place values

To be able to read and write decimal numbers you must be able to know the **place values** to the right of the decimal point. The figure below will help you identify the place values of decimal numbers.

```
        Decimal Point
        │ Tenths
        │ │ Hundredths
        │ │ │ Thousandths
        │ │ │ │ Ten Thousandths
        │ │ │ │ │ Hundred Thousandths
        │ │ │ │ │ │ Millionths
        │ │ │ │ │ │ │
  0  .  6 5 8 0 7 3
```

Notice that the spelling of the place values to the right of the decimal point have a "ths" on the end of the place value name.

> The digit in the thousandths place is an 8.
> The digit in the tenths place is a 6.
> The digit in the ten thousandths place is a 0.
> The digit in the millionths place is a 3.

Exercise A In the following number 0.879325—

1. The digit in the hundredths place is _____7_____.

2. The digit in the tenths place is _____8_____.

3. The digit in the millionths place is _____5_____.

4. The digit in the ten thousandths place is _____3_____.

5. The digit in the hundred thousandths place is _____2_____.

6. The digit in the thousandths place is _____9_____.

Exercise B In the following number .548061—

1. The digit in the _____hundred thousandths_____ place is a 6.

2. The digit in the _____hundredth_____ place is a 4.

3. The digit in the _____millionths_____ place is a 1.

4. The digit in the _____ place is a 0.

5. The digit in the _____ place is a 5.

6. The digit in the _____ place is an 8.

> Check your progress by turning to the answers at the back of the book.

Now that you know the place values on both sides of the decimal place, you are able to read and write decimal numbers. The numbers to the right of the decimal place are read somewhat differently than those on the left.

> **Example 1**
>
> The number .507 is read: Five hundred seven thousandths. (Notice that the number is read, then the label is added on at the end.)

> **Example 2**
>
> The number .9637 is read: Nine thousand, six hundred thirty-seven ten thousandths.

Exercise C   Read the following decimal numbers to yourself.

1. .6057   2. .9871   3. .500

4. .936   5. .8710   6. .9057

Reading a number that has digits on both sides of the decimal point requires that you use the rules presented in chapter 1 along with those that you have just learned. One additional rule is necessary to make the reading complete. When reading the number, the decimal point is read as an "and" or "point."

> **Example 3**
>
> The number 487.903 is read: Four hundred eighty-seven and nine hundred three thousandths.
> *OR* Four hundred eighty-seven point-nine-zero-three.

Exercise D   Read the following numbers to yourself.

1. 1.9673   2. 400.5091   3. 87,365.851

4. 987.53   5. 896.57321

Reading values that include dollars and cents requires that you read all of the dollar values followed by the word "dollars" and then read "and _____ cents."

> **Example 4**
>
> The value $581.39 is read: Five hundred eighty-one dollars and thirty-nine cents.
> (Notice that the hyphens and the comma are still used in the writing of the values just as they were in chapter 1.)

Write the following values in words. Place commas and hyphens in the appropriate places.

1. $823.67 *Eight hundred twenty-three dollars and sixty-seven cents.*

2. $2,105.46 _____

_____

3. $867.28 _____

_____

4. $234.87 _____

_____

5. $3,869.61 _____

_____

Write the following values using numbers. Insert commas and dollar signs where necessary.

1. Nine hundred thirty-five dollars and forty-nine cents.

   $935.49 _____

2. Sixty-three dollars and twenty-six cents.

   _____

3. Five hundred seventy-two dollars and twenty-one cents.

   _____

4. Three thousand, eighteen dollars and seven cents.

   _____

5. Fifty-one thousand, three hundred seven dollars and thirty-six cents.

   _____

Rounding Off

Rounding rule

The rules that you learned in chapter 1 on rounding off will also hold true for decimal numbers.

The **rounding rule** is the same for decimal numbers as it is for whole numbers. If the instructions for rounding are to "round off your answer to the nearest thousandths," then you must be concerned with the digit in the thousandths place and the digit immediately to the right of it (i.e., the ten thousandths place). In the number .07583, the digit 5 is in the thousandths place. The 5 will be changed to a 6 if the digit immediately to the right of it is a 5 or larger. In the example given, the digit is an 8, therefore the answer is .076. All of the digits to the right of the number to be rounded are dropped.

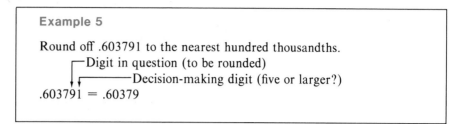

Exercise G   Round off the following numbers to the place value indicated.

1. .60578 to the nearest tenth   .6

2. .4653 to the nearest hundredth

3. .0037 to the nearest tenth

4. .54621 to the nearest thousandth

5. .5467 to the nearest unit

Exercise H   Round off the following values to the nearest cent.

1. $605.837 $605.84

2. $5,867.947

3. $486.938

4. $68,640.273

5. $375.9747

Exercise I   Round off the following numbers to the place value indicated.

1. 607.8035 to the nearest hundredth   607.80

2. 758.9208 to the nearest hundred

3. 759.92749 to the nearest tenth

4. 547,647.8492 to the nearest ten thousand

5. 64,983.987 to the nearest hundredth

Addition The addition of decimal numbers requires the decimal points to be aligned before addition begins.

Example 6

Add the decimal numbers .03; 6.878; 5.67; and 181.006.

.03	.03
6.878	6.878
5.67	5.67
181.006	+181.006
	193.584

Zeros may be added to the numbers if it will aid in the addition process. They should be added to the right of the last digit, thereby not changing the value of the number. The zeros fill in all the columns and, therefore, reduce errors.

Example 7

Find the sum of the following numbers: 6.53; 80.751; .7; 9.543; .00658; and .801.

With zeros added:
```
        6.53000
       80.75100
         .70000
        9.54300
         .00658
    +    .80100
       98.33158
```
(Note: Any whole number has a decimal point to the right of the digit in the units or ones place.)

Exercise J Find the sum in the following problems.

1. 506.375; 9,831.6; 19.6025; 181; and 5,037.62 =
   <u>15,576.1975</u>

2. 56.0983; 86.14; .9573; 658.9401; and 87 =

3. .456; 657.98; 76.98; .86946; and 8.941 =

4. 65.9201; 958; 65.937; and 75.937 =

5. 867; 54,759.136; 86.096; 75.093; and 76.936 =

Exercise K   Find the sum in the following problems.

1. Eight and forty-three ten thousandths; six hundred twelve thousand; eighteen and three hundredths; fifty-seven thousandths.

$$
\begin{array}{r}
8.0043 \\
612{,}000.0000 \\
18.0300 \\
+\phantom{612{,}000}.0570 \\
\hline
612{,}026.0913
\end{array}
$$

2. Three hundred four and six tenths; forty and twenty-seven thousandths; sixty-seven hundredths; and one and four ten thousandths.

3. Fifty-three and six hundred two ten thousandths; four hundred sixteen thousandths; ten and four tenths; and sixteen.

4. Thirty-two and twenty-six thousandths; fifty and ninety-five thousandths; four hundred twenty; and seventy-nine thousandths.

5. One hundred fifty-eight thousand; sixty and twenty-two ten thousandths; four hundred and six thousandths; and three and two hundred four ten thousandths.

Subtraction   Subtraction of decimal numbers also requires the decimal points to be aligned.

Example 8

Subtract 9.853 from 10.1

$$
\begin{array}{r}
10.100 \\
-\ \ 9.853 \\
\hline
.247
\end{array}
$$

Note that zeros may be added to the minuend if it will aid you in the subtraction process.

Exercise L   Find the difference in the following problems.

1. $8.067 - .537 =$
$$
\begin{array}{r}
-\ .537 \\
\hline
7.530
\end{array}
$$

2. $19.6 - 3.167 =$

3. $.9853 - .547 =$
.4383

4. $65 - 8.957 =$

5. $86.958 - 45.095 =$

Exercise M

1. $\$863.47 - \$27.98 =$
$$
\begin{array}{r}
-\ 27.98 \\
\hline
\$835.49
\end{array}
$$

2. $\$875.90 - \$345.85 =$

3. $\$65.86 - \$17.69 =$

4. $\$649.09 - \$52.10 =$

5. $\$756.92 - \$478.00 =$

Multiplication   The multiplication of decimal numbers requires the additional step of the placement of the decimal point. When multiplying the whole numbers 37×8, we find the answer to be:

$$
\begin{array}{rl}
37 & \text{multiplicand} \\
\times\ 8 & \text{multiplier} \\
\hline
296 & \text{product}
\end{array}
$$

Decimal point
placement rule

The **decimal point placement rule** states that the answer should have as many decimal places to the right of the decimal point as the multiplier and the multiplicand have in total.

Example 9

$37 \times .8 =$
$$
\begin{array}{rl}
37 & \\
\times\ .8 & (+1) \\
\hline
29.6 & (1)
\end{array}
$$

Example 10

$3.7 \times .8 =$

$$
\begin{array}{r}
3.7 \quad (+1) \\
\times \ .8 \quad (+1) \\
\hline
2.96 \quad (2)
\end{array}
$$

Example 11

$.0037 \times .00008 =$

$$
\begin{array}{r}
.0037 \quad (+4) \\
\times \quad .00008 \quad (+5) \\
\hline
.000000296 \quad (9)
\end{array}
$$

Notice: Zeros must be added to fill decimal place positions if there are blanks after stepping of the decimal point.

Exercise N   Find the product in the following problems. Pay particular attention to the placement of the decimal point.

1.
$$
\begin{array}{r}
982 \\
\times \ 8.6 \\
\hline
5892 \\
7856 \\
\hline
8,445.2
\end{array}
$$

2.
$$
\begin{array}{r}
.890 \\
\times \ .64
\end{array}
$$

3.
$$
\begin{array}{r}
76.2 \\
\times \ .650
\end{array}
$$

4.
$$
\begin{array}{r}
.150 \\
\times \ .469
\end{array}
$$

5.
$$
\begin{array}{r}
459 \\
\times \ .006
\end{array}
$$

Division   The division of decimal numbers uses the same rules as the division of whole numbers. The placement of the decimal point is the only additional problem in the division of decimal numbers. As shown in Example 12, the division of 42 by 6 requires no decimal point placement, but $42 \div .6$ does require the decimal point placement.

Example 12

$$
6\overline{)42} \quad \begin{array}{c} 7 \end{array}
$$

If the problem would have been to divide 42 by .6, the decimal place would need to be moved, as shown, in order to correctly place the decimal point.

$$.6\overline{)42.0} \qquad .6.\overline{)42.0.} \quad \begin{array}{c} 70. \end{array}$$

Zeros must be added to the end of the dividend in order to fill in the spaces created by moving the decimal point. Additional zeros may be added to the right of the decimal place to aid in division. The number 420 has the same value as 420.0 or 420.000. The decimal point in the answer is placed directly above the decimal point in the dividend after the decimal point has been moved.

Example 13

530.1 ÷ .57 =

$$.57\overline{)530.10.}$$

```
        930.
.57.)530.10.
      513
      171
      171
        0
```

Exercise O

Round off your answers to the nearest tenth in the following problems.

1. 25.0146 ÷ .7 =

```
       35.735
.7.)25.0.146      = 35.7
```

2. .24 ÷ .6 =

3. 4.63 ÷ .015 =
   308.66666 =

4. 9.872 ÷ 5.9 =
   1.6732203 =

5. .045 ÷ 8.2 =
   .0054878 =

Changing Fractions to Decimal Numbers

Any fraction can be changed to a decimal number or its equivalent by dividing the numerator by the denominator.

Example 14

Common Fraction $\frac{3}{4}$ =

```
       .75
4)3.000
  28
  20
  20
```

Improper Fraction

$\frac{13}{8}$ =

```
     1.625
8)13.000
   8
   50
   48
   20
   16
   40
   40
```

Mixed Number

$4\frac{1}{8}$ = 4 plus

```
        .125
8)1.000
  8
  20
  16
  40
  40
```

Answer = 4.125

Exercise P

Change the following fractions into decimal numbers.

1. $\frac{3}{8}$ = .375

2. $\frac{3}{5}$ =

3. $\frac{5}{16}$ =

4. $\frac{12}{5}$ =

5. $2\frac{3}{16}$ =

Assignment
Chapter Three

Name _____ Date _____ Score _____

Skill Problems   Complete the following problems.

1. $9 \div 4.5 =$ 2. $8.02 \times 3.89 =$ 3.
$$
\begin{array}{r}
4.872 \\
12.87 \\
1,095.1037 \\
+\ \ 345.81 \\
\hline
\end{array}
$$

4.
$$
\begin{array}{r}
876.5 \\
-\ 45.860 \\
\hline
\end{array}
$$
    5. $9 \times .095 =$ 6. $47.04 \times 5.9 =$

7. Round off your answer
   to the nearest tenth.
$$
\begin{array}{r}
6.032 \\
\times\ 8.087 \\
\hline
\end{array}
$$

8. Round off your answer to
   the nearest cent.
   $846.13 \div 5.6 =$

9.
$$
\begin{array}{r}
63.08 \\
9. \\
.075 \\
+\ \ .0039 \\
\hline
\end{array}
$$
    10. $3/8 \times .7 =$ 11. Round off your an-
        swer to the nearest
        hundredth.
        $.193 + 6.073 =$

12. $.047 \times 3\ 1/8 =$ 13.
$$
\begin{array}{r}
452.6 \\
\times\ \ \ \ 65.113 \\
\hline
\end{array}
$$
    14. $463 \times 4.2 =$

15.
$$
\begin{array}{r}
1,469. \\
-\ \ \ \ 6.3807 \\
\hline
\end{array}
$$

1. Diana is the unit control manager of a banquet firm. She has been asked to determine the cost of serving a group of twenty-five guests. The price will be $2.87 per pound. Each guest will be served .4 of a pound. What is the cost for the group of twenty-five guests?

2. Fynee is required to check all incoming invoices to make sure that the supplier has extended the totals correctly for each item and totaled the amount. Review her work to be sure that it is correct.

LIGHT

Second Light, Inc.
724 Fifth Avenue
New York, NY 10019
212-582-6552

All reproduction rights to photographs purchased from LIGHT are expressly reserved by the artist. Permission for reproduction must be obtained in writing from LIGHT Gallery.

A photograph is not sold as one of a limited edition unless the contrary is explicitly stated on this invoice.

SOLD TO · Barbara Strong, Inc.
157 W. 42nd Street
New York, NY 10018

SHIP TO · Same

			AMOUNT
11984	24"x36" A. Adams reproduction		$2,500.⁻
9462	Set of three Stahl prints @ $4.80 ea		14.40
10567	Toutain original/frame		127.95
2134	Pavlidis landscape of Mt. Katahdin		200.⁻
		Total	$2,842.35

Please make check payable to Second Light, Inc.

FORM B.5BH

Courtesy of Second Light, Inc., New York, NY.

3. Patricia Barrett worked 7.1 hours at the rate of $4.60 per hour. How much did she earn?

4. The sales staff met to determine the total distance on the route through the city. The distances were: office to the warehouse: 4.6 miles; warehouse to the first stop: 3.2 miles; sales route to the office: 54.1 miles. What is the total mileage?

5. Helene is paid on a piece-rate system that specifies that she will earn 8.3 ($.083) cents for each operation that she completes. Yesterday she did 471 operations. To the nearest cent, how much did she earn?

6. A salesperson for the Wesser Company found that five-eighths of the 17.35 tons of chloride sold each year was used for agricultural purposes. To the nearest tenth of a ton, how much was used for this purpose?

7. Mr. LaFrance paid $10,500 for a piece of land at the rate of $730 an acre. How many full acres did he buy?

8. A manufacturer found that the price of needed raw materials had increased by 1.9 times over the past four years. The old price of four years ago was $14.50 per unit. What is the price increase?

9. Marie Kreger sold her home for $31,000. The balance on the mortgage was $18,546.87. She paid the real estate agent a commission on the sale. The commission was $2,869.95. She also paid the bank a penalty of $567.12 for early payment on the mortgage. She decided to use the money from the sale of the first home to purchase a home that cost $75,800. How much money did she have to borrow to purchase the new home?

10. A representative from the manufacturing department of Olinson Carbides found that 46.8 hours were lost due to accidents over the past month, 85 hours due to sickness, and 46 hours to vacation time. The department had scheduled 820 hours for the month. How many hours were actually worked?

11. Joanne Bacher sold pennants at football games. The pennants cost thirty-seven cents each. They were sold for seventy-five cents. Joanne and her sales team sold 167,759 pennants during the season. What were the total sales for the season?

12. Bill Wilson said that he would like to improve his shop by expanding the size by 1.8 times its current area of 197 square feet. He expects the addition would cost about $15,000. How many square feet would the new portion of the building have?

13. Julie Carstairs was offered a job paying $38.50 a day for eight hours work. She would like to take the job, but she is not sure if the job pays more than the $4.90 an hour she is earning at her present job. What is the highest hourly rate that Julie has as an option?

14. The Lennolda Shoppe is taking inventory of the small pieces in the storage area of the shop. The inventory revealed the following: 45 pieces priced at $.54 each, 144 pieces priced at $.19 each, 20 units priced at $1.95 each, a box of 50 pieces priced at $.39 each and 4 units priced at $.49 each. What is the total value of these small pieces of merchandise?

15. Mr. Ernest Seldon bought a bin of bird seed. The bird seed is made up of seven bushels of oats at $2.13 a bushel, ten bushels of cracked corn at $3.19 a bushel, and five bushels of cracked sunflower seeds at $1.18 a bushel. The mixture was sold for $3.50 a half bushel, which included the 10 cents for the bag in which it was packed. How much profit did he make?

16. The lounge chairs of the Marina Bay Condominium are in need of repair. A review of the grounds indicated that there were 27 chairs and 27 loungers that needed to have new webbing installed. The manager received price quotes from area repair shops. The lowest price was $.71 per replaced web. There are 13 webs on each of the chairs and 22 webs on each lounger. How much will it cost to have the 54 units repaired?

17. The sales staff of the Weston Company has been requested to submit their report for the week. The volume of "firm" and "possible" sales are listed below by sales representative. What is the difference between the firm and possible sales figures if each unit sells for $8.45?

Sales Representative	Firm Sales Orders	Possible Sales Orders
A. Janor	410 Units	650 Units
B. K. Moore	301 Units	800 Units
N. Manoto	285 Units	1,000 Units

18. Fuel for the fleet of trucks operated by Wiise and Company cost $5,689.40 last month. The company is able to purchase fuel at a cost of $1.17 per gallon. To the nearest tenth of a gallon, how many gallons of fuel did the firm purchase last month?

19. A doctors office will begin to deliver a small flower and card arrangement to each of the surgery patients as of the first of next month. There are 162 patients scheduled for surgery next month. The flowers will cost $8.50 and cards will cost $1.25 each. The delivery charge will be $4 on the average. What will be the total cost of this service for the month?

20. The Weirton Company has offered to deduct one eighth of the price off of every unit of their product over a volume of 500,000 per month. The product sells for $627.50 each. What will be the price of units sold over the 500,000 volume level? Round off your answer to the nearest cent.

Challenge Problem

The Whiting Company bought a bolt of material 4 feet wide with a length of 500 feet. The material is to be cut into pieces 4 feet wide by 5.7 feet long. There were 14 pieces that had to be scrapped due to errors made in cutting. The bolt of material cost $4,678.95. If the firm makes a profit of $14.86 on each piece produced, what will be the total profit made from the sale of the full cut pieces?

Name _____ Date _____ Score _____

1. Round off the following values as indicated.

    a. 7.9803 to the nearest ten _____

    b. .08712 to the nearest tenth _____

    c. 647.096 to the nearest hundred _____

    d. 64.0968 to the nearest thousandth _____

    e. 43.916 to the nearest tenth _____

2. Write the following value in words: $385.70

    _____

3. Add 733.042, 8.367, and 13.758

4. Subtract 9.405 from 57.079

5. Multiply 1.2 × .56 and round off your answer to the nearest unit.

6. Divide $3.72 by 8 and round off your answer to the nearest cent.

7. Change the following to decimal form.

    a. $\frac{5}{8}$ = _.625_ b. $\frac{3}{10}$ = _.3_ c. $4\frac{1}{5}$ = _4.2_

8. If a certain industrial product is made from plastic, it costs 6.7 ($.067)
    cents per unit over a volume of 6,000 pieces. If the same product is made
    of rubber, it will cost $450 for the same volume. The company has a
    contract that assures a revenue of $1,560 for the 6,000 pieces made of
    either material. What is the maximum profit per piece rounded to the
    nearest cent?

9. AM Corp. has expanded its business 1.6 times over last year's volume of
    $324,952. What is this year's volume?

10. Anthony James Ureel, the manager of an agribusiness firm, noted that seven-tenths of the 15,479 barrels of herbicide he bought last year was used for soybean production. To the nearest whole barrel, how many were used for soybeans?

11. Total the sales slip shown below.

PARTS INVOICE

04124

NORTHGATE FORD, Inc.

FORD
MERCURY
LINCOLN

3600 Pine Grove
P.O. Box 706
Telephone Area 313-984-5011
PORT HURON, MICHIGAN 48060
REGISTRATION # F-105152

FORD
MERCURY
LINCOLN

ANY WARRANTIES ON THE PRODUCTS SOLD HEREBY ARE THOSE MADE BY THE MANUFACTURER. THIS IS A LIMITED WARRANTY FOR 90 DAYS. THE SELLER HEREBY EXPRESSLY DISCLAIMS ALL WARRANTIES, EITHER EXPRESSED OR IMPLIED, INCLUDING ANY IMPLIED WARRANTY OF MERCHANTABILITY OR FITNESS FOR A PARTICULAR PURPOSE, AND NEITHER ASSUMES NOR AUTHORIZES ANY OTHER PERSON TO ASSUME FOR IT ANY LIABLITY IN CONNECTION WITH THE SALE OF SAID PRODUCTS.

CUST. I.D	SALESMAN	SHIP VIA	WAYBILL NO.	P.O. # OR R.O. #	TERMS	INVOICE DATE	INVOICE NUMBER
	TW					3·6·86	

PAGE / OF /

SOLD TO: John Lump
4640 Lapeer
Wahdams, MI 48060

SHIP TO:

ITEM NO.	ORDERED	SHIPPED	B/O	PART NUMBER	BIN	SR	DESCRIPTION	SUGGESTED LIST	NET	TOTAL NET
				F80643271			Block			730.25
				F98374026			Gasket Set			41.53
				F87304627			Bearing-Valve			36.40
				F91406236			Snap Ring Set			9.68

NO RETURNS WITHOUT THIS INVOICE — NO RETURNS ON ITEMS $10.00 OR LESS
NO RETURNS AFTER 30 DAYS
NO REFUNDS OR EXCHANGES ON ELECTRICAL PARTS
OR SPECIAL ORDERED PARTS   X _____
20% HANDLING CHARGE ON RETURNED MERCHANDISE   RECEIVED BY

Courtesy of Northgate Ford, Inc., Port Huron, MI.

(If you missed problem 1, you need to review Rounding Off; problem 2, you need to review Reading and Writing Decimal Numbers; problems 3 or 11, you need to review Addition; problem 4, you need to review Subtraction; problems 5, 8, or 9, you need to review Multiplication; problem 6, you need to review Division; problem 7, you need to review Changing Fractions to Decimal Numbers; and if you missed problem 10, you need to review Multiplication, Changing Fractions to Decimal Numbers, and Rounding Off.) Record your score on the inside back cover for future reference.

Section

2

Getting Started—
Business Application

4 Banking Records
5 Payroll
6 Measurements

4 Banking Records

Performance Objectives

After mastering the material in this chapter, you will be able to:

1. Identify different types of endorsements.
2. Reconcile a bank statement.
3. Describe how a checking account functions.
4. Understand and use the following:

Depositor	Special Endorsement
Imprinting Checks	Restrictive Endorsement
Deposit Slip	Bank Statement
Check Register	Deposits in Transit
Check Stub	Outstanding Checks
Check	Service Charges
Blank Endorsement	Adjusted Balance

Most debt payments made by business and private individuals are made by check. The checking account provides a convenient as well as a safe payment method, a definite improvement over paying with cash in person.

When a new checking account is opened, the parties who are authorized to sign checks are required to give a sample signature to the bank. A card containing the signature(s) is kept on file and available to bank personnel at all times. This procedure is used in order to provide security by verifying the handwritten signature.

Depositor

The new **depositor** is given a set of deposit slips and blank checks. A personalized set of checks is ordered at this time also. The new, personalized set will contain pertinent information as to the account holder's name, account number, address, telephone number, and possibly driver's license number. These checks are easier for the bank to identify, and will limit use to only the authorized parties whose names are imprinted on them. There is a charge for the **imprinting** process.

Imprinting checks

Deposits and Payments

Deposit slip

When a depositor wants to deposit money in an account, a **deposit slip** is completed. The date, the amount of currency, the amount of coin, as well as each check to be deposited are listed separately on the slip. This slip, along with the monies specified, is given to the bank teller by the depositor. A duplicate deposit slip or some acknowledgment is then given to the depositor. This is to be retained as proof of deposit and recorded in the check register.

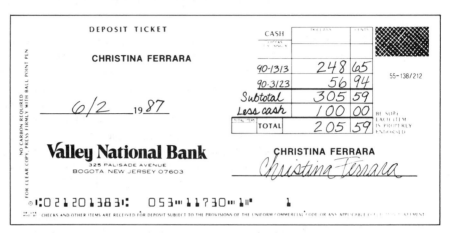

Courtesy of Christina M. Ferrara.

Check register
Check stub

The **check register** or **check stub** provides the form on which the depositor can determine the amount in his account. Deposits are added to the account balance, and checks are subtracted from the account balance. It is important to record the deposits and checks and do the necessary addition or subtraction at the time the transaction occurs. This procedure will insure that there will be sufficient funds in the account at all times to cover issued checks.

PLEASE BE SURE TO **DEDUCT** ANY PER CHECK CHARGES OR SERVICE CHARGES THAT MAY APPLY TO YOUR ACCOUNT

CHECK NO.	DATE	CHECKS ISSUED TO OR DESCRIPTION OF DEPOSIT	(−) AMOUNT OF CHECK	√ T	(−) CHECK FEE (IF ANY)	(+) AMOUNT OF DEPOSIT	BALANCE

Courtesy of Michigan Bank—Port Huron, MI.

Check

When writing a **check,** the depositor must fill in the date, to whom the check is payable (the payee), the amount of the check in numbers as well as words, and lastly an authorized signature. The check register or check stub should also be filled out at this time. This provides a record, duplicating the information on the check itself.

When the bank receives the completed check, it is handled as a demand by the depositor to pay the payee the specified amount.

Types of Endorsements

Before the bank will exchange cash for the completed check, the payee must sign the check. This must be done on the back on the same end that states "Pay to the order of." This signature must be the same name as that specified on the front of the check. If the payee simply signs his name, the check can be cashed by anyone. The check is, therefore, transferable. This type of endorsement is termed a **blank endorsement.** Should a check with a blank endorsement be lost, it could be cashed by any finder. The finder would simply have to sign his name below the endorsement of the payee to receive the specified amount of cash.

Blank endorsement

To provide protection to the payee, the depositor could add to the blank endorsement a limitation such as "Payable to J. Hawkins." With J. Hawkins's signature, only J. Hawkins would be allowed to cash the check. This type of endorsement is termed a **special endorsement.**

Special endorsement

Another restriction can be added to the signature specifying exactly what is to be done with the check. "For deposit only" and the payee's signature will restrict the use of the check to only a deposit in the payee's account. This type of endorsement is termed a **restrictive endorsement.**

Restrictive endorsement

Exercise A

Identify the endorsements below as blank, special, or restrictive.

restrictive	1.	For Deposit to the account of S.S.X. Co. Abe Solen
	2.	Payable to the Green Co. Alice Madison
	3.	James Amos
	4.	P. D. Pierson
	5.	For payment on promissory note #37802 P. Wolver
	6.	For Deposit Only J. J. Adams
	7.	The Big Horn Corp.
	8.	Payable to J. Swage Alp Smith
	9.	P. & K. Turin Co.
	10.	Iverson Co.

Industry Changes

Over the past few years there have been several changes in the banking industry. The checking account was once only available from a full-service bank. Today, due to changes in the law, checking services are available from not only banks, but also from savings and loan associations, credit unions, and investment firms. Not all services are available from each one of these types of firms. It is worthwhile for the individual consumer and the corporate officer to investigate and compare available services.

Much of the "extra" services that are available now are due to the application of the computer to account activities. An account holder is now able to transfer funds from one account to another, receive interest on checking account balances, and make deposits and withdrawals on a 24-hour basis from automatic tellers. Corporations are not allowed to receive some of the services mentioned above. The law and competition will change the services over time.

Reconciliation of Bank Statement

Bank statement

Once a month (or less often by special arrangements) the bank sends a **bank statement** to the depositor. This statement is a record of all of the changes in the account that the bank is aware of since the last statement. It shows the checks that have been paid by the bank, the deposits received by the bank, service charges, if any, as well as other changes in the account balance.

The balance amount on the statement will probably not agree with the balance in the check register or on the last check stub. This may not be due to inaccuracy on the part of either the bank or the depositor because each party is acting on the information available to them at the time. The bank statement must be reconciled. This reconciliation procedure will determine the actual funds available in the account.

When the bank statement is received, the depositor must:

1. Organize the cancelled checks returned with the statement by check number. These checks have been received by the bank, and their amount has been subtracted from the account balance.

2. Review the deposit slips returned with the bank statement. This will identify the deposits made by the depositor but not received by the bank at the time that the statement was prepared. These deposits are termed **"deposits in transit."** The total of their amounts must be added to the bank statement balance.

Deposit in transit

3. Identify which checks have not been received by the bank by using the check register or check stubs. These checks are termed **"outstanding checks."** The total of their amounts must be subtracted from the bank statement balance. They represent a future reduction in the account balance when the check is received by the bank.

Outstanding checks

Service charges

4. Review the bank statement to determine if there are any **service charges** specified. The total of these charges must be subtracted from the depositor's balance on the check register or check stub. The bank has already reduced the account balance for these charges as shown on the statement.
   Service charges may be levied by the bank for:
   a. each check received;
   b. each deposit made;
   c. a monthly account use charge;
   d. imprinting of checks;
   e. an overdraft on the account balance; and/or
   f. a collection charge.

5. Review the bank statement for other changes in the account balance. Some examples of these would be:
   a. an authorized payment made from the account without a check written;
   b. a collection made by the bank and deposited to the account without a deposit slip;

c. a deposit made to the account without a deposit slip (i.e., it is now possible for older Americans to have their Social Security check deposited directly into their account without them even seeing it);

d. checks returned for insufficient funds; and

e. interest earned on the account balance.

Adjusted balance

The result of the above changes in the bank statement balance is the determination of the actual funds available, known as the **adjusted balance.**

Example 1

The J. B. Howland Co. received their bank statement that indicated an $863.70 balance. The check register shows a $682 balance. After organizing the cancelled checks, it is found that check No. 1806 for $145 is still outstanding. A deposit for $28.70, made on the last day of the month, is not shown on the statement. Service charges were $3.60 for use of the account, $8 for imprinting checks, and $3 for an $80 note that was collected by the bank. The bank statement reconciliation appears as follows.

J. B. Howland Company
Bank Statement Reconciliation
May 31, 19XX

Bank Statement Balance	$863.70	Check Register Balance	$682.00
Plus: Deposit in Transit	+ 28.70	Less: Service Charges	− 14.60
	$892.40		$667.40
Less: Outstanding checks No. 1806	− 145.00	Plus: Interest Earned	+ 5.00
		Plus: Note Collected	+ 75.00
Adjusted Balance	$747.40	Adjusted Balance	$747.40

Exercise B

Reconcile the information below to find the adjusted balance.

1. Statement Balance   Checkbook Balance
   $877.98 $778.44
   Service Charge = $3.00
   Checks Outstanding = No. 471— $ 32.00
                                477—   25.17
                                478—   13.00
                                479—   32.37
                                       $102.54

Bank Bal.	Ckbk. Bal.
$877.98	$778.44
−102.54	− 3.00
$775.44	$775.44

2. Statement Balance   Checkbook Balance
     $197.40 $162.30
     Service Charge = $2.50
     Checks Outstanding = No. 213— $14.80   Deposit in
                              220— 75.95   transit = $75.00
                              221— 21.85

3. Statement Balance   Checkbook Balance
     $4,315.17 $3,901.07
     Service Charge = $6.00
     Checks Outstanding = No. 502— $312.00   Deposits in
                              503—   79.50   transit = $62.50
                              504— 131.26   40.16

4. Statement Balance   Checkbook Balance
     $1,430.00 $1,576.00
     Service Charge = $13.00
     Deposits in transit = $397.12   Checks
                         65.36   outstanding = No. 32—$429.00
                      932.52   37— 362.70
                                          41— 336.87
                                          42— 133.43

Assignment

Chapter Four

Name _____ Date _____ Score _____

Skill Problems

1. Bank Statement Balance July 31   = $750.30
    Check Register Balance July 31   = $881.30
    Checks Outstanding =   Service Charge:
    No. 1478—$163.00   Note Collection Charge = $3.50
        1501—   43.70   Note Collected = $472.00
        1502—   21.00   Deposits in transit
                            $102.50 $ 17.00
                            $300.00 $407.70

2. Bank Statement Balance   Checkbook Balance
    $137.00 $92.62
    Service Charge = $1.70
    Checks Outstanding =
        No. 87—$17.90
          88— 51.13
          92—   7.00
    Deposit in transit = $29.95

3. Bank Statement Balance   Checkbook Balance
    $519.20 $798.62
    Service Charge = $8.40
    Check Outstanding = No. 921—$88.20
    Deposits in transit
            $120.36 $80.20
            100.34   58.32

4. Bank Statement Balance   Checkbook Balance
    $1,941.02 $2,048.00
    Checks Outstanding = No. 18— $ 462.00
                              21— $ 190.80
    Note collected by bank = $ 425.00
    Interest earned on account = $ 2.30
    Deposit in transit = $1,187.08

Business Application Problems

Find the adjusted balance in the following problems unless otherwise directed.

1. The Sperryton Manufacturing Company check register shows a balance of
    $1,946.80. The bank statement shows a balance of $2,650.47. After a
    review of the bank statement the following information is determined.

Checks Outstanding:	Service Charges:	Deposits in Transit:
No. 406—$ 63.40	Monthly use Charge	$ 67.33
471—$ 20.00	$4.60	$109.50
472—$720.50	Overdraft Charge	$240.13
481—$327.33	$6.00	

2. The Ace Grocery Company received the bank statement for the month of
    August on the thirty-first. The balance was $3,218.40, which compared to
    a balance of $3,145.68 in the cash account of the balance sheet. The
    $3,145.68 also agreed with the balance in the check register. The
    accountant reviewed the statement and found that the following points
    required reconciliation: check No. 493 for $357.18 had not been cashed,
    the deposits for $195 and $82.19 made on the thirtieth were not shown on
    the bank statement, and the service charge of ????? was not recorded on
    the check register.

3. The bank statement for John Kolerestine revealed:
   a. a balance of $147.30;
   b. a check for $31 deposited by Mr. Kolerestine that was returned because there was insufficient funds in B. Bennett's account;
   c. check No. 141 for $83 was not cashed by the payee;
   d. a deposit for $78 was not received by the bank when the statement was prepared; and
   e. a service charge of $2 has already been subtracted from the bank account balance.
   Mr. Kolerestine's check register shows a $175.30 balance.

4. The Hill Inn has a balance of $5,698.03 on their check register. The bank statement shows a balance of $6,011.80. The following information is determined after a close review of the bank statement and the check register.

Checks Outstanding:	Deposits in Transit:
No. 13—$420.00	$165.00
No. 23—$270.50	$203.60
No. 31—$100.00	$103.03

   Service Charge (Monthly account use charge): $5.10
   Reconcile the bank statement.

5. Cindi found that the bank statement balance and the check register had the same balance of $89. After a review of the statement she found that there was a $13 deposit in transit as well as a $29 outstanding check. She also found that she had failed to subtract a $9 check in her check register. The service charge amount on the statement was unreadable. What was the amount of the service charge?

6. Sally Scanlon noted that there was not a service charge on the bank statement that she received on July 3. She also noted that the $1,937.05 balance did not include the $27.28 deposit that she made on June 30 or the $73.62 check she wrote to the finance company on July 1. The $8.41 interest earned on the account balance was shown on the statement. What should be the current balance in the check register?

7. The Werlot Company's check register balance is $73.60. The bank statement balance is $1,002. The following information is determined after a review of the bank statement and the check register.

Checks Outstanding: Service Charges:
  No. 140—$163.80 $18.00 for imprinting checks
       181—$980.00 $ 3.50 for account use
       185—$ 47.23 $ 5.00 for note collection

Deposits in transit: $18, $482, and $67.41
What was the value of the note collected by the bank?

8. The check register for the Becton Business Service Company is shown below. All of the checks through No. 844 have been returned by the bank the month before. The deposit of October 29 is not shown on the bank statement. The service charge is $4.

PLEASE BE SURE TO **DEDUCT** ANY PER CHECK CHARGES OR SERVICE CHARGES THAT MAY APPLY TO YOUR ACCOUNT

CHECK NO.	DATE	CHECKS ISSUED TO OR DESCRIPTION OF DEPOSIT	(−) AMOUNT OF CHECK	√ T	(−) CHECK FEE (IF ANY)	(+) AMOUNT OF DEPOSIT	BALANCE
							1680 48
839	⁷/₇	ABERESON CO.	16 00	√			− 16 00
							1664 48
840	¹⁰/₆	SMITH CORP.	822 20				− 822 20
							842 28
841	¹⁰/₇	O. PETERSON	327 00				− 327 00
							515 28
842	¹⁰/₁₀	SCHMIDT & SONS	5 00				− 5 00
							510 28
843	¹⁰/₁₆	SMITH CORP.	200 00				− 200 00
							310 28
844	¹⁰/₂₃	H. D. HEBNER	29 50				− 29 50
							280 78
		DEPOSIT				¹⁰/₂₉ 583 00	+583 00
							863 78

The balance on the bank statement is $276.78. What is the adjusted balance?

9. Morning Milk, Inc., received the January bank statement from the Deluxe National State Bank on February 2. Only the deposit shown on the check stub is not shown on the statement. There are no outstanding checks. Using the bank statement and the check stub shown below, reconcile the bank statement.

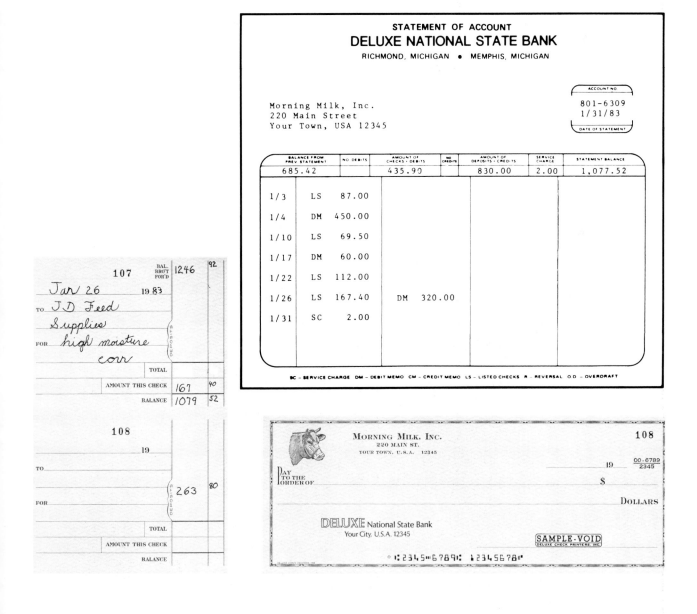

10. K-Lo Products check register shows a $437.90 balance. A smudge on the bank statement conceals the statement balance, but a review of it does reveal the following information:
   a. service charges—$8.50
   b. deposits in transit—$87, $600, and $273
   c. checks outstanding
      No. 87—$ 76.23   No. 88—$185
      No. 98—$632.50

11. The Kromer Travel Agency has a balance of $2,713.63 on their check register. The bank statement shows a balance of $3,027.40. A review of the check register and bank statement shows the following information:

Checks Outstanding:	Deposits in transit:
No. 328—$421.90	$368.60
No. 345—$370.50	$103.03

   Service Charge (Monthly account use charge): $7
   Reconcile the bank statement.

12. The bank statement for the Pondi Company for November is shown below. The statement does not show a deposit made on November 30 for $587.29 or two checks outstanding—No. 862 for $27 and No. 867 for $368.50. What is the adjusted balance for the month? (You will need to complete the bank statement.)

MICHIGAN NATIONAL BANK

CHECKING ACCOUNT STATEMENT

ACCOUNT NUMBER
307-4531-03

Pondi Company
1802 Centerline Road
Debonet, Illinois

PERIOD
FROM Nov. 1
TO Nov. 30

DATE	TRANSACTION CODE		TRANSACTION AMOUNT	TRANSACTION CODE	TRANSACTION AMOUNT	TRANSACTION CODE	TRANSACTION AMOUNT		BALANCE
Nov. 3	1		223 40						1 085 50
Nov. 8	1		750 00	8	1 000 00				835 50
Nov. 10	8		321 80						513 70
Nov. 20	8		40 00	8	125 00	1	300 00		648 70
Nov. 21	1	1	000 00	8	87 50	8	500 00		1 061 20
Nov. 27	1		567 82						1 629 02
Nov. 30	SC		8 50						1 620 52

INCLUDED IN STATEMENT

BEGINNING BALANCE	LOW BALANCE			MO. AVE. AVAILABLE BALANCE
$862.10	DATE Nov. 20	AMOUNT 348.70		$537.20

NO. CREDITS	NO. DEPOSITED ITEMS	TOTAL ADDED FOR CREDITS
0	5	$2,841.22

NO. DEBITS	NO. DR. CHARGED FOR	TOTAL DEDUCTED FOR DEBITS
1	6	$2,082.80

TRANSACTION CODES

CREDITS
1—DEPOSIT
3—CREDIT MEMO
6—CREDIT CASH CONSOLIDATION
7—LIST CORRECTION
10—CHECK CORRECTION
12—CHARGE CORRECTION

BLANK-CHECK
5—DEPOSIT CORRECTION
8—LIST
29—CERTIFIED CHECK MEMO
40—MISC. BANK CHARGE

DEBITS
46—DEBIT CASH CONSOLIDATION
60—DEBIT MEMO
SC—SERVICE CHARGE
30—SERVICE CHARGE MEMO
— —OVERDRAWN BALANCE

PLEASE RECONCILE YOUR STATEMENT PROMPTLY . . . SEE REVERSE SIDE

Courtesy of Michigan Bank—Port Huron, MI.

13. The bank statement for the Carlton family contained the following information: a balance of $45.28 and service charges of $8.50. After a review of the material, the family determined the following: two checks with a total of $85 were not shown on the bank statement, though they were deposited earlier in the week. There were also some checks outstanding that totaled $62.30. The family had failed to maintain the balance in the check register. What would the balance be?

14. John's bank statement showed a charge for use of his automatic teller privileges in the amount of $1.50 per use. John used the auto teller seven times over the course of the month. His account was also charged for a flat service charge of $3.50. If his check book balance is correct at $52.80, what is his adjusted balance?

15. Karen Wallace was notified by her bank that she had not properly endorsed a check for deposit. The check amount was $4,690. The bank indicated over the phone that her balance would be affected by this problem until she could come to the bank and straighten it out. Karen had also made a transfer from her savings account, in the amount of $500, to the checking account just yesterday. The balance shown in the checkbook is $3,852 before the transfer is recorded. What is her real balance at this point?

Challenge Problem

The Polk & Stern Company found that a $63.50 check had not been recorded in the check register. The register's uncorrected balance was $3,684.72. The bank statement balance was $1,990.32. A note had been collected by the bank for $750 and a charge of $5 was levied against the account for this collection service. A $442.50 check deposited by the company was returned because it was improperly endorsed. New checks were imprinted by the bank for a charge of $6.80. The Company had deposited $1,476.60 as the week's receipts since the bank prepared the monthly statement. A $450 monthly interest payment was shown on the bank statement as being automatically withdrawn from the account. There was no monthly use service charge on the account because of the amount of the balance. What is the adjusted balance?

Name _____   Date _____   Score _____

1. Using your name as payee, give an example of:
   a. A restrictive endorsement _____

   b. A blank endorsement _____

   c. A special endorsement _____

2. The Robert Baird Corp. check register shows a $1,063.08 balance. The bank statement shows a balance of $1,088. The accountant reviews the bank statement and the check register and finds the following information:

Checks Outstanding:	Deposits in Transit:
No. 184—$161.92	$165.00
187—$180.00	$ 80.00
188—$105.50	$311.97

   Automatic payment from account   Deposit to account without deposit
   from bank: $100   slip: $234.47

   Reconcile the bank statement and find the adjusted balance.

3. Lee York has a balance of $92.61 in his check register as of April 30. The bank statement that he receives on May 2 indicates a $47 balance. After reviewing both the check register and the bank statement, he finds that the deposit that he made on April 30 for $25 has been omitted. He also finds that a check that he had deposited on April 25 is returned because the account holder did not have enough funds to cover the check. The amount of the check is $47.43. There are also two checks outstanding at this point: No. 103 for $12.80 and No. 107 for $25. The service charge for the period is unreadable on the bank statement. What is the service charge?

4. Jon Sasinowski has received a message from his bank that his account has been overdrawn. The last statement of balance was $89.70. Since the date of the statement there has only been one check written for $97.10. The statement included a service charge of $16. There has not been a deposit made to the account since the statement. By how much has he overdrawn his account?

5. From the information given, reconcile the balance. There is a notation that the deposit on June 13 of a check for $1,962.80 was returned to the account holder due to insufficient funds. A service charge of $9 was also noted. Checks No. 474 and 476 were not shown on the statement. There were no outstanding checks from previous months.

PLEASE BE SURE TO **DEDUCT** ANY PER CHECK CHARGES OR SERVICE CHARGES THAT MAY APPLY TO YOUR ACCOUNT

CHECK NO	DATE	CHECKS ISSUED TO OR DESCRIPTION OF DEPOSIT	(-) AMOUNT OF CHECK	√ T	(-) CHECK FEE (IF ANY)	(+) AMOUNT OF DEPOSIT	BALANCE 940	20
470	6/7	CAMPBELL ASSOC.	50 00	✓			- 50	00
							890	20
471	6/10	BEARDSON CO.	682 40				- 682	40
							207	80
		DEPOSIT				6/13 1962 80	+1962	80
							2170	60
472	6/20	LITTLE & SONS	423 16				- 423	16
							1747	44
473	6/27	PEARSON CORP.	800 00				- 800	00
							947	44
474	6/27	McTAGGART & CO.	12 50				- 12	50
							934	94
475	6/29	R.E. EMERSON	25 60				- 25	60
							909	34
		DEPOSIT				6/29 1827 00	+1827	00
							2736	34
476	6/30	J. OLSONSITE CORP.	10 00				- 10	00
							2726	34

REMEMBER TO RECORD AUTOMATIC PAYMENTS / DEPOSITS ON DATE AUTHORIZED

Record your score on the inside back cover for future reference.

5 Payroll

After mastering the material in this chapter, you will be able to:

1. Determine gross earnings for an employee.
2. Use federal income tax and Social Security tax tables.
3. Determine net pay for an employee.
4. Determine the employer's share of payroll taxes.
5. Use and understand the following:

Pay Systems	Deductions
Gross Earnings	Exemption
Time Card	W-4 Form
Payroll Record	Taxable Base
Net Pay	Tax Rate

Determining Gross Earnings

Pay system

All organizations that have paid employees must maintain payroll records to determine the amount that the employee has earned. The company and the employee enter into an agreement at the time of employment. This agreement determines the type of **pay system** on which the employee will be compensated. The frequency of payment, known as a pay period, is also determined at this time. A pay period may be a week, twice a month, or monthly. There are basically four types of pay systems, which we will look at here.

1. A *salary* is paid to employees for a pay period that may not have a limit to the hours or days to be worked. It is an open-ended agreement that requires the employee to complete specified tasks. This type of pay system is usually limited to managerial employees.

2. A *commission* system is used in conjunction with the selling of goods or services. This system compensates the salesperson for sales made, not how many hours worked. A specified percent of the value of the items sold is paid to the salesperson as a commission. The more items sold, the more earned. Specifics on this topic will be covered in chapter 14, Commission Sales.

3. A *piece-rate* system is used in manufacturing when an operation is repetitious and, therefore, monotonous. This system compensates an employee with more pay for more output. The employee is paid a

specified amount for each operation, piece produced, or cycle completed. The more an employee produces, the more he or she earns. This system was used more frequently in the 1930s than it is today.

4. An *hourly rate* system is used in a variety of situations and is designed to compensate an employee for the amount of time spent on the job. Specified work standards are established to indicate the expected level of output. Under this system, the more hours worked, the more earned. This is the most frequently used pay system. It is almost exclusively found in entry level jobs and often in repetitive work.

These four basic systems are often used in conjunction with each other in order to form a more flexible pay system.

Example 1

1. A combination salary and commission can be used to provide a basic income source for a salesperson in difficult times as well as a motivator to sell more.
2. A combination hourly and piece-rate system can be used for the same purpose.
3. A combination salary and hourly system can be used in order to compensate managerial employees for excessive work hours.

The above are examples of how pay system combinations can be developed in order to meet the needs of the organization and its employees.

Overtime

The Fair Labor Standards Act of 1938 requires payment of one and one-half times the regular wage rate on hours in excess of forty worked by an employee in one week. The effect of this is shown in Example 2.

Example 2

Janie worked 46 hours in a week. Her regular wage rate is $5.50 per hour.

40 hours $\times$ \$5.50/hour =	\$220.00
6 hours $\times$ \$8.25/hour $\left(\$5.50 \times 1\frac{1}{2}\right)$	$\underline{+49.50}$
	\$269.50

Gross earnings

The total, $269.50, is her **gross earnings** for the pay period. This is not the amount that she will receive on her paycheck, but it is the amount that she has earned. Janie's hours are recorded by a time clock. Each time she enters or leaves her place of employment she selects her **time card** from a rack and places it in the time clock. The time clock records the time on the card. The record on the card shows the hours she works and is used to compute her gross pay.

This information—hours worked, hourly rate of pay, and gross earnings— is entered on a **payroll record** sheet (sometimes called a payroll register) by a payroll clerk. This information is used to determine **net pay.**

Time card

Payroll record
Net pay

Exercise A The Easy Accounting Company pays its employees weekly. The hours worked in excess of forty per week are paid at the rate of one and one-half times the regular wages as prescribed by law. Determine the gross earnings for the following employees.

Name	Title	Hourly Wage	Hours Worked	Regular Earnings	Overtime Earnings	Total-Gross Earnings
1. A. Bennett	Accountant	$ 7.58	40	$303.20	$0	$303.20
2. J. Dixon	Accountant	7.20	42	288.00	21.60	
3. L. Pierce	Accountant	8.00	41	320.00	12.00	
4. O. Russell	Supervisor	10.60	42	424.00	31.80	
5. B. Smith	Jr. Accountant	4.20	40	168.00	0	
6. K. Williams	Clerk	3.90	38	148.20	0	
7. J. Wilson	Accountant	6.90	41	276.00	10.35	

Exercise B Williamson Manufacturing pays its employees weekly. The company compensates its employees one and one-half times for all hours worked in excess of eight each day (Monday through Friday), whether or not they work in excess of forty each week. All hours worked on Saturday are one and one-half times regular pay. All Sunday hours are triple time. Determine the gross earnings for the following employees.

Name	M	T	W	Th	F	S	S		Hourly Rate	Regular Earnings	Overtime Earnings	Gross Earnings
1. L. Becker	8	9	7	9	9	8	5	1.	$5.80	$226.20	$182.70	$408.90
2. J. Crimmins	7	6	7	8	8			2.	5.60	201.60	0	
3. B. Fortos	6	8	8	9	9	9	8	3.	6.00	228.00	243.00	
4. T. Jones	9	9	8	7	8			4.	5.00	195.00	15.00	
5. B. Lemis	5	7	8	10	8			5.	4.00	144.00	12.00	
6. K. Mason	10	9	6	8	8	8	5	6.	6.20	235.60	195.30	
7. A. Rust	8	10	7	8	9	9	3	7.	7.00	273.00	189.00	
8. P. Zist	8	9	7	9	9	8		8.	4.50	175.50	74.25	

Determining Net Pay

Deductions

The amount of money that an employee earns is not the amount received on payday. From the total earnings, or gross pay, a variety of **deductions** must be subtracted. After these have been subtracted, the remainder, known as net pay, is payable to the employee.

Deductions are of two types. Payroll taxes, local and state (where applicable), and federal, are mandatory. They are mandatory for the employee to pay, as well as for the employer to collect as an agent for the taxing authority. The second type is voluntary.

Federal Income Tax The laws of the United States require that the federal income tax be paid as wages are earned. The employer is required to collect or withhold from the employee's paycheck a specified amount each pay period. This amount and the amounts withheld from other employees' paychecks are then periodically sent to the federal government's Internal Revenue Service (IRS). A similar procedure is used for state and local income taxes.

To determine the amount of income tax to be withheld, most employers use a set of charts provided by the IRS. The charts are for weekly, monthly, and biweekly pay periods. Income tax is based on an employee's ability to pay (i.e., the more money earned the greater the amount of tax). The tax is computed on the amount of gross earnings and the number of exemptions an employee claims. The employee is entitled to claim one **exemption** for himself or herself and one for each dependent. The employee makes this claim on **Form W-4,** which is shown below.

Exemption
Form W-4

Form **W-4** (Rev. January 1986)	**Employee's Withholding Allowance Certificate** Department of the Treasury—Internal Revenue Service		OMB No. 1545-0010 Expires: 11-30-87
1 Type or print your full name Jacqulyn Sue Retzloff		2 Your social security number 378-58-7122	
Home address (number and street or rural route) 300 Alger		3 Marital Status	☐ Single ☒ Married ☐ Married, but withhold at higher Single rate **Note:** If married, but legally separated, or spouse is a nonresident alien, check the Single box.
City or town, state, and ZIP code Your City, State 00000			

4 Total number of allowances you are claiming (from line F of the worksheet on page 2) **4**

5 Additional amount, if any, you want deducted from each pay . . . . **$**

6 I claim exemption from withholding because (see instructions and check boxes below that apply):

a ☐ Last year I did not owe any Federal income tax and had a right to a full refund of **ALL** income tax withheld, **AND**

b ☐ This year I do not expect to owe any Federal income tax and expect to have a right to a full refund of **ALL** income tax withheld. If both a and b apply, enter the year effective and "EXEMPT" here . . . ▶ **Year** 19

c If you entered "EXEMPT" on line 6b, are you a full-time student? . . . . ☐ Yes ☐ No

Under penalties of perjury, I certify that I am entitled to the number of withholding allowances claimed on this certificate, or if claiming exemption from withholding, that I am entitled to claim the exempt status.

Employee's signature ▶ *Jacqulyn Sue Retzloff*   Date ▶ November 16 , 19 86

7 Employer's name and address (Employer: Complete 7, 8, and 9 only if sending to IRS) | 8 Office code | 9 Employer identification number

Best Wages, Inc.
100 Main St., Big City, MO   00000   42 06 41173

Department of the Treasury—Internal Revenue Service.

This form has been completed for employee Jacqulyn S. Retzloff. She has claimed herself, her spouse, and two children, a total of four. This information with the gross earnings is used to determine the amount of income tax from the chart shown on p. 99.

Example 3

If Ms. Retzloff's earnings for the week is $285, the amount of the income tax would be $19. The amount of tax is found by determining the correct range in which her $285 income for the week would fall and by moving across until the column for the number of exemptions claimed is a 4, to correspond with the W–4 certificate. The value of $19 is then found.

MARRIED Persons–WEEKLY Payroll Period
(For Wages Paid After December 1985)

And the wages are–		And the number of withholding allowances claimed is–										
At least	But less than	0	1	2	3	4	5	6	7	8	9	10
		The amount of income tax to be withheld shall be–										
$0	$54	$0	$0	$0	$0	$0	$0	$0	$0	$0	$0	$0
54	56	1	0	0	0	0	0	0	0	0	0	0
240	250	26	22	19	16	14	11	8	6	3	1	0
250	260	27	24	21	18	15	12	9	7	4	2	0
260	270	29	25	22	19	16	13	11	8	5	3	1
270	280	30	27	24	21	18	15	12	9	7	4	2
280	290	32	29	25	22	19	16	13	10	8	5	3
290	300	34	30	27	24	21	18	15	12	9	7	4
300	310	35	32	28	25	22	19	16	13	10	8	5
310	320	37	33	30	27	23	20	18	15	12	9	6
320	330	39	35	32	28	25	22	19	16	13	10	8
330	340	40	37	33	30	27	23	20	17	14	12	9
340	350	42	38	35	32	28	25	22	19	16	13	10
350	360	44	40	37	33	30	27	23	20	17	14	11
360	370	46	42	38	35	31	28	25	22	19	16	13
370	380	48	44	40	36	33	30	26	23	20	17	14

SINGLE Persons–WEEKLY Payroll Period
(For Wages Paid After December 1985)

And the wages are–		And the number of withholding allowances claimed is–										
At least	But less than	0	1	2	3	4	5	6	7	8	9	10
		The amount of income tax to be withheld shall be–										
$0	$32	$0	$0	$0	$0	$0	$0	$0	$0	$0	$0	$0
32	34	1	0	0	0	0	0	0	0	0	0	0
340	350	54	49	45	40	36	32	28	24	21	18	15
350	360	56	52	47	42	38	34	30	26	23	19	16
360	370	59	54	49	44	40	36	32	28	24	21	18
370	380	62	56	51	47	42	38	34	30	26	23	19
380	390	64	59	54	49	44	40	36	31	28	24	21
$390	$400	$67	$61	$56	$51	$46	$42	$38	$33	$30	$26	$22
400	410	69	64	59	54	49	44	40	35	31	28	24
410	420	72	67	61	56	51	46	42	37	33	29	26
420	430	75	69	64	58	53	49	44	39	35	31	27
430	440	77	72	66	61	56	51	46	41	37	33	29
440	450	80	74	69	64	58	53	48	44	39	35	31
450	460	82	77	72	66	61	55	51	46	41	37	33

SINGLE Persons–MONTHLY Payroll Period
(For Wages Paid After December 1985)

And the wages are–		And the number of withholding allowances claimed is–										
At least	But less than	0	1	2	3	4	5	6	7	8	9	10
		The amount of income tax to be withheld shall be–										
$0	$120	$0	$0	$0	$0	$0	$0	$0	$0	$0	$0	$0
120	124	1	0	0	0	0	0	0	0	0	0	0
3,400	3,440	839	806	773	739	706	673	642	612	581	550	520
3,440	3,480	854	821	787	754	721	687	656	625	595	564	533
3,480	3,520	869	835	802	769	736	702	669	639	608	578	547
3,520	3,560	884	850	817	784	750	717	684	652	622	591	561
3,560	3,600	898	865	832	798	765	732	699	666	635	605	574
3,600	3,640	913	880	847	813	780	747	713	680	649	618	588
3,640	3,680	928	895	861	828	795	761	728	695	663	632	601
3,680	3,720	943	909	876	843	810	776	743	710	676	646	615
3,720	3,760	958	924	891	858	824	791	758	724	691	659	629
3,760	3,800	972	939	906	872	839	806	773	739	706	673	642
3,800	3,840	987	954	921	887	854	821	787	754	721	687	656
3,840	3,880	1,002	969	935	902	869	835	802	769	736	702	669
3,880	3,920	1,017	983	950	917	884	850	817	784	750	717	684

Department of the Treasury-Internal Revenue Service.

F.I.C.A. The Federal Insurance Contributions Act (F.I.C.A.), often known as Social Security, is the second major mandatory deduction. Again the employer is obligated to withhold a specified amount from the employee's earnings. Payment is later made to the government by the employer. F.I.C.A. differs from the federal income tax in that it is not based on an ability to pay, and there are no exemptions to consider. Deductions are made based on the first $42,000 that the employee earns from each employer each year. At year's end he need pay only tax on $42,000 even though he may have had earnings withheld by several employers over the year that exceeded $42,000. The $42,000 represents the **taxable base.** Earnings beyond this amount are not subject to F.I.C.A. tax for that employer in that year.

Taxable base

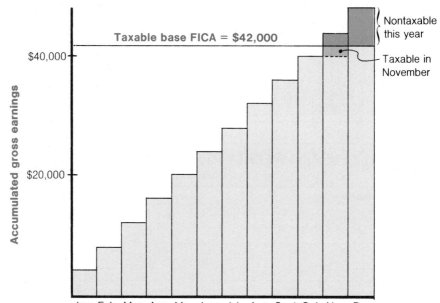

The $42,000 is taxable at a rate of 7.15 percent as it is earned. Charts are also available for determining the amount of this deduction. The taxable amount ($42,000) and **tax rate** (7.15 percent) are subject to change by Congress.

Tax rate

Example 4

Using the previous example of $285 of gross earnings for the week for Ms. Retzloff, her F.I.C.A. tax would be $20.38. This amount is found by determining the number of hundreds in the taxable income. In this example, the number of hundreds would be two. The lower right hand corner of the Social Security Employee Tax Table on the next page shows the tax for $100 amounts of taxable income. For $200, the tax is $14.30. The tax for the remaining amount of taxable income ($85) is found by determining the correct range in which the $85 would fall and reading the amount of the tax. The amount is $6.08. The two amounts then need to be added together to find the total tax deduction ($14.30 + $6.08 = $20.38) for F.I.C.A. for this pay period. The same answer could be determined by a math calculation. The taxable income ($285.00) multiplied by the tax rate (7.15 percent or .0715) yields the same answer.

$285.00
$\times$.0715
$20.38 F.I.C.A. for this pay period.

Social Security Employee Tax Table for 1986
7.15% employee tax deductions

Wages at least	But less than	Tax to be withheld	Wages at least	But less than	Tax to be withheld	Wages at least	But less than	Tax to be withheld	Wages at least	But less than	Tax to be withheld
$0.00	$0.07	$0.00	12.66	12.80	.91	25.39	25.53	1.82	38.12	38.26	2.73
07	21	.01	12.80	12.94	.92	25.53	25.67	1.83	38.26	38.40	2.74
21	35	.02	12.94	13.08	.93	25.67	25.81	1.84	38.40	38.54	2.75
10.14	10.28	.73	22.87	23.01	1.64	35.60	35.74	2.55	48.33	48.47	3.46
10.28	10.42	.74	23.01	23.15	1.65	35.74	35.88	2.56	48.47	48.61	3.47
10.42	10.56	.75	23.15	23.29	1.66	35.88	36.02	2.57	48.61	48.75	3.48
10.56	10.70	.76	23.29	23.43	1.67	36.02	36.16	2.58	48.75	48.89	3.49
10.70	10.84	.77	23.43	23.57	1.68	36.16	36.30	2.59	48.89	49.03	3.50
10.84	10.98	.78	23.57	23.71	1.69	36.30	36.44	2.60	49.03	49.17	3.51
10.98	11.12	.79	23.71	23.85	1.70	36.44	36.58	2.61	49.17	49.31	3.52
11.12	11.26	.80	23.85	23.99	1.71	36.58	36.72	2.62	49.31	49.45	3.53
58.82	58.96	4.21	71.54	71.68	5.12	84.27	84.41	6.03	97.00	97.14	6.94
58.96	59.10	4.22	71.68	71.82	5.13	84.41	84.55	6.04	97.14	97.28	6.95
59.10	59.24	4.23	71.82	71.96	5.14	84.55	84.69	6.05	97.28	97.42	6.96
59.24	59.38	4.24	71.96	72.10	5.15	84.69	84.83	6.06	97.42	97.56	6.97
59.38	59.52	4.25	72.10	72.24	5.16	84.83	84.97	6.07	97.56	97.70	6.98
59.52	59.66	4.26	72.24	72.38	5.17	84.97	85.11	6.08	97.70	97.84	6.99
59.66	59.80	4.27	72.38	72.52	5.18	85.11	85.25	6.09	97.84	97.98	7.00
59.80	59.94	4.28	72.52	72.66	5.19	85.25	85.39	6.10	97.98	98.12	7.01
59.94	60.07	4.29	72.66	72.80	5.20	85.39	85.53	6.11	98.12	98.26	7.02
60.07	60.21	4.30	72.80	72.94	5.21	85.53	85.67	6.12	98.26	98.40	7.03
60.21	60.35	4.31	72.94	73.08	5.22	85.67	85.81	6.13	98.40	98.54	7.04
60.35	60.49	4.32	73.08	73.22	5.23	85.81	85.95	6.14	98.54	98.68	7.05
60.49	60.63	4.33	73.22	73.36	5.24	85.95	86.09	6.15	98.68	98.82	7.06
60.63	60.77	4.34	73.36	73.50	5.25	86.09	86.23	6.16	98.82	98.96	7.07
60.77	60.91	4.35	73.50	73.64	5.26	86.23	86.37	6.17	98.96	99.10	7.08
60.91	61.05	4.36	73.64	73.78	5.27	86.37	86.51	6.18	99.10	99.24	7.09
61.05	61.19	4.37	73.78	73.92	5.28	86.51	86.65	6.19	99.24	99.38	7.10
61.19	61.33	4.38	73.92	74.06	5.29	86.65	86.79	6.20	99.38	99.52	7.11
61.33	61.47	4.39	74.06	74.20	5.30	86.79	86.93	6.21	99.52	99.66	7.12
61.47	61.61	4.40	74.20	74.34	5.31	86.93	87.07	6.22	99.66	99.80	7.13
61.61	61.75	4.41	74.34	74.48	5.32	87.07	87.21	6.23	99.80	99.94	7.14
61.75	61.89	4.42	74.48	74.62	5.33	87.21	87.35	6.24	99.94	100.00	7.15
61.89	62.03	4.43	74.62	74.76	5.34	87.35	87.49	6.25			
62.03	62.17	4.44	74.76	74.90	5.35	87.49	87.63	6.26			
62.17	62.31	4.45	74.90	75.04	5.36	87.63	87.77	6.27			
62.31	62.45	4.46	75.04	75.18	5.37	87.77	87.91	6.28			
62.45	62.59	4.47	75.18	75.32	5.38	87.91	88.05	6.29			
62.59	62.73	4.48	75.32	75.46	5.39	88.05	88.19	6.30			
62.73	62.87	4.49	75.46	75.60	5.40	88.19	88.33	6.31			
62.87	63.01	4.50	75.60	75.74	5.41	88.33	88.47	6.32			
63.01	63.15	4.51	75.74	75.88	5.42	88.47	88.61	6.33			
63.15	63.29	4.52	75.88	76.02	5.43	88.61	88.75	6.34			
63.29	63.43	4.53	76.02	76.16	5.44	88.75	88.89	6.35			
63.43	63.57	4.54	76.16	76.30	5.45	88.89	89.03	6.36			

Wages	Taxes
100	$7.15
200	14.30
300	21.45
400	28.60
500	35.75
600	42.90
700	50.05
800	57.20
900	64.35
1,000	71.50

Department of the Treasury—Internal Revenue Service.

Example 5

Let us say that Ms. Retzloff's earnings for the year-to-date before this pay period for this employer were $41,820. Then only the amount necessary to bring the accumulated taxable earnings to the $42,000 maximum will be taxed this pay period, from her $285 gross.

$42,000
−41,820

$180 taxable this pay period.

Under these circumstances the F.I.C.A. tax for this period would be $12.87.

($180 × .0715) or (F.I.C.A. tax table)

There would not be a deduction for F.I.C.A. at the next pay period because the first $42,000 of earnings have already been taxed for that year.

Note: The tax table or a math calculation will be used in business to determine the tax on a whole pay amount or a partial pay. For the purposes of determining answers, the math calculation approach will be used. The tax table is shown as an equally acceptable method.

State and Local Income Taxes Most states and many cities have an income tax. The structure of the tax specifications differ widely but are similar to the Federal Income Tax or F.I.C.A. They may be a graduated tax (progressive in the sense that the tax rate increases as the gross income increases), a flat rate to be taxed on all gross income, or a rate to be taxed up to a maximum taxable base (similar to F.I.C.A.).

Example 6

Sarah has weekly earnings of $201. She lives in a city that has an income tax of 1 percent of all earnings. The city is in a state that has a progressive income tax. The state tax is 2 percent on the first $150 of earnings a week, an additional $\frac{1}{2}$ percent on the next $200 of earnings a week, and an additional 1 percent on earnings above $350 a week. What is the amount of city and state income tax that Sarah will have deducted from her paycheck? (Note: 2% = .02, and $\frac{1}{2}$% = .005)

$$\$201 \times .01 = \$2.01 \text{ City Income Tax}$$

$$\begin{array}{r} \$201 \\ - \underline{150} \times .02 = \$3.00 \\ \$\ 51 \times .005 = \underline{+.26} \\ \$3.26 \text{ State Income Tax} \end{array}$$

Example 7

Veronica Smathers lives in a state that has an income tax that is a flat 3.7 percent of the first $15,000 earned per year. Veronica has earned $14,849 so far this year. This week's paycheck will be based on gross earnings of $379. What will be the deduction for state income tax for this week? (Note: 3.7% = .037)

$$\begin{array}{r} \$15,000 \\ -\underline{14,849} \\ \$151 \text{ taxable this pay period.} \\ \times \underline{.037} \\ \$5.59 \text{ State Income Tax} \end{array}$$

Voluntary Deductions

The second type of deductions are voluntary deductions authorized by the employee. A payroll deduction authorization slip is signed by the employee and given to the payroll clerk. This okays deductions from gross pay for any one of a variety of purposes specified by the employee.

Some examples of voluntary deductions are: union dues, uniform rental, credit union payments and savings, contributions, savings bonds, retirement program, profit-sharing plans, Individual Retirement Act (IRA's) plans and direct deposits to bank accounts.

Once all of the deductions are calculated, they are subtracted from gross earnings to determine net pay. This amount is made payable to the employee on the paycheck and is the actual amount that the employee has available to spend.

Example 8

Edwin Palmer is paid a salary of $275 a week. He has a wife and two children and claims all of them as exemptions. His earnings previous to this paycheck were $16,250 for the year. He has a deduction of $40 per paycheck for a credit union payment and $10 for the purchase of U.S. savings bonds. What is his net pay?

$275.00 = Gross Earnings
18.00 = Federal Income Tax (four exemptions)
19.66 = F.I.C.A. Tax
40.00 = Credit Union Payment
10.00 = U.S. Savings Bonds
$187.34 = Net Pay

Exercise C Determine the net pay of each employee in the Burson Area Consolidated Schools from the information below.

Employee	Gross Earnings	Federal Income Tax	State Income Tax	F.I.C.A.	Union Dues	Savings Bonds	Net Pay
1. Johnny Biddy	$ 600.00	$118.70	$28.00	$42.90	$6	$ 0	$404.40
2. James Carson	1,263.40	249.00	61.73	90.33	0	40	
3. J. Grason	898.00	173.40	42.88	64.21	6	120	
4. Kay Lasher	756.83	121.60	37.16	54.11	6	0	
5. Sharron Orr	694.20	117.41	34.72	49.64	6	25	

Exercise D Determine net pay for the week from the information below. All of the employees are married.

Employee	Gross Earnings	Exemptions Claimed	Federal Income Tax	Gross Earnings Before Pay Period	F.I.C.A.	Net Pay
1. Sarrah Blair	$268.00	4	$16	$31,000	$19.16	$232.84
2. Jock Lieber	307.00	2		29,795		
3. Fran Smith	296.40	1		42,350		
4. John Ulrick	302.60	5		24,958		
5. Kay Wilson	283.78	0		41,800		
6. Bill Puhl	322.00	1		42,000		
7. A. Lingle	280.00	2		39,400		
8. Jim Seal	282.30	1		41,940		
9. Jean King	325.00	2		38,900		
10. Ed Ely	340.00	4		26,573		

Employers' Payroll Taxes

The employer, like the employee, is obligated to pay taxes based on the employees' gross earnings. The taxes are an extra expense to the employer, increasing the cost of labor.

The most significant of these taxes is the F.I.C.A. tax. The employer is required to pay an amount matching the employee's contribution. Seven point one five percent (7.15 percent) of the first $42,000 each employee earns for each year must be paid to the federal government. When the employer makes the payment, he is really forwarding 14.3 percent of the employee's earnings. The 14.3 percent results from a 7.15 percent deduction from the employee and 7.15 percent additional tax from the employer.

The employer will also be taxed for unemployment insurance by the federal and state government. This tax is computed similar to F.I.C.A. (i.e., a specified tax rate applied to a maximum taxable base).

Other payment taxes levied against the employer are in effect increases in the cost of labor even though these taxes do not appear as part of the employee's gross earnings.

Example 9

Amount of gross earnings taxable for F.I.C.A. this pay period equals $31,859.40. The company must remit the amount necessary for the period to the federal government. How much must be remitted?

$31,859.40 Taxable Earnings this pay period
 $\times$ .143 (7.15% $\times$ 2)
$4,555.89 (Amount to be remitted to federal government)

Assignment

Chapter Five

Name _____ Date _____ Score _____

Skill Problems

Determine the net pay for each employee for the week from the information below.

Employee	Gross Earnings	Federal Income Tax	F.I.C.A.	Cr. Union	Union Dues	Net Pay
1. H. Barker	$273.20	$21.30	$19.53	$ 0.00	$3.50	_____
2. L. Lowery	301.53	60.18	21.56	40.00	4.20	_____
3. P. Norris	268.00	40.71	19.16	17.00	3.50	_____
4. F. Tunks	305.27	31.06	21.83	78.00	3.50	_____
5. B. Willard	286.26	42.18	20.47	25.00	4.00	_____

Determine net pay for each employee for the month from the information below.

Employee	Gross Earnings	Exemptions claimed	Federal Income Tax	Gross Earnings Before Pay Period	F.I.C.A.	Net Pay
6. J. Cousins	$368.20	5	$ 71.12	$ 3,927.80	_____	_____
7. K. Dale	751.00	1	108.47	41,050.00	_____	_____
8. J. Kerns	460.00	0	65.81	38,900.00	_____	_____
9. M. Kurt	421.69	3	49.68	41,650.00	_____	_____
10. P. Wisfal	672.29	3	92.14	24,070.00	_____	_____

Business Application Problems

1. Gwen is single and earns $380 each week. She claims one exemption, but has authorized a deduction for her retirement program of $50 a week. Her gross earnings for this year are $8,085. What is her net pay?

2. Alice Lamson is a sales representative for A. K. Kolan Industries. Her gross earnings this week are made up of a salary of $150 plus $138 of commissions that she earned on sales. She is married, has one child, and claims one exemption. What is her net pay if her gross earnings to date are $25,837?

3. Larry Cashin will earn a $410 salary this week. This is the seventeenth week he has been with the company and the fourth week that he has claimed only himself as an exemption. Larry is single. What is the total amount of deductions made from his paycheck for F.I.C.A. and federal income tax?

4. Ken Smite was paid a salary of $820 a week. He worked each week of the year. What was the deduction for F.I.C.A. on the last (52nd) week of the year?

5. What was the total deduction from Mr. Smite's earnings during the year for F.I.C.A.?

6. The Biggerton Company pays its employees overtime for all hours worked beyond forty per week. If the rate of overtime for J. T. Croswell is one and one-half times his hourly rate of $4.20, what will be his overtime earnings?

Time Card Record

M	T	W	Th	F
9	7.8	10	10.5	8.6

7. Leann Millsworth is paid weekly on an hourly rate of $6.30. She earns overtime (one and one-half) for all hours worked in excess of eight each day. She is married and claims her spouse as a dependent. Her year-to-date earnings are $14,860. What is the deduction for F.I.C.A. for this paycheck?

Time Card Record

M	T	W	Th	F
8	9	8	10	9

8. Sammy Mesner is paid on a piece-rate system. He earns $.50 for each unit that he produces. His W-4 form shows a total of four exemptions and that he is married. His earnings to date are $8,738. What is his net pay?

Output Record

Monday	Tuesday	Wednesday	Thursday	Friday
93	89	109	128	141

9. Darcy had a gross income of $549.35 for the past week. Darcy is single and claims zero dependents. He lives in a city that has an income tax of 1 percent. The state also has an income tax of 2 percent on the first $30,000. Darcy has an accumulated earnings of $41,190 for the year to date. What is Darcy's net income for the week if the deduction for federal income tax is $137.97?

10. What would be the net income for Darcy for the following week if his gross income was the same as problem 9?

11. Yettave had $19.25 deducted from her paycheck for F.I.C.A. on March 20. What was her gross pay?

12. Deductions by the Payroll Office of $18 for union dues, $27.50 for uniform rental, $50 for a savings program, and $10 for tool rental are authorized by Peter Wilson. The payroll clerk also notes that he claims one exemption even though he is married. He has earned $14,900 previous to this pay period. His hourly rate is $6. He worked forty-two hours this week. The company pays double the regular rate for hours in excess of forty. What is his net pay?

13. The earnings for Dixie Brown total $9,867 for the year to date. Dixie is married but claims no exemptions. Her gross earnings for this week are $302.56. She has $50 deducted from her check each week for savings. She also has a $15 deduction for parking each week. The city in which Dixie works has a 1 percent tax for residents and a $\frac{1}{2}$ percent tax for non-residents on the first $10,000 of gross earnings. Dixie is not a resident of the city. What is her net income for the week?

14. The Marxton Corporation payroll for the week of January 26 totaled $34,960.58. What is the amount of F.I.C.A. tax that the corporation will need to submit for the week (employee and employer share combined)?

15. Janice Noteri is considering changing the amount of exemptions that she claims in order to increase her take-home pay. Janice is single and has a salary of $350 per week. She now only claims herself, but she is considering claiming five exemptions. What will be the difference in her take-home pay if she makes the change?

16. Al Derton receives a salary of $2,365 per month. He claims one exemption. This paycheck included a bonus of $1,500. How much will Al receive in this monthly paycheck if his earnings to date total $23,000?

17. If an employee is now earning an annual salary of $41,800 and receives a raise of 10 percent, what will be the additional take-home pay? The W-4 form indicates three exemptions and single. She receives a monthly paycheck.

Challenge Problem

Dave Cich has been employed with the Olton Corporation for six months. He earns a salary of $100 a week as well as a commission of $1\frac{1}{2}$ percent of sales. His commission last month was $840. He will receive one-fourth of that amount this week in his gross earnings. Dave is married, has five children but only claims three exemptions. He also earns $40 a week by doing artwork on the side out of his own home. He collects this income in cash. He has earned $14,900 to date from his sales for the Olton Corporation and $3,880 for his artwork. He has $47 taken out of his paycheck each week for savings and $100 is direct deposited into his bank account. What is his paycheck amount for the week?

Name _____ Date _____ Score _____

True or False

T   F   1.   Gross Earnings + Deductions = Net Pay

T   F   2.   A W-4 form is used to determine the amount of withholding allowances for an employee.

T   F   3.   Overtime pay is not subject to F.I.C.A. tax because it is $1\frac{1}{2}$ the usual rate of pay.

T   F   4.   Net pay is determined from reading the numbers on the time card.

T   F   5.   The hourly rate pay system is usually used for sales people.

T   F   6.   Gross earnings is the amount that is used to determine federal income tax.

7.   Compute the employee's gross earnings from the piece-rate information below.

Output Record

Days	M	T	W	Th	F
Units of Output	74	83	91	59	87
Hours worked	8	6	8	7.5	8.1

Piece-Rate = $1.15 per unit

8.   Determine the amount of federal income tax to be withheld if the gross earnings are $400 for the week, the number of exemptions claimed is one, and the employee is single.

9.   The payroll clerk noted that $911.57 was withheld from the employees of the company for F.I.C.A. for the week. What is the total amount that the employer must send the federal government for F.I.C.A. for the week?

10. Peter earns an hourly rate of $5.80. He is paid weekly and worked forty-seven hours last week. He is paid overtime for hours in excess of forty at the rate of one and one-half times. His earnings to date are $26,280. He is married and claims two exemptions. What is his net pay?

11. Jeff Hazel earns $9 per hour. He worked 42 hours last week. He is paid double time for all hours worked in excess of 40 each week. His earnings to date are $7,947. He is single and claims one exemption. What is his gross pay for the week?

12. Compute the gross earnings for an employee who is paid on a combination hourly and piece-rate system.

Day	M	T	W	T	F
Hours worked	9	7.6	8	7.2	8
Units of output	93	112	141	86	152

    Hourly rate = $4.10
    Piece rate = 7.8¢ per unit

6 Measurements

Performance Objectives

After mastering the material in this chapter, you will be able to:

1. Perform all of the fundamental processes in problems dealing with measurements.
2. Find the solution to problems dealing with linear, surface, and volume measure. (Using the traditional measurement system.)
3. Find the solution to problems dealing with linear, surface, and volume measure. (Using the metric system.)
4. Convert measurements to the metric system or to the traditional measurement system.
5. Understand and use the following terms:
   Linear Measure   Surface Measure   Volume Measure

The topic of measurements is useful to a business student in the application areas of building decoration and landscaping (carpeting, painting, sodding, and seeding), construction (determining the amount of earth removal, insulation required, and the area to be heated or cooled), and establishing retail and wholesale space allocations (determining overhead expenses by area, shelf allocations, and sales by floor space).

This chapter deals with the application of the fundamental processes to problems that require the dimension of measurement. The first part of the chapter includes using some basic fundamental processes on measurement data. The second part introduces the metric measurement system and problems relating to metric conversion as well as metric measurement. You will be able to make use of your knowledge in working with whole numbers, fractions, and decimals in this chapter.

The following is a table of measurements. This table will be useful to you in working the problems in the first part of the chapter.

Measurements Table

Linear or Straight Measure

12 inches	= 1 foot
3 feet	= 1 yard
5½ yards	= 1 rod
16½ feet	= 1 rod
66 feet	= 1 chain
320 rods	= 1 mile
5,280 feet	= 1 mile
1,760 yards	= 1 mile

Cubic or Volume Measure

1,728 cubic inches	= 1 cubic foot
27 cubic feet	= 1 cubic yard
128 cubic feet	= 1 cord of wood

Liquid Measure

4 gills	= 1 pint
2 pints	= 1 quart
4 quarts	= 1 gallon
31½ gallons	= 1 barrel
7½ gallons	= 1 cubic foot
32 ounces	= 1 quart

Dry Measure

2 pints	= 1 quart
8 quarts	= 1 peck
4 pecks	= 1 bushel

Surface or Square Measure

144 square inches	= 1 square foot
9 square feet	= 1 square yard
30¼ square yards	= 1 square rod
160 square rods	= 1 acre
640 acres	= 1 square mile or section

Counting

12 units	= 1 dozen
12 dozen	= 1 gross

Avoirdupois Weight

16 ounces	= 1 pound
100 pounds	= 1 hundredweight
20 hundredweights	= 1 ton
2,000 pounds	= 1 ton
2,240 pounds	= 1 long ton

Time

60 seconds	= 1 minute		100 years	= 1 century
60 minutes	= 1 hour		4⅓ weeks	= 1 month
24 hours	= 1 day		30 days	= 1 month
7 days	= 1 week		52 weeks	= 1 year
365 days	= 1 year		13 weeks	= 1 quarter (year)
366 days	= 1 leap year		12 months	= 1 year

Linear Measure

Linear measure considers only one dimension: length.

$$\longleftarrow \text{Length} \longrightarrow$$

The difficulties that occur with measurement problems are:

1. Performing the basic fundamentals on measurement information.
2. Selecting the proper conversion factor from the measurement table.
3. Reducing or borrowing units from larger or smaller units.

To perform the basic fundamentals on measurement information you must begin in the same manner as you would any other whole number problem. The first step is to set up the problem.

Example 1

4 yd., 1 ft., 5 in. × 2 =

$$\begin{array}{r} 4 \text{ yd., 1 ft., 5 in.} \\ \times\ 2 \\ \hline 8 \text{ yd., 2 ft., 10 in.} \end{array}$$

$C \to mm \times 10$
$mm \to C \div 10$
$m \to C \times 100$
$C \to m \div 100$
$m \to Km \div 1000$
$Km \to m \times 1000$

m	C	M
1	100	1000
1.5144	15.144	151.44
4.5720	45.720	457.20

$1'' = 2.54\, cm$

Example 2

4 hr., 37 min., 14 sec. + 1 hr., 40 sec.

```
  4 hr., 37 min., 14 sec.
+ 1 hr.          40 sec.
  5 hr., 37 min., 54 sec.
```

The examples so far have not required borrowing or reducing in order to complete the problem. In the following examples you must either borrow or reduce in order to find the correct answer.

Example 3

17 yd., 2 ft., 9 in. × 3 =

```
17 yd., 2 ft., 9 in.
             × 3
51 yd., 6 ft., 27 in.
```
This answer must be reduced to lowest terms.

$$\underset{12)\overline{27\ in.}}{\overset{2\ ft.,\ 3\ in.}{}}$$

```
51 yd., 6 ft.
+       2 ft., 3 in.
51 yd., 8 ft., 3 in.
```

$$\underset{3)\overline{8\ ft.}}{\overset{2\ yd.,\ 2\ ft.}{}}$$

```
51 yd.        3 in.
+ 2 yd., 2 ft.
+53 yd., 2 ft., 3 in.
```

When reducing measurement problems, always begin with the smallest measurement (in size) and work up to the largest.

Example 4

7 yd., 1 ft., 3 in. − 5 yd., 2 ft., 10 in.

```
  7 yd., 1 ft., 3 in.
− 5 yd., 2 ft., 10 in.
  1 yd., 1 ft., 5 in.
```

In Example 4, ten inches cannot be subtracted from three inches; so, a foot's worth of inches must be borrowed and added to the three inches. The sum, fifteen inches, is enough to allow the subtraction. The next step is to subtract the feet. A yard's worth of feet must be borrowed and added to the zero feet. The sum, three feet, allows the subtraction of two feet. The last step is to subtract the yards.

Exercise A   Solve the following problems. Remember to reduce your answers.

1. 13 yd., 2 ft., 7 in. × 4 = 52 yd., 8 ft., 28 in.
                                 = <u>55</u> yd., <u>1</u> ft., <u>4</u> in.

2. 8 lb., 6 oz. ÷ 6 = _____ lb. _____ oz.

3. 1 hr., 6 min., 10 sec. ÷ 2 = _____ min. _____ sec.

4. 60 lb., 11 oz. × 7 = _____ lb. _____ oz.

5. 5 hr., 17 min. − 3 hr., 50 min., 13 sec. = _____ hr. _____ min.
    _____ sec.

Surface Measure

Surface (or square) **measure** considers two dimensions: length and width. Answers are labeled as square feet or square yards, etc. Surface measure is the result of finding the product of the length and width (i.e., L × W).

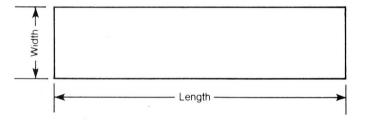

Example 5

How many square feet are there in a room that is 19′ long and 11′ wide?

        19 ft.
    × 11 ft.
        19
      19
      209 sq. ft.

Example 6

Surface measure problems also need to be reduced. In the previous example, the answer should be reduced to square yards and square feet. The measurements table indicates that there are nine square feet in a square yard.

           23 sq. yd., 2 sq. ft.
    9) 209 sq. ft.
       18
       29
       27
        2

Exercise B   Complete the problems below and reduce your answers.

1. 4 sq. yd., 2 sq. ft. + 22 sq. yd.,
    8 sq. ft., 7 sq. in. = 26 sq. yd., 10 sq. ft.,
    7 sq. in. = <u>27</u> sq. yd., <u>1</u> sq. ft., <u>7</u> sq. in.

2. 71 sq. yd. ÷ 3 = _____ sq. yd. _____ sq. ft.

3. $9\frac{1}{2}$ ft. × $6\frac{1}{2}$ ft. = _____ sq. yd. _____ sq. ft.

4. 3.2 mi. × 6.8 mi. = _____ sq. mi.

5. 5 sq. yd. − 3 sq. yd., 2 sq. ft. = _____ sq. yd. _____ sq. ft.

Volume Measure

Volume (or cubic) **measure** considers the three dimensions of length, width, and depth. It is the result of finding the product of the length, width, and depth of an object. In some problems the depth factor may be substituted as height.

$$Volume = L \times W \times D$$

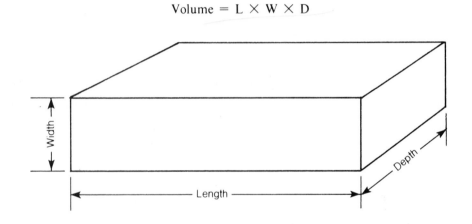

Example 7

How many cubic feet of earth must be removed to dig a ditch $1\frac{1}{2}'$ wide, 16' long, and $3\frac{1}{2}'$ deep?

  L × W × D =
16 ft. × 1.5 ft. × 3.5 ft. = 84 cu. ft.

Volume measure as well as surface measure problems need to be reduced; in the previous problem, the answer could be reduced to cubic yards and cubic feet. After consulting the measurements table, you will find that there are 27 cubic feet in a cubic yard.

$$
\begin{array}{r}
3 \text{ cu. yd., 3 cu. ft.} \\
27\overline{)84 \text{ cu. ft.}} \\
\underline{81} \\
3
\end{array}
$$

Exercise C   Complete the problems below and reduce your answers.

1. 6 yd. × 3 ft. × 2.5 ft. = 135 cu. ft. = <u> 5 </u> cu. yd.

2. 8 ft. × 10 ft. × 1$\frac{1}{8}$ ft. = <u> 90 CF </u> cu. yd., <u> 3,3 </u> cu. ft.

3. 42 sq. ft. by 7 ft. high = <u>   </u> cu. yd., <u>   </u> cu. ft.

4. 16 cu. yd., 19 cu. ft. + 3 cu. yd., 12 cu. ft. = <u>   </u> cu. yd.
<u>   </u> cu. ft.

5. A pool is 40′ long, 20′ wide, and averages 5′ deep. Find the total volume to the nearest cubic foot. <u>   </u> cu. ft.

The Metric System

Our government has committed the nation to the adoption of the metric system. The reason for this is clear; we are one of the very few remaining industrialized nations who are not on this system. And since, from an economic standpoint, exports are becoming more important to our nation, it is imperative that we fully learn this international language of measure. You, as an individual, should also become familiar with the metric system because you will soon be using it.

This portion of the chapter will first look at the metric system and how it is structured. Some traditional measurements will need to be converted to the metric system. The last portion of the chapter will provide some practice problems in measurement conversion.

The liter, meter and the gram are the basic units of measure.

For a rough comparison: 1 liter = approximately 1 quart
                   1 meter = approximately 1 yard
                   1 kilogram = approximately 2 pounds

The Metric Measurement System

Linear Measure

10 millimeters (mm.)	= 1 centimeter (cm.)
10 centimeters	= 1 decimeter (dm.)
10 decimeters	= 1 meter (m.)
10 meters	= 1 decameter (dcm.)
10 decameters	= 1 hectometer (hm.)
10 hectometers	= 1 kilometer (km.)
10 kilometers	= 1 myriameter (mym.)

Square Measure

100 square millimeters (sq. mm.)	= 1 square centimeter
100 square centimeters (sq. cm.)	= 1 square decimeter
100 square decimeters (sq. dm.)	= 1 square meter
100 square meters (sq. m.)	= 1 square decameter
100 square decameters (sq. dcm.)	= 1 square hectometer
100 square hectometers (sq. hm.)	= 1 square kilometer
100 square kilometers (sq. km.)	= 1 square myriameter (sq. mym.)

Cubic Measure

1,000 cubic millimeters (cu. mm.)	= 1 cubic centimeter
1,000 cubic centimeters (cu. cm., c.c.)	= 1 cubic decimeter
1,000 cubic decimeters (cu. dm.)	= 1 cubic meter
1,000 cubic meters (cu. m.)	= 1 cubic decameter
1,000 cubic decameters (cu. dcm.)	= 1 cubic hectometer
1,000 cubic hectometers (cu. hm.)	= 1 cubic kilometer
1,000 cubic kilometers (cu. km.)	= 1 cubic myriameter (cu. mym.)

Liquid and Dry Measure

10 milliliters (mi.)	= 1 centiliter (cl.)
10 centiliters	= 1 deciliter (dl.)
10 deciliters	= 1 liter (l.)
10 liters	= 1 decaliter (dcl.)
10 decaliters	= 1 hectoliter (hl.)
10 hectoliters	= 1 kiloliter (kl.)
10 kiloliters	= 1 myrialiter (myl.)

Weight Measure

10 milligrams (mg.)	= 1 centigram (cg.)
10 centigrams	= 1 decigram (dg.)
10 decigrams	= 1 gram (g.)
10 grams	= 1 decagram (dcg.)
10 decagrams	= 1 hectogram (hg.)
10 hectograms	= 1 kilogram (kg.)
10 kilograms	= 1 myriagram (myg.)
10 myriagrams	= 1 quintal (q.)
10 quintals	= 1 tonneau (T.)

Notice that in all of the units of measure the prefix is the same (i.e., milli, centi, deci, etc.).

milli→centi→deci→BASIC UNIT OF MEASURE→deca→hecto→kilo
(smaller)   (larger)

Factors   Notice that all of the metric system measurements have a base of 10 (i.e., by dividing 1 meter by 10 the result is 1 decimeter, 10 hectometers equals 1 kilometer, and so forth). Once you become familiar with this system it is much easier than the 12 inches to a foot, 3 feet to a yard, 1,760 yards to a mile, etc. that we have been using.

The square measure unit is found by the same method as it is in the traditional measurement system (i.e., length times (×) width). If 1 meter is equal to 10 decimeters, then one square meter must be equal to 100 square decimeters (10 × 10 = 100).

The same holds true for volume or cubic measure. Length × width × depth is the method used to determine cubic measure. This is the reason that 1 cubic meter is equal to 1,000 cubic decimeters (10 × 10 × 10 = 1,000).

The previous explanations should give you a basic understanding of the manner in which the measurement units are found.

The base of 10 allows for easy conversion from meters to, say, decameters; 53.6 meters equals 5.36 decameters, since there are 10 meters to a decameter $(10\overline{)53.6} = 5.36)$.

7.6 square kilometers = 760 square hectometers (100 square hectometers equals one square kilometer—100 × 7.6 = 760)

53,065.2 cubic millimeters = 53.0652 cubic centimeters (53,065.2 ÷ 1,000 = 53.0652)

Exercise D   Convert the following measurements to the base indicated.

1. 963.2 centimeters to meters _____9.632_____

2. 856 square hectometers to square kilometers _____

3. 806,329 cubic centimeters to cubic meters _____

4. .76 liters to centiliters _____

5. 47,357 grams to decigrams _____

It may be necessary for you to convert from the traditional measurement system to the metric system or vice-versa. The table on page 123 will aid in the conversion process.

Example 8

A hole 47 ft. long, 18 in. wide, and 42 in. deep equals _____ cubic meters.

47 ft. $\times$ 1.5 ft $\times$ 3.5 ft. = 246.75 cu. ft.

   246.75 cu. ft.
$\times$ .02832 (1 cu. ft. = .02832 cu. m.) (from table)
  6.98796 cu. m.

Example 9

437 kilometers equals _____ miles.

   437 kilometers
$\times$ .6214 (1 km. = .6214 mi.) from table
271.5518 miles

Conversion Table

Linear Measure

1 in.	= 2.54 cm.	1 mm.	= .03937 in.
1 ft.	= .3048 m.	1 cm.	= .3937 in.
1 yd.	= .9144 m.	1 dm.	= .3281 ft.
1 rd.	= 5.029 m.	1 m.	= 39.37 in.
1 mi.	= 1.6093 km.	1 m.	= 3.281 ft.
		1 m.	= 1.0936 yd.
		1 dcm.	= 1.9884 rd.
		1 km.	= .6214 mi.

Square Measure

1 sq. in.	= 6.452 sq. cm.	1 sq. mm.	= .00155 sq. in.
1 sq. ft.	= .0929 sq. m.	1 sq. dm.	= .1076 sq. ft.
1 sq. yd.	= .8361 sq. m.	1 sq. km.	= .3861 sq. mi.
1 sq. mi.	= 259 ha. or 2.589 sq. km.	1 sq. cm.	= .155 sq. in.
1 sq. rd.	= 25.293 sq. m.	1 sq. m.	= 1.196 sq. yd.
		1 ha.	= 2.471 acre

Cubic or Volume Measure

1 cu. in.	= 16.3872 cu. cm. (c.c.)	1 cu. cm. (c.c.)	= .06102 cu. in.
1 cu. ft.	= 28.317 cu. dm. or .02832 cu. m.	1 cu. dm.	= .0353 cu. ft.
1 cu. yd.	= .7646 cu. m.	1 cu. m.	= 1.308 cu. yd.
1 cd.	= 3.624 steres (st.)	1 st.	= .2759 cd.

Liquid and Dry Measure

1 dry qt.	= 1.101 l.	1 l.	= .908 dry qt.
1 liquid qt.	= .9463 l.	1 l.	= 1.0567 liquid qt.
1 liquid gal.	= .3785 dcl. or 3.785 l.	1 dcl.	= 2.6417 liquid gal.
1 pk.	= .881 dcl. or 8.81 l.	1 dcl.	= 1.135 pk.
1 bu.	= .3524 hl.	1 hl.	= 2.8377 bu.

Weight Measure

1 gr. troy	= .0648 g.	1 g.	= 15.432 gr. troy
1 oz. troy	= 31.104 g.	1 g.	= .03215 oz. troy
1 oz. avoir.	= 28.35 g.	1 g.	= .03527 oz. avoir.
1 lb. troy	= .3732 kg.	1 kg.	= 2.679 lb. troy
1 lb. avoir.	= .4536 kg.	1 kg.	= 2.2046 lb. avoir.
1 T. (short)	= .9072 met. t.	1 met. t.	= 1.1023 T. (short)

Exercise E   Fill in the missing values. Note: Slight variations from the answers in the back of the book may occur due to your choice of conversion factors from the table.

1. 4 yd., 7 in. equals _____3.8354_____ m.

2. 4 yd., 2 ft., 6 in. equals _____ m.

3. 36.1 m. equals _____ yd.   *16.74 Y*

4. 16 liquid qt. equals _____ l.

5. 91 sq. ft. equals _____ sq. m.

6. 7 sq. mi. equals _____ sq. km.

7. 2.6 sq. m. equals _____ sq. yd.

8. 4 cu. ft., 18 cu. in. equals _____ cu. m.

9. 3 lb., 14 oz. avoir. equals _____ kg.

10. 7.6 metric tons equals _____ tons.

Exercise F   Fill in the missing values.

1. 7.6 m. equals ___8.31136___ yd.

2. 69.42 sq. ft. equals _____ sq. m.

3. 6.2 sq. km. equals _____ sq. mi.

4. 334 kg. equals _____ lb. (avoir.).

5. 498 sq. m. equals _____ sq. yd.

6. 56.7 sq. cm. equals _____ sq. ft.

7. 45.08 cu. m. equals _____ cu. yd.

8. 456 cl. equals _____ l.

9. 546.7 cm. equals _____ m.

10. 43.8 dg. equals _____ gm.

Assignment
Chapter Six

Name _____ Date _____ Score _____

Skill Problems

Complete the problems below. Remember to reduce your answer.

1. 3 yd., 2 ft., 8 in. × 2 = __7__ yd. __2__ ft. __4__ in.

2. 36 lb., 8 oz. ÷ 4 = __9__ lb. __2__ oz.

3. 7 min., 20 sec. × 83 = _____ hr. _____ min. _____ sec.

4. 2 sq. yd., 7 sq. ft. × 7 = __19__ sq. yd. __4__ sq. ft.

5. 5 yd., 2 ft. × 4 ft. × 7 yd., 1 ft. = _____ cu. yd. _____ cu. ft.

6. 2.3 sq. ft. × 5 ft. = _____ cu. ft.

7. 627.8 cm. equals _____ m.

8. 18 l. equals _____ cl.

9. 4 yd., 2 ft., 7 in. equals _____ m.

10. 14.6 sq. m. equals __17.4__ sq. yd.

Business Application Problems

1. Miss Huntington was assigned a new task by her supervisor. The task is expected to take her 1 hour and 53 minutes. She must complete the task two times a day. How much time will be left out of an 8-hour day for other activities?

2. Mrs. Young's new house was just completed. She now wants to sod the yard in order to add the finishing touches to the home's exterior. She measures the front yard and finds it is 40 ft. × 100 ft., the side yard is 20 ft. × 15 ft., and the back yard is 60 ft. × 100 ft. A price quotation from a local sod dealer was $7.00 a square yard to have the sod laid. How much will it cost to do the job? Use the nearest square yard.

3. Ed Wilson has a front yard that measures 160 ft. × 147 ft. His local hardware store has a sale on lawn fertilizer. The 50 pound bag is on sale for $1.95. The 50 pounds will cover a 500 square foot area. If Mr. Wilson buys 7 bags, he can get another 5 percent discount off the sale price of all the fertilizer that he buys. How many bags will it take to fertilize Mr. Wilson's lawn? (No partial bags sold.)

4. The Werwin Mail Order Company has decided to refinish the shipping room floor. The room measures 29 ft. × 56 ft. The company has selected linoleum floor tiles 9 in. × 9 in. to cover the cement floor. If the tiles cost $.11 each, how much will the tile cost to do the job? (No partial tiles sold.)

5. The Shaw family is considering a new pool for their summer home. They contact the Cool Pool Company, a local distributor. The pool company representative stated that the first job would be to remove the sod from an area 30 ft. × 60 ft. Next a hole would be dug 25 ft. × 55 ft. × an average of 6 ft. deep. The pool would then be built in the hole. The finished pool would measure 20 ft. × 50 ft. × 5 ft. deep (average). How many square yards of sod must be removed from the lawn before the digging can begin?

6. How much would it cost for earth removal at $21.50 a cubic yard? (Nearest cubic yard.)

7. The Shaws are concerned about the amount of time it would take to fill the pool if their well will only pump 225 gallons per hour. How many hours will it take to fill the pool to within one foot of the top?

8. A room measures 5 meters by $7\frac{3}{10}$ meters. How many square decameters are there in the room?

9. The J. & J. Excavation Co. is preparing a bid on an earth removing project. The earth to be removed measures 160 ft. $\times$ 420 ft. $\times$ 5 ft. J. & J. charges a flat fee of $50 to transport the earth removing machine to the site. A rate of $21.50 per cubic yard is charged for the actual earth removal. Using the nearest cubic yard, what will be the bid on the project for earth removal?

10. The mayor's office must be recarpeted. The room is 30 ft. wide and 32 ft. long. An 8 ft.-by-4 ft. area near the desk in the corner of the room is to be left uncarpeted. The carpet store has suggested a nylon beige tweed at $17 a square yard. The carpet can only be sold in full square yards. How much will it cost to carpet the portion of the room as described?

Challenge Problem

The J. B. Colson Company will build a new building in July. In order to determine the potential utility cost savings by installing insulation, an estimation of costs and savings must be developed. The building will be 75 ft. wide by 260 ft. long. The side walls will be 10 ft. high in the single-story structure. All of the ceilings except for the 40 ft. $\times$ 65 ft. Shipping and Receiving area will be insulated to a depth of 7 in. The local utility company has stated that there will be a $60 per month savings on heating and cooling expenses if the building is insulated to the 7 in. depth in the areas described above. The insulating material will cost $2.78 for each cubic meter bag. How many months of fuel savings will it take to repay the cost of the insulation?

Name _____ Date _____ Score _____

1. The Harry Cornell Co. has just received a contract to construct a bicycle path across a part of the county. The company had three groups of men to work on the project, which was 4 miles, 895 yards long. The company has decided to divide the distance equally among the three groups. To the nearest foot, how long of a distance will each group be responsible?

2. If Clara's job operation requires 37 seconds to complete, how many complete operations can she do in a period of 5 hours?

3. Oscar Krieger is about to remodel his insurance office. The room is 30 ft. × 42 ft. with 8 ft. side walls. He will paint the walls and ceiling all one color. The paint that he picked out will cover 500 square feet per gallon. How many gallons must be purchased to do the job if he does not allow for doors, windows, etc.? (Partially used gallons can not be returned.)

4. A building must have an addition that measures a total of 400 feet (the three sides). The purchasing agent must determine the amount of cement to be used to fill a footing trench $2\frac{1}{2}$ ft. deep by 18 in. wide. Determine, to the nearest cubic yard, how many cubic yards of cement will be needed to fill the trench.

5. 53 sq. m. ÷ 17 equals _____ sq. ft.

6. A dump truck hauls 7.6 cubic yards of gravel per load. How many cubic meters would the truck haul?

7. Ninety pounds of candy is to be sold at $.50 for each seventy-gram box. How many boxes can be made from the ninety pounds? (Use avoir.)

8. 8 yd., 2 ft., 9 in. — 5 yd., 1 ft., 11 in. =

9. Convert 143 square decameters to square meters _____ .

10. A restaurant will consume 950 gallons of water a day. What will be the cost of water to the restaurant if it is priced at $.01 per liter?

11. The owner of a store contacted an air conditioning firm for an estimate. The owner indicated that the dimensions of the store were 60 ft. by 120 ft. with 12 ft. high side walls. The air conditioning firm stated that their Model X-1,000 could handle 75,000 cubic feet. Would the Model X-1,000 be large enough for the store?

12. What will be the cost of operation of a delivery van that consumes gas at the rate of one gallon for each 12 miles driven. Gasoline costs the firm $.326 per liter. What is the gasoline cost per mile (to the nearest tenth of a cent)?

3

Percent and Its Application to Business

7   Percentage
8   Insurance
9   Simple Interest
10 Promissory Notes
11 Consumer Credit and Installment Loans
12 Compound Interest and Present Value

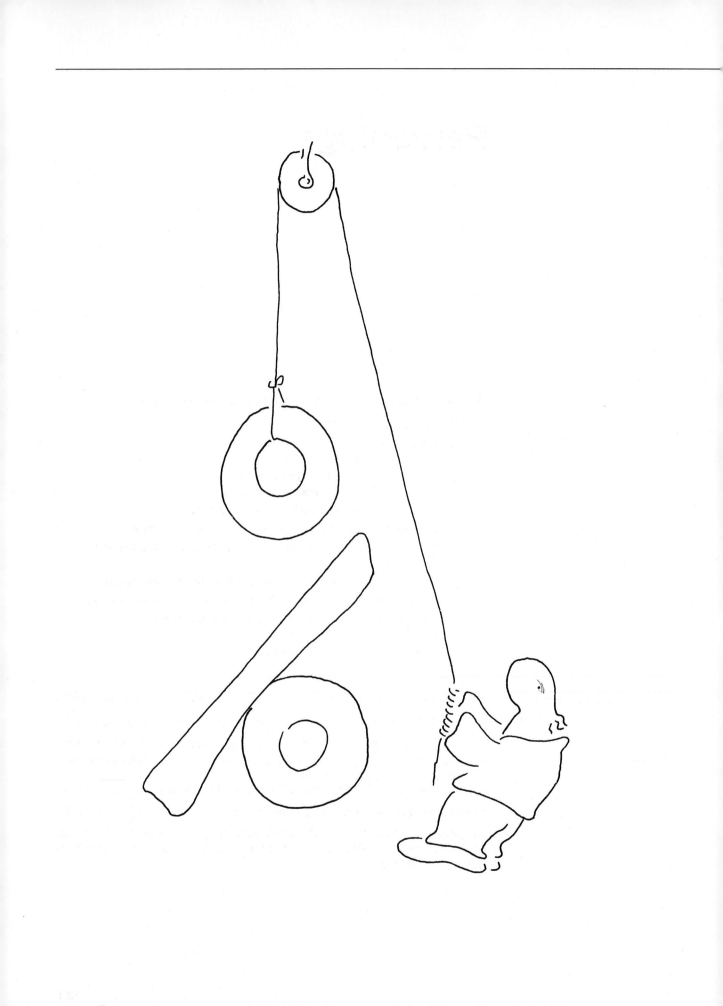

7 Percentage

After mastering the material in this chapter, you will be able to:

1. Define what percent means.
2. Change—percent to a fraction.
      percent to a decimal.
      decimal percent to a fraction.
      decimal number to a percent.
3. Write all of the above with fractional percent.
4. Identify the base, rate, and percentage in word problems.
5. State the formulas to be used to find the base, the rate, and the percentage.
6. Select and use the correct formula to find the unknown factor.
7. Work word problems that apply percentage to business situations.
8. Understand and use the following terms and concepts:

| Percent | Rate |
| Base | Percentage |

What Percent Means

Percent is another way of expressing hundredths; it can be defined as hundredths $\left(\text{i.e., 1 percent is the same as } \frac{1}{100} \right)$. Percent is used throughout business problems in computing payroll deductions, cash and trade discounts, depreciation, interest, returns, markup, and taxes to name just a few. The importance of percent cannot be emphasized too much.

The sign % signifies percent and therefore hundredths. You can also express hundredths as a fraction by showing a denominator of 100 $\left(\text{i.e., } \frac{?}{100} \right)$. In chapter 3, the figure on decimal number place values indicates that the second position to the right of the decimal point is the hundredths position. One hundredth is written .01.

<table>
<tr><td>**Percent to a
Fraction**</td><td>To change a number expressed as a percent to a fraction with a denominator of
100: (1) drop the percent sign, and (2) add a denominator of 100.</td></tr>
</table>

> **Example 1**
>
> $$47\% = \frac{}{100}$$
> $$47\% = \frac{47}{100}$$

<table>
<tr><td>**Percent to a
Decimal**</td><td>In chapter 3, you learned that any fraction can be changed into a decimal number
by dividing the numerator by the denominator. In the previous example, 47 per-
cent was changed into a fraction of $\frac{47}{100}$. This fraction can be changed into a
decimal number by dividing 47 by 100 with an answer of .47 (i.e., forty-seven
hundredths).</td></tr>
</table>

> **Example 2**
>
> $$7\% = .07$$
> $$135\% = 1.35$$

<table>
<tr><td>**Decimal to a
Fraction**</td><td>If a fraction can be changed to a decimal number, we should be able to reverse
the process and change a decimal number to a fraction: (1) drop the decimal
point, and (2) put the number over 100.</td></tr>
</table>

> **Example 3**
>
> $$.76 = \frac{?}{100}$$
> .76 is read as seventy-six hundredths, which can be expressed as
> $\frac{76}{100}$.

> **Example 4**
>
> $$.08 = \frac{8}{100} \qquad 1.53 = \frac{153}{100}$$

<table>
<tr><td>**Decimal to a
Percent**</td><td>Using the same thinking, we should be able to change a decimal to a percent.
Again, recalling the definition of percent as meaning hundredths, .67 can be
changed to 67 percent; .67 is read sixty-seven hundredths or sixty-seven percent.
The process requires: (1) drop the decimal point, and (2) add the percent sign.</td></tr>
</table>

You should now be able to interchange percent, fractions, and decimal numbers in any order. Use the previous pages of this chapter as guides to do the first few problems of exercise A.

Exercise A   Express as a decimal.

1. $17\% = \dfrac{17}{100} = \underline{\quad.17\quad}$

2. $56\% = \dfrac{56}{100} = \underline{\qquad}$

3. $11\% = \dfrac{11}{100} = \underline{\qquad}$

4. $9\% = \dfrac{9}{100} = \underline{\qquad}$

5. $156\% = \dfrac{156}{100} = \underline{\qquad}$

Exercise B   Fill in the blanks in the following problems.

1. $\underline{\quad41\quad}\% = \dfrac{41}{100} = \underline{\quad.41\quad}$

2. $\underline{\qquad} = \dfrac{}{100} = .62$

3. $\underline{\qquad} = \dfrac{}{100} = 1.27$

4. $\underline{\qquad} = \dfrac{}{100} = .1$

5. $21\% = \dfrac{}{100} = \underline{\qquad}$

Fractional Percent   Quite often a percent is expressed as a mixed number such as $8\frac{1}{2}$ percent or $20\frac{1}{4}$ percent. In order to be able to perform the fundamentals, you must be able to change the mixed number or fractional percent to a decimal. The process requires: (1) change the fraction to a decimal, (2) place the decimal behind the whole number, (3) drop the percent sign, and (4) divide by 100.

Example 6

$9\dfrac{3}{4}\% = 9.75\% = \dfrac{9.75}{100} = .0975$

$\dfrac{1}{5}\% = .2\% = \dfrac{.2}{100} = .002$

When you read a fractional percent that does not include a whole number such as $\frac{1}{4}$ percent, the percent can be read as one-fourth percent or more clearly as one-fourth of one percent. One-fourth percent is realistically a fraction of 1 percent. It should not be confused with 25 percent.

Fill in the blanks in the following problems.

1. $8\frac{1}{5}\% = \frac{8.2}{100} = \underline{.082}$

2. $1\frac{3}{8}\% = \frac{}{100} = \underline{\quad}$

3. $\underline{\quad}\% = \frac{}{100} = \underline{\quad}$

4. $52.9\% = \frac{}{100} = \underline{\quad}$

5. $\underline{\quad}\% = \frac{}{100} = .295$

Percentage

In this chapter you will be using three formulas in order to make percent work for you. The formulas will allow you to do a variety of problems.

You should be concerned with the mastery of the identification of the three factors in percentage problems outlined at the beginning of the chapter. The definitions or identification characteristics should be memorized before you attempt to proceed with the problems. Again, it should be emphasized that the factor definitions and identification characteristics are useful for you to learn!

The three factors in percentage problems are the base, the rate, and the percentage. There are always three factors used in the formulas, and they are always those listed above.

Base   The **base** is defined as "the factor of which a certain number of hundredths is taken." The base is always 100 percent, the basis of comparison. The base is not necessarily always the largest factor. Its size will depend on the rate.

Rate   The **rate** is defined as "a certain number of hundredths." The rate will be a percent.

Percentage   The **percentage** is defined as "the result of taking a certain number of hundredths of the base." The percentage is *not* necessarily always the smallest factor. Its size will depend on the rate.

Take time out now to memorize the factor definitions and identification characteristics.

In working percentage problems, two of the factors will always be known or can be easily found. You must find the third unknown factor. In order to find the unknown factor you must memorize the following formulas:

The Formulas

Percentage = Base × Rate $\qquad$ P = B × R

Base = $\dfrac{\text{Percentage}}{\text{Rate}}$ $\qquad$ B = P ÷ R

Rate = $\dfrac{\text{Percentage}}{\text{Base}}$ $\qquad$ R = P ÷ B

The Model

By putting your finger on the factor that you wish to find, the remaining uncovered portion of the model reveals the math operations that are used to find the unknown factor.

Example 7

If you know Percentage and Rate in a problem but need to fin[d] Base, put your finger over B.

Base is found by dividing P by R.

Some example problems will help to make the formulas more meaningful.

Example 8

Base = 400	$P = B \times R$
Rate = 20%	$P = 400 \times .20$
Percentage = unknown	$P = 80$

Example 9

B = 60	$P = B \times R$
R = 140%	$P = 60 \times 1.40$
P = unknown	$P = 84$

Example 10

P = 918	$B = \dfrac{P}{R}$
R = 153%	$B = \dfrac{918}{1.53}$
B = unknown	$B = 600$

Example 11

B = 150	$R = \dfrac{P}{B}$
P = 30	$R = \dfrac{30}{150}$
R = unknown	$R = 20\%$

Four-Step Process

Notice that a four-step process can always be used:

1. Identify the factors (base, rate, and percentage).
2. Select the formula for the unknown.
3. Substitute the values for the factors.
4. Complete the fundamental process called for in the problem.

Exercise D

In the following problems, find the unknown factor. Round off your answer to the nearest unit or nearest percent.

1. B = 93
   R = 107%
   P = 100

2. B = 116
   R = 86%
   P = 100

3. B = 700
   $R = 3\frac{3}{4}\%$ 3.75%
   P = ____

4. B = 492
   R = 14%
   P = 68.88

5. B = 92
   R = ____
   P = 10

6. B = 500
   R = 36%
   P = 180

Exercise E

1. B = $17
   R = 42%
   P = $7.14

2. B = 180
   R = 30%
   P = $54

3. B = $860
   R = ____
   P = $4,400

4. B = 23.20
   R = 250%
   P = $58

5. B = $48
   $R = 14\frac{3}{4}\%$
   P = ____

6. B = $47
   R = 42%
   P = $20

You will find it much easier using this four-step process when working the word problems at the end of this chapter.

Example 12

Forty percent of the students of Bisvern College are in the Vocational Division. There are 6,800 students at the college. How many are in the Vocational Division?

40% of the students are in the Vocational Division.
(R)   (B)
40% of 6,800 = P
40% × 6,800 = P
     2,720 = P

If the same information was placed in the problem with a different unknown value, the approach would be the same regarding the use of the four-step process.

Example 13

Of the 6,800 students at Bisvern College, 2,720 are in the Vocational Division. What is the percent of Vocational Division students?

2,720 students of 6,800 students is _____ percent?
  (P)   (B)
2,720 ÷ 6,800 is equal to _____ percent?
2,720 ÷ 6,800 = R
       40% = R

Again, the same information can be phrased differently to ask for a different unknown value. The four-step approach would still be used.

Example 14

The 2,720 Vocational Division students represent 40 percent of the total students at Bisvern College. What is the total number of students at Bisvern College?

2,720 students represent 40 percent of the total.
2,720 students represent 40 percent of B.
2,720 = 40% × B
6,800 = B

Increases and Decreases

The same formula can be used to find increases and decreases in an amount. The way the problem is worded is very important to the solution. In most cases you will begin by finding the difference in the previous figure and the current figure.

Example 15

Mark is the manager of the produce section of the local grocery store. On Monday he had 14 boxes of lettuce. On Wednesday he had only 5 boxes left. What percent were sold?

14	B = 14	R = P ÷ B
−5	P = 9	R = 9 ÷ 14
9 were sold (difference)	R = ?	R = 64%

Example 16

If the question in Example 15 were to read "What percent were left?", the solution would be a little different.

B = 14	R = P ÷ B
P = 5 (left)	R = 5 ÷ 14
R = ?	R = 36%

Example 17

Due to increased competition the sales of the Morten Company decreased from $459,098 to $398,013 over the period of one year. What is the percent of decrease?

$459,098
$-\ \underline{398,013}$
$\$\ \ 61,085$ (difference or decrease)

$B = \$459,098$ $R = P \div B$
$P = \$61,085$ $R = \$61,085 \div$
$R = ?$ $\$459,098$
                $R = \underline{13\%}$

The same approach is used to find increases.

Example 18

Ellen had 147 credit customers at the beginning of the quarter. At the quarter's end she had 159. What is the percent of increase in credit customers?

159
$-\underline{147}$
  12 (increase or difference)

$B = 147$ $R = P \div B$
$P = \ \ 12$ $R = 12 \div 147$
$R = \ \ ?$ $R = \underline{8\%}$

Example 19

There were 890 items of inventory in the warehouse of the Moeler Corporation at the beginning of the year. During the year the company added 47 new items. What is the percent of increase in inventory items?

$B = 890$
$P = \ \ 47$
$R = \ \ ?$

$R = P \div B$
$R = 47 \div 890$
$R = \underline{5\%}$

Example 20

Jason was earning an hourly rate of $5.20. He asked his boss for a raise. In his next paycheck he noticed his new rate of $5.60. What is the rate of the increase?

$\$\ 5.60$
$-\underline{5.20}$
$\$\ \ \ .40$ (increase or raise)

$B = \$5.20$ $R = P \div B$
$P = \$\ .40$ $R = \$.40 \div \$5.20$
$R = \ \ ?$ $R = \underline{8\%}$

Exercise F   In the following problems, find the unknown factor. Round off your answer to the nearest unit, cent, or percent.

1. Student enrollment grew from 8,000 to 10,000 or a ___25___ percent increase.

2. Sales decreased from $670,000 to $600,000 or a _____ percent decrease.

3. Employment increased from 93 to 106 employees or a _____ percent increase.

4. The state budget increased by 16 million from $633 million or a _____ percent increase.

5. The cost of a computer printer decreased by $100 from $890 or a _____ percent decrease.

6. Serious accidents increased by 10 percent from the 850 from last year or to _____ accidents this year.

7. Jim sold 20 percent less this month than the $500,000 that he sold last month or _____ sales for this month.

8. Advertising increased by 30 percent this month to a level of $150,000. The advertising was _____ last month.

9. The number of clients grew to sixty from fifty last month or a _____ percent increase.

10. The price of a product decreased from $5.50 to $5 or a _____ percent decrease.

Assignment

Chapter Seven

Name _____   Date _____   Score _____

Skill Problems

Fill in the blanks in the following problems. Round off your answer to the nearest unit, cent, or percent.

1. $62\% = \dfrac{}{100}$

2. $17\% = \underline{.17}$

3. $.64 = \dfrac{}{100}$

4. $8.7 = \underline{870}\ \%$

5. $7\% = \underline{}$

6. $\dfrac{3}{4}\% = \underline{.0075\%}$

7. $1.759 = \underline{175.9}$

8. $\dfrac{4.6}{100} = \underline{4.6\%}$

9. $458\% = \underline{4.58\%}$

10. $\dfrac{1}{4}\% = \underline{.0025}$

11. B = 62
    R = 11%
    P = ___

12. B = _____
    R = $6\dfrac{1}{2}\%$
    P = 852

13. B = $17,500
    R = ___ %
    P = $16,000

14. B = $56
    R = ___ %
    P = $62.20

15. B = _____
    R = 125%
    P = $81.00

Business Application Problems

1. Of the 700 high-level executives surveyed by a university, 43 percent had graduate degrees. How many had graduate degrees?

2. The College Business Club decided to spend $292 of the $730 balance in the treasury on a field trip to Toronto. What percent was left?

3. Wilmer Wilcox had 86 customers on Monday; on Tuesday he had an increase of 46 customers. What percent increase did he enjoy?

4. The price of a particular type of yard goods increased 17 percent. The increase brought the price up to $1 per yard. How much did the yard goods originally sell for?

5. Albert E. Hodge planted 47 percent of his land to pasture. Of the remainder, he planted 40 acres in oats and 26 acres in wheat. He found that he still had a field idle. He has a 240-acre farm. How much was left idle?

6. Mr. Otis sold 8 percent of his oat crop. He kept sixty bushels of oats for seed. The amount for seed represented 2 percent of the total crop. How many bushels of oats did he grow?

7. A company wished to buy a building priced at $30,000. They had a down payment of 20 percent. How large of a loan will they have to make?

8. Mrs. Jantz earns $4.20 per hour. She has just been informed that starting next week she will receive a 5 percent raise. What will be her new rate per hour?

9. Nancy Pryor noticed that her paycheck stated that she had earned $247 for last week's work. She also took note of the fact that $32.50 was deducted from her check for taxes. What percent was deducted?

10. Twelve percent of the students at Rerton Technical College were under twenty years old. The enrollment at the college is 950. How many students are under twenty years of age?

11. Sammy is a salesperson at a men's store. Yesterday he sold $865 of merchandise. Sammy stated that this was 110 percent of the amount that he sold on Tuesday. How much did Sammy sell on Tuesday?

12. The Deli section of the grocery store enjoyed sales of $890 last Tuesday. The store had sales of $39,740 on the same day. What percent of the sales came from the Deli?

13. A recently passed law stipulated that the number of federal employees must remain steady at the 1977 level of 2,191,121. Another portion of the law states that the federal work force can increase as the U.S. population increases if the president deems it in the national interest. The 1980 census showed that the number could increase by 53,000. What percent increase would the additional employees represent?

14. A corporate budget was increased by 2.4 percent over the previous year. The previous budget called for expenditures of $45,970,000. What is the new budget amount?

15. If the level of foreign car sales in the U.S. was 30 percent of the total market and the total market consisted of nine million vehicles, what would the foreign car sales be if the market increased to 12 million vehicles?

16. The Home Mortgage Company found that 164 of their clients were in default for the month of July. Those who defaulted represented 2% of the total mortgages held by the company. How many mortgages does the company hold?

17. Carrie spends $480 for rent each month. She has totaled her expenditures on food and has found that she spends $260 or 16 percent of her gross income on food. What percent of her gross income does she spend on rent?

18. If the unemployment rate changed from 7.3 percent to 7.5 percent, how many additional workers were unemployed in a work force of 90,000,000 people?

19. All of the sales staff of the Donaldson Corp. made the quota for the month. The quota was a sales volume of $260,000. Seven of the ten sales representatives went over the quota by 15 percent. One additional sales representative exceeded the quota by 20 percent. What was the excess of quota achievement using the figures given?

20. The class of Economics students were drawn from many geographical sources. Of the total class enrollment, seven were foreign. This group represented $16\frac{2}{3}$ percent of the class. How many students are enrolled in the class?

Challenge Problem   Mr. Bierstottle has 42 percent of his money invested in livestock, 12 percent paid into a home, and the remainder in cash. He has been in the agriculture business for 31 years. He has $42,900 in cash. His productivity increased by 12 percent last year to give him the highest return ever. He has a $22,000 mortgage with the Delta State Bank. How much does he have invested in his home?

Name _____ Date _____ Score _____

Percentage   Fill in the blanks in the following problems.

1. 9% = _____

2. $\dfrac{7}{8}$ = _____

3. .21 = _____

4. $9\dfrac{1}{2}$ = $\dfrac{}{100}$

5. **T F** $P = R \times B$

6. **T F** $R = B \div P$

7. **T F** $250 = 50\%$ of 50

8. B = $600
    R = 25%
    P =

9. The Sales Department of Jacklen Marketing Co. reported that gross sales were $642,800 for the first quarter of the year. Sales returns were $12,856 for the same period. What percent were the returns to gross sales (nearest percent)?

10. The cost of raw materials for the garment industry increased by $8\dfrac{1}{2}$ percent over last year. An item that sells for $24 wholesale this year would have been priced lower last year by what amount?

11. Food is about 16 percent of the average family budget. What will be the expenditures for food by a family that has an income of $1,500 a month?

12. The work force in the U.S. is approximately 85,000,000 people. The unemployment rate recently decreased .7 percent. How many additional people were put to work?

13. An apartment building increased in appraised value by $7,000 over a period of one year to $86,000. What was the percent increase in appraised value?

14. A bank had 40 percent of its holdings in stocks and bonds. The amount invested totaled $68 million in all investments. How much was invested in stocks and bonds?

15. The bank in problem 14 added $816,000 to total investments the following year. What is the percent increase in investments?

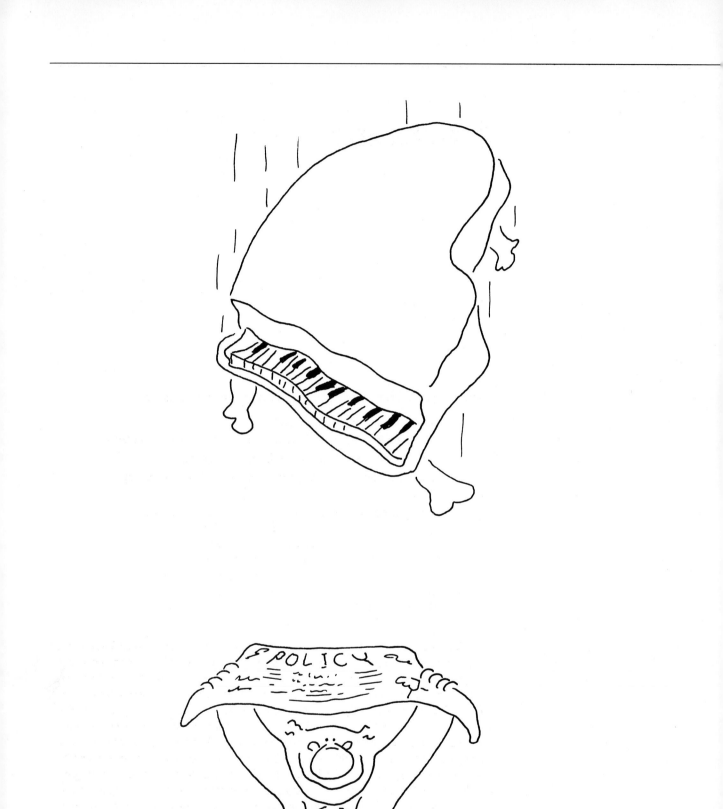

8 Insurance

Performance Objectives

After mastering the material in this chapter, you will be able to:

1. State the purpose of insurance.
2. Calculate premiums in fire, life, and auto insurance problems.
3. Identify different types of life insurance coverage.
4. Calculate the amount of payment on a fire loss covered by coinsurance.
5. Understand and use the following terms and concepts:

Premiums	Limited Pay Life Policy
Policy	Endowment Life Policy
Coinsurance	Comprehensive Insurance
Beneficiary	Property Damage Insurance
Term Life Policy	Collision Insurance
Straight Life Policy	

The purpose of insurance is to minimize the cost of unforeseen losses. If a firm or person foresees a chance of high risk, some type of insurance coverage may be warranted. There are many types of insurance—health, fire, casualty, life, crop, automobile, marine, workmen's compensation, and even rain insurance. This financial protection can be purchased by groups of people, individually, or even for another person. In some instances it can be purchased from the federal government or from privately owned firms. Private firms are either stock companies (owned by stockholders of that firm) or mutual companies (owned by policyholders of that firm). An insurance policy is sold through an insurance agent who is a local representative of an insurance company. Due to the vastness of this topic only a brief coverage of fire insurance, life insurance, and auto insurance will be included.*

*Further information is available from your local insurance agency or by writing the Consumer Information Center, Pueblo, Colorado 81009, for these free booklets: Insurance for Renters and Homeowners 018D, Insurance for your Health, Car, and Life 019D, Questions and Answers about No-Fault Auto Insurance 256D.

Insurance protection is purchased by making fixed payment amounts at periodic intervals. The payment amounts are termed **premiums.** The premium amount is established by the insurance company by considering the chance of loss through statistical analysis and adding on the cost of doing business. Premiums are usually paid quarterly, semiannually, or annually. There is an economic savings to the insured by paying annually due to the reduced costs of handling by the insurance company. A **policy,** or written contract, is then given to the owner that identifies the areas and amount of coverage.

Policy

Property Insurance

Property damage or loss is a common type of insurance. There are many types of property insurance including wind, fire, water, vandalism, and breakage. Fire is the greatest damage threat and is included in most property coverage. Fire insurance rates vary by the amount of fire protection available nearby, age of dwelling, construction materials, and fire extinguishers on the premises, among other factors. Premium rates are stated in terms of $100 of coverage. Rates for coverage over $100 are multiplied by the number of $100s of coverage desired.

Example 1

Determine the fire premium for an office building to be insured for $38,500 that is constructed of masonry materials. The rate is $.325 per $100 of coverage desired.

$38,500 =   385 hundreds
             $\times$ $.325 per $100
             $125.13 annual premium

Property insurance, including fire protection, is often purchased for periods longer than one year. Policies for three to five years offer a reduction in the amount of the premium because of the reduced cost of doing business.

Fire Insurance

A common clause in most fire insurance policies is the **coinsurance** clause. This clause states that the policy holders must provide a minimum percent of coverage on their property. A common coinsurance percent is 80 percent. A building that is valued at $41,000 must be insured for $32,800 ($41,000 $\times$ .80) (Insurance Required) in order to receive maximum payment if a loss occurs. If the property was insured for only $24,600 (60 percent of $41,000; insurance carried) and was damaged by $14,000, the insurance company would not pay for the full amount of the loss. A partial payoff of $10,500 would be made.

Coinsurance

This amount is a prorated payment. It is found by:

$$\frac{\text{Insurance Carried}}{\text{Insurance Required}} \times \begin{array}{l}\text{amount}\\\text{of loss}\end{array}$$

$$\frac{\$24,600}{\$32,800} \times \$14,000 = \$10,500 \text{ (amount of payoff)}$$

James Garison's warehouse is covered by an insurance policy that has an 85 percent coinsurance clause. The building is valued at $120,000. It is insured for $78,000. Fire did $40,000 worth of damage to the building. What is the amount of the settlement from the insurance company?

$120,000 × .85 = $102,000 (insurance required)

$$\frac{\$\ 78,000}{\$102,000} \times \$40,000 = \$30,588.24 \text{ (amount of payoff)}$$

Though the property owner may carry more insurance than the coinsurance clause specifies, the payoff will never exceed the face value of the policy. Also, the payoff will never exceed the value of the loss. The maximum payoff on property insured to the coinsurance limit will always be the face value of the policy or the amount of the loss, whichever is lower. Keep this in mind when completing the assigned problems.

Exercise A Calculate the amount of the annual premium in the problems below.

	Value of Property	Amount of Coverage	Premium Per $100 of Coverage/yr.	Total Premium Per Year
1.	$46,000	$36,000	$.310	$111.60
2.	31,900	24,000	.396	_____
3.	54,000	42,000	.462	_____
4.	67,000	51,000	.332	_____
5.	21,300	16,500	.405	_____
6.	87,000	70,000	.358	_____
7.	36,000	27,000	.490	_____
8.	61,900	50,000	.318	_____
9.	54,800	42,500	.325	_____
10.	21,700	17,000	.431	_____

Calculate the amount of payoff in the problems below. Do not round off the insurance carried to insurance required factor before multiplying the Amount of Loss amount. This will provide the most accurate answer.

	Value of Property	Amount of Coverage	Coinsurance Clause Specification	Amount of Loss	Amount of Payoff
1.	$ 46,000	$ 36,000	80%	$12,000	$11,739.13
2.	65,000	52,000	80	20,000	
3.	41,500	30,000	75	6,000	
4.	60,000	40,000	80	40,000	
5.	23,000	18,000	75	3,000	
6.	95,000	76,000	80	10,000	
7.	120,000	100,000	80	80,000	
8.	62,800	48,000	75	15,000	
9.	60,000	45,000	75	22,500	
10.	30,000	26,000	80	28,500	

Life Insurance

Life insurance has many purposes, the most common of which is to provide some financial security or protection for the survivors of the insured. The survivors that are to receive the financial benefits are named by the insured in the policy. These named persons or organizations are termed **beneficiaries.**

Beneficiary

Life insurance can be purchased in many forms by making monthly, quarterly, semiannual, or annual premium payments. There is an economic savings earned by paying annually. Some of the types of life insurance are discussed here.

Term Life

The **term life** policy is often offered by employers as part of a fringe benefit package. It provides protection only as long as the premiums are paid. This type of policy offers the lowest cost for the amount of protection.

Straight Life

The **straight life** policy is similar to term life. The insured is protected only as long as premiums are made. Straight life insurance premiums are a little higher than term life because part of the premium is saved by the company for the insured. These savings are paid to the insured if the policy is cancelled. The amount paid to the insured is termed cash surrender value. The cost is higher than term life because of the savings factor in this policy.

Limited Pay Life

The **limited pay life** policy is similar to straight life. There is a savings factor in the premium, but the insured is required to make only a limited number of premium payments. This reduces the financial pressure on the insured when earnings decline, such as after retirement. Due to the limited number of premium payments, the premium cost is higher than term or straight life.

Endowment Life

The **endowment life** policy is similar to limited pay life. It has a limited number of premium payments and has a savings factor. The savings factor is larger in this policy than in limited pay life. Endowment life is used to financially prepare for retirement, college, a trip, or a business venture. Due to the increased savings factor the premium payments are the highest of all the types of life insurance discussed.

Premiums are stated per $1,000 of life insurance coverage. The premium amount varies from company to company due to the efficiency of the firm, the quality of investments made, or type of insurance company. A representative schedule of premiums follows.

Annual Premium per $1,000 of Insurance

Age of Insured*	Term Life	Straight Life	Limited Pay Life	Endowment Life
18	$ 4.42	$14.98	$21.35	$35.45
19	4.43	15.09	21.68	35.48
20	4.45	15.11	22.02	35.50
21	4.47	15.46	22.40	35.52
22	4.49	15.80	22.85	35.55
23	4.53	16.17	23.30	35.58
24	4.58	16.55	23.75	35.62
25	4.61	16.96	24.25	35.67
26	4.67	17.40	24.76	35.74
27	4.72	17.82	25.26	35.81
28	4.80	18.27	25.80	35.87
29	4.89	18.75	26.35	35.95
30	4.98	19.26	26.92	36.05
31	5.08	19.75	27.50	36.17
32	5.22	20.33	28.15	36.28
33	5.39	20.95	28.80	36.43
34	5.60	21.55	29.40	36.60
35	5.77	22.20	30.11	36.79
36	6.07	22.91	30.82	36.99
37	6.40	23.62	31.55	37.25
38	6.76	24.40	32.30	37.52
39	7.17	25.20	33.15	37.81
40	7.60	26.05	33.99	38.15
41	8.09	26.95	34.85	38.55
42	8.63	27.85	35.75	38.95
43	9.23	28.84	36.70	39.40
44	9.86	29.92	37.80	39.90
45	10.55	30.99	38.81	40.38
46	11.35	32.10	39.90	40.95
47	12.20	33.35	40.89	41.55
48	13.20	35.70	42.10	42.25
49	14.21	36.00	43.35	43.00
50	15.39	37.50	44.70	43.80

*Premiums for ages two weeks through eighty years old and beyond are also available.

The annual premium for a $15,000 limited pay life insurance policy would be $342.75 if the insured were twenty-two years old at the time the policy was purchased.

$$\$15,000 = \quad 15 = \$1,000 \text{ of coverage}$$
$$\underline{\times \ \$22.85} = \text{Annual premium for twenty-two-year-old}$$
$$\text{limited pay life}$$
$$\$342.75 = \text{Annual Premium}$$

Example 3

What will be the annual premium on a term life policy for $8,000 if the insured is forty-seven years old?

$$8 = \$1,000 \text{ of coverage}$$
$$\underline{\times \ \$12.20} = \text{Annual premium for forty-seven-year-old term life}$$
$$\$97.60 = \text{Annual premium}$$

Exercise C   Calculate the annual premium in the following problems.

	Amount of Insurance Coverage	Type of Insurance	Age of Insured	Annual Premium
1.	$ 20,000	Straight	18	$ 299.60
2.	55,000	Term	23	_____
3.	100,000	Limited Pay	20	_____
4.	20,000	Term	28	_____
5.	60,000	Straight	32	_____
6.	5,000	Endowment	24	_____
7.	20,000	Limited Pay	30	_____
8.	25,000	Straight	45	_____
9.	20,000	Term	26	_____
10.	120,000	Endowment	35	_____

Auto Insurance

Auto insurance is designed to provide coverage for accidents resulting in damage to the automobile and people involved in auto accidents.

Comprehensive Insurance

Insurance can be purchased to provide coverage for loss caused by vandalism, theft, fire, windstorm, etc. This type of coverage is termed **comprehensive insurance.** The insurance premium rate for this type of coverage is dependent on the area that the auto will be used, the age of the auto, and its cost.

Property Damage Insurance

Property damage insurance covers damage done to property other than that of the insured. This type of coverage will pay for damages done to the other auto, buildings, or landscaping when it is determined that the insured is at fault. The driver's age and driving record determine the cost of this type of insurance.

In many states a "No-Fault" insurance system has been enacted into law. This law requires that injuries and property damage be paid for by the coverage of the auto owner, regardless of fault. Payment by the insurance company is limited to the maximum of the insurance coverage.

Collision Insurance

Comprehensive and property damage insurance does not provide coverage to the insured's auto in case of a collision. **Collision insurance** is designed to fix or replace the auto when damaged by a collision with another object. The cost of this type of coverage is based on (1) type of auto, (2) age of auto, (3) record of driver and amount of miles to be driven per year, and (4) the size of the deductible. The deductible clause indicates that the insured pay for the first $50, $100, or $250 of damage. Damages beyond the specified deductible are paid up to the limit of the insurance coverage. The lower the deductible, the higher the premium costs. The deductible clause reduces small claims that would plague the insurance company by putting payment responsibility on the insured. The following are some typical specifications for $100 deductible collision auto insurance.

Age of driver and auto usage:
Class 1A = car not driven to work (for pleasure only).
Class 1B = car driven to work, total round trip distance not to exceed six miles.
Class 1C = car driven to work, total round trip distance will exceed six miles.
Class 2C = driver is a male under twenty-five years of age.

Area of auto usage
Region I = Urban—Made up of cities of moderate or larger size. Populations of 20,000 or more. High concentration of business, industry, and autos; therefore a higher accident rate.
Region II = Suburban—Made up of residential areas. Far less commercial and industrial concentration; therefore less congestion and a moderate accident rate.
Region III = Rural—Made up of areas of very few homes or people. Primarily agricultural areas; therefore fewer accidents.

Age of auto
Group I = all current year autos
Group II = autos of previous year
Group III = autos two or more years old

Annual Premium for Collision Insurance with $100 Deductible

Group	Region	Class 1A	Class 1B	Class 1C	Class 2C
I	I	$57.00	$81.13	$87.20	$110.14
	II	49.80	77.20	81.40	108.30
	III	42.65	72.50	78.00	104.37
II	I	52.20	75.40	79.88	104.20
	II	45.30	71.00	75.70	101.80
	III	37.10	65.00	70.30	97.40
III	I	41.00	62.90	69.00	98.65
	II	31.38	54.10	61.60	92.90
	III	29.30	48.60	55.20	88.45

Example 4

John Billings, age forty-two and living in a suburban area, purchased a one-year-old car yesterday. John indicates that he will drive four miles to work each day. What will be the collision insurance premium cost?

John is: Class 1B
Region II
Group II

The annual premium will be $71.

Example 5

Janis Gifford, age twenty-seven, living in a downtown (urban) area sold her 1974 full-size car and purchased a new compact-size car. She will drive across town fourteen miles each day to get to work. What will be her annual premium for collision insurance?

Janis is: Class 1C
Region I
Group I

The annual premium will be $87.20.

Exercise D   Determine the annual premium in the problems below.

	Age of Insured	Age of Auto (Years Old)	Area of Auto Usage	Amount of Miles to be Driven/ Day to Work	Annual Premium for Collision Insurance
1.	31	new	Rural	17	$ 78.00
2.	64	1	Suburban	42	
3.	19 (female)	5	Urban	7	
4.	42	3	Rural	not to work	
5.	23 (male)	new	Suburban	19	
6.	37	4	Urban	40	
7.	28	2	Rural	12	
8.	37	3	Suburban	10	
9.	49	new	Urban	19	
10.	57	9	Urban	32	

Insurance agencies are in business to make a profit. Clients with good driving records will have fewer accidents and therefore fewer claims against their policy. It is to the advantage of insurance agencies to provide a discount to those good drivers and keep them as their clients. The opposite is true for drivers with poor records. Their record indicates that they should be charged more because they will have more claims on their policy in the future. The agent will want the good drivers.

Some agencies treat all new clients, initially, as if they were poor risk drivers. After the driver has established a record of no claims against their insurance, a discount is offered. This discount remains in effect until the driver's record changes. A poor driver can earn a discount only after a period of no accidents.

Example 6

Diane Moeler has purchased a new automobile. Her agent has quoted her a premium amount of $632 per year. The agent also stated that after the second year of no claims against her insurance she would receive a 5 percent discount and a 10 percent discount after three years of no claims. Diane pays her insurance on a semi-annual basis. What is her six-month premium for the third year? What is her six-month premium for the fourth year? Assume no accidents.

Premium the third year: $632 − $31.60 (5% of $632) = $600.40
$600.40 ÷ 2 = $300.20 each six months
Premium the fourth year: $632 − $63.20 (10% of $632) = $568.80
$568.80 ÷ 2 = $284.40 each six months

Name _____   Date _____   Score _____

Skill Problems   Calculate the amount of annual premium in the problems below.

Fire Insurance

	Value of Property	Amount of Coverage Desired	Premium Per $100 of Coverage	Total Premium Per Year
1.	$40,000	$30,000	$.412	_____
2.	18,000	13,500	.410	_____
3.	60,000	48,000	.359	_____
4.	38,000	31,000	.375	_____
5.	62,500	53,000	.415	_____

Life Insurance

	Amount of Coverage	Type of Insurance	Age of Insured	Annual Premium
6.	$15,000	Term	23	_____
7.	40,000	Limited Pay	27	_____
8.	12,500	Endowment	41	_____
9.	20,000	Straight	32	_____
10.	20,000	Straight	20	_____

Auto Insurance

	Age of Insured	Age of Auto (Years)	Area of Auto Usage	Amount of Miles to be Driven/Day	Annual Premium for Collision Insurance
11.	22 (male)	new	Urban	20	_____
12.	40	1	Rural	16	_____
13.	35	4	Urban	21	_____
14.	39	3	Rural	7	_____
15.	29	new	Rural	19	_____

Calculate the amount of payoff in the problems below. Use the nearest percent of coverage.

	Value of Property	Amount of Coverage	Coinsurance Clause	Amount of Loss	Amount of Payoff
16.	$23,000	$17,250	80%	$10,000	_____
17.	70,000	50,000	80	40,000	_____
18.	62,000	46,500	75	6,500	_____
19.	98,000	80,000	85	90,000	_____
20.	19,600	14,000	80	9,500	_____

Business Application Problems

1. The Burton Corp. wishes to purchase a term life insurance policy on their president, Mrs. Ann Pierson. The company officials feel that if she died there would be a decline in earnings because of the absence of her leadership ability. The company will be named the beneficiary. What will be the cost of a $125,000 term life policy on Mrs. Pierson if her age is fifty?

2. Phil Buckner has decided that he can afford $12 each month for life insurance protection. He is twenty-eight years old, married, and has two children. He is not sure which type of policy to purchase, but has narrowed the decision down to term life or straight life. If he dies at age thirty-five, how much more will his family receive if he decides to purchase term life?

3. Rob, at age forty-seven, realized that he had an extra $120 a month that he could use to buy life insurance with. Rob would like to purchase an endowment policy with the money. To the nearest $1,000, how much endowment life insurance will the $120 buy?

4. Burston and Fischer have inquired about the cost of insuring a building recently purchased for an office. The building costs $47,000. The insurance company has a 75 percent coinsurance clause on fire protection. The current rate is $.371 per $100. What will be the annual premium if the company insures to the 75 percent clause?

5. Polisar Corp. incurred a $35,000 fire loss on an empty warehouse. The building is valued at $100,000. The insurance company specified a 75 percent coinsurance clause in the fire protection policy. What amount of insurance coverage was necessary to receive the maximum payment on the loss?

6. A new automobile was purchased by Cal Weston for use in his company. The driver will be a thirty-one year old sales representative who will drive the car about sixty-five miles a day on company business in rural areas. What will be the annual collision insurance premium amount?

7. The Lawson home burned down at an estimated loss of $42,000. The insurance policy contained an 80 percent co-insurance clause. The face value of the policy was $38,000. What was the amount of the payoff to the Lawson family?

8. Apex Life Insurance Company provides an auto for all of their salespeople. They recently purchased a new auto for their agent, Bud Brown. The auto will be driven approximately 140 miles a day in the city. Bud is thirty-seven years old and has an excellent driving record. What will be the annual premium?

9. A fire destroyed the home of the Brendege family. The total loss was estimated at $38,000. The family had an insurance policy to cover loss from fire with a face value of $29,000. The policy contained a co-insurance clause of 80 percent. What was the amount of the payoff to the Brendege family?

10. A company has added to the staff over the last month. Each new employee will receive a term life insurance policy in the amount of $10,000. The insurance is paid for by the company. The employees are listed below with their respective ages. What is the total cost of the insurance coverage to the company?

Bob Akers, twenty-four years old

Andy Watts, thirty-seven years old

Carla White, forty-five years old

11. A new building was insured for $120,000 for fire protection. After the construction was complete, the structure was appraised at $160,000. A fire in the second story caused $42,000 in damage. What was the payoff to the owner if the insurance policy specified an 80 percent coinsurance clause?

12. Robbie bought a pickup truck that was two years old for $8,400. He lives in a rural setting and will use the vehicle about twenty miles a day on the average. Robbie is twenty-two years old. What will be the cost of collision coverage on the truck?

13. A new commercial building will be completed on the first of the month for Beck and Company. The insurance agent has indicated that the insurance policy will specify a 75 percent coinsurance clause. The building will have a market value of $634,000. What is the amount of insurance coverage that Beck and Company will need to carry? Round off your answer to the nearest ten thousand dollars.

14. Carol Reddy, a forty-three year old, has $200 per month to use for additional insurance coverage. She is considering term and straight life policies. She is interested in the difference in the amount of coverage that she can obtain from the same investment. What is the difference in coverage that she can purchase? Round off your answer to the nearest $1,000 of coverage.

15. A company has decided to provide a new car to an executive employee as a fringe benefit. The new car will cost $23,800. The executive will use the vehicle about 300 miles a week. The executive, a forty-eight-year-old female, travels in an urban setting. What is the cost of the insurance to the company?

Challenge Problem   The Denberton Company pays an annual fire insurance premium of $185.50 at $.35 per $100 of coverage of fire insurance. The building is valued at $85,000. Last week they had a $50,000 fire. There is a 75 percent coinsurance clause. What is the amount of the loss to the Denberton Company?

Name _____ Date _____ Score _____

True or False

T F 1. An insurance policy is a contract that sets forth the rights of the in-sured and the amount of coverage.

T F 2. Endowment life insurance has the highest cost per thousand.

T F 3. Collision insurance provides coverage for loss caused by fire.

T F 4. The money paid at regular intervals to an insurance company is termed coverage.

T F 5. The beneficiary will receive the face value of the life insurance policy.

T F 6. When an insurance company states that the insured must share in the risk of insurance by absorbing part of the losses, the firm is spec-ifying a coinsurance clause.

T F 7. A term life insurance policy will buy more coverage for a stated amount of dollars than any other type of policy.

T F 8. Property damage insurance is aimed at paying for damages done to the insured auto.

T F 9. The purpose of insurance is to reduce the risk of loss.

T F 10. If a homeowner has a total loss and the insurance coverage exceeds the value of the property, the insurance company will pay out the value of the policy to the homeowner.

11. The Wilson Manufacturing Company will purchase term life insurance for its employees up to the amount of their individual annual income. The insurance is a fringe benefit for employees after one year of employment. Beverly Seldon, a forty-year-old receptionist, earns $18,000 a year. What is the annual cost of this fringe benefit to the Wilson Manufacturing Company?

12. How much term life insurance can be purchased by a thirty-year-old female who has an extra $70 per month? Round off your answer to the nearest $1,000.

13. Kevin John, at twenty-two, is the proud owner of a new automobile. He will use the car to drive to work, a distance of sixteen miles. Kevin lives on the family farm. What will be the annual premium for collision insurance on the new car?

14. The Shaw family home burned down at a total loss of $34,000. They had insurance on the property. The insurance company had a 75 percent coinsurance clause in the contract. What will the payout be if the family had only 60 percent coverage?

15. Jane Martin has a new apartment in the city of Shoresville, a community of 965 inhabitants. Jane, twenty-four, took the new apartment because she just accepted a teaching position in a nearby town. She will have to drive, round trip, about four miles to work. She also purchased a new car for driving to work. What will her collision insurance cost per year?

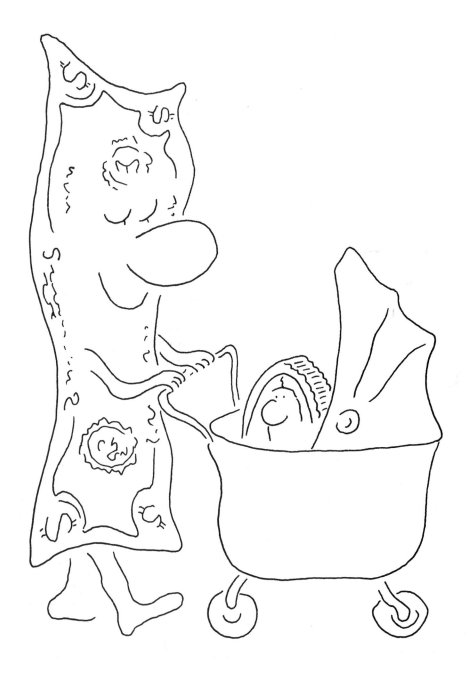

9 Simple Interest

$$T = \frac{I}{P \times R}$$

$$I = P \times R \times \frac{T}{12} \text{ or } \frac{T}{360}$$

$$R = \frac{I}{P \times \frac{T}{12} \text{ or } \frac{T}{360}}$$

$$P = \frac{I}{R \times \frac{T}{12} \text{ or } \frac{T}{360}}$$

Performance Objectives

After mastering the material in this chapter, you will be able to:

1. Explain what interest means.
2. Compute the time factor.
3. Compute both ordinary and exact interest using the principal, rate, and time factors.
4. Work word problems dealing with interest.
5. Understand and use the following terms:

Interest	Leap Year
Principal	The Interest Formula (I = P × R × T)
Rate	Ordinary Interest
Time	Exact Interest
The Calendar	

What Interest Means

Interest

There are undoubtedly many answers to the question "What is **interest?**" The lender may say that it is a return to cover the risk on his investment, a borrower may state that it is a penalty for having to borrow, and the economist would probably state that it is related to the supply and demand of risk capital.

Interest is a rental amount or a charge for the use of money.

Interest is determined by the amount borrowed, the rate of interest or charge rate, and the length of time the amount is to be borrowed.

When borrowing or renting money, the borrower is obligated, at the end of the period, to pay back the amount borrowed as well as the interest or rent on the amount borrowed. It should be noted that both the amount borrowed and the interest are owed by the borrower.

Principal
Rate
Time

In order to be able to compute interest you must know three factors. First the amount of money to be borrowed is termed the **principal.** The charge rate is termed the **rate,** and the length of time the money is to be borrowed is termed the **time.** To solve an interest problem, you must be able to determine the number of days that the money has been borrowed. You may in fact be given the date that the money was borrowed and the date the money was paid back. You will need to compute the number of days that have elapsed.

The Calendar In order to accomplish this task you must be familiar with **the calendar.**

Days per Month

January	31	July	31
February	28 or 29	August	31
March	31	September	30
April	30	October	31
May	31	November	30
June	30	December	31

Leap year   February has twenty-eight days, with the exception of **leap year,** when it has twenty-nine days. Leap year is any year that is evenly divisible by four. When computing the time factor you may find that the dates given for the length of time the money was borrowed may not be at the beginning or the end of a month. You must then compute the elasped time period in order to find the time factor. Below is a model to be used to compute "time."

Time Calculation Model

	Days in the month that borrowing took place
−	Date money is borrowed
	Days that money was borrowed in this month
+	Days in each succeeding month
+	Date of repayment
	Total "Time" factor

Notice that you are actually not counting the day that the money was borrowed, but you are counting, as a full day, the day the money was returned.

Example 1

A loan made on July 16 was repaid on October 22. What is the "time" of the loan?

July has	31 days
loan was made on July	− 16 th
borrowed money for	15 days in July
borrowed money in August for	31 days
borrowed money in September for	30 days
borrowed money in October for	22 days (date of repayment)
total "time" of loan =	98 days

Example 2

Julie borrows $7,000 at 8 percent on December 4 to be repaid on February 16 of the following year.

December has	31 days
loan was made on December	− 4 th
borrowed money for	27 days in December
borrowed money in January for	31 days
borrowed money in February for	16 days (date of repayment)
total "time" of loan =	74 days

The time factor can also be determined by using the Time Table shown below. Each day of the year is assigned a number that begins with the first day of the year.

Time Table

Day of Month	Jan.	Feb.	March	April	May	June	July	Aug.	Sept.	Oct.	Nov	Dec.	Day of Month
1	1	32	60	91	121	152	182	213	244	274	305	335	1
2	2	33	61	92	122	153	183	214	245	275	306	336	2
3	3	34	62	93	123	154	184	215	246	276	307	337	3
4	4	35	63	94	124	155	185	216	247	277	308	338	4
5	5	36	64	95	125	156	186	217	248	278	309	339	5
6	6	37	65	96	126	157	187	218	249	279	310	340	6
7	7	38	66	97	127	158	188	219	250	280	311	341	7
8	8	39	67	98	128	159	189	220	251	281	312	342	8
9	9	40	68	99	129	160	190	221	252	282	313	343	9
10	10	41	69	100	130	161	191	222	253	283	314	344	10
11	11	42	70	101	131	162	192	223	254	284	315	345	11
12	12	43	71	102	132	163	193	224	255	285	316	346	12
13	13	44	72	103	133	164	194	225	256	286	317	347	13
14	14	45	73	104	134	165	195	226	257	287	318	348	14
15	15	46	74	105	135	166	196	227	258	288	319	349	15
16	16	47	75	106	136	167	197	228	259	289	320	350	16
17	17	48	76	107	137	168	198	229	260	290	321	351	17
18	18	49	77	108	138	169	199	230	261	291	322	352	18
19	19	50	78	109	139	170	200	231	262	292	323	353	19
20	20	51	79	110	140	171	201	232	263	293	324	354	20
21	21	52	80	111	141	172	202	233	264	294	325	355	21
22	22	53	81	112	142	173	203	234	265	295	326	356	22
23	23	54	82	113	143	174	204	235	266	296	327	357	23
24	24	55	83	114	144	175	205	236	267	297	328	358	24
25	25	56	84	115	145	176	206	237	268	298	329	359	25
26	26	57	85	116	146	177	207	238	269	299	330	360	26
27	27	58	86	117	147	178	208	239	270	300	331	361	27
28	28	59	87	118	148	179	209	240	271	301	332	362	28
29	29	. .	88	119	149	180	210	241	272	302	333	363	29
30	30	. .	89	120	150	181	211	242	273	303	334	364	30
31	31	. .	90	. . .	151	. . .	212	243	. . .	304	. . .	365	31

One day must be added to dates after February 28 on leap-year problems.

Example 3

Using the information in Example 1, loan made on July 16 and repaid on October 22, what is the "time" of the loan?

October 22 is day	295
July 16 is day	−197
	98 days

Exercise A   In the following problems find the number of days or the term of the loan.

Date of Loan	Date of Repayment	Days
1. July 17	August 21	35
2. May 17	June 30	44
3. March 10	June 1	
4. September 16	December 3	
5. November 22	January 3	

When the date of the loan is known and the number of days or term of the loan is known, you have the necessary parts to compute the date of repayment. The determination of the repayment date is very similar to the approach used in determining the term of the loan.

Example 5

A loan for $3,500 at $7\frac{1}{2}$ percent interest is made to Steve Williams on January 16, 1985 for ninety days. Determine the date of repayment or maturity date.

January has:	31 days
Loan was made on January:	16
Borrowed money for:	15 days in January
There are:	28 days in February
There are:	31 days in March
	74 days in total to date
	16 more days required to make a total of
	90 days

Loan will come due on April 16th:

Example 6

Mark Watson borrowed $562 on June 25 for sixty days at 9 percent interest. What is the date of repayment or maturity date?

June has:	30 days
Loan was made on June:	<u>25</u>
Borrowed money for:	5 days in June
There are:	<u>31 days</u> in July
	36 days in total to date
	<u>24</u> more days required to make total
	60 days

Loan will mature on August 24:

The Time Table can be used to determine the due date on a loan. Using the date of the loan number from the table, add the term of the loan to the number and find the new number (sum) in the table. The new number will be the maturity date.

Example 7

Using the information from Example 6, a loan made on June 25 for sixty days, find the maturity date.

June 25 is day   176

                      <u>+ 60</u> term of note

                      236 number to be found on the Time Table

Day 236 is August 24

Exercise B

In the following problems, find the date of repayment or maturity date. Watch for leap year!

Date of Loan	Term of Loan	Date of Repayment
1. December 8, 1984	90 days	March 8
2. October 12, 1985	45	
3. June 3, 1987	60	
4. August 30, 1986	120	
5. January 23, 1988	60	

The Formula:
I = P × R × T

Ordinary interest

Exact interest

Rate

Time is one of the three factors in the formula to compute interest $(I = P \times R \times T)$. Time is usually expressed as a fraction of a year. The fraction numerator is the length of time that the money is to be borrowed (term of note). The denominator is either 360 or 365. A denominator of 360 is used to compute what is termed **ordinary interest.** This approach earns more interest for the lender. When a 365-day denominator is used to compute interest, the answer is termed **exact interest.** Exact interest earns the lender less interest because the denominator for time is larger.

The **rate** of interest is always expressed as a percent. The percent or interest rate is always for one year. The interest rate is therefore an annual rate. When the loan is for less than one year, the time factor must be used to adjust the annual rate for the shorter time period. The rate factor multiplied by the time factor will result in an adjusted rate factor. (Note: If the loan was for a year the time factor would be $\frac{1}{1}$ or 1.)

The amount of money borrowed is termed the *principal*. This is the amount that the borrower is "renting" and, therefore, the borrower must pay interest or "rent" on this amount. The more that is borrowed, at a given rate and time factor, the higher the interest.

You should now be able to understand all three elements of the interest formula: principal, rate, and time. To compute interest you will be multiplying, dividing, using fractions, decimals, and percent, computing time, and lastly rounding off.

Refer to Appendix.B, page 508, for additional information on short cuts in this area.

Example 8

Principal = $150
Rate   =   6%
Time   =   90 days
Interest = _____ ? (using ordinary interest)
I =   P × R × T
I = $150 × .06 × $\frac{90}{360}$

You can cancel in the above formula as shown below.

$$I = \$\overset{75}{\cancel{150}} \times \overset{.03}{\cancel{.06}} \times \frac{\cancel{90}}{\cancel{360}} \; \overset{\overset{1}{\cancel{2}}}{\underset{1}{\cancel{4}}}$$

$$I = \frac{\$75}{1} \times \frac{.03}{1} \times \frac{1}{1}$$

$$I = \$2.25$$

Example 9

Principal $= \$1,600$
Rate $\quad = \quad 7\%$
Time $\quad =$ June 23 to August 30th
$\qquad$ (using exact interest)

$$I = \quad P \quad \times \quad R \quad \times \quad T$$

$$I = \$1{,}600 \times .07 \times \frac{68}{365}$$

(with 320 written above $\$1{,}600$ and 73 written below 365)

$$I = 320 \times .07 \times \frac{68}{73}$$

$$I = \$20.87$$

Time Calculation
June 30
$-$ June 23
$\qquad$ 7 days in June
$+$ 31 days in July
$+$ 30 days in August
$\qquad$ 68 days in total

Exercise C Compute interest in the following problems (use ordinary interest).

1. Principal $= \$600$
   Rate $\quad = 8\%$
   Time $\quad = 42$ days
   Interest $= \$\underline{\quad 5.60 \quad}$

2. P $= \$1,000$
   R $= 14\%$
   T $= 25$ days
   I $= \$\underline{\qquad}$

   6000

   5232

3. P $= \$6,000$
   R $= 12\frac{1}{4}\%$
   T $= 120$ days
   I $= \$\underline{\qquad}$

4. P $= \$408$
   R $= 9\frac{1}{2}\%$
   T $=$ From June 16 to October 20
   I $= \$\underline{\qquad}$

5. P $= \$260$
   R $= 8\%$
   T $=$ January 17, 1984 to July 3, 1984
   I $= \$\underline{\qquad}$

6. P $= \$3,500$
   R $= 12\%$
   T $=$ February 29, 1988 to May 19, 1988
   I $= \$\underline{\qquad}$

Exercise D   In the following problems, compute interest using the exact interest method (365-day year).

1. P = $600
    R = 8%
    T = 45 days
    I = $ <u> 5.92 </u>

2. P = $3,000
    R = $12\frac{1}{4}$ %
    T = 180 days
    I = <u>   </u>

3. P = $365
    R = 15%
    T = 52 days
    I = <u>   </u>

4. P = $850
    R = $13\frac{1}{2}$ %
    T = 36 days
    I = <u>   </u>

5. P = $1,000
    R = 10%
    T = 36 days
    I = <u>   </u>

6. P = $450
    R = 14%
    T = 75 days
    I = <u>   </u>

Name _____ Date _____ Score _____

Skill Problems   Find the number of days or the term of the loan.

	Date of Loan	Date of Repayment	Days
1.	July 19	September 30	_____
2.	March 23	July 1	_____
3.	July 30	October 16	_____
4.	May 2	June 5	_____
5.	September 1	December 6	_____

Find the date of repayment or maturity date.

	Date of Loan	Term of Loan	Date of Repayment
6.	Jan. 10, 1984	60 days	_____
7.	June 3, 1985	120	_____
8.	May 13, 1988	45	_____
9.	March 6, 1986	40	_____
10.	January 12, 1984	90 ⁻	*13 APR 84*

Compute interest in the following problems.

11. Principal = $2,000
    Rate = $12\frac{1}{2}$ %
    Time = 2 years
    Interest = $ _____ (ordinary)

12. Principal = $1,800
    Rate = 9%
    Time = 13 days
    Interest = $ *5.84* (ordinary)

    $1800 \times 9\% \times \frac{13}{360} =$

13. Principal = $30,000
    Rate = 16%
    Time = 62 days
    Interest = $ _____ (ordinary)

14. Principal = $600
    Rate = 9%
    Time = 60 days
    Interest = $ _____ (exact)

15. Principal = $9,500
    Rate = $15\frac{3}{4}$ %
    Time = 1 year
    Interest = $ _____ (exact)

Business Application Problems

1. Niel Spradley borrowed $1,500 from a friend for a period of 200 days. The loan was based on a 12 percent interest rate. What is the amount of the interest on the loan? (Use ordinary interest.)

2. Dave Cich deposited his bonus check for $2,000 in his savings account on January 15, 1984. He hopes to have enough saved to take a vacation on July 5, 1984. The savings account pays $5\frac{1}{4}$ percent interest. What will his deposit be worth on July 5? (Use ordinary interest.)

3. A ninety-day loan was secured from the National Bank of Norden. The loan was made by Jackie Lee for $7,000. The bank is charging a 14 percent rate. What will be the amount of interest on the loan if it runs the full ninety-day period? (Use exact interest.)

4. Orin T. Southwell places his money in a bank that pays $5\frac{1}{4}$ percent compounded quarterly. James B. Mackie borrowed $4,700 from the same bank. The bank must charge 13 percent interest on loans to make a profit. Mr. Mackie's loan was for ninety-three days. How much interest did the bank earn? (Use ordinary interest.)

5. The Severance National Bank of Adrain, Michigan charged Harold Denlar $9 interest on a loan of $1,000 at $10\frac{1}{2}$ percent interest for ninety days.

    Mr. Denlar went all the way to the bank president, Mr. Ronald Severance, to complain that he was overcharged. After careful examination of the facts, Mr. Severance stated that Mr. Denlar was in fact undercharged. Who was correct; Mr. Denlar or Mr. Severance? (Use exact interest.)

6. June Farson took out a loan for $8,200 on July 18 to be repaid on August 3. She agreed to pay $9\frac{1}{2}$ percent interest. What was the amount due on August 3? (Use exact interest.)

7. Tony Cox borrowed $5,375 from the Rio Credit Union. The credit union charges a $12\frac{3}{4}$ percent interest rate on loans. What is the amount due on the loan if it runs for ninety-five days? (Use exact interest.)

8. A loan for $96 dated July 27, to be repaid on December 20, was paid by check to the bank on December 18. The rate of interest was 16 percent. What was the value of the check? (Use exact interest.)

9. Mike Bruen agreed to repay an education loan of $4,000 to his father plus 9 percent interest. The loan was from a period starting on August 31, 1985 to July 15, 1986. What is the amount due his father on July 15? (Use ordinary interest.)

10. A loan made by the Teachers Credit Union of Mill City was to have run for thirty days. The borrower, S. R. Potter, was unable to repay the loan when it came due on July 5, 1986. The credit union agreed to extend the loan until August 10, 1986. The loan was for $5,500. The interest rate on the loan was stated as 17 percent. What is the total amount of interest due on the loan when it is paid off on August 10? (Use exact interest.)

11. Orson Ingrahm loaned a business associate $5,000 on December 20, 1988. The loan was for three months at $14\frac{3}{4}$ percent. What is the amount of the interest on the loan? (Use ordinary interest.)

12. Babs borrowed $700 from a friend for three years at 10 percent simple interest. What is the amount that she will need to repay at the end of the three years?

13. What is the difference in interest on a loan using ordinary versus exact interest if the loan value is $5,000 for a term of 120 days at $16\frac{1}{2}$ percent?

14. A student loan for $6,000 must be refinanced. The lender had loaned the money to the student two years ago at 14 percent. The student has not made any payments on the principal or interest. How much will the student need to refinance?

15. Sherry borrowed $300 from a loan company on June 23. She repaid the loan on August 30. The loan specified a 15 percent rate (ordinary interest). What is the amount of payoff on the loan?

Challenge Problem　　　The Malon Corporation borrowed $892 from the Manufacturers Commerce Bank. The bank charges $9\frac{3}{4}$ percent interest and pays $4\frac{1}{2}$ percent compounded semiannually on savings. The bank is forty-seven years old and will soon build a new $4.3 million Science and Trade Center. How much interest will the Malon Corporation have to pay for their ninety-day loan? (Use ordinary interest.)

Name _____   Date _____   Score _____

Complete the following problems.

1. Interest can be defined as

    a.   The amount of money borrowed.
    b.   The amount of money that is to be returned to the lender.
    c.   The money that the borrower must pay the lender for the use of the principal.
    d.   The results of time multiplied by rate.

2. Date of loan: March 6
   Date of repayment: August 1
   Days: _____

3. Date of loan: February 20, 1988
   Days of term of loan: Sixty days
   Date of repayment: _____

4. P = $5,000
   R =   16%
   T =   30 days
   I = $ _____ (ordinary)

5. What is the answer to the above problem using exact interest?

   $I = P \times R \times T$

   $I = \$5{,}000 \times .16 \times \dfrac{30}{365}$

   $I = $ _____

6. Viola Austin borrowed $1,000 from a friend at the rate of $10\frac{3}{4}$ percent interest. The loan ran for forty-five days. What is the repayment date for this loan made on May 12?

7. What is the amount of the interest due on the loan in problem 6? (Use ordinary interest.)

8. What is the total amount of money that Viola must repay when the loan comes due in problem 6?

9. Bud Disolli borrowed $600 from a friend for forty-five days at $15\frac{1}{2}$ percent interest. What was the amount of interest on the loan at the repayment date? (Use ordinary interest.)

10. Patty Emerson lent a business associate $5,000 on May 2. The loan was to be repaid on October 12 along with 13 percent interest. What was the amount due on October 12? (Use exact interest.)

11. Julie Snider borrowed $5,000 for sixteen days at 17 percent interest. How much must she pay back? (Use exact interest.)

12. A loan for $900 at 12 percent interest runs for a period of seventy-one days. The borrower asks the bank to indicate the amount of interest due when the loan comes due. How much interest will be due on the loan at the due date? (Use ordinary interest.)

10 Promissory Notes

After mastering the material in this chapter, you will be able to:

1. Describe the legal implications of a promissory note.
2. Compute the maturity value of a promissory note using ordinary or exact interest.
3. Compute the proceeds of a discounted noninterest- or interest-bearing promissory note.
4. Compute any one unknown factor in the interest formula $(I = P \times R \times T)$ when the other three factors are known.
5. Understand and use the following terms:

Promissory Note	Noninterest-bearing Note
Maker	Interest-bearing Note
Payee	Discount Rate
Face Value	Term of Discount
Term of Note	Discount Amount
Maturity Value	Proceeds

Legal Environment

Promissory note
Maker
Payee
Face value

Term of note

A **promissory note** is used in business as an "IOU." It is a legally enforceable written contract. The **maker** is obligated to repay the amount of the note, along with interest to the **payee.** The Uniform Commercial Code defines a promissory note as "an unconditional promise in writing made by one person to another signed by the maker engaging to pay on demand or at a particular future time a certain sum of money to order or to the bearer."

The amount written on the note is known as the **face value** and is equal to the amount borrowed. It is a negotiable instrument (i.e., transferable from one party to another) for cash or merchandise. The time period that the note is to run is known as the **term of note.** This will be the actual number of days from the time the note is made until it is repaid. Some notes run for years and are usually for larger sums of money.

A promissory note can be given, as an example, to the seller of merchandise by the buyer or as an extension of credit by the seller to the buyer. In the above example, the maker, K. Droston, promises to pay the payee, Michigan National Bank, the sum of $1,500 plus 8 percent interest for the ninety-day term of the note. This amount to be repaid is due ninety days after October 1, 1987, the date the note was made. The value of the note on that date will be $1,530 [$1,500 +

Maturity value
($1,500 × .08 × 90/360 = $30)], or known as the **maturity value.** The maker is obligated to pay $1,530, the maturity value, to the payee or bearer on that date. Notice that this loan to a commercial firm uses ordinary interest (360-day year). Loans made to individuals for noncommercial use must be computed using exact interest (365-day year) according to the Truth in Lending Law.

Occasionally, the payee will not charge the drawer interest on the note. This

Noninterest-bearing note
type of note is known as a **noninterest-bearing note.** Otherwise, and most fre-
Interest-bearing note
quently, the note will be an **interest-bearing note,** indicating that the maker must repay both face value and interest at maturity.

Exercise A

Determine the maturity value of the interest-bearing and noninterest-bearing notes described below. Use ordinary interest.

	Face Value	Term of Note	Interest Rate	Maturity Value
1.	$ 6,500	60 Days	15%	$ 6,662.50
2.	4,000	60	12	
3.	13,600	60	17	
4.	25,000	100	$10\frac{3}{4}$	
5.	9,000	40	11	

	Face Value	Term of Note	Interest Rate	Maturity Value
6.	7,000	120 Days	13%	_____
7.	8,500	30	$17\frac{1}{2}$	_____
8.	5,000	30	None	_____
9.	60,000	73	14	_____
10.	3,000	1 Year	18	_____

Discounting

Discount rate
Term of discount

When the payee of a promissory note (noninterest-bearing or interest-bearing) finds that there is a shortage of cash in the firm, a decision to sell a promissory note may be advisable. This will turn a semiliquid asset into spendable cash, allowing the payee to pay invoices, take advantage of cash discounts, and meet payroll obligations. The note is negotiable and, therefore, can be sold to a bank or another firm with ready cash. The payee must determine the rate that the lending institution will charge the firm to gain cash for the note. This rate is called the **discount rate.** The length of time that the note will be discounted at this rate is known as the **term of discount.**

Computing Discount

If the note in the earlier example is discounted for cash on December 10, 1987, then the term of discount will be twenty days.

October has	31 days
−October	1, 1987
	30
November	30
December	30−Maturity Date
	90 days

December 30−Maturity Date
−December 10−Date of Discount
⎯⎯⎯⎯→ 20 days
└── term of discount

Discount amount

If the discount rate was 10 percent, the **discount amount** would be computed as follows:

Discount amount = Maturity value × Discount Rate × Term of Discount
$8.50 = $1,530 × .10 × 20/360

Computing Proceeds

Proceeds

The discount amount is charged by the lending institution for cash and should be subtracted from the maturity value in order to find the amount of cash that the payee will receive, the **proceeds.** The proceeds = $1,530 − $8.50 = $1,521.50. The payee receives $1,521.50 on December 10, 1987, the lending institution will receive the $1,530 maturity value of the note from the maker on December 30, 1987, as the bearer.

Another example should clarify any questions.

Example 1

Information

Face Value of note	$780
Rate of interest	$9\frac{1}{2}\%$
Date of note	June 17, 1985
Term of note	60 days
Interest	$ _____
Maturity Value	$ _____
Discount Rate	$10\frac{1}{4}\%$
Date of Discount	July 30, 1985
Term of Discount	_____
Discount Amount	$ _____
Proceeds	$ _____

Solution

$$I = P \times R \times T$$

$$I = \$780.00 \times .095 \times \frac{60}{360}$$

$$I = \$12.35$$

$780.00 + $12.35 = $792.35 = maturity value

Disc.= Mat. Val. $\times$ Disc. Rate $\times$ Term of Disc.

$$\text{Disc.} = \$792.35 \times .1025 \times \frac{17}{360}$$

$$\text{Disc.} = \$3.84$$

June 30	July has 31
− June 17	− July 30
13	1
+ July 31	+ Aug. 16
44	17 days = term of discount
+ Aug 16 − Maturity Date	
60	

Maturity Value	=	$792.35
Amount of Discount	=	− 3.84
Proceeds	=	$788.51

In the next example, the calculations will be shown in an abbreviated form. This model should be useful for further assignments in this area. The numerical values can be shown graphically as in the example below.

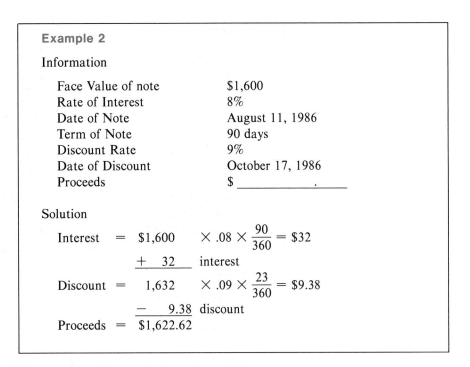

Example 2

Information

Face Value of note	$1,600
Rate of Interest	8%
Date of Note	August 11, 1986
Term of Note	90 days
Discount Rate	9%
Date of Discount	October 17, 1986
Proceeds	$ _____. _____

Solution

$$\text{Interest} \quad = \quad \$1,600 \quad \times .08 \times \frac{90}{360} = \$32$$

$$\underline{+ \quad 32} \quad \text{interest}$$

$$\text{Discount} \quad = \quad 1,632 \quad \times .09 \times \frac{23}{360} = \$9.38$$

$$\underline{- \quad 9.38} \quad \text{discount}$$

$$\text{Proceeds} \quad = \quad \$1,622.62$$

Note: The proceeds may be greater or less than the face value.

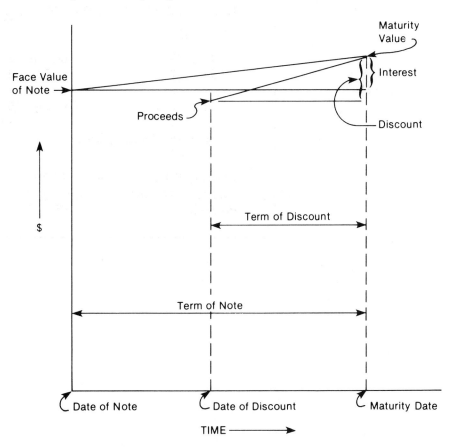

Determine the term of discount in each of the exercises below.

	Date of Note	Term of Note	Date of Discount	Term of Discount
1.	June 4, 1985	60 days	July 11, 1985	23 days
2.	Aug. 20, 1985	60	Sept. 26, 1985	
3.	Sept. 14, 1986	90	Oct. 5, 1986	
4.	May 12, 1987	60	June 20, 1987	
5.	Jan. 7, 1988	95	Mar. 16, 1988	
6.	Dec. 14, 1987	150	Feb. 27, 1988	
7.	April 12, 1986	30	April 20, 1986	
8.	Jan. 30, 1988	60	Feb. 29, 1988	

Exercise C   Compute the answers to the problems below. Use ordinary interest (360-day year).

	1.	2.
Face Value	$450	$5,000
Rate of Interest	10%	16%
Date of Note	Oct. 3, 1986	Mar. 6, 1986
Term	45 days	60 days
Interest	$5.63	
Maturity Value	$455.63	
Disc. Rate	10%	11%
Date of Disc.	Nov. 1, 1986	Mar. 12, 1986
Term of Disc.	16 days	54 days
Discount Am't.	$2.03	
Proceeds	$453.60	

	3.	4.
Face Value	$1,100	$6,000
Rate of Interest	14%	12%
Date of Note	May 3, 1987	July 16, 1987
Term	90 days	60 days
Interest		
Maturity Value		
Disc. Rate	13%	13%
Date of Disc.	July 3, 1987	August 30, 1987
Term of Disc.	29 days	15 days
Discount Am't.		
Proceeds		

Face Value	5. $1,800	6. $170	
Rate of Interest	13%	$13\frac{3}{4}\%$	
Date of Note	March 1, 1986	June 16, 1986	
Term	120 days	19 days	
Interest	_____	_____	
Maturity Value	_____	_____	
Disc. Rate	12%	14%	
Date of Disc.	May 14, 1986	June 30, 1986	
Term of Disc.	46 days	5 days	
Discount Am't.	_____	_____	
Proceeds	_____	_____	

Face Value	7. $800	8. $1,000	
Rate of Interest	11%	12%	
Date of Note	January 3, 1987	April 1, 1986	
Term	40 days	75 days	
Interest	_____	_____	
Maturity Value	_____	_____	
Disc. Rate	$9\frac{3}{4}\%$	9%	
Date of Disc.	Feb. 3, 1987	May 15, 1986	
Term of Disc.	9 days	31 days	
Discount Am't.	_____	_____	
Proceeds	_____	_____	

Face Value	9. $1,000	10. $3,500	
Rate of Interest	13%	$12\frac{1}{2}\%$	
Date of Note	May 3, 1988	May 31, 1987	
Term	60 days	45 days	
Interest	_____	_____	
Maturity Value	_____	_____	
Disc. Rate	$13\frac{1}{2}\%$	15%	
Date of Disc.	June 30, 1988	July 1, 1987	
Term of Disc.	2 days	14 days	
Discount Am't.	_____	_____	
Proceeds	_____	_____	

Other Interest Problems

It may be necessary to determine the amount of principal, rate, or time on a promissory note when the interest and two other factors of the $I = P \times R \times T$ formula are known. The formula $I = P \times R \times T$ can be manipulated to develop the following formulas.

$$P = \frac{I}{R \times T} \quad R = \frac{I}{P \times T} \quad T = \frac{I}{P \times R}$$

You will need to know the above formulas or be able to use the model below.

By putting your finger on the factor that you wish to find, the remaining portion of the model reveals the formula.

Example 3

If you know Interest, Principal, and Time but need to find Rate, place your finger over R for Rate. Rate is found by dividing I by the product of

Computing Principal

The principal amount in a promissory note problem can be found when the other three factors are known.

Example 4

The interest on a promissory note was $30; the note ran for ninety days at an 8 percent interest rate. What was the principal amount?

$$P = \frac{I}{R \times T} \qquad P = \frac{\$30}{.08 \times \dfrac{90}{360}} = \$1,500$$

Computing Rate

When the rate on a promissory note is to be found, the formula $R = I/P \times T$ must be used.

Example 5

The same data from the above example will be used to illustrate this formula.

$$R = \frac{I}{P \times T} \qquad R = \frac{\$30}{\$1,500 \times \dfrac{90}{360}} = .08 = 8\%$$

Computing Time

The time factor can be determined by using the formula from above with one additional step. The decimal results must be multiplied by 360 days to obtain the answer in days.

Example 6

$$T = \frac{I}{P \times R} \qquad T = \frac{\$30}{\$1,500 \times .08} = .25 \quad .25 \times 360 \text{ days} = 90 \text{ days}$$

Exercise D   Fill in the missing information in the problems below. (Use ordinary interest.) Round off your answer to the nearest percent, day, or cent.

$$\frac{14.63}{115 \times 1300} = \frac{14.63}{A5} \times 360 = 27$$

	Interest	Face Value	Rate of Interest	Term of Note
1.	$ 8.00	$ 720.00	8%	50 days
2.	_____	5,500.00	10	20
3.	4.50	400.00	____	30
4.	14.63	1,300.00	15	_____
5.	17.50	_____	14	60
6.	80.00	2,700.00	3.6⅔	90 ,2⁵
7.	_____	10,000.00	17	45
8.	18.00	_____	10	60 .1666
9.	8.98	4,200.00	11	____
10.	40.00	1,200.00	____	90
11.	73.00	_____	12	53 ,1472
12.	100.00	_____	15	40
13.	3.90	450.00	13	_____
14.	70.00	750.00	____	270
15.	83.67	1,000.00	12	____
16.	_____	42,000.00	11	90 ,2⁵
17.	12.00	1,000.00	____	45
18.	75.00	_____	13	45
19.	53.37	2,500.00	13	_____
20.	41.00	_____	14	60

Name _____ Date _____ Score _____

Skill Problems Compute the answers to the problems below. Use ordinary interest.

	1.	2.	3.	4.	5.
Face value	$4,000	$6,400	$750	$900	$3,500
Rate of interest	15%	11%	10%	15%	$14\frac{1}{2}$%
Date of note	May 3	March 8	Oct. 15	Jan. 13	June 10
Term of note	90 days	60 days	45 days	80 days	30 days
Date of discount	June 10	May 1	Nov. 2	Feb. 1	July 1
Rate of discount	16%	$10\frac{1}{2}$%	11%	12%	12%
Proceeds	_____	_____	_____	_____	_____

Compute the answers to the problems below. Use exact interest.

	6.	7.	8.	9.	10.
Face value	$600	$7,000	$6,500	$420	$1,000
Rate of interest	11%	13%	12%	None	10%
Date of Note	July 10	Sept. 30	Oct. 5	May 4	Aug. 19
Term of note	90 days	100 days	90 days	120 days	45 days
Date of discount	Aug. 30	Oct. 15	Dec. 16	July 30	Sept. 3
Rate of discount	12%	15%	15%	16%	11%
Proceeds	_____	_____	_____	_____	_____

Complete the information below. Use ordinary interest. Round off your answer to the nearest percent, day, or cent.

	Interest	Face Value	Rate of Interest	Term of Note
11.	$87.50	_____	15%	30 days
12.	70.00	1,400.00	20%	90
13.	36.00	900.00	16	____
14.	14.70	760.00	10%	68
15.	3.75	500.00	12	____
16.	4.23	317.25	16	30

Business Application Problems

1. The T. J. Purlon Company received a $1,500 note from a customer who was unable to pay for merchandise purchased on account. The note was dated April 7, 1985 and was to run for ninety days without interest. On June 1, 1985, the Purlon Company decided to discount the note at 12 percent for cash. What were the proceeds? (Use ordinary interest.)

2. National City Bank received a check for $16,565.31 on November 1, 1987 from a promissory note customer. The customer had two notes outstanding at the time, and bank officials were not sure which one should be cancelled. Both notes had a $9\frac{1}{2}$ percent interest rate; one was dated October 17, 1987 for $16,500 and the other was dated June 17, 1987 for $16,000. Which note was the check to cover? (Use ordinary interest.)

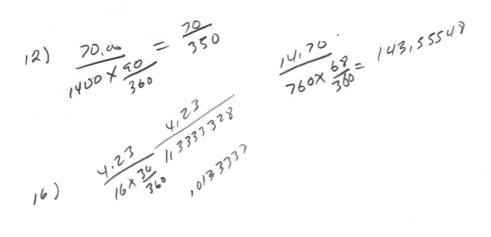

$$12) \quad \frac{70.00}{1400 \times \frac{90}{360}} = \frac{70}{350}$$

$$\frac{14.70}{760 \times \frac{68}{360}} = 143.55547$$

$$16) \quad \frac{4.23}{16 \times \frac{30}{360}} \quad \frac{4.23}{1.3333328} \quad .0133337$$

3. A promissory note dated July 14, 1986 is discounted on November 7 at a rate of 14 percent. The note carried an interest rate of 12 percent for 150 days. What were the proceeds if the face value is $700? (Use ordinary interest.)

4. A promissory note earned $39 at a rate of 13 percent for twenty-four days. What was the principal amount? (Use ordinary interest.) Round off your answer to the nearest dollar.

5. The promissory note below was paid off on April 16, 1987. What was the amount of interest? Use exact interest (365-day year) on this personal promissory note.

No. __546776__ Date __March 4__ , 19 __87__ Due __September 1, 1987__

__One hundred eighty-one__ _____ days after date, I. **XX** promise to pay to the order of

MICHIGAN NATIONAL BANK, __PORT HURON__ , Michigan

the sum of __Thirteen thousand----------------------------------__ Dollars, $ __13,000.00__ .

plus __12__ % simple interest after __3/4/87__ .

This note secured by __Office Equipment__

Holder, upon deeming himself insecure, may, without notice declare the unpaid balance to be immediately due and payable. Holder upon default may realize on or dispose of the collateral. Makers severally waive demand, notice and protest, and any defense due to extension of time or other indulgence by holder and to any substitution or release of collateral. This Note will bear interest on the entire unpaid balance at the rate of __12__ per centum (**12**%) per annum during any period of default hereunder.

Addresses: __2309 Taylor Street__ _____ Signatures: __Bonnie Kurtz__

10-1 REV. 4/70

6. A firm decided to discount a note at 14 percent on July 16, 1987 valued at $1,460 at maturity. The note was made on June 1, 1987 to run for 120 days. What were the proceeds? (Use ordinary interest.)

7. A promissory note for $1,900 dated January 31, 1986 was paid off on June 1, 1986 with a check for $1,944. To the nearest percent, what is the rate of interest on the note? (Use ordinary interest.)

8. The Birk Corp. received a note from Alfred Coloni for a service provided on an industrial machine. The note stated that Mr. Coloni promised to pay $5,000 within ninety days after the date of the note, June 14, 1986. The Birk Corporation discounted the note at 14 percent on July 20, 1986 for cash. What was the amount of the check that Mr. Coloni used to pay off the note if he paid it off on August 18, 1986?

9. The lawyers in the law office of Peterson, Peterson & Snell agreed to accept a promissory note for $1,200 for services on July 14, 1987. The note interest rate was 12 percent and was to be paid off within ninety days. The office manager, Janis Tobian, decided that there was a shortage of cash for payroll and discounted the note on September 11, 1987 at a rate of 14 percent. What were the proceeds? (Use ordinary interest.)

10. A note carrying the interest rate of 10 percent on $1,400 is paid in full with a check for $1,431.11. If the note was paid off on September 16, 1988, on what date was the note made? This note was a commercial loan.

11. The Bot and Orr Company accepted a ninety day promissory note from a customer on October 22, 1987. The face value of the note was $62,500. The note was interest free. The company discounted the note on December 1, 1987 at a rate of 14 percent. What is the amount of the discount? (Use exact interest.)

12. If Bot and Orr had carried the account on the books and charged 12 percent on the account (exact interest), what would they have saved in lost interest charges and discounts?

13. Jameson and Jameson Company took a $45 discount on a noninterest-bearing promissory note on July 16, 1988. The note had a maturity date of August 31, 1988. If the note was discounted at 15 percent, what was the face value of the note? Round off your answer to the nearest dollar. (Use exact interest.)

Challenge Problem   A consumer promissory note was negotiated on January 2, 1986 for $5,100 at $9\frac{3}{4}$ percent for 120 days. On March 18, 1986 the payee discounted the note at a rate of $13\frac{1}{8}$ percent for cash at the State Bank of Burns. The proceeds were used to meet a 15 percent increase in payroll expenses. The maker of the note won a lottery prize of $10,000 on April 6, 1986 and decided to pay off the note on that date. What was the amount that the payee was obligated to pay on April 6, 1986?

Name _____ Date _____ Score _____

Match the terms and correct answers using the following promissory note.

_____ 1. face value of note

_____ 2. maturity date

_____ 3. maturity value

_____ 4. date of note

_____ 5. maker

_____ 6. payee

a. Michigan National Bank
b. $1,850
c. Pilskton Corp.
d. $1,924
e. October 21, 1986
f. 463801
g. 12 percent
h. September 20, 1986
i. $2,072
j. October 20, 1986
k. June 23, 1986

Dalmas Office Equipment Co. accepted a promissory note from Warren Steel for the purchase of $3,580 of office furniture on July 10, 1987. The note had an interest rate of 14 percent and was to run for ninety days. On August 7, Park Dalmas, president, discounted the note at 15 percent for cash. (Use ordinary interest.)

7. What was the term of discount? _____

8. What was the discount amount? _____

9. What were the proceeds? _____

10. How much is the maker required to pay at maturity to the holder of the

note? _____

Using ordinary interest, fill in the missing information below. Round off your answers to the nearest percent, day, or cent.

	Interest	Face Value	Rate of Interest	Term of Note
11.	_____	$5,000	13%	30 days
12.	17.00	_____	10	90
13.	20.00	4,500	16	_____
14.	15.00	800	_____	45

15. A consumer loan earned the bank $117 in interest over ninety days. The rate of the loan was 13 percent. Using exact interest, determine the face value of the loan. Round off your answer to the nearest dollar.

16. The Peters Corp. agreed to sell $900 of industrial supplies to Franton Manufacturing if Franton would sign a promissory note for the amount of the purchase. The interest-free note was to be paid off thirty days after the November 10, 1986 purchase. On November 20, 1986 Peters discounted the note at 14 percent for cash. What were the proceeds? (Use ordinary interest.)

11 Consumer Credit and Installment Loans

Performance Objectives

After mastering the material in this chapter, you will be able to:

1. Describe the obligations of buying on credit.
2. Describe the legal implications of an installment contract.
3. Compute a repayment schedule for an installment contract.
4. Determine the payment amount on an installment contract using a table or when given the amount of a loan, the time period of the loan, and the rate of interest.
5. Describe the use of an escrow account and its effect on a mortgage.
6. Describe the effect of an early payoff on an installment contract.
7. Understand and use the following terms and concepts:

Credit Card	Principal Balance
Store Card	Repayment Schedule
Gasoline Card	Fixed Rate
Bank Card	Variable Rate
Travel or Entertainment Card	Fixed Payment Amount
Monthly Statement	Variable Payment Amount
Minimum Payment Amount	Balloon Payment
Amortizing	Points
Regulation Z	Closing Costs
Down Payment	Escrow Account
Payment Amount	Rule of 78s

Credit Purchases

There are certain circumstances in a consumer's life that result in the purchase of goods and services costing more than the consumer earns. These instances are usually in the early years and again in the later years when, for example, children enter college or are married. Goods and services such as automobiles, furniture, homes, appliances, medical services, petroleum products, and entertainment are often purchased on credit. A credit purchase allows the consumer to own and use the product when it is needed and pay for it while it is being used. Without

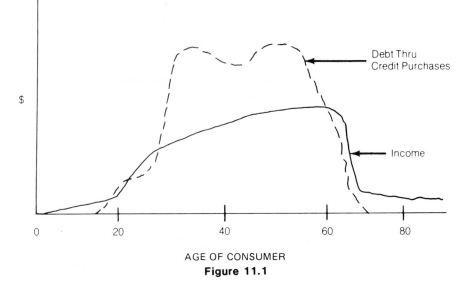

AGE OF CONSUMER

Figure 11.1

such an opportunity consumers would have to go without desired and necessary items until the money is saved for the purchase. As can be seen in figure 11.1, debt through credit purchases is typically incurred in the consumer's early twenties (purchase of an automobile, appliances, and a home), is reduced over a period of the next fifteen to twenty years, and then increases again (weddings, college education, etc.). Most of the debt is paid off by the time of retirement.

The ability to purchase on credit appeals to most Americans, as the majority use some type of credit financing. As with any freedom, there is also a degree of responsibility. The responsibility of repayment and credit management falls into the hands of the consumer. There are many ways a person can buy on credit. We will take a look at two types: credit cards and installment loans.

Credit Cards

Since World War II, the acceptance of **credit cards** has grown to the point that today more than one-half of the families in the U.S. use them. This widespread acceptance is based at least in part on the functions that credit cards provide. Today, a credit card acts to identify a person, allows for credit payment of an item or service, and provides a means to obtain additional credit from other sources. Having one credit card with a good payment record opens up the door to other credit arrangements.

Store Card

There are four types of credit cards. The **store card** can be used in one store or chain of stores.

Gasoline Card

The **gasoline card** is a second type. This type of card was initially issued by gasoline companies to attempt to gain a greater market share and customer loyalty. Today, the oil and gas companies are taking a second look at them due to the high interest rates.

The **bank card,** a third type, is the fastest growing type of credit card. It is replacing the store card and is being sought because of its versatility. It can be used to purchase merchandise, some gasoline stations will accept it, and entertainment establishments often take it.

The **travel** or **entertainment card** is the last type. It is issued on a more selective basis to business people or professionals who are apt to use it more often. The charges per month will exceed $100 on most occasions.

All of the four types described are similar except the travel or entertainment card. This type requires a membership fee. The other three types are free; no charges or obligations for payment until they are used.

The mark ® is a registered trademark of MasterCard International Inc.

A credit card application will ask for information on your income, length of employment, other credit references and banking references.

The obligation for payment begins when a purchase is made with a credit card. The finance charge or service charge agreement is usually printed on the card or on the credit card application. The charge for the use of credit with a credit card ranges from 1 to $1\frac{3}{4}$ percent per month.

Monthly statement

The credit card customer will receive a **monthly statement** of purchases from the card-issuing institutions. This statement will itemize the date of the purchase and amount. Charges for credit will also be shown at the bottom of the statement. The amount owed, or balance, will require payment within a specified time period or a **minimum payment amount** will be specified on the statement. The minimum payment amount will be a percent of the balance or a flat amount such as $10.

Minimum payment amount

```
        5413197000012942              1000     5007    031986

            BARNETT         MASTERCARD
        PLEASE RETURN THIS PORTION AND CHECK, PAYABLE TO:   MASTERCARD
```

ACCOUNT NUMBER	MINIMUM PAYMENT DUE	NEW BALANCE	FOR INFORMATION CALL	INDICATE AMOUNT PAID
	1000	5007	800-342-8472	

```
0000031338                      MICHAEL D TUTTLE
13                              1030 US HWY 1 #203
001700700                      N PALM BEACH  FL   33408
```

PLEASE INDICATE ABOVE ANY CHANGE OF NAME, ADDRESS,
ZIP CODE AND/OR TELEPHONE NUMBER AND AREA CODE.

PLEASE RETAIN THIS PORTION
FOR YOUR RECORDS

STATEMENT SUMMARY

TO AVOID ADDITIONAL FINANCE CHARGE ON MERCHANDISE PURCHASES, PAY YOUR ENTIRE NEW BALANCE BY

PREVIOUS BALANCE	PAYMENTS	CREDIT ADJUSTMENTS	DEBIT ADJUSTMENTS	PURCHASES AND CASH ADVANCES	FINANCE CHARGE	NEW BALANCE	AVERAGE DAILY BALANCE
00	00	00	00	5000	07	5007	555

BILLING DATE	NUMBER OF DAYS IN CYCLE	ANNUAL PERCENTAGE RATE	PAST DUE AMOUNT	CREDIT LIMIT	AVAILABLE CREDIT	PAYMENT DUE DATE	MINIMUM PAYMENT DUE
03/19/86	27	18%	00	1000	949	04/13/86	1000

BARNETT MASTERCARD

SEND INQUIRIES (DISPUTES) TO: BANKCARD CENTER

PAYMENTS OF ANY AMOUNT IN DISPUTE ARE NOT REQUIRED PENDING OUR COMPLIANCE WITH FAIR CREDIT BILLING ACT

```
P.O. BOX 2049
JACKSONVILLE, FL 32231                    5413-1970-0001-2942
```

DATE OF TRANSACTION	REFERENCE NUMBER	DATE PROCESSED BY BANK	IDENTIFICATION	AMOUNT
0317	54115760779014400	0318	BARNETT ATM CASH ADV PALM BCH GDNS FL	5000

```
NOTICE * THE DAILY PERIODIC RATE IS .000493
NOTICE * SEE REVERSE SIDE FOR IMPORTANT INFORMATION      PAGE  1 OF  1
CONTRIBUTIONS TO YOUR IRA CAN BE EASY WITH BARNETT CONVENIENCE CHECKS.
IT IS SAFE AND EASY AND GIVES YOU A TAX DEDUCTION NOW AND SECURITY FOR
YOUR FUTURE.  NEED A CONVENIENCE CHECK.  CALL CUSTOMER SERVICE TODAY.
```

808989 Jul 81

The finance charge is usually based on the unpaid balance at the end of the month. An example of the effects of the minimum payment amount and finance charge are shown in example 1.

Example 1

Martin Stahl has a credit card. The past four monthly statements show the following information.

Month	Previous Balance	Purchases this Month	Payments	Finance Charges	New Balance
1	$42.10	$37.20	$20	_____	_____
2	_____	85.00	20	_____	_____
3	_____	. . .	20	_____	_____
4	_____	7.50	50	_____	_____

The minimum payment amount is $20 and the finance charge is 1 percent. What is the amount of total finance charge for the four months and what is the new balance at the end of the fourth month?

Solution: The new balance for any month is found by (1) computing the finance charge on the previous balance, (2) adding the finance charge to the previous balance, (3) adding the amount of the purchases for the month, and (4) subtracting the payments.

Month
1
$42.10 \times .01 = \$.42$
$42.10 + \$.42 = \$42.52$
$42.52 + \$37.20 = \$79.72$
$79.72 - \$20 = \$59.72$
2
$59.72 \times .01 = \$.60$
$59.72 + \$.60 = \$60.32$
$60.32 + \$85 = \$145.32$
$145.32 - \$20 = \$125.32$
3
$125.32 \times .01 = \$1.25$
$125.32 + \$1.25 = \$126.57$
$126.57 + 0 = \$126.57$
$126.57 - \$20 = \$106.57$
4
$106.57 \times .01 = \$1.07$
$106.57 + \$1.07 = \$107.64$
$107.64 + \$7.50 = \$115.14$
$115.14 - \$50 = \$65.14$

The total finance charge is $3.34 ($.42 + $.60 + $1.25 + $1.07). The new balance at the end of the fourth month is $65.14

Some card-issuing banks/institutions are considering the addition of a monthly service charge. This flat monthly charge would be similar to a checking account service charge. Other firms are considering the addition of interest charges that would begin at the date of the purchase. These variations would increase the cost of a credit purchase to the consumer.

Example 2

Malinda's use of her credit card is shown below. The monthly purchases are for gasoline, clothes, and jewelry. There is a 1 percent finance charge on the unpaid monthly balance, a minimum payment amount of $10, and a flat service charge of $1.00 per month. What is the amount of the new balance at the end of the third month?

Month	Previous Balance	Purchases this Month	Payments	Flat Service Charge and Finance Charges	New Balance
1	$86.40	. . .	$10	$ 1.86 ($86.40 × .01 + $1)	$78.26
2	78.26	$17.58	40	1.78 ($78.26 × .01 + $1)	57.62
3	57.62	. . .	10	1.58 ($57.62 × .01 + $1)	49.20

The new balance at the end of the third month is $49.20.

Exercise A   Compute the new balance in the exercises below.

Month	Previous Balance	Purchases this Month	Payments	Finance (1%) Charges	New Balance
1. 1	$ 48.20	. . .	$10	$ .48 ($48.20 × .01)	$ 38.68
2	38.68	$ 35.00	10	.39 ($38.68 × .01)	64.07
3	64.07	22.60	10	.64 ($64.07 × .01)	77.31
2. 1	187.00	13.00	30		
2	_____	. . .	20		
3	_____	70.00	50		
3. 1	36.50	10.00	30		
2	_____	46.10	10		
3	_____	51.80	50		
4	_____	. . .	10		

4.	1	0.00	53.00	. .	_____	_____
	2	_____	65.50	10	_____	_____
	3	_____	. . .	10	_____	_____
5.	1	56.10	. . .	20	_____	_____
	2	_____	186.50	15	_____	_____
	3	_____	21.50	20	_____	_____
	4	_____	. . .	30	_____	_____

Installment Loans

Consumers and business firms often have need to make credit purchases that are beyond the loan limit of the credit card. When this happens, the bank or other lending institution provides a source of funds through an installment loan.

Legal Environment

An installment contract requires the buyer, to whom credit is extended, to first pay the amount of interest due on the loan at the end of each month, as well as some amount on the principal. The amount of payment on the principal will reduce the amount of the loan to zero over a period of time. This payment process

Amortizing

is termed **amortizing** the loan. This differs from a promissory note that requires only one payment, which includes the face value of the note as well as the interest, at the end of the term of the loan.

The Truth-in-Lending Act states that (1) the buyer must be made aware of all of the finance charges on a loan, and (2) the annual rate of interest on the loan be clearly stated. A monthly rate of interest of $1\frac{1}{2}$ percent is equal to 18 percent annually; 1 percent is equal to 12 percent annually, etc. This rate of interest is determined differently on an installment contract due to the declining amount of principal borrowed over the life of the loan.

Regulation Z

Regulation Z, the implementing phase of the Truth-in-Lending Act, states that total financing charges on credit purchases must be disclosed to the borrower. The amount of financing charges is found by subtracting the amount borrowed from the amount that is to be paid back. The difference is the amount of financing charges.

The annual percentage rate (APR) on an installment contract must be stated according to Regulation Z. The Federal Reserve Board has prepared a table that is used to determine the annual percentage rate. A loan is made for $600 for eight months with interest charges of $28 plus an application fee of $6 and a filing fee of $2. The borrower will pay back:

$600 = amount of loan
28 = interest
6 = application fee
+ 2 = filing fee
$636 = amount to be paid back
− 600 = amount borrowed
$ 36 = finance charges

$$\frac{\$36 \text{ finance charges}}{\$600 \text{ amount of loan}} = \$6 \text{ finance charge per } \$100 \text{ of loan}$$

By referring to the annual percentage rate table on page 218, the annual percentage rate can be determined. Using eight payments along the left-hand edge, look across until you find the $6 amount. The annual percentage rate is 15.75 percent.

Example 3

Jeremy borrowed $500 for 10 months. The lender indicated that the interest charges would be $32.50. There would also be a service charge of $3 and a filing fee of $2.50. What is the Annual Percentage Rate on the loan?

$$
\begin{aligned}
\$500.00 &= \text{loan} \\
32.50 &= \text{interest} \\
3.00 &= \text{service charge} \\
+\quad 2.50 &= \text{filing fee} \\
\hline
\$538.00 &= \text{amount to be paid back} \\
-\;500.00 &= \text{amount borrowed} \\
\hline
\$\;38.00 &= \text{finance charges}
\end{aligned}
$$

$38.00/\$500.00 = \$7.60$ finance charge/$100 of loan $= 16.25\%$ from table.

The Annual Percentage Rate table can also be used to determine the amount of finance charge if the rate is known. The amount per hundred ($7.60 in Example 3) is found in the 16.25 percent column across from the ten payments level. By multiplying $7.60 times the number of hundreds (five), the interest of $38.00 is found.

Annual Percentage Rate

Number of Payments	14.00%	14.25%	14.50%	14.75%	15.00%	15.25%	15.50%	15.75%	16.00%	16.25%	16.50%	16.75%
1	1.17	1.19	1.21	1.23	1.25	1.27	1.29	1.31	1.33	1.35	1.38	1.40
2	1.75	1.78	1.82	1.85	1.88	1.91	1.94	1.97	2.00	2.04	2.07	2.10
3	2.34	2.38	2.43	2.47	2.51	2.55	2.59	2.64	2.68	2.72	2.76	2.80
4	2.93	2.99	3.04	3.09	3.14	3.20	3.25	3.30	3.36	3.41	3.46	3.51
5	3.53	3.59	3.65	3.72	3.78	3.84	3.91	3.97	4.04	4.10	4.16	4.23
6	4.12	4.20	4.27	4.35	4.42	4.49	4.57	4.64	4.72	4.79	4.87	4.94
7	4.72	4.81	4.89	4.98	5.06	5.15	5.23	5.32	5.40	5.49	5.58	5.66
8	5.32	5.42	5.51	5.61	5.71	5.80	5.90	6.00	6.09	6.19	6.29	6.38
9	5.92	6.03	6.14	6.25	6.35	6.46	6.57	6.68	6.78	6.89	7.00	7.11
10	6.53	6.65	6.77	6.88	7.00	7.12	7.24	7.36	7.48	7.60	7.72	7.84
11	7.14	7.27	7.40	7.53	7.66	7.79	7.92	8.05	8.18	8.31	8.44	8.57
12	7.74	7.89	8.03	8.17	8.31	8.45	8.59	8.74	8.88	9.02	9.16	9.30
13	8.36	8.51	8.66	8.81	8.97	9.12	9.27	9.43	9.58	9.73	9.89	10.04
14	8.97	9.13	9.30	9.46	9.63	9.79	9.96	10.12	10.29	10.45	10.62	10.78
15	9.59	9.76	9.94	10.11	10.29	10.47	10.64	10.82	11.00	11.17	11.35	11.53
16	10.20	10.39	10.58	10.77	10.95	11.14	11.33	11.52	11.71	11.90	12.09	12.28
17	10.82	11.02	11.22	11.42	11.62	11.82	12.02	12.22	12.42	12.62	12.83	13.03
18	11.45	11.66	11.87	12.08	12.29	12.50	12.72	12.93	13.14	13.35	13.57	13.78
19	12.07	12.30	12.52	12.74	12.97	13.19	13.41	13.64	13.86	14.09	14.31	14.54
20	12.70	12.93	13.17	13.41	13.64	13.88	14.11	14.35	14.59	14.82	15.06	15.30
21	13.33	13.58	13.82	14.07	14.32	14.57	14.82	15.06	15.31	15.56	15.81	16.06
22	13.96	14.22	14.48	14.74	15.00	15.26	15.52	15.78	16.04	16.30	16.57	16.83
23	14.59	14.87	15.14	15.41	15.68	15.96	16.23	16.50	16.78	17.05	17.32	17.60
24	15.23	15.51	15.80	16.08	16.37	16.65	16.94	17.22	17.51	17.80	18.09	18.37
25	15.87	16.17	16.46	16.76	17.06	17.35	17.65	17.95	18.25	18.55	18.85	19.15
26	16.51	16.82	17.13	17.44	17.75	18.06	18.37	18.68	18.99	19.30	19.62	19.93
27	17.15	17.47	17.80	18.12	18.44	18.76	19.09	19.41	19.74	20.06	20.39	20.71
28	17.80	18.13	18.47	18.80	19.14	19.47	19.81	20.15	20.48	20.82	21.16	21.50
29	18.45	18.79	19.14	19.49	19.83	20.18	20.53	20.88	21.23	21.58	21.94	22.29
30	19.10	19.45	19.81	20.17	20.54	20.90	21.26	21.62	21.99	22.35	22.72	23.08
31	19.75	20.12	20.49	20.87	21.24	21.61	21.99	22.37	22.74	23.12	23.50	23.88
32	20.40	20.79	21.17	21.56	21.95	22.33	22.72	23.11	23.50	23.89	24.28	24.68
33	21.06	21.46	21.85	22.25	22.65	23.06	23.46	23.86	24.26	24.67	25.07	25.48
34	21.72	22.13	22.54	22.95	23.37	23.78	24.19	24.61	25.03	25.44	25.86	26.28
35	22.38	22.80	23.23	23.65	24.08	24.51	24.94	25.36	25.79	26.23	26.66	27.09
36	23.04	23.48	23.92	24.35	24.80	25.24	25.68	26.12	26.57	27.01	27.46	27.90
48	31.17	31.77	32.37	32.98	33.59	34.20	34.81	35.42	36.03	36.65	37.27	37.88
60	39.61	40.39	41.17	41.95	42.74	43.53	44.32	45.11	45.91	46.71	47.51	48.31

Number of Payments	17.00%	17.25%	17.50%	17.75%	18.00%	18.25%	18.50%	18.75%	19.00%	19.25%	19.50%	19.75%
1	1.42	1.44	1.46	1.48	1.50	1.52	1.54	1.56	1.58	1.60	1.63	1.65
2	2.13	2.16	2.19	2.22	2.26	2.29	2.32	2.35	2.38	2.41	2.44	2.48
3	2.85	2.89	2.93	2.97	3.01	3.06	3.10	3.14	3.18	3.23	3.27	3.31
4	3.57	3.62	3.67	3.73	3.78	3.83	3.88	3.94	3.99	4.04	4.10	4.15
5	4.29	4.35	4.42	4.48	4.54	4.61	4.67	4.74	4.80	4.86	4.93	4.99
6	5.02	5.09	5.17	5.24	5.32	5.39	5.46	5.54	5.61	5.69	5.76	5.84
7	5.75	5.83	5.92	6.00	6.09	6.18	6.26	6.35	6.43	6.52	6.60	6.69
8	6.48	6.58	6.67	6.77	6.87	6.96	7.06	7.16	7.26	7.35	7.45	7.55
9	7.22	7.32	7.43	7.54	7.65	7.76	7.87	7.97	8.08	8.19	8.30	8.41
10	7.96	8.08	8.19	8.31	8.43	8.55	8.67	8.79	8.91	9.03	9.15	9.27
11	8.70	8.83	8.96	9.09	9.22	9.35	9.49	9.62	9.75	9.88	10.01	10.14
12	9.45	9.59	9.73	9.87	10.02	10.16	10.30	10.44	10.59	10.73	10.87	11.02
13	10.20	10.35	10.50	10.66	10.81	10.97	11.12	11.28	11.43	11.59	11.74	11.90
14	10.95	11.11	11.28	11.45	11.61	11.78	11.95	12.11	12.28	12.45	12.61	12.78
15	11.71	11.88	12.06	12.24	12.42	12.59	12.77	12.95	13.13	13.31	13.49	13.67
16	12.46	12.65	12.84	13.03	13.22	13.41	13.60	13.80	13.99	14.18	14.37	14.56
17	13.23	13.43	13.63	13.83	14.04	14.24	14.44	14.64	14.85	15.05	15.25	15.46
18	13.99	14.21	14.42	14.64	14.85	15.07	15.28	15.49	15.71	15.93	16.14	16.36
19	14.76	14.99	15.22	15.44	15.67	15.90	16.12	16.35	16.58	16.81	17.03	17.26
20	15.54	15.78	16.01	16.25	16.49	16.73	16.97	17.21	17.45	17.69	17.93	18.17
21	16.31	16.56	16.81	17.07	17.32	17.57	17.82	18.07	18.33	18.58	18.83	19.09
22	17.09	17.36	17.62	17.88	18.15	18.41	18.68	18.94	19.21	19.47	19.74	20.01
23	17.88	18.15	18.43	18.70	18.98	19.26	19.54	19.81	20.09	20.37	20.65	20.93
24	18.66	18.95	19.24	19.53	19.82	20.11	20.40	20.69	20.98	21.27	21.56	21.86
25	19.45	19.75	20.05	20.36	20.66	20.96	21.27	21.57	21.87	22.18	22.48	22.79
26	20.24	20.56	20.87	21.19	21.50	21.82	22.14	22.45	22.77	23.09	23.41	23.73
27	21.04	21.37	21.69	22.02	22.35	22.68	23.01	23.34	23.67	24.00	24.33	24.67
28	21.84	22.18	22.52	22.86	23.20	23.55	23.89	24.23	24.58	24.92	25.27	25.61
29	22.64	22.99	23.35	23.70	24.06	24.41	24.77	25.13	25.49	25.84	26.20	26.56
30	23.45	23.81	24.18	24.55	24.92	25.29	25.66	26.03	26.40	26.77	27.14	27.52
31	24.26	24.64	25.02	25.40	25.78	26.16	26.55	26.93	27.32	27.70	28.09	28.47
32	25.07	25.46	25.86	26.25	26.65	27.04	27.44	27.84	28.24	28.64	29.04	29.44
33	25.88	26.29	26.70	27.11	27.52	27.93	28.34	28.75	29.16	29.57	29.99	30.40
34	26.70	27.12	27.54	27.97	28.39	28.81	29.24	29.66	30.09	30.52	30.95	31.37
35	27.52	27.96	28.39	28.83	29.27	29.71	30.14	30.58	31.02	31.47	31.91	32.35
36	28.35	28.80	29.25	29.70	30.15	30.60	31.05	31.51	31.96	32.42	32.87	33.33
48	38.50	39.13	39.75	40.37	41.00	41.63	42.26	42.89	43.52	44.15	44.79	45.43
60	49.12	49.92	50.73	51.55	52.36	53.18	54.00	54.82	55.64	56.47	57.30	58.13

Number of Payments	20.00%	20.25%	20.50%	20.75%	21.00%	21.25%	21.50%	21.75%	22.00%	22.25%	22.50%	22.75%
1	1.67	1.69	1.71	1.73	1.75	1.77	1.79	1.81	1.83	1.85	1.88	1.90
2	2.51	2.54	2.57	2.60	2.63	2.66	2.70	2.73	2.76	2.79	2.82	2.85
3	3.35	3.39	3.44	3.48	3.52	3.56	3.60	3.65	3.69	3.73	3.77	3.82
4	4.20	4.25	4.31	4.36	4.41	4.47	4.52	4.57	4.62	4.68	4.73	4.78
5	5.06	5.12	5.18	5.25	5.31	5.37	5.44	5.50	5.57	5.63	5.69	5.76
6	5.91	5.99	6.06	6.14	6.21	6.29	6.36	6.44	6.51	6.59	6.66	6.74
7	6.78	6.86	6.95	7.04	7.12	7.21	7.29	7.38	7.47	7.55	7.64	7.73
8	7.64	7.74	7.84	7.94	8.03	8.13	8.23	8.33	8.42	8.52	8.62	8.72
9	8.52	8.63	8.73	8.84	8.95	9.06	9.17	9.28	9.39	9.50	9.61	9.72
10	9.39	9.51	9.63	9.75	9.88	10.00	10.12	10.24	10.36	10.48	10.60	10.72
11	10.28	10.41	10.54	10.67	10.80	10.94	11.07	11.20	11.33	11.47	11.60	11.73
12	11.16	11.31	11.45	11.59	11.74	11.88	12.02	12.17	12.31	12.46	12.60	12.75
13	12.05	12.21	12.36	12.52	12.67	12.83	12.99	13.14	13.30	13.46	13.61	13.77
14	12.95	13.11	13.28	13.45	13.62	13.79	13.95	14.12	14.29	14.46	14.63	14.80
15	13.85	14.03	14.21	14.39	14.57	14.75	14.93	15.11	15.29	15.47	15.65	15.83
16	14.75	14.94	15.14	15.33	15.52	15.71	15.90	16.10	16.29	16.48	16.68	16.87
17	15.66	15.86	16.07	16.27	16.48	16.68	16.89	17.09	17.30	17.50	17.71	17.92
18	16.57	16.79	17.01	17.22	17.44	17.66	17.88	18.09	18.31	18.53	18.75	18.97
19	17.49	17.72	17.95	18.18	18.41	18.64	18.87	19.10	19.33	19.56	19.79	20.02
20	18.41	18.66	18.90	19.14	19.38	19.63	19.87	20.11	20.36	20.60	20.84	21.09
21	19.34	19.60	19.85	20.11	20.36	20.62	20.87	21.13	21.38	21.64	21.90	22.16
22	20.27	20.54	20.81	21.08	21.34	21.61	21.88	22.15	22.42	22.69	22.96	23.23
23	21.21	21.49	21.77	22.05	22.33	22.61	22.90	23.18	23.46	23.74	24.03	24.31
24	22.15	22.44	22.74	23.03	23.33	23.62	23.92	24.21	24.51	24.80	25.10	25.40
25	23.10	23.40	23.71	24.02	24.32	24.63	24.94	25.25	25.56	25.87	26.18	26.49
26	24.04	24.36	24.68	25.01	25.33	25.65	25.97	26.29	26.62	26.94	27.26	27.59
27	25.00	25.33	25.67	26.00	26.34	26.67	27.01	27.34	27.68	28.02	28.35	28.69
28	25.96	26.30	26.65	27.00	27.35	27.70	28.05	28.40	28.75	29.10	29.45	29.80
29	26.92	27.28	27.64	28.00	28.37	28.73	29.09	29.46	29.82	30.19	30.55	30.92
30	27.89	28.26	28.64	29.01	29.39	29.77	30.14	30.52	30.90	31.28	31.66	32.04
31	28.86	29.25	29.64	30.03	30.42	30.81	31.20	31.59	31.98	32.38	32.77	33.17
32	29.84	30.24	30.64	31.05	31.45	31.85	32.26	32.67	33.07	33.48	33.89	34.30
33	30.82	31.23	31.65	32.07	32.49	32.91	33.33	33.75	34.17	34.59	35.01	35.44
34	31.80	32.23	32.67	33.10	33.53	33.96	34.40	34.83	35.27	35.71	36.14	36.58
35	32.79	33.24	33.68	34.13	34.58	35.03	35.47	35.92	36.37	36.83	37.28	37.73
36	33.79	34.25	34.71	35.17	35.63	36.09	36.56	37.02	37.49	37.95	38.42	38.89
48	46.07	46.71	47.35	47.99	48.64	49.28	49.93	50.58	51.23	51.88	52.54	53.19
60	58.96	59.80	60.64	61.48	62.32	63.17	64.01	64.86	65.71	66.57	67.42	68.28

Number of Payments	23.00%	23.25%	23.50%	23.75%	24.00%	24.25%	24.50%	24.75%	25.00%	25.25%	25.50%	25.75%
1	1.92	1.94	1.96	1.98	2.00	2.02	2.04	2.06	2.08	2.10	2.12	2.15
2	2.88	2.92	2.95	2.98	3.01	3.04	3.07	3.10	3.14	3.17	3.20	3.23
3	3.86	3.90	3.94	3.98	4.03	4.07	4.11	4.15	4.20	4.24	4.28	4.32
4	4.84	4.89	4.94	5.00	5.05	5.10	5.16	5.21	5.26	5.32	5.37	5.42
5	5.82	5.89	5.95	6.02	6.08	6.14	6.21	6.27	6.34	6.40	6.46	6.53
6	6.81	6.89	6.96	7.04	7.12	7.19	7.27	7.34	7.42	7.49	7.57	7.64
7	7.81	7.90	7.99	8.07	8.16	8.25	8.33	8.42	8.51	8.59	8.68	8.77
8	8.82	8.91	9.01	9.11	9.21	9.31	9.40	9.50	9.60	9.70	9.80	9.90
9	9.83	9.94	10.04	10.15	10.26	10.37	10.48	10.59	10.70	10.81	10.92	11.03
10	10.84	10.96	11.08	11.21	11.33	11.45	11.57	11.69	11.81	11.93	12.06	12.18
11	11.86	12.00	12.13	12.26	12.40	12.53	12.66	12.80	12.93	13.06	13.20	13.33
12	12.89	13.04	13.18	13.33	13.47	13.62	13.76	13.91	14.05	14.20	14.34	14.49
13	13.93	14.08	14.24	14.40	14.55	14.71	14.87	15.03	15.18	15.34	15.50	15.66
14	14.97	15.13	15.30	15.47	15.64	15.81	15.98	16.15	16.32	16.49	16.66	16.83
15	16.01	16.19	16.37	16.56	16.74	16.92	17.10	17.28	17.47	17.65	17.83	18.02
16	17.06	17.26	17.45	17.65	17.84	18.03	18.23	18.42	18.62	18.81	19.01	19.21
17	18.12	18.33	18.53	18.74	18.95	19.16	19.36	19.57	19.78	19.99	20.20	20.40
18	19.19	19.41	19.62	19.84	20.06	20.28	20.50	20.72	20.95	21.17	21.39	21.61
19	20.26	20.49	20.72	20.95	21.19	21.42	21.65	21.89	22.12	22.35	22.59	22.82
20	21.33	21.58	21.82	22.07	22.31	22.56	22.81	23.05	23.30	23.55	23.79	24.04
21	22.41	22.67	22.93	23.19	23.45	23.71	23.97	24.23	24.49	24.75	25.01	25.27
22	23.50	23.77	24.04	24.32	24.59	24.86	25.13	25.41	25.68	25.96	26.23	26.50
23	24.60	24.88	25.17	25.45	25.74	26.02	26.31	26.60	26.88	27.17	27.46	27.75
24	25.70	25.99	26.29	26.59	26.89	27.19	27.49	27.79	28.09	28.39	28.69	29.00
25	26.80	27.11	27.43	27.74	28.05	28.36	28.68	28.99	29.31	29.62	29.94	30.25
26	27.91	28.24	28.56	28.89	29.22	29.55	29.87	30.20	30.53	30.86	31.19	31.52
27	29.03	29.37	29.71	30.05	30.39	30.73	31.07	31.42	31.76	32.10	32.45	32.79
28	30.15	30.51	30.86	31.22	31.57	31.93	32.28	32.64	33.00	33.35	33.71	34.07
29	31.28	31.65	32.02	32.39	32.76	33.13	33.50	33.87	34.24	34.61	34.98	35.36
30	32.42	32.80	33.18	33.57	33.95	34.33	34.72	35.10	35.49	35.88	36.26	36.65
31	33.56	33.96	34.35	34.75	35.15	35.55	35.95	36.35	36.75	37.15	37.55	37.95
32	34.71	35.12	35.53	35.94	36.35	36.77	37.18	37.60	38.01	38.43	38.84	39.26
33	35.86	36.29	36.71	37.14	37.57	37.99	38.42	38.85	39.28	39.71	40.14	40.58
34	37.02	37.46	37.90	38.34	38.78	39.23	39.67	40.11	40.56	41.01	41.45	41.90
35	38.18	38.64	39.09	39.55	40.01	40.47	40.92	41.38	41.84	42.31	42.77	43.23
36	39.35	39.82	40.29	40.77	41.24	41.71	42.19	42.66	43.14	43.61	44.09	44.57
48	53.85	54.51	55.16	55.83	56.49	57.15	57.82	58.49	59.15	59.82	60.50	61.17
60	69.14	70.01	70.87	71.74	72.61	73.48	74.35	75.23	76.11	76.99	77.87	78.76

Number of Payments	26.00%	26.25%	26.50%	26.75%	27.00%	27.25%	27.50%	27.75%	28.00%	28.25%	28.50%	28.75%
1	2.17	2.19	2.21	2.23	2.25	2.27	2.29	2.31	2.33	2.35	2.37	2.40
2	3.26	3.29	3.32	3.36	3.39	3.42	3.45	3.48	3.51	3.54	3.58	3.61
3	4.36	4.41	4.45	4.49	4.53	4.58	4.62	4.66	4.70	4.74	4.79	4.83
4	5.47	5.53	5.58	5.63	5.69	5.74	5.79	5.85	5.90	5.95	6.01	6.06
5	6.59	6.66	6.72	6.79	6.85	6.91	6.98	7.04	7.11	7.17	7.24	7.30
6	7.72	7.79	7.87	7.95	8.02	8.10	8.17	8.25	8.32	8.40	8.48	8.55
7	8.85	8.94	9.03	9.11	9.20	9.29	9.37	9.46	9.55	9.64	9.72	9.81
8	9.99	10.09	10.19	10.29	10.39	10.49	10.58	10.68	10.78	10.88	10.98	11.08
9	11.14	11.25	11.36	11.47	11.58	11.69	11.80	11.91	12.03	12.14	12.25	12.36
10	12.30	12.42	12.54	12.67	12.79	12.91	13.03	13.15	13.28	13.40	13.52	13.64
11	13.46	13.60	13.73	13.87	14.00	14.13	14.27	14.40	14.54	14.67	14.81	14.94
12	14.64	14.78	14.93	15.07	15.22	15.37	15.51	15.66	15.81	15.95	16.10	16.25
13	15.82	15.97	16.13	16.29	16.45	16.61	16.77	16.93	17.09	17.24	17.40	17.56
14	17.00	17.17	17.35	17.52	17.69	17.86	18.03	18.20	18.37	18.54	18.72	18.89
15	18.20	18.38	18.57	18.75	18.93	19.12	19.30	19.48	19.67	19.85	20.04	20.22
16	19.40	19.60	19.79	19.99	20.19	20.38	20.58	20.78	20.97	21.17	21.37	21.57
17	20.61	20.82	21.03	21.24	21.45	21.66	21.87	22.08	22.29	22.50	22.71	22.92
18	21.83	22.05	22.27	22.50	22.72	22.94	23.16	23.39	23.61	23.83	24.06	24.28
19	23.06	23.29	23.53	23.76	24.00	24.23	24.47	24.71	24.94	25.18	25.42	25.65
20	24.29	24.54	24.79	25.04	25.28	25.53	25.78	26.03	26.28	26.53	26.78	27.04
21	25.53	25.79	26.05	26.32	26.58	26.84	27.11	27.37	27.63	27.90	28.16	28.43
22	26.78	27.05	27.33	27.61	27.88	28.16	28.44	28.71	28.99	29.27	29.55	29.82
23	28.04	28.32	28.61	28.90	29.19	29.48	29.77	30.07	30.36	30.65	30.94	31.23
24	29.30	29.60	29.90	30.21	30.51	30.82	31.12	31.43	31.73	32.04	32.34	32.65
25	30.57	30.89	31.20	31.52	31.84	32.16	32.48	32.80	33.12	33.44	33.76	34.08
26	31.85	32.18	32.51	32.84	33.18	33.51	33.84	34.18	34.51	34.84	35.18	35.51
27	33.14	33.48	33.83	34.17	34.52	34.87	35.21	35.56	35.91	36.26	36.61	36.96
28	34.43	34.79	35.15	35.51	35.87	36.23	36.59	36.96	37.32	37.68	38.05	38.41
29	35.73	36.10	36.48	36.85	37.23	37.61	37.98	38.36	38.74	39.12	39.50	39.88
30	37.04	37.43	37.82	38.21	38.60	38.99	39.38	39.77	40.17	40.56	40.95	41.35
31	38.36	38.76	39.16	39.57	39.97	40.38	40.79	41.19	41.60	42.01	42.42	42.83
32	39.68	40.10	40.52	40.94	41.36	41.78	42.20	42.62	43.05	43.47	43.90	44.32
33	41.01	41.44	41.88	42.31	42.75	43.19	43.62	44.06	44.50	44.94	45.38	45.82
34	42.35	42.80	43.25	43.70	44.15	44.60	45.05	45.51	45.96	46.42	46.87	47.33
35	43.69	44.16	44.62	45.09	45.56	46.02	46.49	46.96	47.43	47.90	48.37	48.85
36	45.05	45.53	46.01	46.49	46.97	47.45	47.94	48.42	48.91	49.40	49.88	50.37
48	61.84	62.52	63.20	63.87	64.56	65.24	65.92	66.60	67.29	67.98	68.67	69.36
60	79.64	80.53	81.42	82.32	83.21	84.11	85.01	85.91	86.81	87.72	88.63	89.54

Number of Payments	29 00%	29 25%	29 50%	29 75%	30 00%	30 25%	30 50%	30 75%	31 00%	31 25%	31 50%	31 75%
1	2 42	2 44	2 46	2 48	2 50	2 52	2 54	2 56	2 58	2 60	2 63	2 65
2	3 64	3 67	3 70	3 73	3 77	3 80	3 83	3 86	3 89	3 92	3 95	3 99
3	4 87	4 91	4 96	5 00	5 04	5 08	5 13	5 17	5 21	5 25	5 30	5 34
4	6 11	6 17	6 22	6 27	6 33	6 38	6 43	6 49·	6 54	6 59	6 65	6 70
5	7 37	7 43	7 49	7 56	7 62	7 69	7 75	7 82	7 88	7 95	8 01	8 08
6	8 63	8 70	8 78	8 85	8 93	9 01	9 08	9 16	9 23	9 31	9 39	9 46
7	9 90	9 98	10 07	10 16	10 25	10 33	10 42	10 51	10 60	10 68	10 77	10 86
8	11 18	11 28	11 38	11 47	11 57	11 67	11 77	11 87	11 97	12 07	12 17	12 27
9	12 47	12 58	12 69	12 80	12 91	13 02	13 13	13 24	13 36	13 47	13 58	13 69
10	13 77	13 89	14 01	14 14	14 26	14 38	14 50	14 63	14 75	14 87	15 00	15 12
11	15 08	15 21	15 35	15 48	15 62	15 75	15 89	16 02	16 16	16 29	16 43	16 56
12	16 40	16 54	16 69	16 84	16 98	17 13	17 28	17 43	17 58	17 72	17 87	18 02
13	17 72	17 88	18 04	18 20	18 36	18 52	18 68	18 84	19 00	19 16	19 33	19 49
14	19 06	19 23	19 41	19 58	19 75	19 92	20 10	20 27	20 44	20 62	20 79	20 96
15	20 41	20 59	20 78	20 96	21 15	21 34	21 52	21 71	21 89	22 08	22 27	22 45
16	21 76	21 96	22 16	22 36	22 56	22 76	22 96	23 16	23 35	23 55	23 75	23 95
17	23 13	23 34	23 55	23 77	23 98	24 19	24 40	24 61	24 83	25 04	25 25	25 47
18	24 51	24 73	24 96	25 18	25 41	25 63	25 86	26 08	26 31	26 54	26 76	26 99
19	25 89	26 13	26 37	26 61	26 85	27 08	27 32	27 56	27 80	28 04	28 28	28 52
20	27 29	27 54	27 79	28 04	28 29	28 55	28 80	29 05	29 31	29 56	29 81	30 07
21	28 69	28 96	29 22	29 49	29 75	30 02	30 29	30 55	30 82	31 09	31 36	31 62
22	30 10	30 38	30 66	30 94	31 22	31 50	31 78	32 07	32 35	32 63	32 91	33 19
23	31 53	31 82	32 11	32 41	32 70	33 00	33 29	33 59	33 88	34 18	34 48	34 77
24	32 96	33 27	33 57	33 88	34 19	34 50	34 81	35 12	35 43	35 74	36 05	36 36
25	34 40	34 72	35 04	35 37	35 69	36 01	36 34	36 66	36 99	37 31	37 64	37 96
26	35 85	36 19	36 52	36 86	37 20	37 54	37 88	38 21	38 55	38 89	39 23	39 58
27	37 31	37 66	38 01	38 36	38 72	39 07	39 42	39 78	40 13	40 49	40 84	41 20
28	38 78	39 15	39 51	39 88	40 25	40 61	40 98	41 35	41 72	42 09	42 46	42 83
29	40 26	40 64	41 02	41 40	41 78	42 17	42 55	42 94	43 32	43 71	44 09	44 48
30	41 75	42 14	42 54	42 94	43 33	43 73	44 13	44 53	44 93	45 33	45 73	46 13
31	43 24	43 65	44 07	44 48	44 89	45 30	45 72	46 13	46 55	46 97	47 38	47 80
32	44 75	45 17	45 60	46 03	46 46	46 89	47 32	47 75	48 18	48 61	49 05	49 48
33	46 26	46 70	47 15	47 59	48 04	48 48	48 93	49 37	49 82	50 27	50 72	51 17
34	47 79	48 24	48 70	49 16	49 62	50 08	50 55	51 01	51 47	51 94	52 40	52 87
35	49 32	49 79	50 27	50 74	51 22	51 70	52 17	52 65	53 13	53 61	54 09	54 58
36	50 86	51 35	51 84	52 33	52 83	53 32	53 81	54 31	54 80	55 30	55 80	56 30
48	70 05	70 74	71 44	72 13	72 83	73 53	74 23	74 93	75 63	76 34	77 04	77 75
60	90 45	91 37	92 28	93 20	94 12	95 04	95 97	96 89	97 82	98 75	99 68	100 62

Number of Payments	32 00%	32 25%	32 50%	32 75%	33 00%	33 25%	33 50%	33 75%	34 00%	34 25%	34 50%	34 75%
1	2 67	2 69	2 71	2 73	2 75	2 77	2 79	2 81	2 83	2 85	2 87	2 90
2	4 02	4 05	4 08	4 11	4 14	4 18	4 21	4 24	4 27	4 30	4 33	4 36
3	5 38	5 42	5 46	5 51	5 55	5 59	5 63	5 68	5 72	5 76	5 80	5 85
4	6 75	6 81	6 86	6 91	6 97	7 02	7 08	7 13	7 18	7 24	7 29	7 34
5	8 14	8 21	8 27	8 33	8 40	8 46	8 53	8 59	8 66	8 72	8 79	8 85
6	9 54	9 61	9 69	9 77	9 84	9 92	9 99	10 07	10 15	10 22	10 30	10 38
7	10 95	11 03	11 12	11 21	11 30	11 39	11 47	11 56	11 65	11 74	11 83	11 91
8	12 37	12 47	12 57	12 67	12 77	12 87	12 97	13 07	13 17	13 27	13 36	13 46
9	13 80	13 91	14 02	14 14	14 25	14 36	14 47	14 58	14 69	14 81	14 92	15 03
10	15 24	15 37	15 49	15 62	15 74	15 86	15 99	16 11	16 24	16 36	16 48	16 61
11	16 70	16 84	16 97	17 11	17 24	17 38	17 52	17 65	17 79	17 93	18 06	18 20
12	18 17	18 32	18 47	18 61	18 76	18 91	19 06	19 21	19 36	19 51	19 66	19 81
13	19 65	19 81	19 97	20 13	20 29	20 45	20 62	20 78	20 94	21 10	21 26	21 43
14	21 14	21 31	21 49	21 66	21 83	22 01	22 18	22 36	22 53	22 71	22 88	23 06
15	22 64	22 83	23 01	23 20	23 39	23 58	23 76	23 95	24 14	24 33	24 52	24 71
16	24 15	24 35	24 55	24 75	24 96	25 16	25 36	25 56	25 76	25 96	26 16	26 37
17	25 68	25 89	26 11	26 32	26 53	26 75	26 96	27 18	27 39	27 61	27 82	28 04
18	27 22	27 44	27 67	27 90	28 13	28 35	28 58	28 81	29 04	29 27	29 50	29 73
19	28 76	29 00	29 25	29 49	29 73	29 97	30 21	30 45	30 70	30 94	31 18	31 43
20	30 32	30 58	30 83	31 09	31 34	31 60	31 86	32 11	32 37	32 63	32 88	33 14
21	31 89	32 16	32 43	32 70	32 97	33 24	33 51	33 78	34 05	34 32	34 60	34 87
22	33 48	33 76	34 04	34 33	34 61	34 89	35 18	35 46	35 75	36 04	36 32	36 61
23	35 07	35 37	35 66	35 96	36 26	36 56	36 86	37 16	37 46	37 76	38 06	38 36
24	36 67	36 99	37 30	37 61	37 92	38 24	38 55	38 87	39 18	39 50	39 81	40 13
25	38 29	38 62	38 94	39 27	39 60	39 93	40 26	40 59	40 92	41 25	41 58	41 91
26	39 92	40 26	40 60	40 94	41 29	41 63	41 97	42 32	42 66	43 01	43 36	43 70
27	41 56	41 91	42 27	42 63	42 99	43 34	43 70	44 06	44 42	44 78	45 15	45 51
28	43 20	43 58	43 95	44 32	44 70	45 07	45 45	45 82	46 20	46 57	46 95	47 33
29	44 87	45 25	45 64	46 03	46 42	46 81	47 20	47 59	47 98	48 37	48 77	49 16
30	46 54	46 94	47 34	47 75	48 15	48 56	48 96	49 37	49 78	50 19	50 60	51 00
31	48 22	48 64	49 06	49 48	49 90	50 32	50 74	51 17	51 59	52 01	52 44	52 86
32	49 91	50 35	50 78	51 22	51 66	52 09	52 53	52 97	53 41	53 85	54 29	54 73
33	51 62	52 07	52 52	52 97	53 43	53 88	54 33	54 79	55 24	55 70	56 16	56 62
34	53 33	53 80	54 27	54 74	55 21	55 68	56 15	56 62	57 09	57 56	58 04	58 51
35	55 06	55 54	56 03	56 51	57 00	57 48	57 97	58 46	58 95	59 44	59 93	60 42
36	56 80	57 30	57 80	58 30	58 80	59 30	59 81	60 31	60 82	61 33	61 83	62 34
48	78 46	79 17	79 88	80 59	81 30	82 02	82 74	83 45	84 17	84 89	85 61	86 34
60	101 56	102 49	103 43	104 38	105 32	106 27	107 21	108 16	109 12	110 07	111 03	111 98

Number of Payments	35.00%	35.25%	35.50%	35.75%	36.00%	36.25%	36.50%	36.75%	37.00%	37.25%	37.50%	37.75%
1	2.92	2.94	2.96	2.98	3.00	3.02	3.04	3.06	3.08	3.10	3.12	3.15
2	4.40	4.43	4.46	4.49	4.52	4.55	4.59	4.62	4.65	4.68	4.71	4.74
3	5.89	5.93	5.97	6.02	6.06	6.10	6.14	6.19	6.23	6.27	6.31	6.36
4	7.40	7.45	7.50	7.56	7.61	7.66	7.72	7.77	7.83	7.88	7.93	7.99
5	8.92	8.98	9.05	9.11	9.18	9.24	9.31	9.37	9.44	9.50	9.57	9.63
6	10.45	10.53	10.61	10.68	10.76	10.83	10.91	10.99	11.06	11.14	11.22	11.29
7	12.00	12.09	12.18	12.27	12.35	12.44	12.53	12.62	12.71	12.80	12.88	12.97
8	13.56	13.66	13.76	13.86	13.97	14.07	14.17	14.27	14.37	14.47	14.57	14.67
9	15.14	15.25	15.37	15.48	15.59	15.70	15.82	15.93	16.04	16.15	16.27	16.38
10	16.73	16.86	16.98	17.11	17.23	17.36	17.48	17.60	17.73	17.85	17.98	18.10
11	18.34	18.47	18.61	18.75	18.89	19.02	19.16	19.30	19.43	19.57	19.71	19.85
12	19.96	20.11	20.25	20.40	20.55	20.70	20.85	21.00	21.15	21.31	21.46	21.61
13	21.59	21.75	21.91	22.08	22.24	22.40	22.56	22.73	22.89	23.05	23.22	23.38
14	23.23	23.41	23.59	23.76	23.94	24.11	24.29	24.47	24.64	24.82	25.00	25.17
15	24.89	25.08	25.27	25.46	25.65	25.84	26.03	26.22	26.41	26.60	26.79	26.98
16	26.57	26.77	26.97	27.17	27.38	27.58	27.78	27.99	28.19	28.39	28.60	28.80
17	28.25	28.47	28.69	28.90	29.12	29.34	29.55	29.77	29.99	30.20	30.42	30.64
18	29.96	30.19	30.42	30.65	30.88	31.11	31.34	31.57	31.80	32.03	32.26	32.49
19	31.67	31.91	32.16	32.40	32.65	32.89	33.14	33.38	33.63	33.87	34.12	34.36
20	33.40	33.66	33.91	34.17	34.43	34.69	34.95	35.21	35.47	35.73	35.99	36.25
21	35.14	35.41	35.68	35.96	36.23	36.50	36.78	37.05	37.33	37.60	37.88	38.15
22	36.89	37.18	37.47	37.76	38.04	38.33	38.62	38.91	39.20	39.49	39.78	40.07
23	38.66	38.96	39.27	39.57	39.87	40.18	40.48	40.78	41.09	41.39	41.70	42.00
24	40.44	40.76	41.08	41.40	41.71	42.03	42.35	42.67	42.99	43.31	43.63	43.95
25	42.24	42.57	42.90	43.24	43.57	43.90	44.24	44.57	44.91	45.24	45.58	45.91
26	44.05	44.40	44.74	45.09	45.44	45.79	46.14	46.49	46.84	47.19	47.54	47.89
27	45.87	46.23	46.60	46.96	47.32	47.69	48.05	48.42	48.78	49.15	49.52	49.89
28	47.70	48.08	48.46	48.84	49.22	49.60	49.98	50.36	50.75	51.13	51.51	51.89
29	49.55	49.95	50.34	50.74	51.13	51.53	51.93	52.32	52.72	53.12	53.52	53.92
30	51.41	51.82	52.23	52.65	53.06	53.47	53.88	54.30	54.71	55.13	55.54	55.96
31	53.29	53.71	54.14	54.57	55.00	55.43	55.85	56.28	56.72	57.15	57.58	58.01
32	55.17	55.62	56.06	56.50	56.95	57.39	57.84	58.29	58.73	59.18	59.63	60.08
33	57.07	57.53	57.99	58.45	58.92	59.38	59.84	60.30	60.77	61.23	61.70	62.16
34	58.99	59.46	59.94	60.42	60.89	61.37	61.85	62.33	62.81	63.30	63.78	64.26
35	60.91	61.40	61.90	62.39	62.89	63.38	63.88	64.38	64.88	65.37	65.87	66.37
36	62.85	63.36	63.87	64.38	64.89	65.41	65.92	66.44	66.95	67.47	67.98	68.50
48	87.06	87.79	88.52	89.24	89.97	90.70	91.44	92.17	92.91	93.64	94.38	95.12
60	112.94	113.90	114.87	115.83	116.80	117.77	118.74	119.71	120.68	121.66	122.64	123.62

Exercise B   Determine the annual percentage rate from the table in the following problems.

	Amount Borrowed	Interest	Other Charges	Term of Loan (in Months)	Annual Percentage Rate
1.	$ 600	$ 22.42	$ 5.00	6	_____
2.	1,000	232.00	25.00	24	_____
3.	450	_____	0	9	18.75
4.	800	27.00	6.60	6	_____
5.	2,500	859.75	31.00	36	_____

The following graph shows a comparison between a promissory note and an installment contract for $500 at 12 percent annual interest rate over a period of ten months. Note that the total amount of interest on the installment contract is less over the ten months because less-average principal has been used.

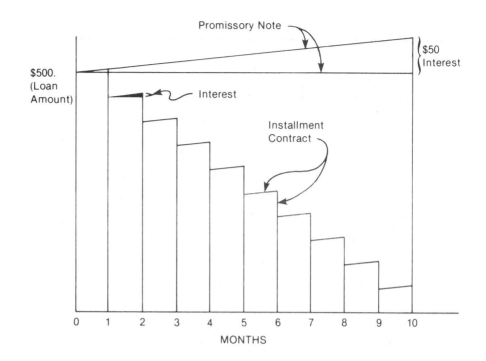

The buyer borrowed $500 and decreases the amount of the principal by making monthly payments. Because the amount of the loan is decreased over its life, the amount of interest also is less. The example shows that the buyer would pay a total of $550 on a promissory note, but only a total of $527.92 if it were financed on an installment contract. (See page 225 for computations on the installment contract.) The borrower should also realize that there is use of only approximately one-half of the principal over the term of the loan on an installment contract.

Down payment

> **Example 4**
>
> Jenny purchased a set of stereo components for a total purchase price of $386.75. She decided to make a **down payment** of $86.75 and finance the remainder. The down payment is made to secure the purchase and to prove the buyer's intentions to the seller.
>
> Jenny borrowed the $300 at 10 percent interest for four months to be repaid at $76.60 per month.
>
> The repayment schedule is computed as follows:
>
> Month #1 = $2.50 = $300 \times .10 \times \dfrac{1}{12}$
>
> $\begin{array}{r} +\quad 2.50 \\ \hline \$302.50 \\ -\quad 76.60 \\ \hline \end{array}$ = interest
>
> = payment
>
> #2 = $1.88 = $225.90 \times .10 \times \dfrac{1}{12}$
>
> $\begin{array}{r} +\quad 1.88 \\ \hline \$227.78 \\ -\quad 76.60 \\ \hline \end{array}$ = interest
>
> = payment

Example 4 *Continued*

$$\#3 = \$1.26 = \quad \$151.18 \times .10 \times \frac{1}{12}$$

$$\frac{+\quad 1.26}{\$152.44} = \text{interest}$$

$$\frac{-\quad 76.60}{} = \text{payment}$$

$$\#4 = \$ .63 = \quad \$ 75.84 \times .10 \times \frac{1}{12} \, {\scriptstyle 1083333}$$

$$\frac{+\quad .63}{\$76.47} = \text{interest}$$
$$\$76.47 = \text{last payment}$$

Repayment Schedule

Payment Number	Payment Amount	Interest Amount	Payment on Principal	Principal Balance
1	$76.60	$2.50	$74.10	$225.90
2	76.60	1.88	74.72	151.18
3	76.60	1.26	75.34	75.84
4	76.47	.63	75.84	0.00

Use of Payment Tables

The previous examples were for small loans for such items as office equipment, appliances, recreation equipment, furniture, and engagement rings. Installment loans are also used for larger loans for such items as machinery, buildings, land, and private homes. Due to the higher costs of these items the loan amortization is usually extended over a period of years in order to allow the buyer to successfully pay off the mortgage or loan. The process of computing the repayment schedule is exactly the same as in the earlier examples. The amount of the monthly payment can be determined by using the following table.

Monthly Payment Amount per $1,000 to Pay Principal and Interest on a Loan

Term of Loan	7%	8%	9%	10%	11%	12%	13%	14%	15%	16%	17%	18%
5 years	$19.81	$20.28	$20.76	$21.25	$21.75	$22.25	$22.76	$23.27	$23.79	$24.32	$24.86	$25.40
10 years	11.62	12.14	12.67	13.22	13.78	14.35	14.94	15.53	16.14	16.76	17.38	18.02
15 years	8.99	9.56	10.15	10.75	11.37	12.01	12.66	13.32	14.00	14.69	15.40	16.11
20 years	7.76	8.37	9.00	9.66	10.33	11.02	11.72	12.44	13.17	13.92	14.67	15.44
25 years	7.07	7.72	8.40	9.09	9.81	10.54	11.28	12.04	12.81	13.59	14.38	15.18
30 years	6.66	7.34	8.05	8.78	9.53	10.29	11.07	11.85	12.65	13.45	14.26	15.08

Computing the Principal Balance

Payment amount

Principal balance
Repayment schedule

Example 5

Let us use an example of a firm that wishes to purchase an office machine. The firm will finance or borrow $500 in order to make the purchase. A lending institution, bank, or finance company has agreed to lend the $500 at an annual rate of 12 percent for a period of ten months. A **payment amount** of $52.75, which will pay back the $500 principal and the 12 percent interest over the ten months of the loan, is established. A record is kept of payments, interest, and the amount due after each payment, which is known as the **principal balance.** This record is termed a **repayment schedule.** It is developed as follows:

Computing the Interest

$$\text{Interest} = \$500 \text{ (Principal)} \times 12\% \text{ (annual rate)} \times \frac{1}{12} \text{ (time)}$$

(Monthly payments)

$$\$5 = \$500 \times .12 \times \frac{1}{12}$$

$$
\begin{aligned}
+\quad 5 &= \text{interest for the first month} \\
\$505.00 &= \text{amount owed at the end of the first month} \\
-\ 52.75 &= \text{amount of monthly payment} \\
\$452.25 &= \text{amount of loan after the first monthly payment or principal balance}
\end{aligned}
$$

$$\$4.52 = \$452.25 \times .12 \times \frac{1}{12}$$

$$
\begin{aligned}
+\quad 4.52 &= \text{interest for the second month} \\
456.77 &= \text{amount owed at the end of the second month} \\
-\ 52.75 &= \text{amount of monthly payment} \\
\$404.02 &= \text{amount of loan after the second monthly payment}
\end{aligned}
$$

$$\$4.04 = \$404.02 \times .12 \times \frac{1}{12}$$

$$
\begin{aligned}
+\quad 4.04 &= \text{interest for the third month} \\
\$408.06 &= \text{amount owed at the end of the third month} \\
-\ 52.75 &= \text{monthly payment} \\
\$355.31 &= \text{amount of loan after the third monthly payment}
\end{aligned}
$$

This process is continued until the principal balance is reduced to zero. The completed repayment schedule for the $500 loan follows.

Repayment Schedule

Payment Number	Payment Amount	Interest Amount	Payment on Principal	Principal Balance
1	$52.75	$5.00	$47.75	$452.25
2	52.75	4.52	48.23	404.02
3	52.75	4.04	48.71	355.31
4	52.75	3.55	49.20	306.11
5	52.75	3.06	49.69	256.42
6	52.75	2.56	50.19	206.23
7	52.75	2.06	50.69	155.54
8	52.75	1.56	51.19	104.35
9	52.75	1.04	51.71	52.64
10	53.17	.53	52.64	0.00

Note that the last payment may be a few cents more or less than the established payment amount.

Example 6

A boat was sold for $23,800. The buyers agreed to make a $2,800 down payment and finance the balance at 10 percent over five years. The amount of monthly payment on the boat would be found as follows:

$$\begin{array}{rl} \$23,800 = & \text{purchase price} \\ - \ 2,800 = & \text{down payment} \\ \hline \$21,000 = & \text{amount to be financed} \end{array}$$

From the table on page 224 (Monthly Payment Amount Per $1,000), the amount of $21.25 can be found (10 percent, 5 years). This amount should be multiplied by twenty-one (the number of $1,000 in the loan) to find a payment amount of $446.25.

Example 7

A piece of land was purchased for $58,300. A down payment of $6,000 was made with the balance to be financed at 12 percent over twenty years. What is the payment amount?

$$\begin{array}{ll} \begin{array}{r} \$58,300 \\ -6,000 \\ \hline \$52,300 \end{array} & \begin{array}{rl} \$ \ 11.02 = & \text{payment per \$1,000} \\ \times \ \ \ 52.3 = & \text{the number of \$1,000 in loan} \\ \hline \$576.35 = & \text{monthly payment amount} \end{array} \end{array}$$

Exercise C   In the following problems, compute the monthly payment amount. Use the table.

	Amount of Purchase	Down Payment	Rate of Interest	Term of Loan	Monthly Payment Amount
1.	$ 13,600	$ 3,000	7%	5 years	$ 209.99
2.	40,000	6,000	13	15	_____
3.	69,900	21,000	10	25	_____
4.	23,000	4,000	14	5	_____
5.	21,500	3,100	15	5	_____
6.	129,000	35,000	12	10	_____
7.	45,800	5,400	16	25	_____
8.	56,500	10,000	10	30	_____

Home Mortgages

Developed property is purchased by both business (stores, office buildings, research centers, manufacturing plants, and warehouses) and individuals (single family homes, multi-unit complexes, and condominiums). The information and problems that follow, although applicable to both business and individuals, deal with purchasing a home—a decision relevant to most Americans.

Maximum Monthly Cost

As a guide, the maximum amount that should be spent on shelter by a family is about $\frac{1}{4}$ of the gross income of the household. A family with a combined income of $60,000 could spend a maximum of $15,000 per year on shelter or $1,250 per month. That amount must include the payment, taxes (if applicable), insurance, utilities, and repairs. This guide applies to those renting or buying.

Advantages

There are some advantages to both buying and renting. Examples follow.

Buying:

1. Interest and tax expenses are deductible for federal income tax purposes.
2. There may be some appreciation in the value of the property over the period that it is owned.
3. The property is being purchased. At some point in time, there will be no more payments!

Renting:

1. No or little effort needed to maintain the property.
2. Renter is free to move when the lease expires. No need to sell. This is an important factor for those who have jobs that require relocation.

Over half of the homes sold in the U.S. in recent years are financed by the seller. This is an important factor to consider because you, as a potential buyer through this method, will need to know exactly what you are facing in terms of interest rates, term of the loan, and how the balance is affected by each payment. The remainder of homes are financed by savings and loan associations and commercial banks, which have more conservative loan terms and payment schedules.

The average new single family home costs about $100,000. Financing can be obtained by qualified buyers for up to 100 percent of the purchase price. Most buyers will put a 10 or 20 percent down payment on the property in order to reduce the monthly payment amount.

Effect of Interest Rate Difference

Interest rates are competitive and therefore a prospective buyer should shop around or try to negotiate a lower rate. The difference of one percentage point can result in several thousand dollars in additional payments over the term of the agreement.

Example 8

A family decides to purchase a home that is priced at $75,000. They put a $25,000 down payment on the home. The balance of $50,000 will be financed by a commercial bank. One bank will provide 11 percent financing on a twenty-year term. Another bank will provide 12 percent financing for the same term. What is the difference in the amount of the total payments if the loan goes to term?

$	10.33 (11%, 20 years)		$	11.02 (12%, 20 years)	
×	50 = thousands		×	50 = thousands	
$	516.50 = payment per month		$	551 = payment per month	
×	240 = (12 months × 20 years)		×	240 = (12 months × 20 years)	
$123,960	= total repayment		$132,240	= total repayment	

$$\begin{array}{rl} \$132,240 & = (12\%, \ 20 \ \text{years}) \\ -\ 123,960 & = (11\%, \ 20 \ \text{years}) \\ \hline \$\ \ 8,280 & \text{difference} \end{array}$$

The family in Example 8 has a combined household income of $30,000. The payment amount and other household expenses total $650 per month. It does not appear that they could afford this home because the total shelter expense exceeded the $\frac{1}{4}$ maximum guideline ($30,000 × $\frac{1}{4}$ = $7,500 and $7,500 ÷ 12 = $625 per month).

Effect of Term Difference

Example 9

Another lender was found that would provide financing at 11 percent for a thirty-year term. Would the extra ten years of term allow the buyers to fit the guideline of $\frac{1}{4}$ of gross income? How much additional cost would be incurred over the life of the loan for the expanded amortization period?

$$\begin{array}{rl} \$\ \ 9.53 & (11\%, \ 30 \ \text{years}) \\ \times \ \ \ \ \ 50 & = \text{thousands} \\ \hline \$476.50 & = \text{payment per month} \end{array}$$

$$\begin{array}{rl} \$516.50 & = (11\%, \ 20 \ \text{years}) \\ -\ 476.50 & = (11\%, \ 30 \ \text{years}) \\ \hline \$\ 40.00 & = \text{less per month} \end{array}$$

$$\begin{array}{rl} \$650 & = \text{monthly household expenses with 20-year mortgage} \\ -\ \ \ 40 & = \text{reduction in monthly mortgage payment} \\ \hline \$610 & = \text{this would allow the buyer to meet the guidelines} \end{array}$$

$$\begin{array}{rl} \$476.50 & = \text{payment per month} \\ \times \ \ \ \ 360 & = (12 \ \text{months} \times 30 \ \text{years}) \\ \hline \$171,540 & = \text{total repayment over 30 years} \\ -\ 123,960 & = \text{total repayment over 20 years} \\ \hline \$\ 47,580 & = \text{additional cost over the term of the loan} \end{array}$$

Example 9 points out very clearly that time does cost money. In this case $47,580 more! The student, however, must consider another factor in order to put the information into proper perspective. Since the average family moves every five years, the family in Examples 8 and 9 probably won't take the payments on the property to term. The family will more than likely sell the home after making only sixty payments!

Because lenders are aware that consumers are looking for a variety of financing plans to fit their individual family needs, they have formulated several plans that will fit both their needs and the needs of the borrower. Some of the variations follow.

Fixed Rate:
The rate on the loan remains the same over the term of the loan. This is a traditional type of loan and the type that will be used in the problems in the assignment section unless otherwise indicated.

Variable Rate:
The rate on the loan will change, usually on an annual basis. The change in the rate will usually be based on some interest indicator such as Treasury Bills.

Fixed Payment Amount:
This is the traditional method of amortizing the loan and the method used in the assignment section unless otherwise indicated. The payment amount remains the same over the term of the loan.

Variable Payment Amount:
This type of loan begins with low payments and increases the payment amount as the loan begins to mature. This allows the new, and usually younger buyer, to get into a home early in life. The loan is designed to anticipate the increase in household income in future years (see figure 11.1). In this type of loan, the balance may increase due to the low payment amount. This is termed negative amortization.

Balloon Payment:
This specification may be used with any of the above variations. A balloon payment indicates that the total amount of the balance of the loan must be paid on the balloon date. The balloon date is usually five years after the original loan begins. The loan will therefore have to be refinanced by the balloon date or paid in full.

When the buyer applies for a loan from a financial institution (commercial bank or savings and loan), there may be an application fee. The lender may be allowed to also charge fees for a legal review of the papers, an appraisal, filing fees, prorated taxes, and points. A **point** is one percent of the amount of the loan. The points assessed on the loan may be paid for by the buyer or the seller, or both. Points can be negotiable and should be reviewed by legal counsel.

Closing Costs   When the buyer makes the final financial commitment to purchase the property, the buyer and seller go through what is known as closing. At the closing meeting, the appropriate papers are signed and fees and monies are transferred to the lender, seller, and other parties. The total of these fees is termed **closing costs** because they are paid at closing. These costs are above the amount of the loan. Often, the buyer is not aware of the exact amount of the closing costs until the day or week before the closing date.

Escrow Account   When a piece of property is mortgaged, the lending institution may, at the request of the buyer, collect money from the buyer to cover the yearly property taxes and fire insurance. This predetermined amount, which is over and above the regular monthly payment, is put into an **escrow account** for the buyer.

As the tax and insurance payments are due, the lender draws money from the escrow account and makes the payments for the buyer. The escrow account money, which does not earn or pay interest, is a reserve for the buyer to insure that there will always be money to make the tax and insurance payments. In this way, too, the escrow account provides some protection to the lender by insuring that the payments will be made.

Example 10

James E. Willard purchased a home for his family for $43,000. They made a down payment of $10,800 and financed the balance on a mortgage at 11 percent for thirty years. The lending institution stated that the home must be insured at a cost of $960 over three years. The property taxes were $1,470 per year. What would the monthly payment amount be in order to pay taxes, insurance, and amortize the loan?

$$\begin{array}{rl} \$43,000 = & \text{purchase price} \\ -\ 10,800 = & \text{down payment} \\ \hline \$32,200 = & \text{amount of loan} \end{array}$$

$$\begin{array}{rl} \$\ \ 9.53 = & \text{payment per \$1,000} \\ 32.2 = & \text{the number of \$1,000 in loan} \\ \hline \$306.87 = & \text{monthly payment amount} \end{array}$$

$$\begin{array}{rrl} & \$306.87 = & \text{monthly payment amount} \\ \$960 \text{ (insurance for 3 years)} \div 36 = & 26.67 = & \text{insurance per month} \\ \$1,470 \text{ (taxes for 1 year)} \div 12 = & 122.50 = & \text{taxes per month} \\ \hline & \$456.04 = & \text{monthly payment amount including escrow amount} \end{array}$$

To develop a repayment schedule or determine the balance on the loan, the payment amount without escrow is used.

Exercise D

In the following problems, compute the monthly payment amount including the amount for escrow. Use the table.

	Amount of Purchase	Down Payment	Rate of Interest	Term of Loan	Insurance Cost/year	Taxes per year	Monthly Payment Amount (Including Escrow)
1.	$31,500	$ 0	9%	15 years	$147	$ 600	$381.98
2.	49,000	5,000	13	25	458	1,942	
3.	18,000	3,000	7	5	92	480	
4.	41,600	5,600	13	10	186	1,520	
5.	94,000	20,000	12	25	—	1,800	
6.	21,000	13,000	10	15	108	165	
7.	33,500	5,800	11	20	160	478	

Early Payoff Penalties

The development of a repayment schedule earlier in the chapter provided a complete analysis of the amount of interest, payment on the principal, and payment amount, as well as the balance after each monthly payment. This information is useful and necessary on an installment contract. There may be an instance when the loan is paid off before the end of the term. There is usually some type of penalty that the borrower must pay in order to receive credit for complete payment. For example, on a long-term mortgage the penalty may be a simple 1 percent of the original amount of the loan. This must be spelled out in the loan agreement.

Example 11

On a $42,000 loan with a principal balance of $7,860 at 8 percent for twenty-five years, the borrower may find enough money to pay off the loan before the end of the twenty-five years. After reviewing the contract, a penalty clause reveals that the borrower must pay a $\frac{3}{4}$ percent penalty on the balance if an early payoff is made. The payoff amount would be computed as follows:

$$\$7,860 \times .08 \times \frac{1}{12} = \begin{array}{r} \$7,860.00 = \text{principal balance} \\ +\quad 52.40 = \text{interest for month} \\ +\quad 58.95 = \frac{3}{4}\ \% \text{ on balance for early} \\ \text{payoff penalty} \\ \hline \$7,971.35 = \text{payoff amount} \end{array}$$

Rule of 78s   On a shorter-term loan a bank may use the Rule of 78s. This rule states that more of the interest is earned in the earlier months of a loan's life. To compute the amount of payoff on a loan using the **Rule of 78s,** the number of the months in the term of the loan must be totaled. In a twelve-month loan the total is 78, that is,

$$12 + 11 + 10 + 9 + 8 + 7 + 6 + 5 + 4 + 3 + 2 + 1 = 78$$

The bank uses $\frac{12}{78s}$ of the principal to compute the first month's interest for payoff purposes; the second month uses $\frac{11}{78s}$, etc. This results in a higher payoff amount than most consumers expect.

Note: The formula $\frac{n(n+1)}{2}$ can be used to find the sum of the months. "n" is equal to the number of months of the loan. In a twelve-month loan it would be solved as $\frac{12(12+1)}{2} = 78$

Example 12

Fred Jabcubus borrowed $780 to be repaid in eighteen monthly payments of $47 each. The total to be repaid was $846. At the end of the fifteenth month, Fred inquired about the payoff amount. By using the Rule of 78s the bank indicated the amount to be $138.68. The amount was found as follows:

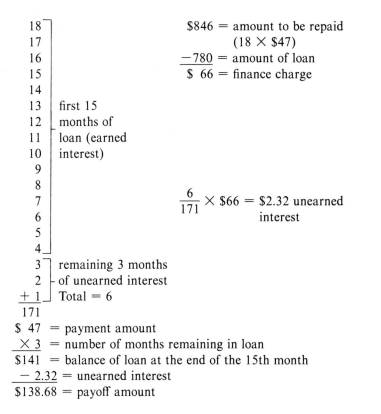

$$
\begin{array}{l}
\$846 = \text{amount to be repaid} \\
\quad\quad (18 \times \$47) \\
-780 = \text{amount of loan} \\
\overline{\$\ 66} = \text{finance charge}
\end{array}
$$

$$\frac{6}{171} \times \$66 = \$2.32 \text{ unearned interest}$$

18, 17, 16, 15, 14, 13, 12, 11, 10, 9, 8, 7, 6, 5, 4 — first 15 months of loan (earned interest)

3, 2, +1 — remaining 3 months of unearned interest — Total = 6

$$
\begin{array}{l}
171 \\
\$\ 47 = \text{payment amount} \\
\underline{\times\ 3} = \text{number of months remaining in loan} \\
\$141 = \text{balance of loan at the end of the 15th month} \\
\underline{-\ 2.32} = \text{unearned interest} \\
\$138.68 = \text{payoff amount}
\end{array}
$$

Computer Applications

It should be realized that even though the calculations in this chapter seem lengthy, they are very easily programmed into a computer. The repayment schedule, as an example, can be developed for the full term of a twenty-five-year loan in a matter of seconds. The computer only needs the principal, interest rate, and payment amount, as well as a simple set of instructions in order to develop the complete repayment schedule.

This task is typical of many business problems that are repetitious and, therefore, easily automated. Other examples of computer applications are depreciation, payroll, compound interest, and monthly billing.

Large firms that have their own computers or a computer service need trained employees to aid in the programming of the computers, while small firms need trained personnel to do the calculations on office calculating machines. Individual consumers need training in the topic of installment contracts in case they purchase or sell property or merchandise on a land contract.

National bank credit cards and retail merchants selling on credit all use a similar installment contract repayment analysis. The variations, though small, are numerous and should be understood by the consumer before authorizing a purchase on credit.

Estimating the Total Interest on an Installment Contract

The Truth-in-Lending Act requires that the total amount of finance charges and the effective annual rate be stated on a loan. In order to compute the total amount of interest on a loan and the amount of the monthly payment, it will be necessary to be able to use the formula below:

$$\text{Estimating Total Interest on an Installment Contract} = \frac{\text{the interest for the first month} \times (\text{the months in the contract} + 1)}{2}$$

This estimating formula is used for short-term installment contracts only.

For installment contracts that have a term of years, use the table on page 224.

Note that this formula is different than the $I = P \times R \times T$ used with single-payment promissory notes.

Example 13

Betty bought her husband two sport coats and a suit for his birthday gift. The merchandise totaled $218. The men's store where the purchase was made requires 20 percent down and charges 11 percent interest. As the store manager, you are asked to determine the amount of monthly payment required to pay the loan off within eight months. The calculations are as follows:

$218 = amount of purchase
$\times$ .20
$ 43.60 = down payment

$218.00
$-$ 43.60
$174.40 = amount to be financed

$$\text{Total interest} = \frac{\$174.40 \times .11 \times \frac{1}{12} \times (8 + 1)}{2}$$

$$= \frac{\$1.60 \times 9}{2} = \$7.20$$

$174.40 = principal
$+$ 7.20 = interest on contract over 8 months
$181.60 = total to be repaid

$181.60 $\div$ 8 payments = $22.70 (monthly payment amount)

Example 14

Sandy Reidda purchased living room furniture for her condominium from Bestway as shown on the following sales slip. She decided to take the credit terms that were offered by store manager Chuck Sale. She will finance the balance at 11 percent for twelve months. What will be the monthly payment amount?

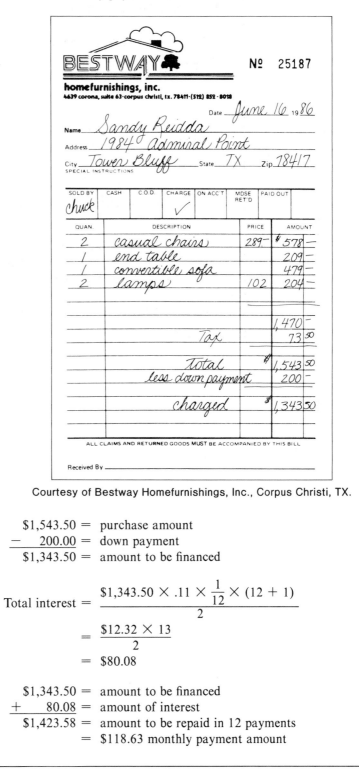

Courtesy of Bestway Homefurnishings, Inc., Corpus Christi, TX.

$1,543.50 = purchase amount
− 200.00 = down payment
$1,343.50 = amount to be financed

$$\text{Total interest} = \frac{\$1,343.50 \times .11 \times \frac{1}{12} \times (12 + 1)}{2}$$

$$= \frac{\$12.32 \times 13}{2}$$

$$= \$80.08$$

$1,343.50 = amount to be financed
+ 80.08 = amount of interest
$1,423.58 = amount to be repaid in 12 payments
= $118.63 monthly payment amount

Assignment

Chapter Eleven

Name _____ Date _____ Score _____

Skill Problems

1. Amount of purchase = $14,900
   Rate of interest = 12%
   Term of loan = 10 years
   Monthly payment = $ _____

2. Amount of purchase = $50,000
   Down payment = $8,000
   Rate of interest = 15%
   Term of loan = 25 years
   Monthly payment = $ _____

3. Amount of purchase = $21,000
   Down payment = $0.00
   Rate of interest = 13%
   Term of loan = 30 years
   Monthly payment = $ _____

4. Amount of purchase = $28,750
   Down payment = $12,000
   Rate of interest = 12%
   Term of loan = 15 years
   Taxes per year = $540
   Insurance for 3 years = $906
   Monthly payment = $ _____ (total)

5. Amount of purchase = $25,000
   Down payment = $8,000
   Rate of interest = 14%
   Term of loan = 15 years
   Taxes per year = $768
   Insurance per year = $261
   Monthly payment = $ _____ (total)

6. Amount of purchase = $8,000
   Rate of interest = 12%
   Monthly payment = $180
   Principal balance after the second monthly payment $ _____

7. Amount of purchase = $8,640
   Rate of interest = 9%
   Monthly payment = $120
   Interest amount for fourth month = $ _____

8. Amount of purchase = $26,000
   Rate of interest = 8%
   Monthly payment = $305
   Principal balance after the third monthly payment = $ _____

9. Amount of purchase = $13,100
   Rate of interest = 16%
   Monthly payment = $260
   Interest for first two months = $ _____

10. Amount of purchase = $26,000
    Rate of interest = 9%
    Monthly payment = $390 (including $106 for escrow account)
    Principal balance after the third monthly payment $ _____

11. Amount borrowed = $4,000
    Interest charges = $1,640.40
    Service charge = $40
    Filing fee = $10
    Term of loan = 48 months
    Annual percentage rate = _____

12. Amount of purchase = $26,000
    Down payment = $0.00
    Rate of interest = 10%
    Monthly payment = $236.34
    Term of loan = _____ years

13. Amount of purchase = $14,700
    Down payment = $3,000
    Monthly payment = $90.32
    Term of loan = 25 years
    Rate of interest = _____

14. Amount of purchase = $380
    Monthly payments = $48
    Amount to be repaid = $384
    8 monthly payments
    Amount of payoff at end of 6th month = $ _____
    (Use Rule of 78s)

15. Amount of purchase = $286
    Rate of interest = $16\frac{1}{2}$%
    Term of loan = 8 months
    Down payment = $36
    Monthly payment = $ _____

1. Sugar's Confectionary will add on to their existing store with a loan from the American State Bank. The loan will be for $31,500. The owner negotiated a 10 percent rate and an amortization over twenty years. What is the payment amount?

2. As cash payments clerk of the Accounting Department, you are asked to develop a repayment schedule on a loan of $22,800. The rate of interest is 12 percent and the loan will run for fifteen years. Taxes on the property are $640 a year. The insurance coverage for a year will be $230. Complete the repayment schedule through the third month.

Repayment Schedule

Payment Number	Payment Amount	Interest Amount	Payment on Principal	Principal Balance
1	_____	_____	_____	_____
2	_____	_____	_____	_____
3	_____	_____	_____	_____

3. The teller of the Mid-State Bank referred a customer to the loan manager to explain the payoff amount on an installment loan for $600. The amount to be repaid was $684 over eight months. The customer has paid four payments and feels that the loan balance should be $328. Using the rule of 78s, determine the correct payoff amount.

4. Marilyn bought a television for $580. She paid $80 down and charged the balance on her credit card. She paid $150 a month until it was paid off. The service charge was $1 \frac{1}{2}$ percent per month. What was the amount of the last payment?

5. In problem 4 what were the finance charges?

6. Alice Baid paid off the mortgage on her home early. The amount of the mortgage was initially $26,000. The balance at the date of payoff was $3,626.80. The mortgage contract stipulated a 1 percent penalty charge on the original amount of the contract for early payoff or payments in excess of 10 percent of the principal. What is the payoff amount?

7. Predmore Associates purchased a piece of land for future development at a price of $46,000. They paid $10,000 down and financed the balance at 15 percent interest. The payments are $600 per month. The land was purchased four months ago. No formal record or repayment schedule has been established to date. As secretary to the Budget Director, you are asked to prepare the figures for this month's interest expense on the loan. What is the interest for the fourth month?

8. Ricardo Perez purchased living room furniture for $860. He paid $150 down and financed the balance through the furniture store credit card at 1 percent interest per month. He paid $200 a month on the loan. What will be the finance charges on the loan?

9. What will be the last monthly payment amount in problem 8?

10. Blanche Olsen selected an apartment condo to purchase. She decided to put down $12,500 as a down payment on the purchase price of $79,500. She will amortize the loan over a period of fifteen years at 11 percent. What will be the principal balance after the second monthly payment?

11. If Banche in problem 10 had elected to take a 10 percent, thirty-year loan with Marlin Mortgage, how much more would it have cost her over the term of the loan?

12. Julie Smith purchased a typewriter on a credit card. The typewriter was priced at $302. She paid $50 down and financed the balance. The credit card stipulated a finance charge of 1 percent plus a flat charge of $2 per month. Her previous balance was $63. What is the balance that she will owe after a $30 payment is made on the balance that includes the typewriter purchase?

13. Lloyd must obtain a mortgage on a home in the amount of $80,000. He has the choice of a 12 percent, thirty-year mortgage, or a 11 percent, twenty-five-year mortgage. What is the difference on the first month's interest?

14. What is the difference in the interest over the term of the mortgage in problem 13?

15. Marin and Associates will build a new home on a piece of land. The finished home will sell for $84,900. A loan company will finance 90 percent of the value of the home. If a buyer finances the 90 percent at 13 percent interest over a twenty-year period, what will be the amount of interest for the first month?

Challenge Problem   The accountant for the Vilper Corporation must determine the principal balance for a loan negotiated six months ago on a piece of property. The property purchase price was $24,000. The rate of interest on the loan was 9 percent. The payment amount of $263 per month will pay off the loan and the $300 tax bill per year. The vacant land required a down payment of $6,000 before the bank would finance the loan. A penalty charge of 1 percent on the balance of the loan was agreed upon by Vilper should they decide to pay off the loan early. What is the principal balance?

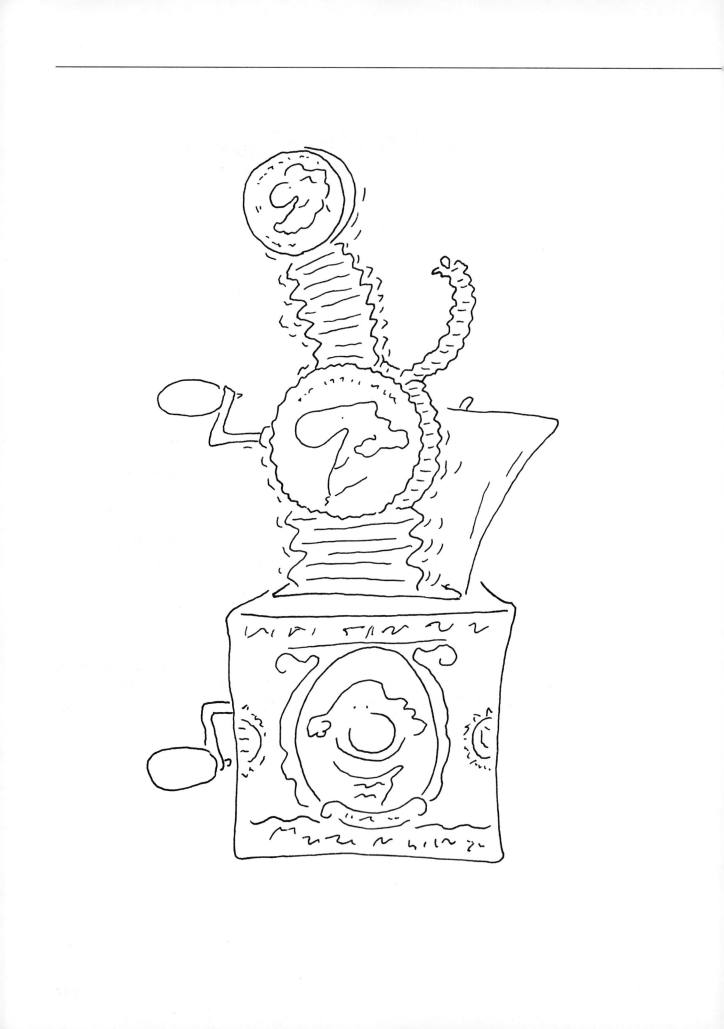

12 Compound Interest and Present Value

Performance Objectives

After mastering the material in this chapter, you will be able to:

1. Compute the balance on a savings account.
2. Compute the compounded amount in an investment problem using compound interest tables.
3. Compute the present value in an investment problem using present value tables.
4. Compute the cash value of two types of annuities in an investment problem using an annuity table.
5. Determine the payment amount in a sinking fund problem.
6. Understand and use the following terms and concepts:

Compound Interest	Ordinary Annuity
Compounded Amount	Annuity Due
Present Value	Sinking Fund
Annuity	

Compound Interest

Compound interest is another way the chapter on Simple Interest can be applied to solve business problems. The math procedure is only slightly different, but the results are dramatically different. To calculate **compound interest** the interest from the previous period becomes part of the new principal amount; that is, the interest is added to the principal before the interest for the next period is calculated.

Example 1

An example will help illustrate the dramatic affect that compounding has on the principal. Under three sets of circumstances, $1,000 invested at 4 percent for a year will show a difference in the amount returned to the investor, termed the **compounded amount.**

$1,000 at 4% simple interest

Interest = $40 = $1,000 × .04 × 1

$$\begin{array}{ll} \$ \quad 40 & - \text{ interest} \\ +1,000 & - \text{ principal} \\ \hline \$1,040 & = \text{ return to investor} \end{array}$$

$1,000 at 4% interest compounded semiannually

$$\begin{array}{l} \text{Int} = \$20.00 = \$1,000 \times .04 \times \frac{1}{2} \text{ (first six months)} \\ \qquad\qquad\quad \underline{+\ 20} \end{array}$$

$$\begin{array}{l} \text{Int} = \$20.40 = \$1,020 \times .04 \times \frac{1}{2} \text{ (second six months)} \\ \qquad\qquad\quad \underline{+\ 20.40} \\ \qquad\qquad\quad \$1,040.40 = \text{ return to investor (compounded amount)} \end{array}$$

$1,000 at 4% interest compounded quarterly

$$\text{Int} = \$10.00 = \$1,000 \times .04 \times \frac{1}{4} \text{ (first three months)}$$

$$\underline{+\ 10.}$$
$$\text{Int} = \$10.10 = \$1,010. \times .04 \times \frac{1}{4} \text{ (second three months)}$$

$$\underline{+\ 10.10}$$
$$\text{Int} = \$10.20 = \$1,020.10 \times .04 \times \frac{1}{4} \text{ (third three months)}$$

$$\underline{+\ 10.20}$$
$$\text{Int} = \$10.30 = \$1,030.30 \times .04 \times \frac{1}{4} \text{ (fourth three months)}$$

$$\underline{+\ 10.30}$$
$$\$1,040.60 = \text{ return to investor (compounded amount)}$$

In this first-year period the investor has earned an additional 40 cents by selecting an opportunity to invest at 4 percent compounded semiannually as opposed to 4 percent at simple interest. The investor would receive 60 cents more by compounding quarterly rather than using simple interest. Notice that the more frequently the principal is compounded a year, the greater the return or compounded amount. Notice also that the increase in interest earnings from compounding twice a year to 4 times a year is not as great as simple interest to compounding twice a year. The amount of increase in interest earnings declines as the principal is compounded more frequently.

Savings Accounts   Often banks, savings and loan associations, and credit unions indicate monthly or even daily interest. The computer has made such frequent compoundings fast and inexpensive to these firms. The resulting additional return to the investor is small compared to the return from compounding semiannually or quarterly.

Use of Tables   This type of problem is repetitive and, therefore, open to a shortcut. Tables have been developed to reduce the number of these calculations.

Example 2

An investment of $600 at 4 percent compounded semiannually for a period of five years can be calculated as follows using the table.
Interest = $600 (principal) × 4 percent interest (annual rate)

$$\times \frac{1}{2} \text{ (compounded semiannually)}$$

Consider for a moment only the rate and time factors in the above formula.

R × T

$$4\% \times \frac{1}{2} = \overset{2\%}{\cancel{4\%}} \times \frac{1}{\underset{1}{\cancel{2}}}$$

The reduced factors indicate that the investment is actually compounded 2 percent each six-month period. Therefore, the effective rate of interest is 2 percent per period for the ten six-month periods of the five-year investment. By using the effective rate of 2 percent (across top) and the ten periods (along the edge) that the investment is to be compounded in the compound interest table, a factor of 1.21899442 can be found. This factor is the amount returned to the investor for each dollar invested. In the example $600 was invested.

$600   = investment
×1.21899442   = factor/$1.00
$731.40   = returned to investor (compounded amount)

Note: If you are using a calculator, enter the maximum number of digits possible.

Example 3

Let's check our answer in the first example of an investment of $1,000 at 4 percent compounded quarterly.

R × T   1%

$$4\% \times \frac{1}{4} \qquad = \overset{1\%}{\cancel{4\%}} \times \frac{1}{\underset{1}{\cancel{4}}}$$

One percent is the effective rate for the four quarter periods in one year. Using the table, 1 percent (across top) and four periods (along the edge) show a factor equal to 1.04060401 for each dollar invested.

$1,000   = investment
×1.04060401   = factor/$1.00
$1,040.60   = returned to investor (compounded amount)

Compound Interest

Periods	¾%	1%	1½%	2%	2½%	3%	3½%	4%	4½%	5%	5½%	6%	7%
1	1.00750000	1.01000000	1.01500000	1.02000000	1.02500000	1.03000000	1.03500000	1.04000000	1.04500000	1.05000000	1.05500000	1.06000000	1.07000000
2	1.01505625	1.02010000	1.03022500	1.04040000	1.05062500	1.06090000	1.07122500	1.08160000	1.09202500	1.10250000	1.11302500	1.12360000	1.14490000
3	1.02266917	1.03030100	1.04567837	1.06120800	1.07689062	1.09272700	1.10871788	1.12486400	1.14116612	1.15762500	1.17424137	1.19101600	1.22504300
4	1.03033919	1.04060401	1.06136355	1.08243216	1.10381289	1.12550881	1.14752300	1.16985856	1.19251860	1.21550625	1.23882465	1.26247696	1.31079601
5	1.03806673	1.05101005	1.07728400	1.10408080	1.13140821	1.15927407	1.18768631	1.21665290	1.24618194	1.27628156	1.30696001	1.33822558	1.40255173
6	1.04585224	1.06152015	1.09344326	1.12616242	1.15969342	1.19405230	1.22925533	1.26531902	1.30226012	1.34009564	1.37884281	1.41851911	1.50073035
7	1.05369613	1.07213535	1.10984491	1.14868567	1.18868575	1.22987387	1.27227926	1.31593178	1.36086183	1.40710042	1.45467916	1.50363026	1.60578148
8	1.06159885	1.08285671	1.12649259	1.17165938	1.21840290	1.26677008	1.31680904	1.36856905	1.42210061	1.47745544	1.53468651	1.59384807	1.71818618
9	1.06956084	1.09368527	1.14338998	1.19509257	1.24886297	1.30477318	1.36289735	1.42331181	1.48609514	1.55132822	1.61909427	1.68947896	1.83845921
10	1.07758255	1.10462213	1.16054083	1.21899442	1.28008454	1.34391638	1.41059876	1.48024428	1.55296942	1.62889463	1.70814446	1.79084770	1.96715136
11	1.08566441	1.11566835	1.17794894	1.24337431	1.31208666	1.38423387	1.45996972	1.53945406	1.62285305	1.71033936	1.80209240	1.89829856	2.10485195
12	1.09380690	1.12682503	1.19561817	1.26824179	1.34488882	1.42576089	1.51106866	1.60103222	1.69588143	1.79585633	1.90120749	2.01219647	2.25219159
13	1.10201045	1.13809328	1.21355244	1.29360663	1.37851104	1.46853371	1.56395606	1.66507351	1.77219610	1.88564914	2.00577390	2.13292826	2.40984500
14	1.11027553	1.14947421	1.23175573	1.31947876	1.41297382	1.51258972	1.61869452	1.73167645	1.85194492	1.97993160	2.11609146	2.26090396	2.57853415
15	1.11860259	1.16096896	1.25023207	1.34586834	1.44829817	1.55796742	1.67534883	1.80094351	1.93528244	2.07892818	2.23247649	2.39655819	2.75903154
16	1.12699211	1.17257864	1.26898555	1.37278571	1.48450562	1.60470644	1.73398604	1.87298125	2.02237015	2.18287459	2.35526270	2.54035168	2.95216375
17	1.13544455	1.18430443	1.28802033	1.40024142	1.52161826	1.65284763	1.79467555	1.94790050	2.11337681	2.29201832	2.48480215	2.69277279	3.15881521
18	1.14396039	1.19614748	1.30734064	1.42824625	1.55965872	1.70243306	1.85748920	2.02581652	2.20847877	2.40661923	2.62146627	2.85433915	3.37993228
19	1.15254009	1.20810895	1.32695075	1.45681117	1.59865019	1.75350605	1.92250132	2.10684918	2.30786031	2.52695020	2.76564691	3.02559950	3.61652754
20	1.16118414	1.22019004	1.34685501	1.48594740	1.63861644	1.80611123	1.98978886	2.19112314	2.41177402	2.65329771	2.91775749	3.20713547	3.86968446
21	1.16989302	1.23239194	1.36705783	1.51566634	1.67958185	1.86029457	2.05943147	2.27876807	2.52024116	2.78596259	3.07823415	3.39956360	4.14056237
22	1.17866722	1.24471586	1.38756370	1.54597967	1.72157140	1.91610341	2.13151158	2.36991879	2.63365201	2.92526072	3.24753703	3.60353742	4.43040174
23	1.18750723	1.25716302	1.40837715	1.57689926	1.76461068	1.97358651	2.20611448	2.46471554	2.75216635	3.07152376	3.42615157	3.81974966	4.74052986
24	1.19641353	1.26973465	1.42950281	1.60843725	1.80872595	2.03279411	2.28332849	2.56330416	2.87601383	3.22509994	3.61458990	4.04933464	5.07236695
30	1.25127176	1.34784892	1.56308022	1.81136158	2.09756758	2.42726247	2.80679370	3.24339751	3.74531813	4.32194238	4.98395129	5.74349117	7.61225504

Compound Interest

Periods	8%	9%	10%	11%	12%	13%	14%	15%	16%	17%	18%	19%	20%
1	1.08000000	1.09000000	1.10000000	1.11000000	1.12000000	1.13000000	1.14000000	1.15000000	1.16000000	1.17000000	1.18000000	1.19000000	1.20000000
2	1.16640000	1.18810000	1.21000000	1.23210000	1.25440000	1.27690000	1.29960000	1.32250000	1.34560000	1.36890000	1.39240000	1.41610000	1.44000000
3	1.25971200	1.29502900	1.33100000	1.36763100	1.40492800	1.44289700	1.48154400	1.52087500	1.56089600	1.60161300	1.64303200	1.68515900	1.72800000
4	1.36048896	1.41158161	1.46410000	1.51807041	1.57351936	1.63047361	1.68896016	1.74900625	1.81063936	1.87388721	1.93877776	2.00533921	2.07360000
5	1.46932808	1.53862395	1.61051000	1.68505816	1.76234168	1.84243518	1.92541458	2.01135719	2.10034166	2.19244804	2.28775776	2.38635366	2.48832000
6	1.58687432	1.67710011	1.77156100	1.87041455	1.97382269	2.08195175	2.19497262	2.31306077	2.43639632	2.56516420	2.69955415	2.83976086	2.98598400
7	1.71382427	1.82803912	1.94871710	2.07616015	2.21068141	2.35260548	2.50226879	2.66001988	2.82621973	3.00124212	3.18547390	3.37931542	3.58318080
8	1.85093021	1.99256264	2.14358881	2.30453777	2.47596318	2.65844419	2.85258642	3.05902286	3.27841489	3.51145328	3.75885920	4.02138535	4.29981696
9	1.99900463	2.17189328	2.35794769	2.55803692	2.77307876	3.00404194	3.25194852	3.51787629	3.80296127	4.10840033	4.43545386	4.78544856	5.15978035
10	2.15892500	2.36736367	2.59374246	2.83942099	3.10584821	3.39456739	3.70722131	4.04555774	4.41143508	4.80682839	5.23383555	5.69468379	6.19173642
11	2.33163900	2.58042641	2.85311671	3.15175729	3.47854999	3.83586115	4.22623230	4.65239140	5.11726469	5.62398922	6.17592595	6.77667371	7.43008371
12	2.51817012	2.81266478	3.13842838	3.49845060	3.89597599	4.33452310	4.81790482	5.35025011	5.93602704	6.58006738	7.28759263	8.06424172	8.91610045
13	2.71962373	3.06580461	3.45227121	3.88328016	4.36349311	4.89801110	5.49241149	6.15278762	6.88579137	7.69867884	8.59935930	9.59644764	10.69932054
14	2.93719362	3.34172703	3.79749834	4.31044098	4.88711229	5.53475255	6.26134910	7.07570576	7.98751799	9.00745424	10.14724397	11.41977269	12.83918465
15	3.17216911	3.64248246	4.17724817	4.78458949	5.47356576	6.25427038	7.13793798	8.13706163	9.26552087	10.53872146	11.97374789	13.58952950	15.40702157
16	3.42594264	3.97030588	4.59497299	5.31089433	6.13039365	7.06732553	8.13724930	9.35762087	10.74800420	12.33030411	14.12902251	16.17154011	18.48842589
17	3.70001805	4.32763341	5.05447028	5.89509271	6.86604089	7.98607785	9.27646420	10.76126400	12.46768488	14.42645581	16.67224656	19.24413273	22.18611107
18	3.99601950	4.71712042	5.55991731	6.54355291	7.68996580	9.02426797	10.57516918	12.37545361	14.46251446	16.87895329	19.67325094	22.90051795	26.62333328
19	4.31570106	5.14166125	6.11590904	7.26334373	8.61276169	10.19742280	12.05566287	14.23177165	16.77651677	19.74837535	23.21443611	27.25161636	31.94799994
20	4.66095714	5.60441077	6.72749995	8.06231154	9.64629309	11.52308776	13.74348987	16.36653739	19.46075945	23.10559916	27.39303460	32.42942347	38.33759992
21	5.03383372	6.10880774	7.40024994	8.94916581	10.80384826	13.02108917	15.66757845	18.82151800	22.57448097	27.03355102	32.32378083	38.59101393	46.00511991
22	5.43654041	6.65860043	8.14027494	9.93357404	12.10031006	14.71383077	17.86103944	21.64744570	26.18639792	31.62925470	38.14206138	45.92330658	55.20614389
23	5.87146365	7.25787447	8.95430243	11.02662719	13.55234726	16.62662897	20.36158496	24.89145756	30.37622159	37.00622799	45.00763243	54.64873482	66.24737267
24	6.34118074	7.91108317	9.84973268	12.23915658	15.17862893	18.78809051	23.21220685	28.62517619	35.23641704	43.29728675	53.10900627	65.03199444	79.49684720
30	10.06265689	13.26768847	17.44940227	22.89229657	29.95992212	39.11589796	50.95015858	66.21177196	85.84987691	111.06465001	143.37063844	184.67531215	237.37631380

Exercise A   Complete the following problems to find the compounded amount.

	Amount Invested	Annual Interest Rate	Term of Investment (years)	Compound Frequency	Compounded Amount
1.	$ 1,400	5%	5 2.5%	Semi.(10)	$ 1,792.12
2.	4,000	5	12 6%	Semi.(24)	
3.	5,500	4	8 2%	Semi.(16)	
4.	8,950	4	4 1%	Qtr. (16)	
5.	20,000	4	20 4%	Annual (20)	
6.	7,500	3	5 1.5%	Semi. (10)	
7.	19,500	6	$5\frac{1}{2}$ 1.5%	Qtr. (22)	
8.	5,000	4	6 1%	Qtr. (24)	
9.	5,000	5	18 5%	Annual (20)	
10.	9,000	4	9 2%	Semi. (18)	

Present Value   Money has a "time value." That is, a given amount of money can be invested today with the expectation that it will be worth more in the future. That was just proven in Exercise A. An opposite question could also be asked. "What is the current value of an amount of money to be received at some date in the future?" The current value of the future amount is termed its **present value.** Present value is the exact opposite of compound interest. We are asking what amount of money today will be equal to the amount to be received in the future if an investment can be made with the amount received today.

Example 4

Acrodin, Incorporated, will receive the sum $15,600 three years from this date. The treasurer realizes that money can safely be invested at a 8 percent annual interest rate compounded semiannually. What is the equivalent amount (present value) of $15,600 to be received three years from today?

The present value table will aid in the solution to the example problem in very much the same way as did the compound interest table.

Present Value of 1

Periods	¾%	1%	1½%	2%	2½%	3%	3½%	4%	4½%	5%	5½%	6%	7%
1	0.99255583	0.99009901	0.98522167	0.98039216	0.97560976	0.97087379	0.96618357	0.96153846	0.95693780	0.95238095	0.94786730	0.94339623	0.93457944
2	0.98516708	0.98029605	0.97066175	0.96116878	0.95181440	0.94259591	0.93351070	0.92455621	0.91572995	0.90702948	0.89845242	0.88999644	0.87343873
3	0.97783333	0.97059015	0.95631699	0.94232233	0.92859941	0.91514166	0.90194271	0.88899636	0.87629660	0.86383760	0.85161366	0.83961928	0.81629788
4	0.97055417	0.96098034	0.94218423	0.92384543	0.90595064	0.88848705	0.87144223	0.85480419	0.83856134	0.82270247	0.80721674	0.79209366	0.76289521
5	0.96332920	0.95146569	0.92826033	0.90573081	0.88385429	0.86260878	0.84197317	0.82192711	0.80245105	0.78352617	0.76513435	0.74725817	0.71298618
6	0.95615802	0.94204524	0.91454219	0.88797138	0.86229687	0.83748426	0.81350064	0.79031453	0.76789574	0.74621540	0.72524583	0.70496054	0.66634222
7	0.94904022	0.93271805	0.90102679	0.87056018	0.84126524	0.81309151	0.78599096	0.75991781	0.73482846	0.71068133	0.68743681	0.66505711	0.62274974
8	0.94197540	0.92348322	0.88771112	0.85349037	0.82074657	0.78940923	0.75941156	0.73069021	0.70318513	0.67683936	0.65159887	0.62741237	0.58200910
9	0.93496318	0.91433982	0.87459224	0.83675527	0.80072836	0.76641673	0.73373097	0.70258674	0.67290443	0.64460892	0.61762926	0.59189846	0.54393374
10	0.92800315	0.90528695	0.86166723	0.82034830	0.78119840	0.74409391	0.70891881	0.67556417	0.64392768	0.61391325	0.58543058	0.55839478	0.50834929
11	0.92109494	0.89632372	0.84893323	0.80426304	0.76214478	0.72242128	0.68494571	0.64958093	0.61619874	0.58467929	0.55491050	0.52678753	0.47509280
12	0.91423815	0.88744923	0.83638742	0.78849318	0.74355589	0.70137988	0.66178330	0.62459705	0.58966386	0.55683742	0.52598152	0.49696936	0.44401196
13	0.90743241	0.87866260	0.82402702	0.77303253	0.72542038	0.68095134	0.63940415	0.60057409	0.56427164	0.53032135	0.49856068	0.46883902	0.41496445
14	0.90067733	0.86996297	0.81184928	0.75787502	0.70772720	0.66111781	0.61778179	0.57747508	0.53997286	0.50506795	0.47256937	0.44230096	0.38781724
15	0.89397254	0.86134947	0.79985150	0.74301473	0.69046556	0.64186195	0.59689062	0.55526450	0.51672044	0.48101710	0.44793305	0.41726506	0.36244602
16	0.88731766	0.85282126	0.78803104	0.72844581	0.67362493	0.62316694	0.57670591	0.53390818	0.49446932	0.45811152	0.42458109	0.39364628	0.33873460
17	0.88071231	0.84437749	0.77638526	0.71416256	0.65719506	0.60501645	0.55720378	0.51337325	0.47317639	0.43629669	0.40244653	0.37136442	0.31657439
18	0.87415614	0.83601731	0.76491159	0.70015937	0.64116591	0.58739461	0.53836114	0.49362812	0.45280037	0.41552065	0.38146590	0.35034379	0.29586392
19	0.86764878	0.82773992	0.75360747	0.68643076	0.62552772	0.57028603	0.52015569	0.47464242	0.43330179	0.39573396	0.36157906	0.33051301	0.27650833
20	0.86118985	0.81954447	0.74247042	0.67297133	0.61027094	0.55367575	0.50256588	0.45638695	0.41464286	0.37688948	0.34272896	0.31180473	0.25841900
21	0.85477901	0.81143017	0.73149795	0.65977582	0.59538629	0.53754928	0.48557090	0.43883360	0.39678743	0.35894236	0.32486158	0.29415540	0.24151309
22	0.84841589	0.80339621	0.72068763	0.64683904	0.58086467	0.52189250	0.46915063	0.42195539	0.37970089	0.34184987	0.30792567	0.27750510	0.22571317
23	0.84210014	0.79544179	0.71003708	0.63415592	0.56669724	0.50669175	0.45328563	0.40572633	0.36335013	0.32557131	0.29187267	0.26179726	0.21094688
24	0.83583140	0.78756613	0.69954392	0.62172149	0.55287535	0.49193374	0.43795713	0.39012147	0.34770347	0.31006791	0.27665656	0.24697855	0.19714662
30	0.79918690	0.74192292	0.63976243	0.55207089	0.47674269	0.41198676	0.35627841	0.30831867	0.26700002	0.23137745	0.20064402	0.17411013	0.13136712

Present Value of 1

Periods	8%	9%	10%	11%	12%	13%	14%	15%	16%	17%	18%	19%	20%
1	0.92592593	0.91743119	0.90909091	0.90090090	0.89285714	0.88495575	0.87719298	0.86956522	0.86206897	0.85470085	0.84745763	0.84033613	0.83333333
2	0.85733882	0.84167999	0.82644628	0.81162243	0.79719388	0.78314668	0.76946753	0.75614367	0.74316290	0.73051355	0.71818443	0.70616482	0.69444444
3	0.79383224	0.77218348	0.75131480	0.73119138	0.71178025	0.69305016	0.67497152	0.65751623	0.64065767	0.62437056	0.60863087	0.59341581	0.57870370
4	0.73502985	0.70842521	0.68301346	0.65873097	0.63551808	0.61331873	0.59208028	0.57175325	0.55229110	0.53365005	0.51578888	0.49866875	0.48225309
5	0.68058320	0.64993139	0.62092132	0.59345133	0.56742686	0.54275994	0.51936866	0.49717674	0.47611302	0.45611115	0.43710922	0.41904937	0.40187757
6	0.63016963	0.59626733	0.56447393	0.53464084	0.50663112	0.48031853	0.45558655	0.43232760	0.41044225	0.38983859	0.37043154	0.35214233	0.33489798
7	0.58349040	0.54703424	0.51315812	0.48165841	0.45234922	0.42506064	0.39963732	0.37593704	0.35382953	0.33319538	0.31392503	0.29591792	0.27908165
8	0.54026888	0.50186628	0.46650738	0.43392650	0.40388323	0.37615986	0.35055905	0.32690177	0.30502546	0.28478237	0.26603816	0.24867052	0.23256804
9	0.50024897	0.46042778	0.42409762	0.39092477	0.36061002	0.33288483	0.30750794	0.28426241	0.26295298	0.24340374	0.22545607	0.20896683	0.19380670
10	0.46319349	0.42241081	0.38554329	0.35218448	0.32197324	0.29458835	0.26974381	0.24718471	0.22668360	0.20803738	0.19106447	0.17560238	0.16150558
11	0.42888286	0.38753285	0.35049390	0.31728331	0.28747610	0.26069765	0.23661738	0.21494322	0.19541690	0.17780973	0.16191904	0.14756502	0.13458799
12	0.39711376	0.35553473	0.31863082	0.28584082	0.25667509	0.23070589	0.20755910	0.18690715	0.16846284	0.15197413	0.13721953	0.12400422	0.11215665
13	0.36769792	0.32617865	0.28966438	0.25751426	0.22917419	0.20416450	0.18206939	0.16252796	0.14522659	0.12989242	0.11628773	0.10420523	0.09346388
14	0.34046104	0.29924647	0.26333125	0.23199482	0.20461981	0.18067655	0.15970999	0.14132866	0.12519534	0.11101916	0.09854893	0.08756742	0.07788657
15	0.31524170	0.27453804	0.23939205	0.20900435	0.18269626	0.15989075	0.14009648	0.12289449	0.10792701	0.09488817	0.08351604	0.07358606	0.06490547
16	0.29189047	0.25186976	0.21762914	0.18829220	0.16312166	0.14149624	0.12289165	0.10686477	0.09304053	0.08110100	0.07077630	0.06183703	0.05408789
17	0.27026895	0.23107318	0.19784467	0.16963262	0.14564434	0.12521791	0.10779969	0.09292589	0.08020735	0.06931709	0.05997992	0.05196389	0.04507324
18	0.25024903	0.21199374	0.17985879	0.15282218	0.13003959	0.11081231	0.09456113	0.08080512	0.06914427	0.05924538	0.05083044	0.04366713	0.03756104
19	0.23171206	0.19448967	0.16350799	0.13767764	0.11610678	0.09806399	0.08294836	0.07026532	0.05960713	0.05063708	0.04307664	0.03669507	0.03130086
20	0.21454821	0.17843089	0.14864363	0.12403391	0.10366677	0.08678229	0.07276172	0.06110028	0.05138546	0.04327955	0.03650563	0.03083619	0.02608405
21	0.19865575	0.16369806	0.13513057	0.11174226	0.09255961	0.07679849	0.06382607	0.05313068	0.04429781	0.03699107	0.03093698	0.02591277	0.02173671
22	0.18390451	0.15018171	0.12284597	0.10066870	0.08264251	0.06796327	0.05598778	0.04620059	0.03818776	0.03161630	0.02621778	0.02177544	0.01811393
23	0.17031528	0.13778139	0.11167816	0.09069252	0.07378796	0.06014448	0.04911209	0.04017443	0.03292049	0.02702248	0.02221845	0.01829869	0.01509494
24	0.15769934	0.12640494	0.10152560	0.08170498	0.06588210	0.05322521	0.04308078	0.03493428	0.02837973	0.02309614	0.01882920	0.01537705	0.01257912
30	0.09937733	0.07537114	0.05730855	0.04368282	0.03337792	0.02556505	0.01962702	0.01510305	0.01164824	0.00900376	0.00697493	0.00541491	0.00421272

$$R \times T \qquad 4\%$$
$$4\% \times \frac{1}{2} = \quad \cancel{8}\%^{4} \times \frac{1}{\cancel{2}_{1}}$$

The effective rate for the six six-month periods is 4 percent. Using the present value table, 4 percent (across top) and six periods (along edge) gives a factor of .79031453.

$15,600	= expected sum
×.79031453	= factor/$1.00
$12,328.91	= present value

This means that $12,328.91 received today is equal to $15,600 received three years from now if the $12,328.91 can be invested at 4 percent compounded semiannually. This can be checked by using the compound interest table.

$$\$12,328.91 \times 1.26531902 \text{ (4 percent, six periods)} = \$15,600$$

Example 5

What is the present value of $2,680 to be received five years from today if an investment can be made at 6 percent compounded quarterly?

$$R \times T \qquad 1\frac{1}{2}\%$$
$$6\% \times \frac{1}{4} \quad = \quad \cancel{6}\%^{1\frac{1}{2}} \times \frac{1}{\cancel{4}_{1}}$$

The effective rate for twenty periods is $1\frac{1}{2}$ percent. Using the table, the factor equals .74247042.

$2,680	= expected sum
×.74247042	= factor/$1
$1,989.82	= present value

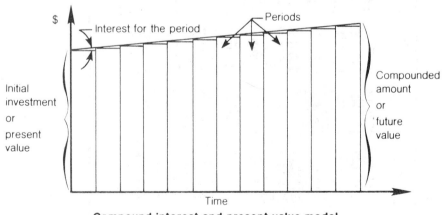

Compound interest and present value model

Exercise B

Complete the following problems to find the present value.

Investment Opportunity

	Expected Sum	Annual Interest Rate	Compound Frequency	Term before Receipt	Present Value
1.	$ 1,600	4% 2%.	Semi.	4 years (8)	$ 1,365.58
2.	2,000	6	Qtr.	3	
3.	5,000	5 2,5	Semi.	5 (10)	3905.99
4.	2,800	9	Annually	7	
5.	1,000	8 4%.	Semi.	6 (12)	624.60
6.	16,000	6	Semi.	8	
7.	6,000	5 2.5%.	Semi.	2 (4)	5435.70
8.	8,500	10	Qtr.	$3\frac{1}{2}$	
9.	10,000	5 2,5	Semi.	8 (6)	6736.25
10.	12,500	4	Semi.	$5\frac{1}{2}$	

Annuities

An annuity is very similar to the concept of compound interest. Money invested over a period of time accumulates interest at a compound rate on the investment. The important difference is that the **annuity** has a series of investments, usually of an equal amount and at regular intervals. The value of an annuity will grow at the stated compound rate and the amount of regular investment.

Annuities are used by business, religious, and financial firms to save money to pay off a bond issue, large note, or a piece of property. Individuals use annuities to save money for their children's education, for a planned trip, or for retirement. An annuity can be purchased from an insurance agent or securities broker.

There are two types of annuities. An Annuity Certain is the type in which the number of payments is stated in the annuity agreement. A Contingent Annuity is open-ended and can include as many payments as the investor chooses to make.

Ordinary annuity
Annunity due

The point at which the payment is made in the time period further classifies an annuity. In an **ordinary annuity** the payment is made at the end of the period. In an **annuity due** the payment is made at the beginning of the period. This can make a difference of one period of interest when using the annuity table.

Ordinary Annuity   An annuity can be calculated over a four-year period at 4 percent as is shown in Example 6.

Example 6

An ordinary annuity for $200 at 4 percent for four years will result in what amount or cash value?

Investment	End of First Year Value	End of Second Year Value	End of Third Year Value	End of Fourth Year Value
1 = $200	(no interest) $200			
2 = $200		$200 × 1.04 = $208 (no interest) + 200 $408		
3 = $200			$408 × 1.04 = $424.32 (no interest) + 200.00 $624.32	
4 = $200				$624.32 × 1.04 = $649.29 (no interest) + 200.00 $849.29 (Cash Value)

Growth of an Annuity   The compound interest table can be used to compute the same cash value.

Investment
1—$200 invested for 3 years
   at 4% compounded annually = 1.12486400 (factor)
2—$200 invested for 2 years
   at 4% compounded annually = 1.08160000 (factor)
3—$200 invested for 1 year
   at 4% compounded annually = 1.04000000 (factor)
4—$200 invested for 0 years
   at 4% compounded annually = <u>1.00000000</u> (factor)
                               4.24646400 = factor or
                                            return/$1

$200   = payment
<u>×4.24646400</u> = factor or return/$1
$849.29   = cash value

The ordinary annuity table simplifies the problem as in the compound interest and present value problems.

The effective interest rate (across top) of 4 percent and four periods (along the edge) gives you a factor of 4.24646400.

Annuity

Periods	¾%	1%	1½%	2%	2½%	3%	3½%	4%	4½%	5%	5½%	6%	7%
1	1.00000000	1.00000000	1.00000000	1.00000000	1.00000000	1.00000000	1.00000000	1.00000000	1.00000000	1.00000000	1.00000000	1.00000000	1.00000000
2	2.00750000	2.01000000	2.01500000	2.02000000	2.02500000	2.03000000	2.03500000	2.04000000	2.04500000	2.05000000	2.05500000	2.06000000	2.07000000
3	3.02255625	3.03010000	3.04522500	3.06040000	3.07562500	3.09090000	3.10622500	3.12160000	3.13702500	3.15250000	3.16802500	3.18360000	3.21490000
4	4.04522542	4.06040100	4.09090338	4.12160800	4.15251563	4.18362700	4.21494287	4.24646400	4.27819112	4.31012500	4.34226638	4.37461600	4.43994300
5	5.07556461	5.10100501	5.15226693	5.20404016	5.25633852	5.30913581	5.36246588	5.41632256	5.47070973	5.52563125	5.58109103	5.63709296	5.75073901
6	6.11363135	6.15201506	6.22955093	6.30812096	6.38773673	6.46840988	6.55015218	6.63297546	6.71689166	6.80191281	6.88805103	6.97531854	7.15329074
7	7.15948358	7.21353521	7.32299419	7.43428338	7.54743015	7.66246218	7.77940751	7.89829448	8.01915179	8.14200845	8.26689384	8.39383765	8.65402109
8	8.21317971	8.28567056	8.43283911	8.58296905	8.73611590	8.89233605	9.05168677	9.21422626	9.38001362	9.54910888	9.72157300	9.89746791	10.25980257
9	9.27477856	9.36852727	9.55933169	9.75462843	9.95451880	10.15910613	10.36849581	10.58279531	10.80211423	11.02656432	11.25625951	11.49131598	11.97798875
10	10.34433940	10.46221254	10.70272167	10.94972100	11.20338177	11.46387931	11.73139316	12.00610712	12.28820937	12.57789254	12.87535379	13.18079494	13.81644796
11	11.42192194	11.56683467	11.86326249	12.16871542	12.48346631	12.80779569	13.14199192	13.48635141	13.84117879	14.20678716	14.58349825	14.97164264	15.78359932
12	12.50758636	12.68250301	13.04121143	13.41208973	13.79555297	14.19202956	14.60196164	15.02580546	15.46403184	15.91712652	16.38559065	16.86994120	17.88845127
13	13.60139325	13.80932804	14.23682960	14.68033152	15.14044179	15.61779045	16.11303030	16.62683768	17.15991327	17.71298285	18.28679814	18.88213767	20.14064286
14	14.70340370	14.94742132	15.45038205	15.97393815	16.51895284	17.08632416	17.67698636	18.29191119	18.93210937	19.59863199	20.29257203	21.01506593	22.55048786
15	15.81367923	16.09689554	16.68213778	17.29341692	17.93192666	18.59891389	19.29586088	20.02358764	20.78405429	21.57856359	22.40866350	23.27596988	25.12902201
16	16.93228183	17.25786449	17.93236984	18.63928525	19.38022483	20.15688130	20.97102971	21.82453114	22.71933673	23.65749177	24.64113999	25.67252808	27.88805355
17	18.05927394	18.43044314	19.20135539	20.01207096	20.86473045	21.76158774	22.70501575	23.69751239	24.74170689	25.84036636	26.99640269	28.21287976	30.84021730
18	19.19471849	19.61474757	20.48933572	21.41231238	22.38634871	23.41443537	24.49969130	25.64541288	26.85508370	28.13238467	29.48120483	30.90565255	33.99903251
19	20.33867888	20.81089504	21.79671636	22.84055863	23.94600743	25.11686844	26.35718050	27.67122940	29.06356246	30.53900391	32.10267110	33.75999170	37.37896479
20	21.49121897	22.01900399	23.12366710	24.29736980	25.54465761	26.87037449	28.27968181	29.77807858	31.37142277	33.06595410	34.86831801	36.78559120	40.99549232
21	22.65240312	23.23919403	24.47052211	25.78331719	27.18327405	28.67648572	30.26947068	31.96920172	33.78313680	35.71925181	37.78607550	39.99272668	44.86517678
22	23.82229614	24.47158598	25.83757994	27.29898354	28.86285590	30.53678030	32.32890215	34.24796979	36.30337795	38.50521440	40.86430965	43.39229028	49.00573916
23	25.00096336	25.71630183	27.22514364	28.84496321	30.58442730	32.45288370	34.46041373	36.61788858	38.93702996	41.43047512	44.11184669	46.99582769	53.43614090
24	26.18847059	26.97346485	28.63352080	30.42186247	32.34903798	34.42647022	36.66652821	39.08260412	41.68919631	44.50199887	47.53799825	50.81557735	58.17667076
25	27.38488412	28.24319950	30.06302361	32.03029972	34.15776393	36.45926432	38.94985669	41.64590829	44.56521015	47.72709882	51.15258816	54.86451200	63.24903772
26	28.59027075	29.52563150	31.51396896	33.67090572	36.01170803	38.55304225	41.31310168	44.31174462	47.57064460	51.11345376	54.96598051	59.15638272	68.67647036
27	29.80469778	30.82088781	32.98667850	35.34432383	37.91200073	40.70963352	43.75906024	47.08421440	50.71132361	54.66912645	58.98910943	63.70576568	74.48382328
28	31.02823301	32.12909669	34.48147867	37.05121031	39.85980075	42.93092252	46.29062734	49.96758298	53.99333317	58.40258277	63.23351045	68.52811162	80.69769091
29	32.26094476	33.45038766	35.99870085	38.79223451	41.85629577	45.21885020	48.91079930	52.96628630	57.42303316	62.32271191	67.71135353	73.63979832	87.34652927
30	33.50290184	34.78489153	37.53868137	40.56807921	43.90270316	47.57541571	51.62267728	56.08493775	61.00706966	66.43884750	72.43547797	79.05818622	94.46078632

Ordinary Annuity Table Rate for Each Interest Period

Periods	8%	9%	10%	11%	12%	13%	14%	15%	16%	17%	18%	19%	20%
1	1.00000000	1.00000000	1.00000000	1.00000000	1.00000000	1.00000000	1.00000000	1.00000000	1.00000000	1.00000000	1.00000000	1.00000000	1.00000000
2	2.08000000	2.09000000	2.10000000	2.11000000	2.12000000	2.13000000	2.14000000	2.15000000	2.16000000	2.17000000	2.18000000	2.19000000	2.20000000
3	3.24640000	3.27810000	3.31000000	3.34210000	3.37440000	3.40690000	3.43960000	3.47250000	3.50560000	3.53890000	3.57240000	3.60610000	3.64000000
4	4.50611200	4.57312900	4.64100000	4.70973100	4.77932800	4.84979700	4.92114400	4.99337500	5.06649600	5.14051300	5.21543200	5.29125900	5.36800000
5	5.86660096	5.98471061	6.10510000	6.22780141	6.35284736	6.48027061	6.61010416	6.74238125	6.87713536	7.01440021	7.15420976	7.29659821	7.44160000
6	7.33592904	7.52333456	7.71561000	7.91285957	8.11518904	8.32270579	8.53551874	8.75373844	8.97747702	9.20684825	9.44196752	9.68295187	9.92992000
7	8.92280336	9.20043468	9.48717100	9.78327412	10.08901173	10.40465754	10.73049137	11.06679920	11.41387334	11.77201245	12.14152167	12.52271273	12.91590400
8	10.63662763	11.02847380	11.43588810	11.85943427	12.29969314	12.75726302	13.23276016	13.72681908	14.24009307	14.77325456	15.32699557	15.90202814	16.49908480
9	12.48755784	13.02103644	13.57947691	14.16397204	14.77565631	15.41570722	16.08534658	16.78584195	17.51850797	18.28470784	19.08585477	19.92341349	20.79890176
10	14.48655247	15.19292972	15.93742460	16.72200896	17.54873507	18.41974915	19.33729510	20.30371824	21.32146924	22.39310817	23.52130863	24.70886205	25.95868211
11	16.64548746	17.56029339	18.53116706	19.56142995	20.65458328	21.81431654	23.04451641	24.34927597	25.73290432	27.19993656	28.75514419	30.40354584	32.15041853
12	18.97712646	20.14071980	21.38428377	22.71318724	24.13313327	25.65017769	27.27074871	29.00166737	30.85016901	32.82392578	34.93107014	37.18021955	39.58050224
13	21.49529658	22.95338458	24.52271214	26.21163784	28.02910926	29.98470079	32.08865353	34.35191748	36.78619605	39.40399316	42.21866276	45.24446127	48.49660269
14	24.21492030	26.01918919	27.97498336	30.09491800	32.39260238	34.88271190	37.58106503	40.50470510	43.67198742	47.10267200	50.81802206	54.84090891	59.19592323
15	27.15211393	29.36091622	31.77248169	34.40535898	37.27971466	40.41746444	43.84241413	47.58041086	51.65950541	56.11012623	60.96526603	66.26068160	72.03510787
16	30.32428304	33.00339868	35.94972986	39.18994847	42.75328042	46.67173482	50.98035211	55.71747249	60.92502627	66.64884769	72.93901392	79.85021111	87.44212945
17	33.75022569	36.97370456	40.54470285	44.50084281	48.88367407	53.73906035	59.11760141	65.07509336	71.67303048	78.97915180	87.06803642	96.02175122	105.93055534
18	37.45024374	41.30133797	45.59917313	50.39593551	55.74971496	61.72513819	68.39406560	75.83635737	84.14071536	93.40560761	103.74028298	115.26588395	128.11666640
19	41.44626324	46.01845839	51.15909045	56.93948842	63.43968075	70.74940616	78.96923479	88.21181097	98.60322981	110.28456090	123.41353392	138.16640190	154.73999969
20	45.76196430	51.16011964	57.27499949	64.20283215	72.05244244	80.94682896	91.02492766	102.44358262	115.37974658	130.03293626	146.62797002	165.41801826	186.68799962
21	50.42292144	56.76453041	64.00249944	72.26514368	81.69873554	92.46991672	104.76841753	118.81012001	134.84050604	153.13853542	174.02100463	197.84744173	225.02559955
22	55.45675516	62.87333815	71.40274939	81.21430949	92.50258380	105.49100590	120.43599598	137.63163801	157.41498700	180.17208644	206.34478546	236.43845566	271.03071946
23	60.89329557	69.53193858	79.54302433	91.14788353	104.60289386	120.20483667	138.29703542	159.27638372	183.60138492	211.80134114	244.48684684	282.36176223	326.23686335
24	66.76475922	76.78981305	88.49732676	102.17415072	118.15524112	136.83146543	158.65862038	184.16784127	213.97760651	248.80756913	289.49447928	337.01049706	392.48423602
25	73.10593995	84.70089623	98.34705943	114.41330730	133.33387006	155.61955594	181.87082723	212.79301747	249.21402355	292.10485588	342.60348554	402.04249150	471.98108322
26	79.95441515	93.32397689	109.18176538	127.99877110	150.33393446	176.85009821	208.33274304	245.71197009	290.08826732	342.76268138	405.27211294	479.43056488	567.37729986
27	87.35076836	102.72313481	121.09994191	143.07865592	169.37400660	200.84061098	238.49932707	283.56876560	337.50239009	402.03233722	479.22109327	571.52237221	681.85275984
28	95.33882983	112.96821694	134.20993611	159.81728587	190.69888739	227.94989040	272.88923286	327.10408044	392.50277250	471.37783454	566.48089006	681.11162293	819.22331180
29	103.96593622	124.13535646	148.63092972	178.39718732	214.58275388	258.58337616	312.09372546	377.16969250	456.30321610	552.51206642	669.44745027	811.52283129	984.06797417
30	113.28321111	136.30753855	164.49402269	199.02087793	241.33268434	293.19921506	356.78684702	434.74514638	530.31173068	647.43911771	790.94799132	966.71216923	1181.88156900

Annuity Due

The cash value of an annuity due can also be found by using an ordinary annuity table. Remember that an annuity due requires that the payment be made at the beginning of the period. This will make a difference in the cash value compared to an ordinary annuity.

By referring to the ordinary annuity table you will find the effective interest rate of 4 percent (across top) and five periods (along the edge). Five periods is used because the payment is being made at the beginning of the period. The effect is the same as starting an ordinary annuity one period earlier. The factor is 5.41632256. Subtract 1.00000000 from this factor, which will compensate for *not* making the fifth payment with no interest, and the factor 4.41632256 will be found. This compares to the 4.41632256 factor found by using the compound interest table.

Example 9

Find the cash value of an annuity due for $380 at 3 percent with annual payments for eleven years. The effective interest rate (across top) is 3 percent, and there are 12 periods (along the edge), so the factor is 14.19202956.

$$
\begin{array}{rl}
14.19202956 & \\
-\ \underline{1.00000000} & \\
13.19202956 & = \text{factor or return/\$1.00} \\
\times\ \underline{\$380} & = \text{payment} \\
\$\ \ 5{,}012.97 & = \text{cash value}
\end{array}
$$

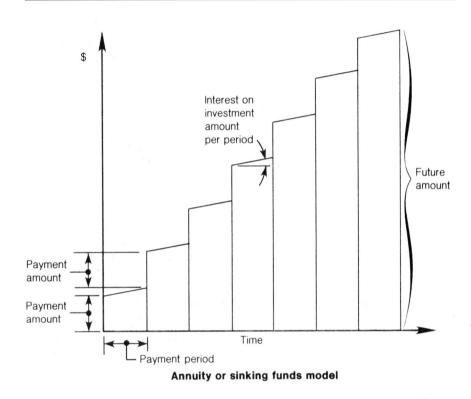

Annuity or sinking funds model

Example 10

To make the distinction between an ordinary annuity and annuity due even clearer, this example will solve the answer to both using the same information.

   Find the cash value of an annuity for $200 at 7 percent with annual payments for five years.

Annuity Due		*Ordinary Annuity*	
7.15329074	factor for 7%,	5.75073901	factor for 7%,
−1.00000000	6 periods	×$200	5 periods
6.15329074		$ 1,150.15 Cash Value	
× $200			
$ 1,230.66 Cash Value			

Example 11

Find the cash value of an annuity for $350 at 16 percent with semi-annual payments for six years.

Annuity Due			*Ordinary Annuity*	
21.49529658	factor for 8%,		18.97712646	factor for 8%,
− 1.00000000	13 periods		× $350	12 periods
20.49529658			$ 6,641.99 Cash Value	
× $350				
$7,173.35 Cash Value				

Be careful to distinguish which type of annuity is specified.

Exercise C   Using the ordinary annuity table, determine the cash value in the following problems.

	Payment Amount	Payment Frequency	Annuity Term	Type of Annuity	Interest Rate	Cash Value
1.	$3,000	Semi. (12)	6 years	Ordin.	3%6%	$42,576.09
2.	500	Annual (11)	10	Due	5%5	6603.39
3.	1,800	Semi. (8)	4	Ordin.	2%4	
4.	2,000	Semi. (11)	5	Due	2%4	
5.	750	Annual (8)	8	Ordin.	6%6	
6.	1,500	Semi. (6)	3	Ordin.	3%6	
7.	3,600	Annual (4)	3	Due	4%4	
8.	5,000	Annual (13)	12	Due	3%3	
9.	875	Semi. (10)	5	Ordin.	2%4	
10.	3,750	Semi. (7)	3	Due	3%6	

Sinking Funds   When a company has future plans to replace worn equipment, expand their facilities, or retire a bond issue, they often establish a **sinking fund**. Payments are made at the end of each period into an investment that pays interest. These payments, along with interest, accumulate over several periods in order to provide the desired amount. The money set aside in the form of payments and its accumulation is termed a sinking fund.

A sinking fund is very much like an annuity except:

1. Sinking fund problems require a solution to the payment question, not the maturity value question.
2. Sinking fund problems usually require payments at the end of each period and are therefore similar to ordinary annuities.

To compute the payment amount in a sinking fund problem the following information is needed:

1. the amount desired;
2. the interest rate;
3. the frequency that the investment is to be compounded; and
4. the length of time before the desired amount is required.

Example 12

What payment amount will be required if $58,000 is needed ten years from now if the interest rate is 6 percent compounded annually?

$58,000   = amount desired
× .07586796 = (6%, 10 periods)—sinking funds table
$ 4,400.34   = payment at the end of each year

Example 13

What payment amount will be required every six months if a $150,000 office addition will be needed in three years and if the interest rate is 8 percent compounded semiannually?

$150,000   = amount desired
× .15076190 = (4%, 6 periods)
$ 22,614.29 = payment at the end of each six months

Exercise D   Using the sinking funds table, determine the payment amount in the problems below.

	Required Value	Payment Frequency	Sinking Fund Term	Interest Rate	Payment Amount
1.	$ 43,000	Annual	14 yrs.	6%	$ 2,046.15
2.	16,500	Semi.	5	6	_____
3.	122,000	Annual	12	5	_____
4.	42,500	Semi.	6	4	_____
5.	65,000	Semi.	10	6	_____
6.	25,000	Annual	3	3	_____
7.	140,000	Annual	12	5	_____
8.	75,000	Semi.	7	4	_____
9.	62,000	Annual	4	5	_____
10.	57,500	Semi.	12	6	_____

Sinking Funds Table

Periods	¾%	1%	1½%	2%	2½%	3%	3½%	4%	4½%	5%	5½%	6%	7%
1	1.00000000	1.00000000	1.00000000	1.00000000	1.00000000	1.00000000	1.00000000	1.00000000	1.00000000	1.00000000	1.00000000	1.00000000	1.00000000
2	0.49813200	0.49751244	0.49627792	0.49504950	0.49382716	0.49261084	0.49140049	0.49019608	0.48899756	0.48780488	0.48661800	0.48543689	0.48309179
3	0.33084579	0.33002211	0.32838296	0.32675467	0.32513717	0.32353036	0.32193418	0.32034854	0.31877336	0.31720856	0.31565407	0.31410981	0.31105167
4	0.24720501	0.24628109	0.24444479	0.24262375	0.24081788	0.23902705	0.23725114	0.23549005	0.23374365	0.23201183	0.23029449	0.22859149	0.22522812
5	0.19702242	0.19603980	0.19408932	0.19215839	0.19024686	0.18835457	0.18648137	0.18462711	0.18279164	0.18097480	0.17917644	0.17739640	0.17389069
6	0.16356891	0.16254837	0.16052521	0.15852581	0.15654997	0.15459750	0.15266821	0.15076190	0.14887839	0.14701747	0.14517895	0.14336263	0.13979580
7	0.13967488	0.13862828	0.13655616	0.13451196	0.13249543	0.13050635	0.12854449	0.12660961	0.12470147	0.12281982	0.12096442	0.11913502	0.11555322
8	0.12175552	0.12069029	0.11858402	0.11650980	0.11446735	0.11245639	0.11047665	0.10852783	0.10660965	0.10472181	0.10286401	0.10103594	0.09746776
9	0.10781929	0.10674036	0.10460982	0.10251544	0.10045689	0.09843386	0.09644601	0.09449299	0.09257447	0.09069008	0.08883946	0.08702224	0.08348647
10	0.09667123	0.09558208	0.09343418	0.09132653	0.08925876	0.08723051	0.08524137	0.08329094	0.08137882	0.07950457	0.07766777	0.07586796	0.07237750
11	0.08755094	0.08645408	0.08429384	0.08217794	0.08010596	0.07807745	0.07609197	0.07414904	0.07224818	0.07038889	0.06857065	0.06679294	0.06335690
12	0.07995148	0.07884879	0.07667999	0.07455960	0.07248713	0.07046209	0.06848395	0.06655217	0.06466619	0.06282541	0.06102923	0.05927703	0.05590199
13	0.07352188	0.07241482	0.07024036	0.06811835	0.06604827	0.06402954	0.06206157	0.06014373	0.05827535	0.05645577	0.05468426	0.05296011	0.04965085
14	0.06801146	0.06690117	0.06472332	0.06260197	0.06053652	0.05852634	0.05657073	0.05466897	0.05282032	0.05102397	0.04927912	0.04758491	0.04434494
15	0.06323639	0.06212378	0.05994436	0.05782547	0.05576646	0.05376658	0.05182507	0.04994110	0.04811381	0.04634229	0.04462560	0.04296276	0.03979462
16	0.05905879	0.05794460	0.05576508	0.05365013	0.05159899	0.04961085	0.04768483	0.04582000	0.04401537	0.04226991	0.04058254	0.03895214	0.03585765
17	0.05537321	0.05425806	0.05207966	0.04996984	0.04792777	0.04595253	0.04404313	0.04219852	0.04041758	0.03869914	0.03704197	0.03544480	0.03242519
18	0.05209766	0.05098205	0.04880578	0.04670210	0.04467008	0.04270870	0.04081684	0.03899333	0.03723690	0.03554622	0.03391992	0.03235654	0.02941260
19	0.04916740	0.04805175	0.04587847	0.04378177	0.04176062	0.03981388	0.03794033	0.03613862	0.03440734	0.03274501	0.03115006	0.02962086	0.02675301
20	0.04653063	0.04541531	0.04324574	0.04115672	0.03914713	0.03721571	0.03536108	0.03358175	0.03187614	0.03024259	0.02867933	0.02718456	0.02439293
21	0.04414543	0.04303075	0.04086550	0.03878477	0.03678733	0.03487178	0.03303659	0.03128011	0.02960057	0.02799611	0.02646478	0.02500455	0.02228900
22	0.04197748	0.04086372	0.03870332	0.03663140	0.03464661	0.03274739	0.03093207	0.02919881	0.02754565	0.02597051	0.02447123	0.02304557	0.02040577
23	0.03999846	0.03888584	0.03673075	0.03466810	0.03269638	0.03081390	0.02901880	0.02730906	0.02568249	0.02413682	0.02266965	0.02127848	0.01871393
24	0.03818474	0.03707347	0.03492410	0.03287110	0.03091282	0.02904742	0.02727283	0.02558683	0.02398703	0.02247090	0.02103580	0.01967900	0.01718902
30	0.02984816	0.02874811	0.02663919	0.02464992	0.02277764	0.02101926	0.01937133	0.01783010	0.01639154	0.01505144	0.01380539	0.01264891	0.01058640

Sinking Funds Table

Periods	8%	9%	10%	11%	12%	13%	14%	15%	16%	17%	18%	19%	20%
1	1.00000000	1.00000000	1.00000000	1.00000000	1.00000000	1.00000000	1.00000000	1.00000000	1.00000000	1.00000000	1.00000000	1.00000000	1.00000000
2	0.48076923	0.47846890	0.47619048	0.47393365	0.47169811	0.46948357	0.46728972	0.46511628	0.46296296	0.46082949	0.45871560	0.45662100	0.45454545
3	0.30803351	0.30505476	0.30211480	0.29921307	0.29634898	0.29352197	0.29073148	0.28797696	0.28525787	0.28257368	0.27992386	0.27730789	0.27472527
4	0.22192080	0.21866866	0.21547080	0.21232635	0.20923444	0.20619420	0.20320478	0.20026535	0.19737507	0.19453311	0.19173867	0.18899094	0.18628912
5	0.17045645	0.16709246	0.16379748	0.16057031	0.15740973	0.15431454	0.15128355	0.14831555	0.14540938	0.14256386	0.13977784	0.13705017	0.13437970
6	0.13631539	0.13291978	0.12960738	0.12637656	0.12322572	0.12015323	0.11715750	0.11423691	0.11138987	0.10861480	0.10591013	0.10327429	0.10070575
7	0.11207240	0.10869052	0.10540550	0.10221527	0.09911774	0.09611080	0.09319238	0.09036036	0.08761268	0.08494724	0.08236200	0.07985490	0.07742393
8	0.09401476	0.09067438	0.08744402	0.08432105	0.08130284	0.07838672	0.07557002	0.07285009	0.07022426	0.06768989	0.06524436	0.06288506	0.06060942
9	0.08007971	0.07679880	0.07364054	0.07060166	0.06767889	0.06486890	0.06216838	0.05957402	0.05708249	0.05469051	0.05239482	0.05019220	0.04807946
10	0.06902949	0.06582009	0.06274539	0.05980143	0.05698416	0.05428956	0.05171354	0.04925206	0.04690108	0.04465660	0.04251464	0.04047131	0.03852276
11	0.06007634	0.05694666	0.05396314	0.05112101	0.04841540	0.04584145	0.04339427	0.04106898	0.03886075	0.03676479	0.03477639	0.03289090	0.03110379
12	0.05269502	0.04965066	0.04676332	0.04402729	0.04143681	0.03898608	0.03666933	0.03448078	0.03241473	0.03046558	0.02862781	0.02689602	0.02526496
13	0.04652181	0.04356656	0.04077852	0.03815099	0.03567720	0.03335034	0.03116366	0.02911046	0.02718411	0.02537814	0.02368621	0.02210215	0.02062000
14	0.04129685	0.03843317	0.03574622	0.03322820	0.03087125	0.02866750	0.02660914	0.02468849	0.02289797	0.02123022	0.01967806	0.01823456	0.01689306
15	0.03682954	0.03405888	0.03147378	0.02906524	0.02682424	0.02474178	0.02280896	0.02101705	0.01935752	0.01782209	0.01640278	0.01509191	0.01388212
16	0.03297687	0.03029991	0.02781662	0.02551675	0.02339002	0.02142624	0.01961540	0.01794769	0.01641362	0.01500401	0.01371008	0.01252345	0.01143614
17	0.02962943	0.02704625	0.02466413	0.02247148	0.02045673	0.01860844	0.01691544	0.01536686	0.01395225	0.01266157	0.01148527	0.01041431	0.00944015
18	0.02670210	0.02421229	0.02193022	0.01984287	0.01793731	0.01620085	0.01462115	0.01318629	0.01188485	0.01070600	0.00963946	0.00867559	0.00780539
19	0.02412763	0.02173041	0.01954687	0.01756250	0.01576300	0.01413439	0.01266316	0.01133635	0.01014166	0.00906745	0.00810284	0.00723765	0.00646245
20	0.02185221	0.01954648	0.01745962	0.01557564	0.01387878	0.01235379	0.01098600	0.00976147	0.00866703	0.00769036	0.00681998	0.00604529	0.00535653
21	0.01983225	0.01761663	0.01562439	0.01383793	0.01224009	0.01081433	0.00954486	0.00841679	0.00741617	0.00653004	0.00574643	0.00505440	0.00444394
22	0.01803207	0.01590499	0.01400506	0.01231310	0.01081051	0.00947948	0.00830317	0.00726577	0.00635264	0.00555025	0.00484626	0.00422943	0.00368962
23	0.01642217	0.01438188	0.01257181	0.01097118	0.00955996	0.00831913	0.00723081	0.00627839	0.00544658	0.00472141	0.00409020	0.00354156	0.00306526
24	0.01497796	0.01302256	0.01129978	0.00978721	0.00846344	0.00730826	0.00630284	0.00542983	0.00467339	0.00401917	0.00345430	0.00296727	0.00254787
30	0.00882743	0.00733635	0.00607925	0.00502460	0.00414366	0.00341065	0.00280279	0.00230020	0.00188568	0.00154455	0.00126431	0.00103443	0.00084611

Chapter Twelve

Name _____ Date _____ Score _____

Skill Problems

In problems 1 through 10 fill in the missing information. Use the compound interest and present value tables.

		Present Value	Annual Rate of Interest	Term of Investment	Compound Frequency	Future Value
1.142950281	1.	$ 5,000.00	6% (1.5%)	6 years	Qtrly. (24)	7147.51
1.268241779	2.	9,000.00	4 (2%)	6	Semi. (12)	11414.18
0.675564(7	3.	29049.26	8 (4%)	5	Semi. (10)	43,000.00
0.170238674	4.	16159.49	4 (4)	9 (9)	Annual	23,000.00
1.21840290	5.	5,860.00	10 (2.5)	2 (8)	Qtrly.	7139.84
0.820746576	6.	13542.32	5 (2.5)	4 (8)	Semi.	16,500.00
1.67710011	7.	19,200.00	9 (9)	6 (6)	Annual	32200.32
.61391325	8.	1792.63	5 (5)	10 (10)	Annual	2,920.00
1.34488882	9.	3,600.00	10 (2.5)	3 (12)	Qtrly.	4841.60
1.17257864	10.	9,000.00	4 (1%)	4 (16)	Qtrly.	10553.21

In problems 11 through 20 fill in the missing information. Use the ordinary annuity table or sinking funds table.

	Payment Amount	Payment Frequency	Annuity Term	Sinking Fund or Type of Annuity	Interest Rate	Cash Value— Required Value
11.	$ 400.00	Annual	10 years	Ordin.	5%	_____
12.	160.00	Semi.	7	Due	6	_____
13.	_____	Semi.	5	Sink. Fund	9	36,500.00
14.	_____	Annual	12	Sink Fund	5	14,000.00
15.	900.00	Annual	3	Due	3	_____
16.	_____	Semi.	4	Sink. Fund	4	67,000.00
17.	500.00	Semi.	6	Ordin.	6	_____
18.	1,250.00	Annual	9	Ordin.	5	_____
19.	_____	Annual	13	Sink. Fund	6	190,400.00
20.	_____	Annual	11	Sink. Fund	3	53,000.00

1. If $4,320 was deposited in a savings account that paid 6 percent compounded quarterly $5\frac{1}{2}$ years ago, what would be the value of the account today?

2. The Rayton Company wishes to pay off a promissory note due in 8 years. The firm decides to establish a sinking fund and invest money at 11 percent compounded annually. The payments will be made once a year. The promissory note maturity value is $46,380. What will be the payment amount?

3. A promissory note for $5,600 including interest is due in 2 years to the Bulster Company. What is the present value of the note if money can be invested at 6 percent compounded semiannually?

4. A 6 percent contingent ordinary annuity was purchased by James D. Armour seven years ago. The semiannual payment was $175. What is the cash value of the annuity today?

5. The parents of Janie Coldron wished to save some money for her college education. They felt that if they could save $20,000 by the time she became 18 years old the balance of the education cost could be earned by part-time jobs, possible scholarships, etc. Janie will soon have her twelfth birthday. What will be the payment amount on an ordinary annuity at a 6 percent rate if payments are made annually?

6. Phil Orel deposited $1,700 in his savings account on July 1, 1975. The bank paid 4 percent compounded semiannually. On March 21, 1981 he deposited $3,100 in his account. The bank began compounding deposits quarterly on January 1, 1985. On June 30, 1986 Phil withdrew the total amount in his savings account to take a trip to Europe. What was the value of the withdrawal?

7. Genny Portan was recently widowed. She and her husband had made twelve annual payments of $325 on an annuity due at 6 percent. What is the value of the annuity before the next payment is due?

8. Silvia Ryan is a widow. Her husband left $20,000 for her living expenses. She placed the $20,000 in a savings account that paid 4 percent compounded semiannually. At the beginning of each year she transferred $3,000 from her savings account to her checking account. Each month she wrote herself a check for $250. How many monthly $250 checks will she be able to use before the $20,000 is used up? She made the first transfer at the end of the first year.

9. The Porter Products Co. purchased a note for $9,846 due in five years. The current rate of interest on investments is 9 percent compounded semiannually. What is the present value of the note?

10. A firm invested $16,000 four years ago at 12 percent compounded annually. In order to earn this rate the money must be deposited for five years. What will be the compounded amount at the end of the deposit period?

11. The Wycoff Corporation will need to retire a bond debt that is due to mature in six years. The bond issue has a total face value of $6,300,000. The treasurer has recommended that a sinking fund be set up to retire the debt. The funds can be invested at 11 percent compounded semiannually. What will be the amount of the semiannual payment to the sinking fund?

12. Lester placed $5,000 in a cash account with his stockbroker. The account pays an annual rate of 9 percent compounded monthly. After five months, he decided to purchase 300 shares of a stock at a price of $15.50 per share. The broker charged a fee of $\frac{1}{2}$ percent of the total purchase price. Lester used the money from his cash account to pay for the stock. How much was left in the account after the shares were bought and the broker had been paid?

13. A savings and loan association is paying depositors 9 percent interest on savings deposits and compounds the interest every six months. The funds are then lent to home buyers at 12 percent for home mortgages (monthly repayments). The savings and loan association has computed that the annualized rate of return on the home mortgage loans is 14 percent. This savings and loan association has deposits and loans totaling $51,000,000. The overhead for office operations is maintained at 1 percent of deposits. What is the amount of profit for a one-year period?

Challenge Problem

The P. H. Rickton Corporation borrowed $67,500 from Villance Trust Company on a promissory note at 6 percent for five years. The Rickton Corporation negotiated an ordinary annuity at 4 percent on the same date. Payments will be made at six-month intervals. What will the payment amount be in order to repay the maturity value of the note to Villance Trust Company in five years? (Use the sinking funds table.)

Complete the following problems. Use the appropriate tables.

	Present Value	Annual Rate of Interest	Term of Investment	Compound Frequency	Future Value
1.	$ 2,000.00	8%	4 years	Qtrly.	_____
2.	_____	9	6	Annual	5,000.00
3.	19,000.00	10	7	Semi.	_____
4.	_____	8	3	Qtrly.	9,500.00

	Payment Amount	Payment Frequency	Annuity Term	Type of Annuity or Sinking Fund	Interest Rate	Cash Value— Required Value
5.	$ 400.00	Annual	7 years	Due	9%	_____
6.	_____	Semi.	5	Sink. Fund	8	30,000.00
7.	375.00	Semi.	6	Due	10	_____
8.	_____	Annual	2	Sink. Fund	6	50,000.00

9. Dolores Heine placed $300 in a new savings account that paid 5 percent interest compounded semiannually. Her money has been on deposit for $4\frac{1}{2}$ years. What is the value of Ms. Heine's account at the present time if no other deposits or withdrawals have been made?

10. The Blackburn Corp. purchased a contingent annuity due eight years ago with payments of $750 annually. The rate of interest on the annuity was 7 percent. The treasurer of the firm decided to terminate the annuity and purchase bonds with the cash value. What was the cash value of the annuity?

13 Discounts
14 Commission Sales
15 Markup

13 Discounts

After mastering the material in this chapter, you will be able to:

1. Compute the selling price of merchandise subject to a trade discount.
2. Compute a single equivalent trade discount.
3. Compute the net price of merchandise subject to a cash discount using several methods.
4. Compute the net price in problems that include cash discounts and transportation charges using F.O.B. or C.O.D.
5. Understand and use the following terms and concepts:

Trade Discount	E.O.M.
List Price	R.O.G.
Selling Price	Common Carriers
Direct Method	Contract Carriers
Equivalent Trade Discount	F.O.B.
Cash Discount	F.O.B. Destination
Terms of Trade	F.O.B. Shipping Point
Net Price	C.O.D.

Trade Discounts

Manufacturers, wholesalers, and other middlemen often offer their customers discounts based on the buyer providing some marketing functions. These discounts are termed **trade discounts.** The seller offers this price reduction if the buyer purchases in large quantities, transports or stores the merchandise for the seller, promotes the product to the final consumer, gathers sales information for the seller, or if the buyer simply negotiates successfully. The number of the above marketing functions performed will determine the size of the trade discounts offered. The size of the discounts vary from seller to seller.

Finding the Selling Price

List price
Selling price

The trade discount is computed from a **list price** established by the seller in a catalogue or on a price sheet. Since not all buyers will perform the same marketing functions, the trade discounts are not listed. The trade discount is subtracted from the list price in order to find the **selling price.** This is the amount that the seller is willing to accept for the merchandise when a buyer provides the agreed-upon marketing functions.

Example 1

A piece of office equipment is listed at $1,460. The seller agrees to offer the buyer a 15 percent trade discount if the buyer transports and installs the equipment. What is the selling price of the equipment?

$$\begin{array}{rl}
\$1,460 & = \text{list price (base)} \\
\times \quad .15 & = \text{trade discount percent (rate)} \\
\hline
\$ \ 219 & = \text{trade discount amount (percentage)}
\end{array}$$

$$\begin{array}{rl}
\$1,460 & = \text{list price} \\
- \quad 219 & = \text{trade discount amount} \\
\hline
\$1,241 & = \text{selling price}
\end{array}$$

The same problem can be solved in another shorter approach by subtracting the trade discount percent from 100 percent and then multiplying.

Example 2

$$\begin{array}{rl}
\$1,460 & = \text{list price} \\
\times \quad .85 & = (100\% - 15\% \text{ trade discount}) \\
\hline
\$1,241 & = \text{selling price}
\end{array}$$

Example 3

If the selling firm in the previous example were to offer an additional 10 percent trade discount for allowing on-site inspections of the equipment by other prospective customers, the new selling price would be calculated as follows:

$$\begin{array}{rl}
\$1,460.00 & = \text{list price} \\
- \quad 219.00 & = \text{trade discount amount (15\%)} \\
\hline
\$1,241.00 & = \text{(base)} \\
\times \quad\quad .10 & = \text{trade discount percent (rate)} \\
\hline
\$ \ \ 124.10 & = \text{trade discount amount (10\%) (percentage)}
\end{array}$$

$$\begin{array}{rl}
\$1,241.00 & \\
- \quad 124.10 & = \text{trade discount amount (10\%)} \\
\hline
\$1,116.90 & = \text{selling price}
\end{array}$$

When two or more trade discounts are offered, it is termed a series of trade discounts. Notice that the series of trade discounts, 15 percent and 10 percent is *not* the same as a 25 percent discount.

$$\begin{array}{rr}
\$1,460 \qquad\qquad & \$1,460 \\
\times \ .25 \qquad\qquad & - \ \ 365 \\
\hline
\$ \ 365 \qquad\qquad & \$1,095
\end{array}$$

Direct Method

The **direct method** is much quicker and effective in finding the selling price. Each discount is subtracted from 100 percent and is then used to multiply, beginning with the list price, to find the selling price.

Example 4

An 8 percent and 20 percent discount are offered to the Nantalahala Outing Company for their purchase of 20 canoes. The canoes are listed at $340 each. Brund Corporation, the seller, offered the discount due to the size of the order. What is the price of the 20 canoes?

$ 340 each
× 20
$6,800 total

$6,800 (list price) × .92 = $6,256
$6,256 × .80 = $5,004.80 (selling price)

100%   100%
− 8   − 20
92%   80%

This method will be used to determine the answers to the problems in this chapter.

Example 5

Monson Distributing purchased 25 printers that would be interchangeable with several existing computers. The list price of this printer was $1,200. J. Bonner, the distributor, agreed to allow a series of 10, 5, and 20 percent discounts to the buyer for quantity, promotional considerations, and user feedback reasons. What will be the selling price of the lot of 25 printers?

$ 1,200
× 25
$30,000 total list price

$30,000 × .90 = $27,000
$27,000 × .95 = $25,650
$25,650 × .80 = $20,520 selling price

INVOICE

THE Jack Bonner Co.

"South Texas' Largest Office Supplier"
MAIN OFFICES, SALES ROOMS AND PRINTING DEPT
P. O. DRAWER H
CORPUS CHRISTI, TEXAS 78469

BOOKKEEPING
DIAL 883-9219

SOLD TO: Monson Distributors
412 Commercial
San Antonio, TX 78250

Date 12-16-86
Customers P. O. 4031
Sales Ticket No. 7856

Shipped To Same / F.O.B. San Antonio

Terms: 30 Days Net

QUANTITY	UNIT	DESCRIPTION	UNIT PRICE	AMOUNT
25	53071	Micro-Max high speed printers list @ $1,200 ea. less 10,5 ;20% trade discount	$820.10	$20,520.—

Any errors in price, differentials or extensions quoted or invoiced are unintentional and will be corrected

Courtesy of The Jack Bonner Co., Corpus Christi, TX.

Find the total selling price in each of the following problems.

	List Price Per Unit	Units Purchased	Trade Discount Offered	Total Selling Price
1.	$ 64.00	100	20%	$ 5,120.00
2.	1,693.00	40	15	57562.00
3.	42.50	17 722.50	19	585.23
4.	96.00	60 5760	25	4320
5.	23.50	12 = 282.00	10	253.80
6.	48.00	12	25	432.00
7.	120.00	144	10	15552.00
8.	18.00	50	5 and 20	684.00
9.	185.00	3	10 and 10	449.55
10.	24.95	100	20 and 10	1796.40

Equivalent trade discount

There is a method that can be used to find one single discount percent equal to a series of trade discounts. This is termed an **equivalent trade discount.** It is found by subtracting the product of two trade discounts from their sum. This method is useful when a series of discounts are used repeatedly.

Example 6

An 8 percent and a 20 percent discount are offered to the A. J. Rislone Corporation for purchasing 1,500 vertical hydrators listed at $46 each. A & K Distributing, the seller, offered the discounts due to the size of the purchase and because Rislone will be penetrating a new market area. The single equivalent discount and the selling price are computed as follows:

```
  20%
+  8%
  28%    = sum of trade discounts
-  1.6%  = product of trade discounts
  26.4%  = single Equivalent Discount (20% and 8%)
```

$$
\begin{array}{ccc}
20\% & = & .20 \\
\times\ 8\% & = & \times .08 \\
\hline
& & .0160 = 1.6\% \text{ product of trade discounts}
\end{array}
$$

When there are three or more trade discounts offered, a single equivalent discount can also be found. The equivalent discount of two of the trade discounts with the third discount will provide an equivalent of all three discounts.

Find the total selling price of the following problems.

	List Price Per Unit	Units Purchased	Trade Discount Offered	Total Selling Price
1. $	45.00	200	5 and 8%	$ 7,866.00
2.	60.00	100	10 and 15	
3.	25.00	25	5 and 12	
4.	525.00	144	10 and 20	
5.	1,200.00	65	20 and 5	
6.	80.00	100	7, 5, and 10	
7.	42.00	500	10, 10, and 20	
8.	130.00	25	5, 8, and 30	
9.	125.00	20	5, 10 and 10	
10.	7.50	81	10, 5, and 17	_431.11_

Cash Discounts

Manufacturers, wholesalers, and other middlemen also offer their customers **cash discounts.** These discounts are not based on the customer providing marketing functions, but are designed to motivate the customer to promptly pay for the merchandise. The motivating tool is a reduction in the selling price if the payment is made at an early date. The date (or dates) is specified in the **terms of trade** by the seller. Examples of terms of trade are 3/10,n/30 or 2/30,n/60, and are shown on the invoice or bill. In each of the previous examples the first number represents a percent discount. The second number following the slash mark represents the last day after the billing date that the discount is available.

Terms of trade

Example 7

Terms of trade 1/10,n/60 mean that a 1 percent cash discount off of the selling price of the merchandise is offered for the first 10 days after the billing date. The n/60 means that the customer has 60 days after the billing date to pay the bill; in the first 10 days a 1 percent discount is offered, in the next 50 days no discount is offered. Sixty days after the billing date the unpaid bill may be placed in the hands of a collection agent. This would result in a financial penalty to the buyer.

INVOICE

PRINTERS LITHOGRAPHERS

PROGRESS **P**RESS, INC

2328 W. TOUHY AVE. • CHICAGO, ILL. 60645 • 465-5601 — 743-1565

WBC Systems, Inc.
1000 Nagle
Chicago, IL 60606

DATE 6-15-86
YOUR P.O. NO. 4781
SHIPPED Pickup
VIA
TERMS 2/10, n/30
SALESMAN Sam

1,000	Brochures with inserts	$846.00
1,500	Stationery/envelopes	750.00
1,000	Business cards	23.00
	Typesetting	16.00
		$1,635.00
	less 2% cash discount	− 32.70
	net	$1,602.30

Courtesy of Progress Press, Inc., Chicago, IL.

Example 8

Goods purchased on May 26, terms of trade, 3/5,2/30,n/60 would mean that the buyer would have until May 31 to receive a 3 percent discount from the selling price, until June 25 to receive a 2 percent discount from the selling price, or until July 25 to receive no discount with no penalty on the selling price.

Finding the Net Price

Net price

When the cash discount is subtracted from the selling price the balance is termed the **net price.** If there is no cash discount available in the terms of the sale, the selling price may also be called the net price. The net price paid to the seller will complete the financial obligation.

$LP = SP + DISC.$

$DISC = LP - SP$

$SP = L.P - DISC$

$COST + MARKUP = Sell$

$MARKUP = Sell - COST.$

$COST = SP - MARK UP$

$M = MARKUP$

Example 9

Merchandise is sold for a selling price of $1,650 with terms of trade of 4/10,1/30,n/90 on October 17. What is the net price if payment is made on November 6?

$$\begin{array}{r} \$1,650 \\ \times \quad .01 \\ \hline \$ \quad 16.50 \end{array}$$

$$\begin{array}{rl} \$1,650.00 & = \text{selling price} \\ - \quad 16.50 & = \text{cash discount} \\ \hline \$1,633.50 & = \text{net price} \end{array}$$

OR

$$\begin{array}{rl} \$1,650 & = \text{selling price} \\ \times \quad .99 & = \text{percent of net price} \\ & \quad (100\% - 1\%) \\ \hline \$1,633.50 & = \text{net price} \end{array}$$

Note that the buyer did not pay for the merchandise by October 27, and, therefore, did not qualify for the 4 percent cash discount.

Cash discounts are an important financial consideration even though the discount rates sound small. Terms of trade of 2/10,n/30 equal a potential 36 percent annual discount rate.

The proof is shown by the following: 2 percent discount if payment is made within ten days. By not paying on the tenth day, the money is, in effect, borrowed for the next twenty-day periods in a year. Eighteen periods times 2 percent equals 36 percent annually.

Exercise C   Find the net price in the following problems. Note the dates.

	Selling Price	Terms of Trade	Invoice Date	Payment Date	Net Price (Payment Amount)
1.	$ 675.00	3/15,n/30	July 26	Aug. 8	$ 654.75
2.	900.00	2/10,n/30	Nov. 10	Nov. 17	
3.	200.00	1/10,n/90	Sept. 16	Oct. 30	
4.	52.00	2/10,1/30,n/60	Aug. 20	Sept. 12	
5.	175.00	1/30,n/60	May 13	July 1	
6.	1,400.00	n/30	Sept. 15	Oct. 10	
7.	850.00	2/15,1/60,n/90	Jan. 3	Feb. 16	
8.	500.00	2/10,n/120	June 30	July 2	
9.	120.00	1/20,n/45	Aug. 1	Aug. 13	
10.	38.50	1/30,n/60	Dec. 2	Dec. 30	

End of Month (E.O.M.)

A variation in terms of trade is the end of month or **E.O.M.** stipulation. Terms of trade of 2/10,n/60,E.O.M. indicate that the buyer computes the days of discount beginning at the end of the month in which the purchase was made.

Example 10

A $595 purchase of merchandise at selling price is made on June 12, with terms of trade of 2/10,n/60,E.O.M. What is the last date that a cash discount is available?

In this example, E.O.M. means the end of the month of June (month in which the purchase is made). Ten days after the end of the month of June is July 10. The 2 percent discount is offered until July 10.

If the purchase is made after the twenty-fifth of the month, then an additional month is allowed in the discount time period.

Example 11

An invoice for $69.80 is dated March 28 with terms of 3/20,n/30,E.O.M. What is the latest date that a cash discount is available?

Here, E.O.M. means the end of the month of March. Because the purchase was made after the twenty-fifth of the month an additional month is added (April). Twenty days after the month of April is May 20. The 3 percent discount is offered until May 20.

If payment was made before May 20 the net price on this purchase would be $67.71.

Exercise D   Find the net price in the following problems.

	Selling Price	Terms of Trade	Invoice Date	Payment Date	Net Price (Payment Amount)
1.	$ 190.00	2/10,n/30,E.O.M.	Oct. 15	Nov. 20	$ 190.00
2.	150.00	1/20,n/60,E.O.M.	July 20	Sept. 26	_____
3.	60.00	1/10,n/30,E.O.M.	April 30	June 10	_____
4.	750.00	2/20,E.O.M.	Feb. 28	April 16	_____
5.	600.00	1/15,n/30,E.O.M.	May 10	June 30	_____
6.	260.00	3/10,n/60,E.O.M.	Aug. 31	Oct. 7	_____
7.	550.00	2/10,n/20,E.O.M.	Jan. 16	Mar. 28	_____

	Selling Price	Terms of Trade	Invoice Date	Payment Date	Net Price (Payment Amount)
8.	1,530.00	1/30,E.O.M.	Dec. 23	Jan. 25	_____
9.	32.50	4/10,2/30,E.O.M.	June 30	Aug. 3	_____
10.	700.00	2/20,1/30,E.O.M.	July 3	Aug. 25	_____

Receipt of Goods (R.O.G.)

Another variation in terms of trade is the receipt of goods or **R.O.G.** stipulation. This, like E.O.M., also specifies an extension of the time period that the buyer has to pay for the goods and still receive the cash discount. Terms of trade of 3/0,n/30,R.O.G. indicate that the buyer computes the days of discount beginning with the date that the merchandise is actually received by the buyer. The R.O.G. stipulation is often used when goods are not available for immediate shipment by the seller. By specifying R.O.G. the buyer has an opportunity to inspect the goods received before payment is made.

Example 12

A $1,385 purchase of equipment on August 20 is received on October 6. The terms of trade are 2/5,n/60,R.O.G. What is the latest date that a discount is available and what is the net price?

R.O.G. means that the discount period will be computed starting on the date that the goods are received: Oct. 6 plus five days equals October 11. Net Price equals:

$$\begin{aligned} \$1,385 &= \text{selling price (base)} \\ \underline{\times .02} &= \text{cash discount rate (rate)} \\ \$27.70 &= \text{cash discount amount (percentage)} \end{aligned}$$

$$\begin{aligned} \$1,385.00 &= \text{selling price} \\ \underline{- 27.70} &= \text{cash discount amount} \\ \$1,357.30 &= \text{net price} \end{aligned}$$

Exercise E

Find the net price in the following problems.

	Selling Price	Terms of Trade	Invoice Date	Date Received	Payment Date	Net Price (Payment Amount)
1.	$620.00	3/10,n/30,R.O.G.	August 6	Sept. 10	Sept. 17	$601.40
2.	85.00	2/5,n/10,R.O.G.	June 25	July 20	July 22	_____
3.	120.00	1/10,n/60,R.O.G.	Jan. 16	Feb. 1	Feb. 13	_____
4.	450.00	2/5,n/30,R.O.G.	April 3	May 30	June 16	_____

	Selling Price	Terms of Trade	Invoice Date	Date Received	Payment Date	Net Price (Payment Amount)
5.	327.00	1/10,n/20,R.O.G.	Sept. 1	Sept. 3	Sept. 11	_____
6.	700.00	1/30,n/60,R.O.G.	July 5	July 27	Aug. 13	_____
7.	175.00	2/10,n/45,R.O.G.	Oct. 26	Nov. 30	Dec. 7	_____
8.	78.00	2/20,n/30,R.O.G.	May 1	June 16	July 3	_____
9.	325.00	1/20,R.O.G.	Feb. 28	March 26	March 31	_____
10.	802.00	1/5,n/30,R.O.G.	Nov. 2	Nov. 16	Nov. 30	_____

Combination of Cash and Trade Discounts

When both cash and trade discounts are offered the trade discount is subtracted before the cash discount is computed. The model below shows the relationship.

List Price
− Trade Discounts
Selling Price
− Cash Discount
Net Price

Example 13

P. T. Koller purchased 125 "Pulmers" from the Watson Corp. at $32 each list price. Koller was offered a series of trade discounts of 10 percent and 20 percent on terms of trade of 3/10,n/60,E.O.M. The purchase was made on July 12, delivery was made on July 18, and payment was made on July 21. What was the net price on the purchase?

$$
\begin{array}{rl}
\$ 32 & = \text{price per unit at list price} \\
\times 125 & = \text{units purchased} \\
\hline
\$4{,}000 & = \text{total list price} \\
\times .28 & = \text{single equivalent discount (10\% and 20\%)} \\
\hline
\$1{,}120 & = \text{trade discount amount} \\
\end{array}
$$

$$
\begin{array}{rl}
\$4{,}000 & = \text{total list price} \\
- 1{,}120 & = \text{trade discount amount} \\
\hline
\$2{,}880 & = \text{total selling price} \\
\times .03 & = \text{cash discount rate} \\
\hline
\$86.40 & = \text{cash discount amount} \\
\end{array}
$$

$$
\begin{array}{rl}
\$2{,}880.00 & = \text{total selling price} \\
- 86.40 & = \text{cash discount} \\
\hline
\$2{,}793.60 & = \text{net price} \\
\end{array}
$$

Exercise F

Find the net price in the following problems.

	Total List Price	Trade Discounts	Terms of Trade	Invoice Date	Date Received	Payment Date	Net Price
1.	$ 582	10 and 5%	1/10,n/30,E.O.M.	July 5	July 7	July 12	$ 492.63
2.	1,600	10 and 7	2/10,n/60	May 3	May 6	June 5	
3.	270	5 and 7	2/10,n/60,R.O.G.	March 1	March 19	March 25	
4.	950	15 and 10	3/5,n/60,E.O.M.	July 29	Aug. 17	Sept. 3	
5.	2,800	10 and 10	1/10,n/90	Dec. 2	Dec. 9	Dec. 11	

Transportation Charges

The price of merchandise varies due to discounts made available by the seller. Much of the discount variation depends on the negotiating ability of the two parties. Another factor included in the negotiations that has an influence on the final price is transportation charges.

Transportation firms can be classified as common carriers or contract carriers. **Common carriers** are authorized by the federal government to operate over specified routes on an established schedule at approved rates. In effect, a common carrier receives a franchise to operate on the routes, schedules, and rates controlled by the federal government.

Common carriers

Contract carriers

Contract carriers are free to negotiate a contract to carry merchandise over any route, with no specific schedule (except as agreed upon with the individual customer) and at negotiable rates. These firms are free agents that operate independently.

Both types of carriers are important and necessary to our economy.

Whatever the method of delivery, there is a transportation cost that must be paid by one of the parties. Either the seller will include the transportation cost in the quoted price or the buyer will have to add the cost to the negotiated price. The transportation cost may be as high as the cost of the merchandise itself depending on the distance traveled, means of delivery, and weight. The businessperson should consider this cost as an important price factor.

F.O.B.

F.O.B. is an abbreviation for "free on board." It means that the seller will include in his quoted price the service of placing the merchandise on the transportation device—truck, boat, plane, train, etc.—for free. From a cost standpoint F.O.B. does not mean very much. The transportation device will be located near the seller's place of business. The real meaningful portion of F.O.B. follows the abbreviation by indicating to what location the merchandise is free of transportation costs.

F.O.B. Destination

When the buyer and seller agree that the merchandise will be shipped to a location specified by the buyer, and all of the transportation costs will be paid by the seller, the term **F.O.B. destination** is used. This means that the seller will ship the merchandise free to the buyer's place of business. The price per unit quotation will always include transportation. The buyer will usually not be aware of the transportation costs.

mary maxim INC

2001 HOLLAND AVE.
PORT HURON, MICHIGAN 48060

TELEPHONE
987-2000
AREA CODE 313

No. 32005

SOLD TO: *Antoinette Art Forms, Inc.*
600 Enterprise Way
Los Angeles, CA 90274

SHIPPED TO: *Same*

CODE
B · BACK ORDERED
D · DISCONTINUED
O · OTHER

| F.O.B. PORT HURON-TERMS 2/10, n/45 NO ANTICIPATION ALLOWED | IMPORTANT INVOICE NUMBER MUST SHOW ON ALL PAYMENTS AND CORRESPONDENCE-NO DISCOUNT ON FREIGHT | ORDER IS ✓ COMPLETE | BALANCE TO FOLLOW |

ORDER DATE	CUSTOMER ORDER NO.	SEND VIA	CUST. ACCOUNT NO.	INVOICE DATE
9-23-86	50671	U.P.S.	4809	10-1-86

CATALOG NO	DESCRIPTION	QUANTITY ORDERED	QUANTITY SHIPPED	CODE	PRICE	AMOUNT
mm 4261	904 Yarn	24	24		6.72	161.28
mm 3604	Purse Kit	10	10		17.40	174.00
mm 5069	Wall Decor Panels #53	20	20		36.00	720.00
mm 2417	Hook Latch #78	15	15		7.25	108.75
						1,164.03
					POSTAGE	36.80
				PLEASE PAY LAST AMOUNT IN THIS COLUMN ➝		1,200.83

THESE GOODS ARE NOT RETURNABLE FOR CREDIT UNLESS WRITTEN ARRANGEMENTS ARE FIRST MADE

CONTINUING GUARANTEE UNDER THE TEXTILE FIBER PRODUCTS IDENTIFICATION ACT FILED WITH THE FEDERAL TRADE COMMISSION #RN 28126

Thank You

INVOICE

Courtesy of Mary Maxim, Inc., Port Huron, MI.

Example 14

Downson & Patrick sold twenty-six pairs of women's slacks to the Tops and Bottoms Shop in Palo Alto, California. The price of the slacks was $12 each. Freight costs for the shipment were $43.72. Downson & Patrick agreed to ship F.O.B. Palo Alto (the destination) from New York. How much will the Tops and Bottoms Shop pay the seller; terms of 2/10,n/60 if payment is within the discount period?

$$
\begin{array}{rl}
\$\ 12 & \text{pair of slacks} \\
\times\ \ 26 & \text{pairs of slacks} \\
\hline
\$312 & \text{total selling price} \\
\times\ \ .02 & \text{(2\% cash discount)} \\
\hline
\$6.24 &
\end{array}
$$

$$
\begin{array}{rl}
\$312.00 & = \text{total selling price} \\
-\ \ \ 6.24 & = \text{cash discount} \\
\hline
\$305.76 & = \text{net price}
\end{array}
$$

The net price of $305.76 will be paid by Tops & Bottoms to Downson & Patrick for the merchandise including transportation. Downson & Patrick owes the freight company $43.72 for the transportation.

Sometimes the buyer specifies several locations if the merchandise is to be shipped to all of their plants, retail locations, or warehouses. The results are the same if F.O.B. destination is specified. The seller pays the freight costs to the multiple locations that the buyer specifies.

F.O.B. Shipping Point

When the buyer and seller agree that the price of the merchandise does not include the transportation charges, **F.O.B. shipping point** is specified. Under these terms the buyer is responsible for all of the costs associated with moving the merchandise from the seller's location. F.O.B. in this case indicates that the seller will place the merchandise on the transportation device free. From that point on the costs are to be borne by the buyer. This allows the buyer to negotiate the transportation method and cost separately. This may aid in reducing costs and speeding up delivery. Each cost can be identified using F.O.B. shipping point. Transportation charges will not be part of the seller's invoice amount.

Example 15

The Hilltop Inn purchased forty-two sets of tables and chairs for their dining room. Each set was priced at $268, F.O.B. shipping point, n/30. Rustic Pine, the seller, indicated that the best method of shipment would be by truck—common carrier—at $38 a set. What would be the total cost of the forty-two sets delivered?

$$
\begin{array}{rl}
\$ \quad 268 & = \text{price per set} \\
+ \quad\quad 38 & = \text{transportation cost per set} \\
\hline
\$ \quad 306 & = \text{total cost per set delivered} \\
\times \quad\quad 42 & = \text{sets} \\
\hline
\$12,852 & = \text{total cost/42 sets delivered}
\end{array}
$$

The amount paid to Rustic Pine would be:

$$
\begin{array}{rl}
\$ \quad 268 & = \text{price per set} \\
\times \quad\quad 42 & = \text{sets} \\
\hline
\$11,256 & = \text{total cost/42 sets}
\end{array}
$$

The amount paid to the common carrier would be:

$$
\begin{array}{rl}
\$ \quad 38 & = \text{price of delivery per set} \\
\times \quad\quad 42 & = \text{sets} \\
\hline
\$1,596 & = \text{total cost of delivery/42 sets}
\end{array}
$$

Exercise G

Fill in the missing amount in the problems below. Assume the payment is made within the discount period.

	Price Per Unit	Units Purchased	Freight Cost F.O.B. Destination	Terms of Trade	Cost to Buyer (total)
1.	$14.65	144	$ 16.46	2/10,n/30	$2,067.41
2.	_____	90	135.68	n/60	765.00
3.	18.00	150	72.00	3/10,n/30	_____

	Price Per Unit	Units Purchased	Freight Cost F.O.B. Destination	Terms of Trade	Amount Due Seller
4.	6.00	30	27.00	—	_____
5.	60.00	_____	32.00	1/10,n/60	1,782.00

Exercise H Fill in the missing amount in the problems below. Assume that payment is made within the discount period.

	Price Per Unit	Units Purchased	Freight Cost F.O.B. Shipping Point	Terms of Trade	Cost to Buyer (total)
1.	$ 1.44	1,500	$ 162.50	3/10,n/20	$ 2,257.70
2.	15.00	80	2,359.00	n/60	_____
3.	1,950.00	12	493.51	1/10,n/30	_____

	Price Per Unit	Units Purchased	Freight Cost F.O.B. Shipping Point	Terms of Trade	Amount Due Seller
4.	84.90	_____	125.00	n/60	12,735.00
5.	_____	71	792.00	3/10,n/45	5,234.12

F.O.B. Cost Comparison

Item Priced at $500.; Transportation: $35.

F.O.B. DESTINATION

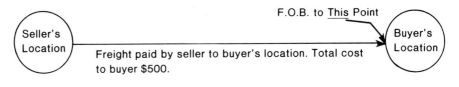

F.O.B. SHIPPING POINT

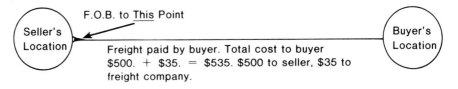

C.O.D. C.O.D. means cash on delivery. The buyer must pay for the merchandise in cash upon delivery or it is returned to the seller's location.

C.O.D. prices tend to be higher than F.O.B. destination because the seller is risking that the buyer will pay for the merchandise at delivery. If the buyer refuses to pay, the seller must pay for the transportation cost for both directions and lose the sale. This type of pricing is used when selling impulse consumer merchandise and when dealing with middlemen with poor or new credit ratings. The merchandise will be quoted "C.O.D." or "plus C.O.D. charges."

Example 16

The Palderson Company sold Mrs. Alma Dickinson four bolts of material for her new upholstery business. The bolts were quoted at $268 per bolt C.O.D. What is the amount that the delivery firm will collect when the merchandise is accepted by Mrs. Dickinson?

$$\begin{array}{rl} \$ \ \ 268 & = \text{price per bolt/C.O.D.} \\ \times \ \ \ \ \ 4 & = \text{bolts} \\ \hline \$1{,}072 & = \text{total price for 4 bolts} \end{array}$$

Example 17

The Watson family was watching television and noticed an announcement that stated an item could be purchased for $29.95 plus C.O.D. charges. The family decided to order one. When the delivery man came to the home, he indicated that the cost of delivery was $4.50. How much is due the delivery man?

$$\begin{array}{rl} \$29.95 & = \text{price of merchandise} \\ + \ \ \ 4.50 & = \text{C.O.D. charges} \\ \hline \$34.45 & = \text{total amount due} \end{array}$$

Assignment

Chapter Thirteen

Name _____ Date _____ Score _____

Skill Problems   Find the total selling price in the following problems.

	List Price Per Unit	Units Purchased	Trade Discounts Offered	Total Selling Price
1.	$ 50.00	10	10%	_____
2.	42.00	144	10 and 20	_____
3.	125.00	25	5	_____
4.	65.00	30	5 and 15	_____
5.	90.00	100	10, 20, and 5	_____

Find the net price in the following problems.

	Selling Price	Terms of Trade	Invoice Date	Date Received	Payment Date	Net Price
6.	$ 29.50	3/10,n/20	July 12	July 15	July 20	_____
7.	890.00	1/20,n/90,E.O.M.	August 29	Sept. 2	Oct. 15	_____
8.	59.50	2/15,n/60,R.O.G.	Oct 21	Nov. 3	Nov. 16	_____
9.	120.00	2/10,n/60,E.O.M.	Feb. 12	March 1	March 7	_____
10.	856.00	n/30	April 22	April 26	May 10	_____

	Total List Price	Trade Discounts	Terms of Trade	Invoice Date	Date Received	Payment Date	Net Price
11.	$1,200.00	5 and 10%	2/10,n/30	July 6	July 9	July 20	_____
12.	768.45	12%	2/5,n/30,R.O.G.	Jan. 5	Feb. 16	Feb. 20	_____

Determine the missing amount in the problems below. Assume that the payment is made within the discount period.

	Amount of Invoice	Transportation Agreement	Terms of Trade	Transportation Costs	Amount Due Seller
13.	$ 453.80	F.O.B. Destination	2/10,n/60	$32.80	_____
14.	980.00	C.O.D.	—	62.68	_____
15.	1,698.00	F.O.B. Shipping Point	1/10,n/45	—	_____

1. The Sales Furniture Store ordered twenty dining sets at a list price of $230 each. The manufacturer offered a 15 percent discount for the size of the order. What is the sales price of the total order?

2. Billings and Alpert Co. received a price quotation from two firms for 900 units of a processing tool used in the canning business. A representative of the Bernwalther Corp. quoted $3.91 per unit F.O.B. destination with terms of trade 2/10,n/60. A spokesperson for the Altron Digital Corp. quoted a price of $3.78 per unit F.O.B. shipping point with terms of trade 3/15,n/45. Total shipping costs were expected to be $93.60 for the 900 units. Which price quotation should be accepted considering the price of the merchandise, transportation costs, and cash discounts?

3. Kelly bought 50 units of raw materials for her manufacturing firm at $17 per unit list price. Terms of trade were 3/10,n/20,E.O.M. The purchase was made on March 12, the goods were delivered on April 6, and payment was made on April 16. What was the amount of the check sent by the company?

4. Karen Liscomb was instructed to pay for a purchase made on September 1 for thirty pieces of office furniture that were listed at $174 each. A trade discount of 15 percent was offered as well as terms of trade of 2/10,n/30. What is the net price if payment is made on September 12?

5. The Aikman Office Furniture Company ordered three desks and matching chairs for their inventory. The items were priced at $1,900 for each set (desk and chair). The manufacturer offered a 10 and 15 percent discount if the Aikman Office Furniture Company would handle and ship the merchandise themselves. What is the selling price of a set to the buyer?

6. The Fredrick Insurance Agency purchased six new electric typewriters listed at $480 each. They received a 10 percent discount because they purchased more than five and an additional 5 percent discount because they took immediate delivery. Terms of trade were 2/5,n/30. What was the net price if payment was made within the discount period?

7. A check for the net amount of $84.28 is received from a customer who was extended terms of 2/10,n/30. The check is past the discount period. You must contact the customer and indicate the correct amount due. What is the amount due?

8. Sharon Sadlowski, payments clerk and secretary for the Tog and Slumber Shop, made out a check to the P. K. Worth Company for a purchase made on July 14. The purchase was for thirty travel wear sets priced at $23 per set. The P. K. Worth Company extended terms of 2/10,n/45, E.O.M. The price quoted was F.O.B. shipping point. Freight on the purchase was $21.80. The check will have the date of August 5. What should be the amount of the check?

9. Peter Frank ordered twenty men's suits at the Apparel Center in Chicago for his men's shop. The suits were priced at $90 each less terms of trade of 2/20,1/30,n/45,R.O.G. The purchase was made on March 12 for fall delivery. The merchandise was received on August 5 and payment was made on August 22. What was the net price for the lot of twenty suits?

10. John Cooper purchased a kitchen utensil from an ad in a magazine. The item was priced at $47.50. The ad further specified that the utensil would be shipped C.O.D. and that charges would be $2.50. What is the amount that John must pay the delivery person?

11. Pulver and Company sold three video machines to Tec-Rec, Inc. The price was $1,680 per machine F.O.B. the buyer's locations in St. Paul, Boston, and Atlanta. Terms of 3/15,n/90 were offered. The transportation costs totalled $567.80. How much did Pulver and Company receive for the machines after the cash discount and transportation costs were considered?

12. Patio Encounters paid $658.75 each for a table and four-chair set after the supplier provided a 15 percent trade discount. What was the original price of the set?

13. Randy Marsh paid an invoice with a check in the amount of $509.25. The vendor had agreed to a 25 percent trade discount and terms of 3/10,n/60. Randy made sure that he paid the invoice within the first ten days. What was the original amount of the goods before the trade and cash discounts?

14. A payment of $1,162.80 was made for merchandise purchased on July 13 and paid for on August 30. The merchandise was purchased through a wholesaler that allowed a series of 15 percent, 10 percent, and 5 percent trade discounts as well as terms of 3/10,E.O.M. What was the original price of the merchandise?

15. The Jackson and Fulmer Company will need to borrow the necessary money to pay for the $56,850 detailed on the invoice from Acme Corp. The terms of trade are 2/10,n/30. The company will receive enough revenue on the twenty-fifth day after the invoice date to repay the lender. The lender will charge 17 percent for the short-term loan. Will the company save any money by borrowing the payment amount for the fifteen days? How much? Use exact interest.

Challenge Problem

Deanna purchased 1,200 pounds of a food additive for the Ideal Food Company at a list price of $9 per pound. The purchase was made on February 12. Delivery was made on March 31. Deanna negotiated a series of trade discounts of 10 percent, 10 percent, and 7 percent. Terms of trade were 3/10,1/30,n/45,R.O.G. $1,300 of the additive at list price was returned to the supplier on April 16 because of over purchase. A partial payment of $500 was made on May 7 with the balance paid on May 28. What was the amount of the payment on May 28? The supplier uses E.O.M.

Name _____ Date _____ Score _____

Match the following terms and phrases.

_____ 1. Equivalent trade discount

_____ 2. Cash discount

_____ 3. Trade discount

_____ 4. Seller pays transportation costs

_____ 5. Independent transportation firms

_____ 6. Buyer pays the transportation costs to the seller who pays the transportation firm

_____ 7. Terms of trade

_____ 8. R.O.G.

_____ 9. Net price

_____ 10. Rates, schedules, and routes controlled by the federal government

_____ 11. Buyer pays the transportation costs to the transportation firm

_____ 12. E.O.M.

_____ 13. List price

_____ 14. Sellling price

A. discount period begins at end of the month
B. Contract carrier
C. C.O.D.
D. abbreviation of cash discount agreement
E. offered for buyer aiding the seller
F. list price less trade discounts
G. Common carrier
H. F.O.B. destination
I. F.O.B. shipping point
J. a reduction in the selling price
K. usually found in a catalogue or price sheet
L. equal to two or more trade discounts
M. discount period begins when the goods are received
N. amount due after cash discount is subtracted

Compute the selling price in the following problems.

	List Price	Trade Discounts Offered	Selling Price
15.	$600	18%	_____
16.	890	10 and 20%	_____

Compute the net price in the following problems. Assume discounts taken.

	Amount of Invoice	Transportation Agreement	Terms of Trade	Transportation Costs	Amount Due Seller
17.	$900	F.O.B. destination	1/10,n/60	$12.00	_____
18.	748	F.O.B. shipping point	2/10,n/30,R.O.G.		_____

Compute the net price in the following problems. Assume discounts taken.

	Total List Price	Trade Discounts	Terms of Trade	Purchase Date	Payment Date	Date Rec'd	Net Price
19.	$ 800	10 and 20%	2/10,n/30,R.O.G.	Dec. 3	Jan. 5	Dec. 28	_____
20.	1,000	5, 5, and 10%	1/20,n/60	May 10	May 31	May 12	_____
21.	650	5, 10, and 8%	2/15,n/60,E.O.M.	July 16	Aug. 12	July 20	_____

22. The accounts payable clerk of the A-K Marketing Company made out a check for the amount due on the purchase of ten file cabinets. The list price of the cabinets was $92 each. The firm had received an 18 percent trade discount on terms of 2/30,n/60. What is the amount of the check if payment is made within the discount period?

23. What is the amount due on a $600 purchase of merchandise bought on April 22? There is a 10 and 12 percent trade discount offered on terms of 2/5,1/20,n/60, R.O.G. The goods were received on May 2 and the payment is made on May 18.

14 Commission Sales

After mastering the material in this chapter, you will be able to:

1. Compute net sales given gross sales, sales returns, and sales allowances.
2. Compute the gross earnings of an employee paid on a straight commission basis.
3. Compute the gross earnings of an employee paid on a commission formula basis.
4. Understand and use the following terms and concepts:

Gross Sales	Net Sales
Sales Returns	Straight Commission
Sales Allowances	Gross Earnings

In chapter 5, Payroll, four basic pay systems—salary, commission, piece rate, and hourly—are discussed. This chapter will increase your understanding of the commission system and its variations. Commission is a means of motivating a salesperson to sell more by paying more for additional sales. In order to determine the amount earned by the salesperson, we must first determine net sales.

Determining Net Sales

Gross sales

The value of the merchandise sold by an employee is used to determine compensation. The value of the sale is termed **gross sales.** The product of price per unit and the number of units sold will determine gross sales. Occasionally the amount of the sale is changed due to circumstances after the sale is completed. Should a customer find that the product is not what was expected—the wrong color, size, or quantity, or other such circumstances—the merchandise may be returned to the seller. The seller gives the buyer credit for the return by reducing the total invoice amount. This action also reduces the gross sale amount for the salesperson. This reduction in gross sales is termed **sales returns.**

Sales returns
Sales allowances

Another factor that may reduce gross sales is termed **sales allowances.** Instead of asking the buyer to return the merchandise for credit, the seller may choose to offer a price reduction to the buyer. If the buyer keeps and sells merchandise that may be damaged, the wrong color, size, etc., the buyer is given a sales allowance.

Sales returns and sales allowances both reduce the amount of actual merchandise sold and therefore the amount of commission earned. By subtracting the value of sales returns and sales allowances from gross sales, the amount on which a commission is due can be determined. This amount is termed **net sales.**

Net sales

gross sales
− sales returns
− sales allowances
net sales

Example 1

Sharon Pierson sold 4,072 units of her firm's product, "The Barton," in one week. The selling price per Barton was $4.95. The selling firm had twenty-eight units returned and made a 20 percent price allowance on another forty units. What were the net sales for Sharon for the week?

4,072	= units sold
×$ 4.95	= price per unit
$20,156.40	= gross sales
− 138.60	= less sales returns (28 units × $4.95 per unit)
− 39.60	= less sales allowances (40 units × $4.95 × 20%)
$19,978.20	= net sales for the week

Exercise A   Determine net sales in the following exercises.

Employee	Units Sold	Price/Unit	Units Returned	Sales Allowance Units	Sales Allowance Percent	Net Sales
1. L. Potter	963	$60.00	12	2	10%	$ 57,048.00
2. M. Wierick	900	2.20	420	10	18	_____
3. T. Bowden	2,500	8.00	0	9	7	_____
4. M. Maxwell	9,500	41.75	2	0	—	_____
5. N. Hildredth	700	23.80	35	80	50	_____
6. J. Stewart	400	35.00	10	6	10	_____
7. G. Thomas	5,500	17.50	156	120	30	_____
8. J. Ureel	19,760	19.82	2,390	20	10	_____
9. J. Sahtout	2,952	23.60	543	175	15	_____
10. D. Yost	53,000	46.00	7	0	—	_____

Determining Gross Earnings

The amount of commission earned for each sale varies from firm to firm and also by product. The more difficult the sale, the higher the dollar value of the product, the more widespread the customers, the higher the commission. The commission system is designed to provide more income for selling more merchandise. There are two types of commission systems: straight commission and a commission formula.

Straight Commission

Straight commission
Gross earnings

A salesperson compensated by a specified percent of sales is paid on a **straight commission** basis. Net sales are multiplied by a percent agreed upon by the firm and the salesperson. The product of net sales and the percent of commission rate determine **gross earnings.**

Example 2

Dale Kirkby is a manufacturer's representative for Patio Playtime Furniture. He earns a commission of 3 percent on all net sales. Net sales for the quarter ended June 30 were $230,000. What is his commission for the period?

$$
\begin{array}{rl}
\$230,000 & = \text{net sales} \\
\times \quad\quad .03 & = \text{straight commission rate} \\
\hline
\$ \quad 6,900 & = \text{gross earnings}
\end{array}
$$

Example 3

Net sales for Bill Wilson for the month were $126,850. Bill is paid a 1.3 percent commission rate. What are Bill's gross earnings?

$$
\begin{array}{rl}
\$ \quad 126,850 & = \text{net sales} \\
\times \quad\quad .013 & = \text{straight commission rate} \\
\hline
\$1,649.05 & = \text{gross earnings}
\end{array}
$$

Exercise B

Determine the gross earnings in the exercise below.

	Gross Sales	Sales Returns	Sales Allowances	Net Sales	Straight Commission Rate	Gross Earnings
1.	$ 84,600	$400	$ 710	$ 83,490	3%	$2,504.70
2.	137,000	700	1,950	134,350	2.5	
3.	138,000	260	0	137,740	4	
4.	97,000	300	1,250	95,450	4	
5.	98,520	850	13,570	84,100	3.5	
6.	46,900	120	2,800	43,980	2	

	Gross Sales	Sales Returns	Sales Allowances	Net Sales	Straight Commission Rate	Gross Earnings
7.	$ 89,800	$ 0	$ 1,500	$ 88,300	4%	_____
8.	83,500	55	2,690	80,755	5	_____
9.	63,350	0	1,620	61,730	4.7	_____
10.	112,600	260	190	112,150	3.6	_____

Commission Formula

Extra sales beyond a certain level may be more difficult to achieve. A salesperson may not feel that the extra effort is really worth the extra compensation. In these cases an additional incentive may be necessary in order to gain the extra sales. The additional incentive is in the form of a salary or a commission rate that increases as sales increase. This makes every extra sale worth even more to the salesperson.

Example 4

Joan Bulock is paid a commission of 1 percent on net sales and an additional 3 percent on net sales above $140,000 a month. Joan's net sales this month were $185,000. What were her gross earnings?

$$
\begin{array}{rl}
\$185,000 & = \text{net sales} \\
\times \quad .01 & = \text{commission rate on all sales} \\
\hline
\$\ \ 1,850 & = \text{commission}
\end{array}
$$

$$
\begin{array}{rl}
\$185,000 & \\
-\ 140,000 & \\
\hline
\$\ 45,000 & = \text{net sales above } \$140,000 \\
\times \quad .03 & = \text{commission rate on sales above } \$140,000 \\
\hline
\$\ \ 1,350 & = \text{commission}
\end{array}
$$

$$
\begin{array}{rl}
\$1,850 & = (1\% - \text{commission}) \\
+\ 1,350 & = (3\% - \text{commission}) \\
\hline
\$3,200 & = \text{gross earnings}
\end{array}
$$

Example 5

Raye Dellis sold $141,850 of electronic merchandise for Piedmont & Co. Raye is paid a commission of 1 percent on sales up to $100,000, 2.5 percent on sales between $100,000 and $150,000, and 4 percent on sales above $150,000. What were Raye's gross earnings this month?

$$
\begin{array}{rl}
\$100,000 & \text{(first } \$100,000 \text{ of sales)} \\
\times \quad .01 & \text{(1\% commission rate)} \\
\hline
\$\ \ 1,000 & \text{commission}
\end{array}
$$

Example 5 *Continued*

```
   $ 41,850     (sales between $100,000 and $150,000)
×       .025     (2.5% commission rate)
   $  1,046.25   commission


          $1,000.00     (1% commission)
        +  1,046.25     (2.5% commission)
          $2,046.25     gross earnings
```

Example 6

Lori Driscol has been the top sales representative for Piedmont & Co. for the past six years. Lori is on the same commission formula as Raye. Lori's sales for the month totaled $164,000. What are her gross earnings for this month?

```
   $100,000     (first $100,000 of sales)
×        .01     (1% commission rate)
   $   1,000     commission


   $  50,000     (sales between $100,000 and $150,000)
×        .025     (2.5% commission rate)
   $   1,250     commission


   $  14,000     (sales above $150,000)
×        .04     (4% commission rate)
   $      560     commission


        $1,000     (1% commission)
         1,250     (2.5% commission)
       +    560     (4% commission)
        $2,810     gross earnings
```

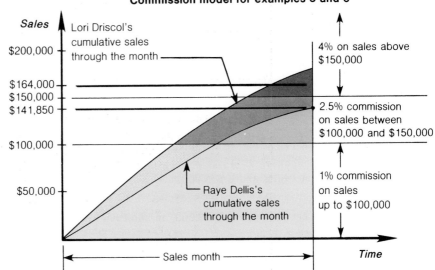

Commission model for examples 5 and 6

Example 7

John is paid on a combination salary and commission basis. He receives a $500 a month salary plus a $\frac{1}{2}$ percent commission on sales between $50,000 and $140,000, 3 percent commission on sales between $140,000 and $200,000, and a 5 percent commission on sales above $200,000. John had net sales of $168,000 this month. What were John's gross earnings for the month?

$$
\begin{array}{rl}
\$90,000 & \text{(sales between \$50,000 and \$140,000)} \\
\times \quad .005 & (\tfrac{1}{2}\ \%\ \text{commission rate}) \\
\hline
\$ \quad 450 & \text{commission}
\end{array}
$$

$$
\begin{array}{rl}
\$28,000 & \text{(sales between \$140,000 and \$200,000)} \\
\times \quad .03 & \text{(3\% commission rate)} \\
\hline
\$ \quad 840 & \text{commission}
\end{array}
$$

$$
\begin{array}{rl}
\$ \ 500 & \text{salary} \\
450 & (\tfrac{1}{2}\ \%\ \text{commission}) \\
+ \quad 840 & \text{(3\% commission)} \\
\hline
\$1,790 & \text{gross earnings}
\end{array}
$$

As you can see, there are many different possible commission formulas. Each formula has an advantage to the salesperson and the firm.

Exercise C   Determine the gross earnings in the exercises below.

	Net Sales	Commission Formula	Gross Earnings
1.	$ 86,000	1% on net sales and 2% on sales over $60,000	$1,380.00
2.	74,000	3% on net sales above $35,000	_____
3.	134,900	1% on net sales and 3.5% on sales over $120,000	_____
4.	208,500	2% on net sales between $150,000 and $200,000, 3% on net sales over $200,000	_____
5.	168,300	1.5% on net sales above $150,000 and 2% on net sales above $200,000	_____
6.	86,950	$720 salary plus 2% on net sales above $75,000	_____
7.	131,500	1% on net sales between $50,000 and $150,000, 2% on net sales above $150,000	_____
8.	92,600	5% on net sales above $75,000	_____
9.	176,950	2% on net sales above $100,000, an additional $2\frac{1}{2}$ % on net sales above $150,000	_____
10.	120,000	1.7% on net sales plus 2% on net sales above $100,000	_____

Assignment

Chapter Fourteen

Name _____ Date _____ Score _____

Skill Problems Determine the net sales in the problems below.

	Units Sold	Price Per Unit	Units Returned	Sales Allowance Units	Sales Allowance Percent	Net Sales
1.	1,215	$ 7.00	0	7	40	_____
2.	1,580	23.50	74	41	10	_____
3.	1,420	8.75	8	0	17	_____
4.	758	15.00	144	8	10	_____
5.	2,830	16.70	10	1	30	_____

Determine gross earnings in the problems below.

	Gross Sales	Sales Returns	Sales Allowances	Net Sales	Straight Commission Rate	Gross Earnings
6.	$105,400	$405	$ 75	_____	3%	_____
7.	85,690	0	980	_____	4	_____
8.	81,240	140	193	_____	3.7	_____
9.	134,740	580	0	_____	2.5	_____
10.	68,090	425	53	_____	4	_____

	Net Sales	Commission Formula	Gross Earnings
11.	$ 72,300	2% on net sales above $20,000	_____
12.	93,600	1% on net sales plus $1\frac{1}{2}$ % on sales above $75,000	_____
13.	68,400	3% on net sales above $70,000	_____
14.	85,600	$300 salary plus 1% on net sales above $50,000	_____
15.	127,000	$500 salary plus 1% on all net sales above $80,000	_____

1. Tom made the sale indicated on the sales invoice below. He is paid a straight commission of 5 percent on all sales. What commission will Tom earn on this sale?

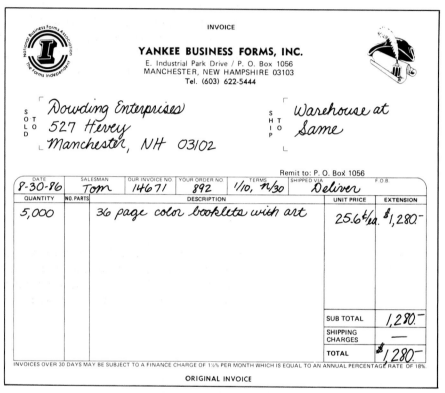

INVOICE

YANKEE BUSINESS FORMS, INC.
E. Industrial Park Drive / P. O. Box 1056
MANCHESTER, NEW HAMPSHIRE 03103
Tel. (603) 622-5444

SOLD TO: *Dowding Enterprises* *527 Hevey* *Manchester, NH 03102*

SHIP TO: *Warehouse at Same*

Remit to: P. O. Box 1056

DATE	SALESMAN	OUR INVOICE NO.	YOUR ORDER NO.	TERMS	SHIPPED VIA	F.O.B.
8-30-86	Tom	14671	892	1/10, n/30	Deliver	

QUANTITY	NO. PARTS	DESCRIPTION	UNIT PRICE	EXTENSION
5,000		36 page color booklets with art	25.6¢/ea.	$1,280.—
		SUB TOTAL		1,280.—
		SHIPPING CHARGES		—
		TOTAL		$1,280.—

INVOICES OVER 30 DAYS MAY BE SUBJECT TO A FINANCE CHARGE OF 1½% PER MONTH WHICH IS EQUAL TO AN ANNUAL PERCENTAGE RATE OF 18%.

ORIGINAL INVOICE

Courtesy of Yankee Business Forms, Manchester, NH.

2. Monty Perez was paid a salary of $500 for the month. His paycheck indicated gross earnings of $2,080. Besides the salary, Monty earns a commission of 1 percent on all sales. What were his sales for the month?

3. The average sale at the Belelor Corporation is $510. Each sales representative makes about three sales a day. Belelor pays a commission of 4 percent on all sales. What will the average sales representative earn a day?

4. Charlie was paid a $472 commission for selling $9,440 of promotional material. What was the rate of commission?

5. The Kieth Steele Company pays all of its salespeople a 3 percent commission on net sales with a bonus of 1 percent commission on net sales above $140,000. Kit Russel sold $162,873 of merchandise this month. The inspection department of a customer's company refused to accept a forty-unit shipment valued at $28 per unit. These units were returned. What were Kit's gross earnings for the month?

6. Edmund Perkel is currently paid a salary of $1,500 a month. He has been offered a sales position that pays a $500 salary plus 2 percent commission on the first $50,000 of sales and 4 percent on sales above $50,000. How much will he have to sell in order to equal his current job?

7. Phyllis earned a commission of $459 for her sales last week. Her commission rate is 4 percent. She had $460 of returns last week. What were her gross sales for the week?

8. The Bridgeton Manufacturing Company pays a commission of 3 percent on all sales and an extra $1\frac{1}{2}$ percent on sales above $250,000. The top salesperson sold $267,970 last month. There were thirty-five units returned during the month. Each unit is priced at $659.00. What was the commission earned by the top salesperson this month?

9. Betty has been offered a sales position with Norton Sales Co. The sales manager has indicated that the company pays a commission rate of 5 percent on net sales. The average salesperson makes $260 a week selling Norton products. What will be the average net sales required to earn $260 a week?

10. Rob is paid a salary of $600 a month plus a 2 percent commission on net sales over $40,000 and an additional 1 percent on net sales over $100,000. Rob sold $164,800 of merchandise this month with only $3,200 of returns. What were Rob's gross earnings?

11. Paul works on a commission basis for a firm that charges a fee. The fee is based on a percent of the cost of the service. The service that The First Federal Bank purchased cost $45,000. The fee was 25 percent of the service. Paul earns 40 percent of the fee as a commission. What is Paul's commission on the First Federal Bank service?

12. Mr. Delano offered the Northeast territory of the U.S. to Haber, a recent college graduate. Haber needs to earn $25,000 a year in order to pay off his college student loan and pay for the usual household expenses. The product that Haber will sell pays a $\frac{1}{2}$ % commission. The price of the product is $86.00. Haber will also receive a salary of $500 per month. How many units of the product will he need to sell in order to reach his earnings objective of $25,000 per year?

13. Raymond had returns last month totaling $4,200. This was the biggest amount of returns ever and constituted 2 percent of his gross sales. Raymond is paid a straight commission of $3\frac{1}{2}$ percent on net sales. What were his earnings for the month?

Challenge Problem

Fredricka is paid a salary of $450 a month plus a 1 percent commission on net sales between $100,000 and $150,000 and 3 percent on net sales above $150,000. Sales returns on Fredricka's accounts this month were $2,700. The firm also gave a 30 percent sales allowance on 180 units of an item priced at $62.50 each. Her gross earnings for the month were $1,300. What were her gross sales for the month?

Name _____ Date _____ Score _____

True or False

T   F   1. Net sales + sales returns + sales allowances = gross sales.

T   F   2. Sales returns are items that are returned to the selling firm due to some type of discrepency in color, size, amount, or some other factor.

T   F   3. Sales returns will reduce the commission of a representative that is paid on net sales.

T   F   4. A commission formula will pay the representative a fixed rate on all net sales. The salary is subtracted from the commission to find gross earnings.

T   F   5. Sales allowances are done to increase the amount of the sale at the time that the sale is made.

6. Determine net sales in the problem below.
   Units Sold = 1,200
   Price Per Unit = $20
   Units Returned = 20

   Net Sales = $ _____

7. Determine gross earnings in the problem below.
   Units Sold = 320
   Price Per Unit = $40
   Sales Allowance
       Units = 10
       Percent = 30
   Commission Rate = 4%

   Gross Earnings $ _____

8. Determine gross earnings in the problem below.
   Units Sold = 1,000
   Price Per Unit = $32
   Sales Returns = 20 units
   Commission Formula = $500 salary plus 1% on sales above $20,000 and an additional 1% on sales above $25,000.

   Gross Earnings $ _____

9. Sue is paid a commission rate of 3 percent on net sales. Her gross earnings for the week were $960. What were her net sales?

10. Ken is salaried at $1,000 a month and earns a $1\frac{1}{2}$ % commission on all sales above $70,000 and a 1 percent bonus commission on sales above $100,000. This month he sold $132,000 of merchandise. What were his gross earnings?

11. Sally Kwasnic sold eighty-five units at $1,350 during the last month. The accounting department indicated that four of the units were returned. She earns a 3.2 percent commission on net sales. What is her commission for the month?

12. The Ferrara Corp. pays its sales representatives a commission of 4 percent on all sales above $50,000. The sales staff all receive a salary of $600.00 a month. Sales for the past month were $589,880. There are five sales representatives in the firm. What is the average monthly commission per representative?

13. Toni sold the big screen TV shown on the following invoice. Her compensation is based on 4 percent of all sales. What is the amount of commission that she will earn on this sale?

THE BEST SERVICE COSTS NO MORE

WILTON'S
TV & APPLIANCE , INC.

2703 PINEGROVE
982-9549
PORT HURON, MICHIGAN 48060

Customer's Order No. _____

Date *12-3* 19 *86*

Sold To *Mark Watson & Associates*

Address *2306 Pine Grove Avenue*

City *Port Huron, MI 48060*

SOLD BY	CASH	C O D	CHARGE	ON ACCT	MDSE RETD	PAID OUT	
T	✓						

Quantity	DESCRIPTION	Price	Amount
1	*Super Screen TV w/ rmt. controls and base*		*$2,195 —*
	Deliver Tuesday AM		
	non taxable	**TAX**	*—*

THANK YOU -Please keep this copy for reference.

TOTAL *$2,195 —*

ALL claims and returned goods MUST be accompanied by this bill.

29500 **Received by**

BEE LINE BUSINESS SYSTEMS - MT. CLEMENS, MICHIGAN 48043

83525

Courtesy of Wilton's TV & Appliances, Inc., Port Huron, MI.

15 Markup

After mastering the material in this chapter, you will be able to:

1. Calculate cost based on cost or sales.
2. Calculate markup based on cost or sales.
3. Calculate sales based on cost or sales.
4. Convert a markup on cost to a markup on sales.
5. Convert a markup on sales to a markup on cost.
6. Calculate the markdown or new selling price.
7. Determine wholesale catalog prices when a trade discount and a markup are to be considered.
8. Understand and use the following terms:
   Markup   Selling Price
   Cost Price   List Price

In order for a merchandising firm to stay in business it must sell its merchandise for more than it pays for it. The merchant must increase the price enough to cover overhead, such as the cost of utilities, rent, taxes, wages, and insurance. There must be an incentive to risk the capital investment required to go into business. This incentive or profit is a return on the capital investment, a reward for the risk taken, and in some cases, compensation for hours worked by the

Markup
owners. Overhead and profit are grouped together and termed **markup** by merchants. Markup is the difference between the amount that is paid for the merchandise and the amount that it is sold for by the merchant.

Markup is used by all members of the channel of distribution, such as retailers, wholesalers, distributors, manufacturers, and independent salespeople. Any firm or person dealing with the flow of goods or materials through the channel of distribution comes into contact with markup. Members of the channel of distribution are often termed middlemen. This term is used because their activities are between the manufacturer of the product and its use or consumption by the final consumer.

Cost price
The price that the firm pays for an item is termed the **cost price.** Cash and trade discounts must be subtracted to find the cost price, which is the net price paid for merchandise.

Selling price
The **selling price** is the amount for which merchandise is sold. This is the amount after trade discounts have been subtracted. The selling price is found by adding a markup to a cost price (i.e., cost price + markup = selling price).

Example 1

A merchant purchased a desk for $165 and marked it up by $70. What is the selling price on the desk?

$$\begin{array}{rl} \$165 & = \text{cost price} \\ +\ \ 70 & = \text{markup} \\ \hline \$235 & = \text{selling price} \end{array}$$

Often the markup is not a specific dollar amount but a percent. The percent is determined by considering the amount of overhead and profit that the firm must earn to stay in business. The percent of markup must be based on one of the two factors in the formula: cost price + markup = selling price.

Markup on Cost

Middlemen often mark up goods based on cost. The cost price of the merchandise is increased by the markup rate. The markup rate is based, in this case, on the cost price of the merchandise. The cost price is, therefore, 100 percent (the base). The selling price percent is the total of the cost price (100 percent) and the markup rate.

Example 2

A gift wholesaler purchased a carload of decorative radios for a price of $15 per item. The goods were priced to sell using the company's standard markup rate of 40 percent. What is the selling price?

100%	40%	140%
Cost Price	+ Markup	= Selling Price
$15		

The selling price in this example is the percentage. The 140% is the rate and the $15 cost price is the base. The percentage is found by:

$P = B \times R$
$P = \$15 \times 1.40\ (100\% + 40\%)$
$P = \$21$ (selling price)

Example 3

A swimming pool accessory firm marks up its merchandise 55 percent on cost. A pool cleaner is purchased for $8. What is the selling price?

100%	55%	155%
Cost Price	+ Markup	= Selling Price
$8.00		

$P = B \times R$
$P = \$8.00 \times 1.55$
$P = \$12.40$ (selling price)

Determine the selling price and markup amount in the exercises. Round off your answer to the nearest cent.

	Cost Price	Markup	Markup Percent on Cost	Selling Price
1.	$ 40.00	$20.00	50%	$ 60.00
2.	60.00	12.00	20	$72.00
3.	100.00	35.00	35	$135.00
4.	125.00	50.00	40	$175.00
5.	48.50	11.16	23	$59.60

Markup on Sales

Goods are either marked up based on cost price or on selling price. If the markup is based on the selling price or sales, then the selling price is 100 percent (the base).

Example 4

Using the information in Example 2, what is the selling price of an item that cost $15 if it will be marked up 40 percent on sales?

$$60\% \quad + \quad 40\% \quad = \quad 100\%$$
Cost Price + Markup = Selling Price
$15

The selling price in this example is the base (100 percent). The 60 percent is the rate, and $15 is the percentage. The base is found by:

$$B = P \div R$$
$$B = \$15 \div .60$$
$$B = \$25 \text{ (selling price)}$$

Notice that a problem that indicates a markup on sales is both handled differently and results in a different answer than one that is marked up on cost.

Example 5

A gift shop bought a piece of glassware for $42. The owner marked up the item 20 percent on sales. What was the selling price?

$$80\% \quad + \quad 20\% \quad = \quad 100\%$$
Cost Price + Markup = Selling Price
$42

Base = Percentage ÷ Rate
Base = $42 ÷ .80
Base = $52.50 (selling price)

Determine the selling price and markup amount in the exercises. Round off your answer to the nearest cent.

	Cost Price	Markup	Markup Percent on Sales	Selling Price
1.	$150	$ 37.50	20%	$187.50
2.	250		35	
3.	80		40	
4.	48		50	
5.	13		45	

Exercise C Determine the selling price in the following exercises. Note the basis of the markup rate. Round off your answers to the nearest cent.

	Cost Price	Markup Rate	Markup on:	Selling Price
1.	$ 90.00	10%	Cost Price	$ 99.00
2.	30.00	40	Cost Price	
3.	160.00	25	Cost Price	$ 200.00
4.	146.00	60	Selling Price	
5.	12.00	50	Selling Price	$ 24.00
6.	14.50	40	Cost Price	
7.	8.00	60	Selling Price	$ 20.00
8.	780.00	45	Cost Price	
9.	19.00	25	Selling Price	$ 25.33
10.	46.00	70	Selling Price	

Finding Cost, Sales, Markup, or Markdown

There are occasions when a middleman needs to know an answer other than the selling price in a markup problem. The information needed may be the cost price, the markup amount, the markup percent, the percent of cost to sales, etc. The possible questions are numerous. These problems require the student to understand the markup formula and percentage. It would be difficult to memorize the procedure for all the problem types. The following examples are designed to provide a guide to work the many types of markup problems. You should determine if the problem is a markup on cost or on sales, then solve for either base, rate, or percentage.

Notice that in all of the examples a basic procedure is followed: (1) the markup formula is used, (2) the markup base is identified with 100 percent, (3) the dollar values available are included in the formula, (4) the percent values available are included in the formula, and (5) the unknown factor is determined. This procedure is an excellent method to solve markup problems. It is recommended that the student adopt this procedure until another method proves to be more workable.

Example 6

To find the cost price when the markup is on cost—What is the cost price on an article priced to sell at $40 if the merchant has marked it up 20 percent on cost?

$$100\% \quad + \quad 20\% \quad = \quad 120\%$$
$$\text{Cost Price} \quad + \quad \text{Markup} \quad = \quad \text{Selling Price}$$
$$\$40$$

Base = Percentage ÷ Rate
Base = $40 ÷ 1.20
Base = $33.33 (answer)

Example 7

To find the cost price when the markup is on sales—What is the cost price on an item priced to sell at $65 if the markup is 30 percent on sales?

$$70\% \quad + \quad 30\% \quad = \quad 100\%$$
$$\text{Cost Price} \quad + \quad \text{Markup} \quad = \quad \text{Selling Price}$$
$$\$65$$

Percentage = Base × Rate
Percentage = $65 × .70
Percentage = $45.50 (answer)

Example 8

To find the markup when the markup percent is on sales—What is the markup on an item priced to sell at $50 if the markup percent is 20 percent on sales?

$$80\% \quad + \quad 20\% \quad = \quad 100\%$$
$$\text{Cost Price} \quad + \quad \text{Markup} \quad = \quad \text{Selling Price}$$
$$\$50$$

Percentage = Base × Rate
Percentage = $50 × .20
Percentage = $10 (answer)

Example 9

To find the markup when the markup percent is on cost—What is the markup on an item priced to sell at $80 if the markup percent is 30 percent on cost?

$$100\% \quad + \quad 30\% \quad = \quad 130\%$$
$$\text{Cost Price} + \text{Markup} = \text{Selling Price}$$
$$\$80$$

Base = Percentage ÷ Rate
Base = $80 ÷ 1.3
Base = $61.54 (cost price)

Percentage = Base × Rate
Percentage = $61.54 × .30
Percentage = $18.46 (answer)

Example 10

To find the markup when the markup percent is on cost—What is the markup on an item that costs $40 and is to be marked up 20 percent on cost?

$$100\% \quad + \quad 20\% \quad = \quad 120\%$$
$$\text{Cost Price} + \text{Markup} = \text{Selling Price}$$
$$\$40$$

Percentage = Base × Rate
Percentage = $40 × .20
Percentage = $8 (answer)

Example 11

To find the markup percent on cost—What is the markup percent on cost of an item that costs $30 and is priced to sell for $125?

$$100\%$$
$$\text{Cost Price} + \text{Markup} = \text{Selling Price}$$
$$\$30 \quad + \quad \$95 \quad = \quad \$125$$

Rate = Percentage ÷ Base
Rate = $95 ÷ $30
Rate = 317% (answer)

Example 12

To find the markup percent on sales—What is the markup percent on sales of an item that costs $40 and is priced to sell at $70?

$$100\%$$

Cost Price + Markup = Selling Price

$40 + $30 = $70

Rate = Percentage ÷ Base
Rate = $30 ÷ $70
Rate = 43% (answer)

Example 13

To find the percent of cost to sales—What is the percent of cost to sales of an item that has a 40 percent markup on sales? The item is priced to sell at $50.

60% + 40% = 100%
Cost Price + Markup = Selling Price
$50

Answer: 60%

Example 14

To find the percent of cost to sales—What is the percent of cost to sales of an item that has a 25 percent markup on cost? The item is priced to sell at $80.

100% + 25% = 125%
Cost Price + Markup = Selling Price
$80

Base = Percentage ÷ Rate
Base = $80 ÷ 1.25
Base = $64 (cost price)
Rate = Percentage ÷ Base
Rate = $64 ÷ $80
Rate = 80% (answer)

Determine the answer in the exercises below. Note the markup base—cost or sales. Round off your answers to the nearest percent or cent.

	Cost Price	Selling Price	Markup Percent	Markup on:	Markup
1.	$128.00	$160.00	20	Sales	$ 32.00
2.		50.00	30	Sales	
3.	40.00		70	Sales	
4.	93.00		20	Cost	
5.		46.00	35	Cost	
6.		47.50	30	Sales	
7.	22.00	39.95		Cost	
8.	45.00	65.50		Sales	
9.			25	Sales	57.00
10.			35	Cost	80.00
11.	20.00	48.00		Cost	
12.	36.00	48.00		Sales	
13.	125.50	200.00		Cost	
14.		56.00	20	Sales	
15.	42.00		350	Cost	

Markdown or Loss

There are times that a retailer may decide to mark down the current inventory in order to move the merchandise. The retailer usually decides on a rate of markdown and has the price tags marked accordingly. The markdown is always based on the previous selling price.

Example 15

Find the sale price on an item that was previously marked $30 and that is now to be part of the store-wide 10 percent sale.

```
   90%           10%           100%
Sale Price + Markdown = Selling Price (previous)
                              $30
```

$30

Percentage = Base × Rate
Percentage = $30 × .90
Percentage = $27 (Sale Price)

When merchandise is sold at an actual loss (less than the cost price), the percent of loss must be caculated. The loss is always based on the cost price.

Example 16

Find the percent of loss on an item that cost $50 and is sold for $40.

100%
Cost Price + Loss = Selling Price
   $50 $10 $40

Rate = Percentage ÷ Rate
Rate = $10 ÷ $40
Rate = 20% (loss)

Exercise E

Determine the answer in the exercises below. Round off your answer to the nearest cent or percent.

	Selling Price	Markdown	Sale Price
1.	$85.00	30%	$59.50
2.	17.00	40	*10.20*
3.	40.00	25	*30.00*
4.	17.95	20	*14.36*

	Cost Price	Selling Price	Loss
5.	$ 68	$40	*41%*
6.	35	20	*43%*
7.	80	50	*38%*
8.	129	89	*31%*

68−40=28÷68=41 (handwritten beside row 5)

Conversion of Markup Rate

A markup of 20 percent on sales is not the same amount as a markup of 20 percent on cost. When a merchant wishes to compare various markups, the markups must be stated using the same base. This will allow for a direct comparison of markup rates. The markup rate on one base can be changed to another base by using the same markup formula.

To change the markup rate on one base (cost or sales) to another base, divide the current markup percent by the new base percent.

Example 17

What is the markup percent on sales if the markup percent on cost is 30 percent?

$$\begin{array}{ccc} 100\% & + & 30\% & = 130\% \\ \text{Cost Price} & + & \text{Markup} & = \text{Selling Price} \end{array}$$

$$\text{Markup percent on sales} = \frac{30\% \text{ (current markup percent)}}{130\% \text{ (new base percent) sales}}$$

Markup percent on sales = 23% (answer)

The new markup percent on sales in the above example can be used in the markup formula as follows.

$$\begin{array}{ccc} 77\% & + & 23\% & = & 100\% \\ \text{Cost Price} & + & \text{Markup} & = & \text{Selling Price} \end{array}$$

The two markup values (30 percent on cost and 23 percent on sales) are equal. To prove this, use a cost price of $3 in each case to determine the selling price.

on Cost	*on Sales*
100% + 30% = 130%	77% + 23% = 100%
Cost + Markup = Selling	Cost + Markup = Selling
Price Price	Price Price
$3	$3
Percentage = Base × Rate	Base = Percentage ÷ Rate
Percentage = $3 × 1.30	Base = $3 ÷ .77
Percentage = $3.90 (the selling price)	Base = $3.90 (the selling price)

Example 18

What is the markup percent on cost if the markup percent on sales is 20 percent?

$$\begin{array}{ccc} 80\% & + & 20\% & = & 100\% \\ \text{Cost Price} & + & \text{Markup} & = & \text{Selling Price} \end{array}$$

$$\text{Markup percent on cost} = \frac{20\% \text{ (current markup percent)}}{80\% \text{ (new base percent) cost}}$$

Markup percent on cost = 25% (answer)

In the previous example a markup of 20 percent on sales is equal to a markup of 25 percent on cost. Proof—What is the selling price of a product that costs $85.60 (using 20 percent on sales and 25 percent on cost)?

on Cost	*on Sales*
100% + 25% = 125%	80% + 20% = 100%
Cost + Markup = Selling Price	Cost + Markup = Selling Price
$85.60	$85.60

Percentage = Base × Rate   Base = Percentage ÷ Rate

Percentage = $85.60 × 1.25   Base = $85.60 ÷ .80

Percentage = $107 (answer)   Base = $107 (answer)

Exercise F   Determine the markup percent on the new base in the exercises below. Round off your answers to the nearest percent.

	Markup Percent on Cost	*Markup Percent on Sales*		*Markup Percent on Cost*	*Markup Percent on Sales*
1.	40%	29%	6.	30	_____
2.	50	_____	7.	_____	40
3.	_____	30	8.	20	_____
4.	_____	50	9.	45	_____
5.	80	_____	10.	_____	20

Catalog Pricing

Merchandise sold by wholesalers or manufacturers is often priced in a catalog and may be subject to a discount (see chapter 13—Discounts). Trade discounts are available for larger purchases and for the buyer performing marketing functions for the seller. The seller must determine the price to be shown in a catalog in order to allow for trade discounts. This price is known as a **list price.** Trade discounts are subtracted from the list price to find the selling price. The relationship of cost price, selling price, and list price is shown below.

List price

(Cost Price + Markup) = Selling Price

Selling Price + Trade Discount = List Price

Example 19

What is the list price on an item that cost a wholesaler $17 if the wholesaler will mark it up 20 percent on sales and allow for a 10 percent trade discount?

   0% + 20% =   100%

Cost Price + Markup = Selling Price

   $17

Base = Percentage ÷ Rate

Base = $17 ÷ .80

Base = $21.25 (the selling price)

   90%   +   10%   =   100%

Selling Price + Trade Discount = List Price

   $21.25

Base = Percentage ÷ Rate

Base = $21.25 ÷ .90

Base = $23.61 (list price)

Example 20

What is the list price on a piece of furniture that cost the distributor $145? The markup is 35 percent on cost; 20 percent and 15 percent trade discounts will be available.

    100%   +   35%   =   135%
Cost Price + Markup = Selling Price
   $145

Percentage = Base $\times$ Rate
Percentage = $145 $\times$ 1.35
Percentage = $195.75 (the selling price)

     68%   +   32%   =   100%
               (20% and 15%)
Selling Price + Trade Discount = List Price
   $195.75

Base = Percentage $\div$ Rate
Base = $195.75 $\div$ .68
Base = $287.87 (list price)

Exercise G   Determine the list prices in the exercises below. Round off your answers to the nearest cent.

	Cost Price	Markup Percent	Markup on:	Trade Discount	List Price
1.	$ 40	150	Cost	15%	$ 117.65
2.	25	35	Sales	10	
3.	163	40	Cost	15 and 10	
4.	47	60	Cost	21	
5.	80	55	Cost	17	
6.	65	7	Sales	20 and 15	
7.	72	42	Cost	15	
8.	1,530	80	Sales	10 and 15	
9.	96	12	Cost	10	
10.	120	17	Sales	20	

Additional Trade Discounts

When a middleman finds another source for a product at a lower price, the middleman may decide not to issue a new catalog immediately. The lower cost price would provide a higher profit for the seller. However, in order to stay competitive, the middleman may decide to offer an additional trade discount passing along to the customer the cost price reduction. The percent of additional trade discount that can be passed on is shown in Example 21.

Example 21

A wholesaler pays $146 for an industrial machine knife. The knife is marked up 40 percent on cost and a 15 percent trade discount is allowed. What is the list price?

$$100\% \quad + \quad 40\% \quad = \quad 140\%$$
Cost Price + Markup = Selling Price
  $146

Percentage = B × R
Percentage = $146 × 1.4
Percentage = $204.40 (selling price)

$$85\% \quad + \quad 15\% \quad = \quad 100\%$$
Selling Price + Discount = List Price
  $204.40

Base = P ÷ R
Base = $204.40 ÷ .85
Base = $240.47 (list price)

  A new supplier can provide the same quality knife to the wholesaler for a cost of $120. What is the additional trade discount that can be offered to customers?
  The solution begins with the new cost price. This price must be marked up, then the answer is compared to the old selling price to determine the additional trade discount.

$$100\% \quad + \quad 40\% \quad = \quad 140\%$$
Cost Price + Markup = Selling Price
  $120

Percentage = B × R
Percentage = $120 × 1.40
Percentage = $168 (new selling price)

    $204.40 —selling price (old)
  − 168.00 —selling price (new)
    $ 36.40 —additional discount

$$\frac{\$\ 36.40 —\text{additional discount}}{\$204.40 —\text{old selling price}} = 18\% \text{ additional trade discount}$$
(answer)

The additional trade discount can also be found by: (1) determining the difference in the old and new cost prices, and (2) dividing the difference by the old cost price.

Example 22

The cost price of a toy robot is $190. A new supplier can reduce the cost price to $172. What will be the additional trade discount the seller can offer if the markup rate and trade discounts remain the same?

$190 old cost price
− 172 new cost price
$ 18 difference

$$\frac{\$18}{\$190} = 9\% \text{ additional trade discount}$$

Exercise H   Determine the list price and additional trade discount. Round off your answer to the nearest percent or cent.

	Cost Price	Markup Percent	Markup on:	Trade Discount	List Price	New Cost Price	Additional Trade Discount Percent
1.	$127.00	15%	Sales	10%	$166.01	$120.00	6%
2.	427.00	35	Cost	20	_____	360.70	_____
3.	320.00	20	Sales	10 and 15	_____	268.00	_____
4.	95.50	38	Cost	$7\frac{1}{2}$	_____	76.00	_____
5.	147.00	80	Cost	22	_____	138.60	_____

Skill Problems Complete the following problems to find the answer indicated. Round off your answers to the nearest percent or cent.

	Cost Price	Selling Price	Markup Percent	Markup on:	Markup
1.	$140.00	_____	35%	Cost	_____
2.	47.50	62.00	____	Cost	_____
3.	60.00	85.00	____	Sales	_____
4.	_____	188.00	20	Cost	_____
5.	_____	_____	40	Sales	60.00
6.	_____	_____	30	Sales	80.00
7.	72.00	_____	60	Cost	_____
8.	_____	27.50	40	Sales	_____
9.	40.00	_____	30	Sales	_____
10.	_____	12.80	120	Cost	_____

	Cost Price	Markup Percent	Markup on:	Selling Price	Trade Discount	List Price
11.	$30.00	40%	Sales	_____	15%	_____
12.	_____	75	Cost	_____	15	147.50
13.	46.00	30	Cost	_____	6	_____
14.	25.50	30	Sales	_____	17	_____
15.	_____	20	Sales	_____	20	60.00

	Cost Price	Markup Percent	Markup on:	Trade Discount	List Price	New Cost Price	Additional Trade Discount Percent
16.	$ 42.00	20%	Cost	12%	_____	$37.50	_____
17.	23.60	70	Cost	10	_____	21.90	_____
18.	126.00	35	Sales	15 and 10	_____	93.70	_____

1. The Carnes Gift Shop purchased an antique for $40 and resold it for $90. To the nearest percent, what is the markup percent on sales?

2. The Merrimack St. Garage, Inc. prices all repair parts to sell at a 60 percent markup based on cost. The counter parts salesperson must price out the item listed below. The cost price is listed on the video display unit as $4.00. Place the selling price in the invoice below.

								2562
NAME	*ann Poole*			DATE	*4-30*	19	*86*	
ADDRESS	*1906 Spranger*			CUST. ORDER NO.	—			
CITY STATE	*Boston, MA*		ZIP					

CASH	CHARGE	RETD. GOODS	RETAIL	WHOLESALE	SALESMAN		CODE
✓							

QUAN.	PART NO.	DESCRIPTION	LIST	NET	AMOUNT
1	*G108643197*	*Relay connector*			

PSP-85-CUST. NP-13526

MERRIMACK ST. GARAGE, INC.
40-56 Merrimack Street
MANCHESTER, N.H. 03101
Phone 623-8015 (Area Code 603)

OLDSMOBILE **VOLVO**

DISCLAIMER OF WARRANTIES
ANY WARRANTIES ON THE PRODUCTS SOLD HEREBY ARE THOSE MADE BY THE MANUFACTURER. THE SELLER/DEALER HEREBY EXPRESSLY DISCLAIMS ALL WARRANTIES, EITHER EXPRESS OR IMPLIED, IN-CLUDING ANY IMPLIED WARRANTY OF MERCHANTABILITY OR FITNESS FOR A PARTICULAR PURPOSE, AND MERRIMACK ST. GARAGE, INC. NEITHER ASSUMES NOR AUTHORIZES ANY OTHER PERSON TO ASSUME FOR IT ANY LIABILITY IN CONNECTION WITH THE SALE OF SAID PRODUCTS.

ABSOLUTELY
NO RETURNS AFTER 30 DAYS
NO REFUNDS OR RETURNS ON SPECIAL ORDER ITEMS
NO REFUNDS OR RETURNS ON ELECTRICAL PARTS
NO REFUNDS WITHOUT THIS INVOICE
15% RESTOCKING CHARGE

RECEIVED BY X _____

	SALES TICKET NO.	CONTROL NO.	KEY
	No. **2562**		
		AMOUNT	
	PARTS & ACC. RETAIL		
	PARTS & ACC. WHOLESALE		
	PARTS & ACC. INTERNAL		
	GAS, OIL GREASE		
	TIRES		
	TAX		
CHARGE SALES			
CASH SALES			

by Reynolds · Reynolds   LITHO IN U.S.A

Courtesy of Merrimack St. Garage, Inc., Manchester, NH.

3. Sarah marked some out-of-season boots to sell for $31 a pair. The boots cost the store $26.80 a pair and had been marked up 23 percent on sales. Rita asked Sarah to determine the percent of markdown on the original selling price. Round off your answer to the nearest percent.

4. Alice's Kitchen and Bath sold two convection ovens to the Colwell Nursing Home, a nonprofit organization. The ovens cost the firm $179 each. They were marked to sell for $229 each. Alice offered to give the buyer a discount as shown on the invoice below. How much markup was made on the sale?

Alice's Kitchen & Bath

221 Huron Avenue
Port Huron, Mich. 48060
Phone: (313)-984-5385

Present this bill on exchanges or returned goods within 10 days of purchase

CUSTOMER'S ORDER NO.	PHONE NUMBER		DATE	
	985 4220		1-19 1986	

SOLD TO *Colwell's Nursing Home*

ADDRESS *1664 Military Street*

CITY *Marysville, MI 48040*

SOLD BY	CASH	CHECK	LAYAWAY	SPECIAL ORDER	MDSE RET'D	PAID OUT	
		✓					

QUANTITY	DESCRIPTION	PRICE	AMOUNT
1 2	GE Convection Ovens	229	458 —
2	less 10% discount		45 80
3			
4			412 20
5			
6			
7			
8			
9			
10			
11	*non taxable*	TAX	
12		TOTAL	412 20

70601

Thank You

REC'D BY X

OUR BUSINESS DEPENDS ON YOUR SATISFACTION

Courtesy of Alice's Kitchen & Bath, Port Huron, MI.

5. The Stork Shop realized a 42 percent markup on sales on all products sold last year. The merchandise bought for resale cost $37,860. There was $17,354 worth of overhead during the year to be paid, such as utilities, rent, insurance, etc. What was the amount of the owner's profit for the year? (overhead + profit = markup)

6. Whitican & Associates, art dealers, planned to mark down a painting 20 percent. The painting was purchased from an artist for $40. They wish to maintain a 35 percent markup on sales after the markdown. What was the pre-marked-down price?

7. Linda's Natural Foods buys dried fruit for resale. A single package of dried apples costs $1.80. The package is marked up 60 percent on sales. How many packages need to be sold in order for the store to realize a total markup of $240?

8. Janis has a markup of 100 percent on cost in her dress shop. A business associate, Cyndi, indicates that she does better than Janis because she earns a 60 percent markup on sales. Who earns more per sale, Janis or Cyndi?

9. For what price must a merchant sell a desk that cost him $90 in order to earn a markup of 30 percent on sales after a 10 percent trade discount has been offered to his customers?

10. The Cabinet Corporation bought a buffet for $60 from the Stillo Manufacturing Company on July 17. The Cabinet Corporation operates under a policy of a 40 percent markup on sales. The corporation allows a 10 percent trade discount to its customers. What will be the list price on the buffet that costs $60?

11. A dress marked 25 percent off is on sale for $180. The dress was originally marked up 150 percent on cost. What was the cost of the dress?

12. A diamond ring is marked $890. The diamond cost the jeweler $200 and is marked up 250 percent on cost. The setting cost the jeweler $114. What is the percent of markup on cost on the setting? Round off your answer to the nearest percent.

13. If the markup on food items at a convenience store is 5 percent on cost, how much merchandise must be sold to have total markups of $8,000 per week?

14. Angelo sells popcorn at all of the athletic games at Bucken Stadium. His popcorn sells for $1.25 a bag. Angelo marks up the ingredients (popcorn oil, salt, etc.) 400 percent on cost. What is the cost of the ingredients?

15. Desmond and Associates have taken an inventory of the stock of materials in their storage facility. The value of the items at their cost is $853,980. The accountant said that these items will be sold at an average markup of 22 percent of the selling price. If Desmond and Associates sell the complete inventory, what will they receive in revenue?

Challenge Problem

The Cronton & Trion Company purchased seventy special timers at a list price of $37.80 each. The Burrs Corporation allowed a 15 percent trade discount as well as terms of 2/15,n/30, E.O.M. The purchase was made on July 18. The timers were back ordered and actually arrived on September 29. Four were found to be defective and were returned. The invoice was paid on October 17. The timers were sold through the Cronton & Trion catalog. The markup rate of 40 percent on cost was made.

A second purchase of seventy timers was made on November 2, C.O.D. at $31 each with no trade discount. They were marked up in the same way as the first purchase. What is the total dollar amount of markup realized by Cronton & Trion on the two purchases? Round your answer off to the nearest cent.

Complete the fifteen problems below. Round off your answer to the nearest cent or percent.

1. Markup = 30% on Cost
   Cost price = $50
   Selling price = $ _____

2. Markup = 60% on Sales
   Cost price = $38
   Selling price = $ _____

3. Markup = 40% on Cost
   Selling price = $200
   Cost price = $ _____

4. Markup = 50% on Sales
   Selling price = $47
   Cost price = $ _____

5. Selling price = $60
   Cost price = $25
   Markup = _____ % on Cost

6. Selling price = $35
   Cost price = $20
   Markup = _____ % on Sales

7. Markup = 40% on Sales
   Markup = _____ % on Cost

8. Markup = 50% on Cost
   Markup = _____ % on Sales

9. Markup = $80
   Markup = 12% on Cost
   Selling price = $ _____

10. Markup = $30
    Markup = 8% on Sales
    Cost price = $ _____

11. Cost price = $120
    Markup = 38% on Sales
    Trade discount = 25%
    List price = $ _____

12. List price = $380
    Trade discount = 15 and 22%
    Markup = 25% on Sales
    Cost price = $ _____

13. Out-of-Doors, Inc. purchased a tent for $280. The tent was then marked up 40 percent on cost. What is the selling price of the tent?

14. The Shipe Ice Cream Parlour marks up half-gallon containers 20 percent on cost. What is the highest cost the firm can pay for the item and sell it for $2.29? Round off your answer to the nearest cent.

15. Richard Yake's mens store purchased suits for $105 each. They were marked to sell for $249. The last of the suits were put on sale for $89. What is the percent of loss on the last suits sold?

5 Math of Accounting

16 Inventory and Turnover

17 Depreciation

18 Taxes

19 Investments

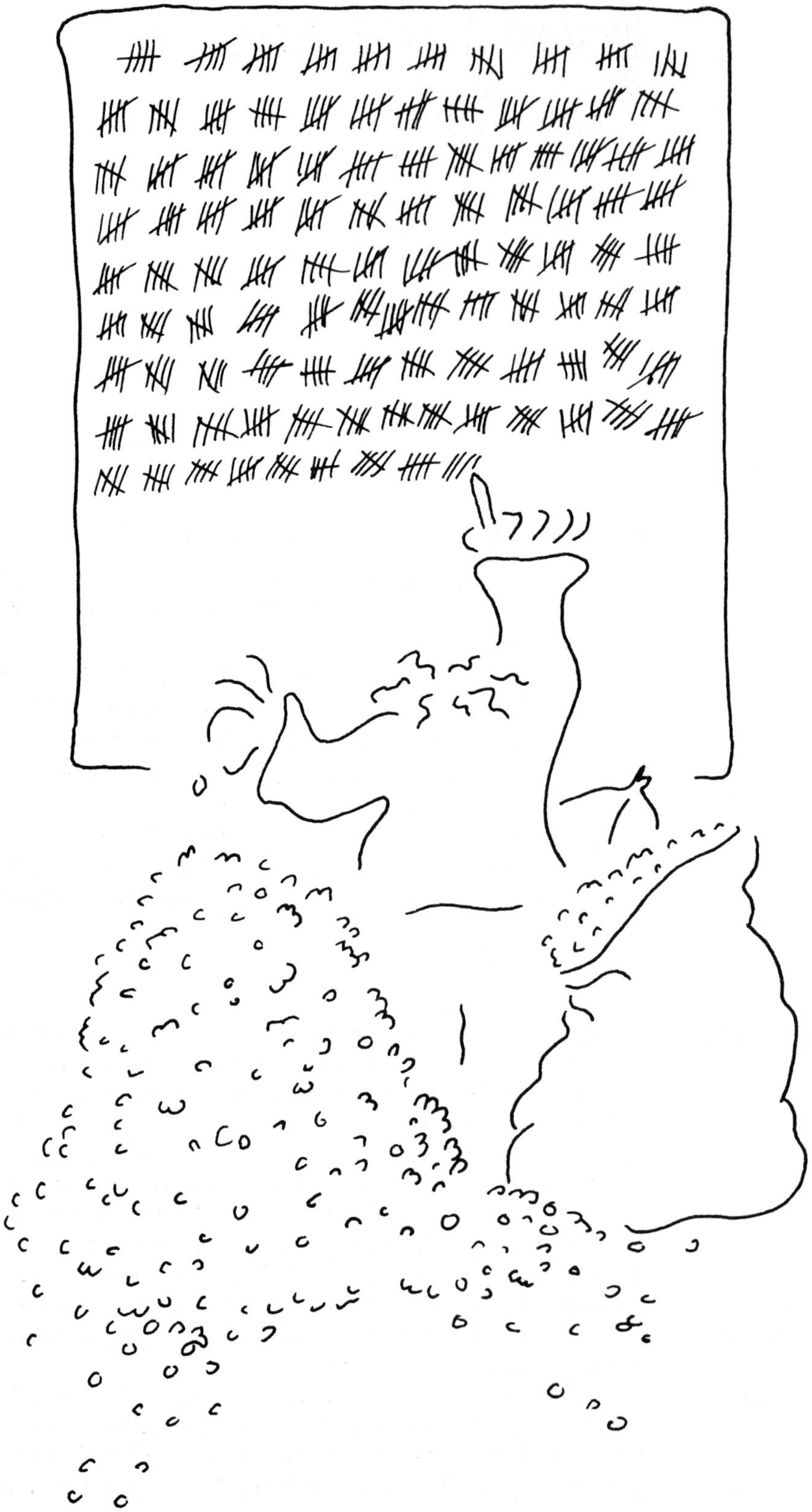

16 Inventory and Turnover

Performance Objectives

After mastering the material in this chapter, you will be able to:

1. Determine the value of ending inventory using the L.I.F.O., F.I.F.O., average cost, specific identification, or retail inventory estimating method.
2. Determine the cost of goods sold using the L.I.F.O., F.I.F.O., average cost, specific identification, or retail inventory estimating method.
3. Determine the rate of merchandise turnover for a firm.
4. Understand and use the following terms or concepts:

   Beginning Inventory   F.I.F.O.
   Purchases   Average Cost
   Goods Available for Sale   Retail Inventory Estimating Method
   Ending Inventory   Specific Identification Method
   Cost of Goods Sold   Turnover
   L.I.F.O.

Inventory Methods

For firms that buy merchandise for resale, the value of the merchandise on hand at tax time or inventory time is very important. Several methods of determining that value will be presented in this chapter. Each method has it own advantage and special purpose. Knowledge of these methods is useful for students studying for clerical, merchandising, distribution, or accounting positions.

Beginning inventory

At the beginning of an accounting time period a firm has an inventory of merchandise on hand to sell. This amount is termed **beginning inventory,** the value of inventory that the firm begins with in a period. During the period the firm will buy more merchandise to add to the inventory. The total value bought is termed **purchases.** Beginning inventory plus purchases equal **goods available for sale,** all of the merchandise that can be sold during this period; not necessarily all available at one time in that period.

Purchases
Goods available for sale

Ending inventory

The value of the goods on hand at the end of the period is termed **ending inventory.** By subtracting the ending inventory from the goods available for sale, the value of the goods that were sold during the period can be found. The cost price of the goods that were sold during the period is termed **cost of goods sold.**

Cost of goods sold

mary maxim

2001 HOLLAND AVENUE
P.O. BOX 5019
PORT HURON, MI. 48061-5019
TELEX 756-775

PURCHASE ORDER

47569

THIS NO. MUST APPEAR ON INVOICES, B/L, CASES, BUNDLES, PACKING LISTS ETC. AND ALL CORRESPONDENCE.

T O
Peter Dea, Inc.
1700 Mountain Air
Portland, OR 97216

S H I P T O
Same

ORDER DATE	DATE REQUIRED	TERMS	FOB	SHIP VIA	VENDOR NO.
6-18-86	7-1-86	1/10, n/30	P.H.	Air Express	1983

CATALOG NO.	VENDOR ITEM NO.	QUANTITY ORDERED	U/M	DESCRIPTION	DEPT.	UNIT COST	AMOUNT
MW 8046 07		100		Mens sweaters	3	8.70	870.—
WW 7361 90		144		Shawls	3	4.10	590.40
WW 8041 07		24		Women's gloves	3	3.90	93.60

TERMS:
ALL ORDERS SUBJECT TO CANCELLATION PRIOR TO SHIPMENT.
PACKING SLIP MUST ACCOMPANY ALL SHIPMENTS.

Pauline Bauer
BUYER

G.B.
MERCHANDISING MANAGER

VENDOR COPY

Courtesy of Mary Maxim, Inc., Port Huron, MI.

Note that (1) the period covered may be a year, six months, a month, or even one day; (2) all of the values in the example are at cost price, not selling price; (3) the ending inventory from one period becomes the beginning inventory for the next period; and (4) that this inventory model repeats itself every period.

Example 1

Inventory Model

    Beginning Inventory
\+ Purchases
    Goods Available for Sale
− Ending Inventory
    Cost of Goods Sold

> **Example 2**
>
> The Dosen Paper Company had 147,000 units of inventory on hand valued at $123 each on June 1. During the month another 46,000 units were purchased at the same price. On June 30, the Accounting Department found that there were $15,922,350 of goods on hand. What is the value of the goods that were sold?
>
> | | |
> |---|---|
> | $18,081,000 | Beginning Inventory (147,000 units × $123/unit)—June 1 |
> | + 5,658,000 | Purchases (46,000 units × $123/unit) |
> | $23,739,000 | Goods Available for Sale |
> | − 15,922,350 | Ending Inventory—June 30 |
> | $ 7,816,650 | Cost of Goods Sold |

In the previous example the cost price per unit of beginning inventory and purchases was the same amount.

For income tax purposes the cost value of ending inventory or cost of goods sold is very important. A firm can legally increase the cost of the goods sold, thereby reducing the taxable income. Income taxes are reduced because the taxable base, gross income, is reduced.

Revenue from Sales
− Cost of Goods Sold
Gross Income
− Operating and Selling Expenses
Net Income Before Taxes
× Tax Rate
Taxes

Inventory Valuation

Valuation of inventory costs considers units of the same product being purchased at different unit cost prices during the period. In order to determine the value of inventory, you must first determine the unit prices to be assigned to the items on hand (ending inventory) at the end of the period. It is necessary to assume an arbitrary flow of costs of merchandise through the company. The three most frequently used methods in valuation of inventory are:

1. L.I.F.O.
2. F.I.F.O.
3. Average Cost

L.I.F.O.

L.I.F.O. is an abbreviation for last in-first out. The **L.I.F.O.** concept considers that the most recently puchased goods (costs incurred) are sold first and their costs should be charged against revenue. The units remaining in the ending inventory come from the earliest purchases at their respective costs.

The L.I.F.O. method will reduce gross income in times of rising prices (unit cost of the most recently acquired merchandise is higher than the unit cost of the earlier purchases). This higher unit cost is used in calculating the "cost of goods sold."

L.I.F.O.
Flow of Costs

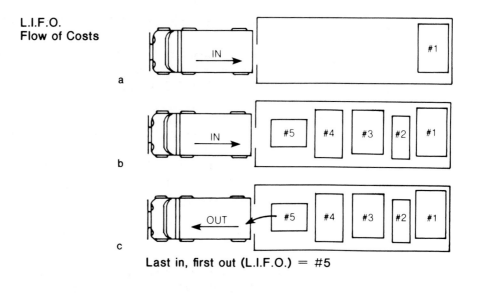

Last in, first out (L.I.F.O.) = #5

Example 3

The Carlton Company made the following purchases of a new item during the year:

January	10	10 units @ $5 each
March	3	20 units @ $6 each
May	30	15 units @ $7 each
September	3	5 units @ $8 each

The accounting department has determined that there were twelve units of the item on hand on December 31.

A. What was the quantity and value of units available for sale:

Units	Price per Unit	Total Price
10	× $5	= $ 50
20	× 6	= 120
15	× 7	= 105
5	× 8	= 40

Total quantity and dollar value of units available for sale.   50 units (Quantity) $315 (Value)

B. What was the value of ending inventory of the 12 units, using L.I.F.O.?

January	10	10 units @ $5 each	= $ 50
March	3	2 units @ $6 each	= 12
Total		12 (Quantity)	$ 62 (Value)

C. What is the value of the cost of goods sold?

Goods Available for Sale	50 units	$315
− Ending Inventory	12 units	62
Cost of Goods Sold	38 units	$253 (Value)

OR

September 3	5 units	@ $8 each =	$ 40
May 30	15 units	@ 7 each =	105
March 3	18 units	@ 6 each =	108
Cost of Goods Sold	38 units		$253 (Value)

Example 4

A new firm, Websters Incorporated, made the following purchases during the first quarter year of operations.

January	16	450 units @ $21.70 each
	21	600 units @ 22.00 each
	28	250 units @ 22.00 each
February	5	300 units @ 21.90 each
	17	600 units @ 22.10 each
	23	225 units @ 22.10 each
March	6	730 units @ 22.15 each
	11	400 units @ 21.95 each
	16	350 units @ 22.20 each
	28	600 units @ 22.20 each
	31	400 units @ 22.21 each

The firm sold 2,600 units during the quarter.

A. How many units were on hand at the end of the quarter?

Total Purchases	4,905 units	
− Less units sold	− 2,600 units	
Ending Inventory	2,305 units	Notice that the inventory model was used above with alterations.

B. What was the value of ending inventory of 2,305 units, using L.I.F.O.?

Purchase of January 16 of 450 units at $21.70 each = $ 9,765.00
        (first purchase)

January 21	600 units @ $22.00 each =	13,200.00
January 28	250 units @ $22.00 each =	5,500.00
February 5	300 units @ $21.90 each =	6,570.00
February 17	600 units @ $22.10 each =	13,260.00
February 23	105 units @ $22.10 each =	2,320.50
	(of the 225 units)	

Value of ending inventory of 2,305 units, using L.I.F.O. = $50,615.50

Example 4 *Continued*

C. What is the value of cost of goods sold of 2,600 units, using L.I.F.O.?

Purchase on March 31 of 400 units at $22.21 each = (most recent purchase)	$ 8,884.00
March 28 of 600 units @ $22.20 each=	13,320.00
March 16 of 350 units @ $22.20 each=	7,770.00
March 11 of 400 units @ $21.95 each=	8,780.00
March 6 of 730 units @ $22.15 each=	16,169.50
February 23 of 120 units @ $22.10 each= (of the 225 units)	2,652.00
Value of cost of goods sold of 2,600 units, using L.I.F.O. =	$57,575.50

Example 5

The Ulmac and Sterver Co. made the following purchases during the month of June.

June	4	120 units @ $9.02 each
	16	200 units @ $9.05 each
	21	310 units @ $9.06 each
	30	150 units @ $9.10 each

The beginning inventory on June 1 of 175 units was made up of 80 units purchased in May at $8.90 each and 95 units purchased in April at $8.55 each; 750 units were sold during June.

A. How many units were on hand at the end of the month?

175 units—Beginning Inventory (June 1)
+ 780 units—Purchases during June
955 units—Goods Available for Sale
− 750 units—Sold during June
205 units—Ending Inventory (June 30)

B. What is the value of ending inventory of 205 units, using L.I.F.O.?

Value of ending inventory, using L.I.F.O.

95 units of beginning inventory purchased in April @ $8.55 each	= $ 812.25
80 units of beginning inventory purchased in May @ $8.90 each	= 712.00
30 units purchased June 4 @ $9.02 each	= 270.60
Value of ending inventory of 205 units, using L.I.F.O.	= $1,794.85

Example 5 *Continued*

C. What is the value of the cost of goods sold, 750 units, using L.I.F.O.?

Value of cost of goods sold, using L.I.F.O.

Purchase on June 30 of 150 units @ \$9.10 each = \$1,365.00
(most recent purchase)

June 21	310 units @ \$9.06 each =	2,808.60
16	200 units @ \$9.05 each =	1,810.00
4	90 units @ \$9.02 each =	811.80

Value of cost of goods sold of 750 units, using L.I.F.O. = \$6,795.40

F.I.F.O.

F.I.F.O. is an abbreviation for first-in, first-out. The **F.I.F.O.** concept considers that the goods are sold in order of their purchase. Therefore, the units remaining in the ending inventory come from the most recent purchases at their respective costs.

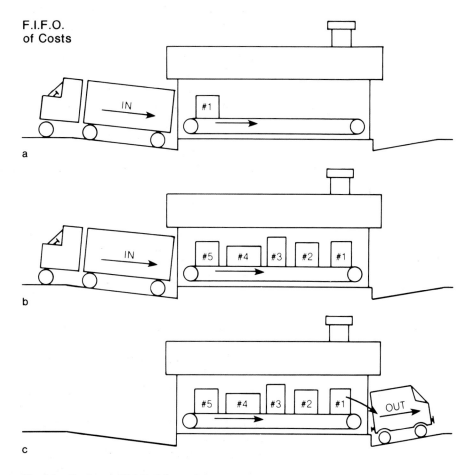

F.I.F.O.
of Costs

a

b

c

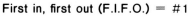

First in, first out (F.I.F.O.) = #1

Example 6

Using the data from the Carlton Company in Example 3;

A. What was the quantity and value of units available for sale? The answer to this question is the same as it would be in Example 3.

    Total quantity <u>50 units</u>   Dollar value <u>$315</u>

B. What was the value of ending inventory of the twelve units, using F.I.F.O.?

September 3	5 units @ $8 each	= $40
May 30	<u>7</u> units @ $7 each	= <u>$49</u>
Total	<u>12</u> (Quantity)	<u>$89</u> (Value)

C. What is the value of the cost of goods sold?

Goods Available for Sale	50 units	$315
− Ending Inventory	12 units	89
Cost of Goods Sold	38 units	$226 (Value)

or

January	10	10 units @ $5 each	= $50
March	3	20 units @ $6 each	= 120
May	30	8 units @ $7 each	= 56
Cost of Goods Sold		38 units	$226 (Value)

Example 7

Using the purchase data from Websters, Inc. in Example 4;

A. What was the value of ending inventory of 2,305 units using F.I.F.O.?

Value of ending inventory, using F.I.F.O.

Purchase on March 31 of 400 units @ $22.21 each = $ 8,884.00
(most recent purchase)
March 28 of 600 units @ $22.20 each = $13,320.00
16 of 350 units @ $22.20 each = $ 7,770.00
11 of 400 units @ $21.95 each = $ 8,780.00
6 of 555 units @ $22.15 each = <u>$12,293.25</u>
(of the 730 units)
Value of 2,305 units, using F.I.F.O. = $51,047.25

Example 7 *Continued*

B. What is the value of the cost of goods sold, 2,600 units, using F.I.F.O.?

Value of cost of goods sold, using F.I.F.O.

Purchase on January 16 of 450 units @ $21.70 each =	$ 9,765.00
(first purchase)	
January 21 of 600 units @ $22.00 each =	13,200.00
28 of 250 units @ $22.00 each =	5,500.00
February 5 of 300 units @ $21.90 each =	6,570.00
17 of 600 units @ $22.10 each =	13,260.00
February 23 of 225 units @ $22.10 each =	4,972.50
March 6 of 175 units @ $22.15 each =	3,876.25
(of the 730 units)	

Value of cost of goods sold of 2,600 units, using F.I.F.O. = $57,143.75

Exercise A — Determine answers in the exercises below.

	1.	2.	3.	4.
Beginning Inventory (units)	38	300	140	650
Cost per Unit	$1.27	$4.75	$40.00	$12.50
Purchases:				
January 16	600 @ $1.28	75 @ $4.90	20 @ $35.00	130 @ $10.00
February 3	350 @ $1.28	200 @ $4.88	35 @ $34.60	150 @ $10.00
15	90 @ $1.30	150 @ $4.95	60 @ $34.70	275 @ $9 59
22	400 @ $1.30	200 @ $4.95	40 @ $35.60	300 @ $10.05
March 2	250 @ $1.35	225 @ $5.00	75 @ $36.10	500 @ $10.25
Goods Available for Sale (units)	1,728			
Goods Sold (units)	1,428			
Ending Inventory (units)	300	350	180	732
Inventory Method	L.I.F.O.	F.I.F.O.	L.I.F.O.	F.I.F.O.
Ending Inventory	$ 383.62			
Cost of Goods Sold	$1,855.14			

Average Cost   Average cost is another method of determining inventory values. This method does not identify any specific units that were sold, but instead uses a weighted average of all units available for sale. The **average cost** is calculated by dividing the total dollar value of units available for sale by the total number of units available.

Example 8

Using the data from the Carlton Company in Example 3,

A. What was the quantity and value of the units available for sale? The answer to this question is the same as it would be in Example 3.

Total quantity 50 units   Dollar value $315

B. What was the value of ending inventory of the twelve units, using average cost?

$$\frac{\text{Total Dollar Value}}{\text{Units Available}} = \frac{\$315}{50} \times 12 \text{ units} = \$75.60$$

C. What is the value of cost of goods sold?

Goods Available for Sale	50 units	$315.00
− Ending Inventory	12 units	75.60
Cost of Goods Sold	38 units	$239.40

or

Goods Available for Sale	$315.00
− Value of Ending Inventory	75.60
Cost of Goods Sold	$239.40

Example 9

Durst & Associates had 400 units of a file separator in stock at the end of the year. At the beginning of the year there were 350 units in stock at an average cost of 87 cents each. Two purchases were made during the year: on July 16, 800 units at 93 cents each were bought and on November 12, 250 units at 94 cents each were obtained.

A. How many units were sold during the year?

350	—Beginning Inventory (units)
+ 1,050	—Purchases (800 + 250 units)
1,400	—Goods Available for Sale (units)
− 400	—Ending Inventory (units)
1,000	—Cost of Goods Sold (units)

1,000 units were sold during the year.

Example 9 *Continued*

B. What is the value of ending inventory, using average cost?

Value of ending inventory using average cost

350 Units of beginning inventory	@ 87¢ each =	$	304.50
800 Units purchased	@ 93¢ each =		744.00
250 Units purchased	@ 94¢ each =		235.00
1,400 total units available	total cost		$1,283.50

$$\frac{\$1,283.50}{1,400} = \frac{\text{Total Cost}}{\text{Total Units}} \times \frac{400 \text{ units ending}}{\text{inventory}} = \frac{\$366.71 \text{ value of}}{\text{ending inventory}}$$

Available

C. What is the value of the cost of goods sold, using average cost?

Value of cost of goods sold, using average cost.

$$\frac{\$1,283.50}{1,400} = \frac{\text{Total Cost}}{\text{Total Units}} \times \frac{1,000 \text{ units of}}{\text{goods sold}} = \frac{\$916.79 \text{ cost of}}{\text{goods sold}}$$

Available

Exercise B

Notice that the average cost method considers the number of units purchased, not the number of purchases. Determine the answers in the exercises below using the average cost method.

	1.	2.
Beginning Inventory—Units	720	300
Beginning Inventory (Cost per Unit)	$9.80	$1.27
Purchases:		
July 24	400 @ $7.90/unit	7,200 @ $1.30/unit
August 10	250 @ $8.40/unit	4,000 @ $1.31/unit
November 26	600 @ $9.70/unit	5,500 @ $1.36/unit
Ending Inventory—Units	730	200
Ending Inventory Value	$ 6,720.45	
Cost of Goods Sold Value	$11,415.55	

	3.	4.
Beginning Inventory—Units	60	550
Beginning Inventory (Cost per Unit)	$32.00	$18.50
Purchases:		
July 24	90 @ $32.00/unit	650 @ $19.00/unit
August 10	50 @ $32.25/unit	400 @ $19.20/unit
November 26	125 @ $31.75/unit	750 @ $18.70/unit
Ending Inventory—Units	50	400
Ending Inventory Value		
Cost of Goods Sold Value		

Retail Inventory Estimating Method

Occasionally, the manager may need only an estimation of the value of inventory. The **retail inventory estimating method** provides that estimate. This approach replaces the need for an actual physical inventory of the merchandise in order to estimate its value. In order for this method to be close to the actual value of inventory, the markup rate for all of the products of the firm must be similar and consistent. The percent of cost to the selling price is used with the sales for the period to estimate the cost price of goods sold and ending inventory.

The comparison of cost to sales is made from goods available for sale. Sales are made from goods available for sale. With a consistent markup rate an estimate of inventory value at cost can be made. The information in the inventory model in Example 1 must be available at selling price. Again, the inventory model has been altered to find ending inventory.

Example 10

	Cost Price	Selling Price
Beginning Inventory	$ 62,580	$ 97,427
+ Purchases	+ 158,690	+ 229,352
Goods Available for Sale	$221,270	$326,779
− Sales		− 261,408
Ending Inventory		$ 65,371

Find the value of ending inventory at cost price from the above information.

$$\text{Percent of cost to sales of Goods Available for Sale} = \frac{\text{Cost Price}}{\text{Selling Price}} = \frac{\$221,270}{\$326,779} = 67.7\%$$

67.7 percent of the ending inventory of $65,371 at selling price must be the cost price.

```
$65,371      —ending inventory at selling price
 × .677      —percent of cost to sales
$44,256.17 —ending inventory at cost price
```

Exercise C

Determine the answers to the exercises below using the retail inventory estimating method. Round off the percent of cost to sales to the nearest tenth of a percent.

		Cost Price	Selling Price
1.	Beginning Inventory	$ 4,762	$ 9,827
	+ Purchases	+ 3,846	+ 7,842
	Goods Available for Sale	$ 8,608	$ 17,669
	− Sales		−$ 13,931
	Ending Inventory	$ 1,820.41	$ 3,738

		Cost Price	Selling Price
2.	Beginning Inventory	$ 8,662	$ 10,421
	+ Purchases	+ 37,356	+ 43,930
	Goods Available for Sale		
	− Sales		− $ 35,567
	Ending Inventory		

		Cost Price	Selling Price
3.	Beginning Inventory	$ 42,618	$ 60,247
	+ Purchases	+ 38,065	+ 57,348
	Goods Available for Sale		
	− Sales		− $103,900
	Ending Inventory		

		Cost Price	Selling Price
4.	Beginning Inventory	$ 3,421	$ 5,608
	+ Purchases	+ 132,641	+ 215,648
	Goods Available for Sale		
	− Sales		− $ 21,432
	Ending Inventory		

Specific Identification Method

When the amount of sales are few, the merchandise may be marked with the date and cost of the purchase. This method allows the middleman to identify which items were sold or are part of ending inventory. The **specific identification method** is used when the price of the merchandise is high or only a few items are sold.

Example 11

The B. J. Abbott Laboratory identified the following units in the storage room at the end of the month.
3 units purchased on July 16 at $82 each
1 unit purchased on April 23 at $78.64 each
5 units purchased on September 7 at $77.90 each
2 units purchased on June 30 at $81.45 each

What is the value of ending inventory?

```
 3 units × $82.00 each = $246.00
 1 unit  × $78.64 each =   78.64
 5 units × $77.90 each =  389.50
 2 units × $81.45 each =  162.90
11 units purchased at      $877.04 = ending inventory value
```

Turnover

Turnover is the number of times the average inventory is sold during the year. Turnover $= \frac{\text{Sales}}{\text{Average inventory}}$. The average inventory is found by totaling the value of all inventories taken during the year and dividing by the number of inventories taken. Both average inventory and sales values must be at cost price. The answer is a number, not a dollar amount or a percent, though the number can be changed to a percent.

Example 12

A firm had sales of $66,000 during the year with a markup of 20 percent on cost. Inventory taken at cost on January 1 was valued at $16,400, on June 30 it was $18,600, and on December 31 it was $13,000. What was the turnover?

Average inventory

$16,400
18,600
+ 13,000
$48,000 ÷ 3 inventories = $16,000

$$\$66,000$$
Cost Price + Markup = Selling Price
100%   +   20%   =   120%

Cost Price $= 1.20\overline{)\$66,000} = \$55,000$

Turnover $= \dfrac{\$55,000}{\$16,000} = \dfrac{\text{Sales (at Cost)}}{\text{Average Inventory (at Cost)}} = 3.4$ times

---

Exercise D   Determine the turnover rate at cost price in the following problems.

	1.	2.	3.	4.	5.
Inventories	$ 47,682.00	$ 23,050.00	$ 40,600.00	$ 2,800.00	$ 3,490.00
	53,802.00	65,400.00	42,400.00	4,380.00	6,660.00
	49,681.00	61,325.00	49,000.00	3,670.00	4,658.00
	57,304.00		50,600.00		5,360.00
Sales	$426,380.00	$117,430.00	$172,480.00	$24,000.00	$31,680.00
Markup %	23%	30%	40%	35%	50%
Markup on	Cost	Cost	Sales	Cost	Sales
Cost of Sales	$346,650.41	$	$	$	$
Average Inventory	$ 52,117.25	$	$	$	$
Turnover (nearest tenth)	6.7				

Assignment

Chapter Sixteen

Name _____ Date _____ Score _____

Skill Problems Determine the value of ending inventory in the problems below.

	Beginning Inventory at Cost	Purchases at Cost	Net Sales	Markup on Cost	Cost of Goods Sold	Ending Inventory at Cost
1.	$13,560	$ 47,390	$ 62,800	35%	$ _____	$ _____
2.	2,658	12,256	13,560	40	_____	_____
3.	91,420	51,200	76,352	45	_____	_____

4. Beginning Inventory = 420 units at $3.60 each
    Purchases = November 2   1,500 units @ $3.70 each
                        10   2,360 units @ $3.75 each
                        23   1,500 units @ $3.72 each
                        28   1,700 units @ $3.76 each
    Ending Inventory = 360 units

    Cost of Goods Sold   L.I.F.O = $ _____

    Ending Inventory   L.I.F.O = $ _____

    Cost of Goods Sold   F.I.F.O. = $ _____

    Ending Inventory   F.I.F.O. = $ _____

    Cost of Goods Sold   Average Cost = $ _____

    Ending Inventory   Average Cost = $ _____

5. Beginning Inventory = 47 units at $1.20 each
    Purchases = April 3   150 units @ $1.23 each
                     26   250 units @ $1.26 each
               May   7   300 units @ $1.28 each
                     30   200 units @ $1.28 each
              June 13   350 units @ $1.29 each
                     19   200 units @ $1.29 each
    Ending Inventory = 320 units

    Cost of Goods Sold   F.I.F.O. = $ _____

    Ending Inventory   F.I.F.O. = $ _____

    Cost of Goods Sold   L.I.F.O. = $ _____

    Ending Inventory   L.I.F.O. = $ _____

    Cost of Goods Sold   Average Cost = $ _____

    Ending Inventory   Average Cost = $ _____

6. Beginning Inventory = 1,366 units @ $14 each
    Purchases = January 5   600 units @ $13.96 each
                    18 4,500 units @ $13.95 each
                    22 3,100 units @ $14.26 each
                    26 8,450 units @ $14.35 each
    Ending Inventory = 1,580 units

Cost of Goods Sold	Average Cost =	_____
Ending Inventory	Average Cost =	_____
Cost of Goods Sold	L.I.F.O. =	_____
Ending Inventory	L.I.F.O. =	_____
Cost of Goods Sold	F.I.F.O. =	_____
Ending Inventory	F.I.F.O. =	_____

Determine the value of ending inventory at cost in problems 7 through 9 using the retail inventory estimating method. Use a cost to sales percent rounded off to the nearest tenth of a percent.

7.
	Cost Price	Selling Price
Beginning Inventory	$ 368.40	$ 605.00
Purchases	943.30	1,736.80
Goods Available for Sale	_____	_____
Sales		$ 2,141.60
Ending Inventory	_____	_____

8.
	Cost Price	Selling Price
Beginning Inventory	$ 46,356.00	$ 51,840.00
Purchases	117,540.00	136,983.00
Goods Available for Sale	_____	_____
Sales		$102,421.00
Ending Inventory	_____	_____

9.
	Cost Price	Selling Price
Beginning Inventory	$ 40,100.00	$108,560.00
Purchases	54,980.00	126,950.00
Goods Available for Sale	_____	_____
Sales		$180,670.00
Ending Inventory	_____	_____

Determine the turnover in the following problems to the nearest tenth.

10. Inventories taken: July   1 = $13,560
                        October   1 =   14,388
                        December 31 =   13,840
                        Sales at cost = $38,645

11. Inventories taken: January   1 = $68,542
                              March 31 =   72,840
                              June 15 =   65,473
                              August 20 =   69,568
                              October 31 =   73,869
                              December 31 =   62,438
    Sales   = $587,364
    Markup = 40% on sales

12. Inventories taken: April   2 = $32,480
                                9 =   36,400
                               16 =   35,931
                               28 =   33,560
    Sales   = $149,680
    Markup = 30% on cost

Business Application Problems

1. A firm has a turnover rate of 7.2 and a markup of 40 percent on cost. Sales are $321,840 for the year. What is the average inventory that the firm carries in order to maintain this level of sales?

2. Kirkby and Co. found that the value of inventory on January 1 was $147,368, and on March 31 it was $153,820. Sales for the period were $413,875. Goods were marked up 40 percent on cost. What was the turnover to the nearest tenth?

3. The Jonesburg Corporation had a beginning inventory for the year of 275 units valued at $14,307.50. At the end of the year there were 265 units remaining. A purchase was made on March 16 for 360 units at $65 each and on September 1 for 800 units at $71.40 each. What is the amount of sales for the period if the firm used a F.I.F.O. system and a 30 percent markup on cost?

4. Dawn's Discount enjoyed a fourth quarter sales record of $69,800 at a markup of 40% on sales. The purchases for the period were $32,590. The ending inventory was $21,730. What was the beginning inventory?

5. Barton Wholesalers had a fire that damaged a portion of their warehouse on June 23. Inventory was taken on June 1 and totaled $85,642. Only one purchase, for $38,650, was made in June. Sales for the first twenty-three days of the month were $95,391 at a 30 percent markup on sales. A physical inventory of the undamaged merchandise totaled $41,365. What is the approximate value of the loss?

6. Benson and Co. started the firm with a purchase of ten units at $14 each. During the month they purchased an additional twenty units at $14.50 each. In the second month they purchased fifty units at a total cost of $727.50. At the end of the second month they had twenty-five units left in stock. If the firm elects to use a F.I.F.O. system, what is the value of ending inventory?

7. If Benson and Co. in problem 6 elects a L.I.F.O. system, what is the value of the cost of goods sold?

8. Benson and Co., from problem 6, sells the merchandise at a markup of 30 percent on the selling price. What was the turnover for the two-month period?

9. The Sterling Corporation had sales of $589,630 for the month. At the beginning of the month the inventory was $184,980. At the end of the month the inventory was $203,568. The firm marks up on sales, and they use a 40 percent rate. To the nearest tenth, what is the turnover for the month?

10. Dalton Distributors uses a L.I.F.O. system for inventory. The firm has a beginning inventory of $190,000. Their purchases for the month totaled 8,500 units at $16.20 each. The purchases brought the total units available for sale to 20,120. The end-of-the-month inventory, as displayed on the computer printout, said that there were 5,890 units available. A physical inventory of the warehouse showed that there were only 5,600 units available. The accountant decided to write off the missing units as "stock shrink." What is the amount of the write-off?

Challenge Problem   The Saranac Producers Association had a beginning inventory of 682 units of a feeder on June 13. The inventory had cost Saranac $947.30. During the next six months the following purchases were made:

September 1   200 units at $1.47 each; terms 3/10,n/30
October 21   450 units at $1.51 each; terms 3/10,n/30
November 13 600 units at $1.52 each; terms 2/10,n/60

All discounts were taken.

1,508 units were sold during the six months at $2.39 each.

What is the value of ending inventory using L.I.F.O.?

Name _____   Date _____   Score _____

True or False

T　F　1.　Goods available for sale less ending inventory equals purchases.

T　F　2.　Ending inventory equals the previous period's beginning inventory.

T　F　3.　Turnover measures the number of times that the average inventory is sold.

T　F　4.　Specific identification is a method of determining the actual value of inventory.

Complete the following matrix for the missing values.

	Beginning Inventory	Purchases	Ending Inventory	C.O.G.S.
5.	$ 42,000	$175,000	$32,000	_____
6.	_____	243,980	56,835	345,600
7.	39,800	156,000	_____	178,000

Determine the value of ending inventory in the problems below using the method indicated.

Beginning inventory = 890 units at $41.00 each
Purchases = January 17　　400 units at $41.20 each
May 30　　650 units at $41.20 each
September 16　　300 units at $41.30 each
November 3　　650 units at $41.50 each
Ending Inventory = 970

8.　Ending Inventory using L.I.F.O. = _____

9.　Ending Inventory using F.I.F.O. = _____

10.　Ending Inventory using average cost = _____

11. Sales are made at a 25 percent markup on sales. What is the turnover in the problem just given if L.I.F.O. is used? Round off the answer to the nearest tenth.

12. Estimate the value of ending inventory at cost using the Retail Inventory Estimating Method.

	Cost Price	Selling Price
Beginning Inventory	$ 38,500	$ 84,600
Purchase	153,750	301,230
Goods Available for Sale		
Sales		$260,900
Ending Inventory		

13. Humbert and Associates found the value of inventory on July 1 to be $96,800. An additional inventory taken on August 1 totaled $42,690. The sales for the period were $120,970 at a markup of 40 percent on sales. What was the turnover to the nearest tenth?

14. The Woodard Company took inventory on January 1 and found that they had 345,587 meters of their wire product. The value was set at $251,873. The warehouse was broken into on January 12. All of the inventory was stolen. The value of the sales for the twelve days was $34,980 at a 40 percent markup on sales. What is the value of merchandise that was stolen? There were no purchases during the period.

17 Depreciation

After mastering the material in this chapter, you will be able to:

1. Explain the concept of depreciation and depletion.
2. Calculate book value, accumulated depreciation, and depreciation using four methods.
3. Explain the advantages of each of the depreciation methods.
4. Calculate the depreciation amount for a partial year using three methods.
5. Understand and use the following terms and concepts:

Depreciation	Straight-Line Method
Expected Life	Units-of-Production Method
Total Cost	Sum-of-Years'-Digits
Salvage Value	(S.O.Y.D.) Method
Total Depreciation	Declining-Balance Method
Accumulated Depreciation	Accelerated Cost Recovery
Book Value	System (A.C.R.S.) Method
Market Value	

Depreciation

Depreciation is an estimate of the amount of decrease in market value of an item over a period of time. A depreciation expense is allowed by taxing authorities, such as the federal government, for the decline in the item value. The depreciation expense, in effect, reduces the amount of income tax to be paid by the firm. The passage of the Economic Recovery Act of 1981 was seen in part as an incentive to business to invest in new machinery, plants, and equipment. These investments would then receive a favorable tax break in the form of a faster depreciation of the asset. This allows for a greater depreciation expense per year in the early years of the asset's life. Fixed assets, such as buildings, office equipment, trucks, and furniture, decline in value due to wear, an outdating of the style, or obsolescence. An office machine may have a useful life of only two or three years, whereas a building's life may exceed fifty years. The useful life of an asset is termed the **expected life.** The number of years of expected life will be stated by the selling firm or provided through industry or government guidelines.

Expected life

The amount of costs to be depreciated include all of those costs necessary to make the item operational. Item costs, transportation costs, and installation costs make up the **total cost** of an item. Consider an item that was purchased at a price that included transportation and installation, such as a computer. If the buyer had agreed instead to purchase the computer without transportation or installation, those costs would still be incurred by the buyer before the computer would be operative. In the final analysis the total costs would be approximately the same.

Total cost

All of the total costs are depreciable over the expected life unless the firm feels that the item can be sold at the end of its expected life. The sales price at the end of the expected life of the item is termed the **salvage value.** Terms such as scrap value, trade-in value, residual value, or end value are also used. An estimate of the salvage value can be gained from the selling firm.

Salvage value

The **total depreciation** or the amount that the item is depreciated over its expected life is found by subtracting the salvage value from the total cost. A portion of the total depreciation is subtracted from the total cost each year. This amount is termed depreciation. By totaling the depreciation to date, the amount of **accumulated depreciation** can be determined. By subtracting the accumulated depreciation from the total cost, the amount of book value can be found. **Book value** is an estimate of an item's market value. The book value is the amount at which the item is valued on the firm's accounting records.

Total depreciation

Accumulated depreciation

Book value

The **market value** is the amount that the item can be sold for at a given point in its expected life.

Market value

The terminology of depreciation is rather extensive but at the same time important to the understanding of depreciation. The following figure may aid you.

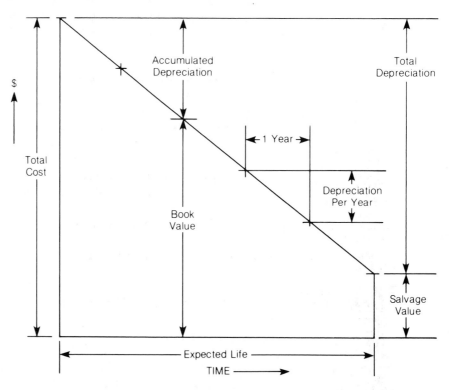

Straight-Line Method

There are four basic methods that are used to determine depreciation. The **straight-line method** is the easiest to understand. This method establishes an equal amount of depreciation per year for an item. It is found by dividing the total depreciation by the years of expected life. Total depreciation is found by subtracting the salvage value from the total cost.

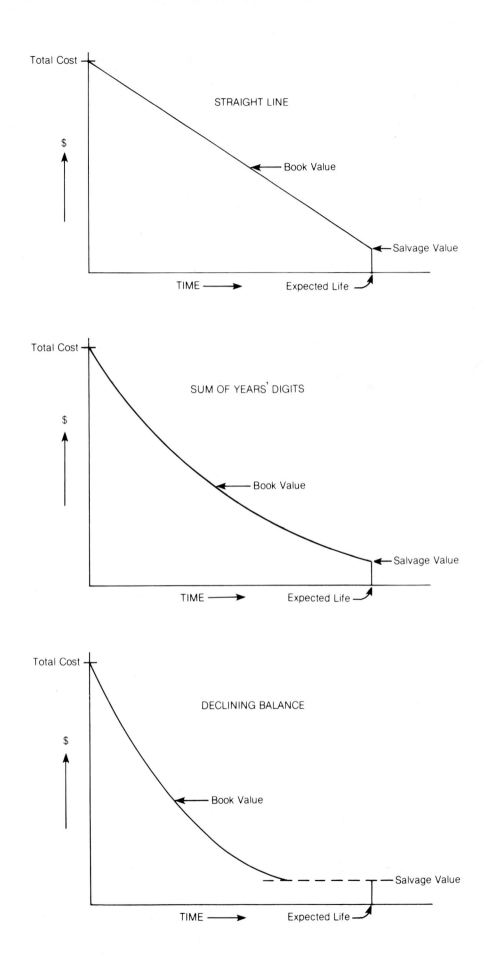

Example 1

A typewriter was purchased for $600 with an expected life of eight years and a salvage value of $100. What is the depreciation per year?

$$\text{Depreciation} = \frac{\text{total depreciation}}{\text{expected life}} \text{ or } \frac{\text{total depreciation}}{n}$$

(n = the number of years of expected life)

$$\text{Depreciation} = \frac{\$500}{8} = \$62.50 \text{ (per year)}$$

The book value at the end of the second year in the above example is found by subtracting the accumulated depreciation ($62.50 per year $\times$ 2 years = $125) from the total cost ($600). Book Value = $600 − $125 = $475.

Example 2

What is the book value at the end of the sixth year of an asset that originally cost $300? The purchasing firm was required to pay $14 for transportation and $26 for installation on top of the $300 purchase price. The asset is expected to be useful for ten years at which time its trade-in value is estimated to be $60.

```
   $300  item cost
 +   14  transportation cost
 +   26  installation cost
   $340  total cost
 −   60  salvage value
   $280  total depreciation
```

$$\text{Depreciation} = \frac{\$280 \text{ (total depreciation)}}{10 \text{ years expected life}} = \$28 \text{ per year}$$

```
   $ 28 = per year depreciation
 ×    6 = years
   $168 = accumulated depreciation at the end of the sixth year
```

```
   $340 = total cost
 −  168 = accumulated depreciation
   $172 = book value—sixth year
```

Exercise A Determine the missing values in the exercises below using the straight-line method.

	Item Cost ①	Trans-portation Cost ②	Installation Cost ③	Salvage Value	Expected Life	Year No.	Depreciation Per Year ①+②+③	Accumulated Depreciation	Book Value
1.	$14,350 +	$95 +	$16,585 −	$3,210	12 years =	4	$2,318.33 ×4=	$9,273.32	$21,756.68
2.	19,000	0	1,757	1,257	30	7	$ 650.00	4550.00	16207.00
3.	625	26	249	200	7	3	100.00	300.00	600.00
4.	42,600	0	10,380	1,980	17	2	3000	6000	46980
5.	965	85	75	325	8	3	100	300	825

(handwritten margin notes: 2057, 900, 52980, 1125*)*

Exercise B Determine the missing values in the exercises below using the straight-line method. Use the formula Depreciation/year = $\dfrac{\text{Total depreciation}}{\text{Expected life}}$ to solve these exercises.

	Total Cost	Expected Life	Salvage Value	Year No.	
1.	$70,000	10	$20,000	3	$55,000 Book Value
2.	10,000	8	2,000	___	$ 3,000 Book Value
3.	4,000	___	1,000	6	$ 1,800 Accumulated Depreciation
4.	20,000	10	___	2	$17,000 Book Value
5.	___	7	6,000	3	$ 2,000 Depreciation per year

Units-of-Production Method

The straight-line method determines the depreciation expense to be a constant per year. Some assets are not used an equal amount every year. Their use varies and, therefore, the depreciation amount should also vary. The **units-of-production method** allows for an unequal usage. The amount of depreciation is equal for each unit produced, but not necessarily an equal total each year. This method is also termed the hours-of-production method.

Example 3

A machine was purchased for $680 and is expected to produce 1,000 units over its useful life. The amount of production this period was 390 units. The salvage value is estimated to be $90. What is the depreciation for this period?

$$\text{Depreciation} = \frac{\text{Total depreciation}}{\substack{\text{Expected total output} \\ \text{capacity over life} \\ \text{of asset}}} \times \text{Output this period}$$

$$\text{Depreciation} = \frac{\$590}{1,000} \times 390 \text{ units} = \$230.10 \text{ for } 390 \text{ units}$$

The book value at the end of 760 units of production would be found as follows:

$$\frac{\$590}{1,000 \text{ units}} \times 760 \text{ units} = \$448.40 \text{ for } 760 \text{ units}$$

$$\begin{array}{rl} \$680.00 = & \text{Total cost} \\ - \ 448.40 = & \text{Accumulated depreciation} \\ \hline \$231.60 = & \text{Book value after 760 units have been produced} \end{array}$$

Exercise C   Determine the missing values in the exercises below using the units-of-production method.

	Total Cost	Salvage Value	Expected Life (in Units)	Units this Period	Units to Date	Depreciation this Period	Book Value
1.	$43,000	$1,500	140,000	1,980	35,923	$ 586.93	$32,351.40
2.	975	65	1,400	350	895		
3.	23,680	1,180	30,000	3,500	19,600		
4.	8,646	966	16,000	950	2,860		
5.	1,270	220	21,000	610	13,548		

Sum-of-Years'-Digits (S.O.Y.D.) Method

The market values of some assets do not decline by an equal amount each year. In order to develop a book value that approximates the market value of an item, the **sum-of-years'-digits (S.O.Y.D.) method** is often used. This method accelerates the depreciation by allowing for the greater decline in the market value in the first years of an asset's life and a lesser decline in the later years of its life. It is similar to the straight-line method. The total depreciation is multiplied by a fraction to determine the depreciation for the year. Each year the fraction becomes smaller in order to develop a lower depreciation amount. The fraction is made up of a denominator (the sum of the years of expected life) and a numerator (the value assigned to a particular year).

Example 4

An asset has an expected life of eight years. What is the fraction used to determine the depreciation for the second year using the S.O.Y.D. method?

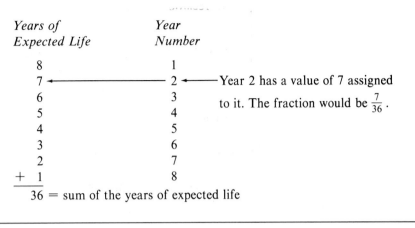

Years of Expected Life	Year Number	
8	1	
7	2	Year 2 has a value of 7 assigned to it. The fraction would be $\frac{7}{36}$.
6	3	
5	4	
4	5	
3	6	
2	7	
+ 1	8	
36 = sum of the years of expected life		

Example 5

An asset has an expected life of twelve years. What is the fraction used to determine the depreciation for the fifth year using the S.O.Y.D. method?

Years of Expected Life	Year Number	
12	1	
11	2	
10	3	
9	4	
8	5	Year 5 has a value of 8 assigned to it. The fraction would be $\frac{8}{78}$.
7	6	
6	7	
5	8	
4	9	
3	10	
2	11	
+ 1	12	
78 = sum of the years of expected life		

The sum of the years can also be found as follows:

$$\frac{n \times (n + 1)}{2} \qquad n = \text{the number of years of expected life}$$

Example 6

The expected life of an asset is thirty years. What is the sum of the years' digits?

$$\frac{n \times (n + 1)}{2} = \frac{30 \times (30 + 1)}{2} = 465$$

This formula is very useful for assets with a long life expectancy.

Exercise D

Determine the fraction to be used in the following exercises.

Years of Expected Life	Sum of Years	Year Number	Fraction to be used
1. 14	105	3	$\frac{12}{105}$
2. 20	___	2	___
3. 13	___	4	___
4. 15	___	6	___
5. 10	___	10	___

To determine the depreciation amount for a year, the fraction is multiplied by the total depreciation. Each year the fraction will change and will provide a different depreciation amount.

Example 7

A building purchased for $42,000 five years ago has an expected life of twenty years. The salvage value is estimated to be $3,000. What is the depreciation for each of the five years and what is the book value?

Years of Expected Life	Year Number	
20	1	$42,000 − $3,000 = $39,000
19	2	(total
90 ── 18	3	depreciation)
17	4	
16	5	

$$+ \quad 1$$
$$\overline{210} = \text{sum of the years of expected life}$$

Example 7 *Continued*

Depreciation

$$\text{Year 1} = \$39,000 \times \frac{20}{210} = \$\ 3,714.29$$

$$\text{Year 2} = \$39,000 \times \frac{19}{210} = \ 3,528.57$$

$$\text{Year 3} = \$39,000 \times \frac{18}{210} = \ 3,342.86 \quad \text{OR} \ \frac{90}{210} \times \$39,000$$

$$\text{Year 4} = \$39,000 \times \frac{17}{210} = \ 3,157.14 \qquad\qquad = \$16,714.29$$

$$\text{Year 5} = \$39,000 \times \frac{16}{210} = \ 2,971.43$$

Accumulated Depreciation $= \$16,714.29$ years 1–5
Book Value $= \$42,000 - \$16,714.29 = \$25,285.71$

Exercise E   Determine the missing values in the exercises below using the S.O.Y.D. method.

	Total Cost	Salvage Value	Expected Life (Years)	Year Number	Depreciation	Accumulated Depreciation	Book Value
1.	$48,500	$4,000	20	10	$2,330.95	$32,845.24	$15,654.76
2.	21,000	600	14	4			
3.	15,875	50	15	6			
4.	8,900	1,000	10	9			
5.	7,600	200	20	15			

Declining-Balance Method

The **declining-balance method** is similar to the sum-of-years'-digits method because this method provides an accelerated amount of depreciation in the early years of an asset's life. This method is even more accelerated than the sum-of-years'-digits method, and there are also some similarities to the straight-line method. The declining-balance method term is very descriptive of the procedure used to determine the depreciation amount.

Using this method, the straight-line rate of depreciation is doubled. This rate is then multiplied by the current book value. The depreciation amount is subtracted from the book value to find a new book value or declined balance. The book value must not drop below the salvage value.

Note that the total cost the first year and the book value or declined value in subsequent years, not the total depreciation, is used to determine the amount of depreciation.

Exercise F   Determine the missing values in the exercises below using the declining-balance method. Use a factor rounded off to three decimal places.

	Total Cost	Salvage Value	Expected Life (Years)	Year Number	Depreciation	Accumulated Depreciation	Book Value
1.	$ 3,800	$ 500	4	2	$ 950.00	$ 2,850.00	$ 950.00
2.	45,000	0	5	2			
3.	16,900	600	8	3			
4.	10,000	1,000	6	4			
5.	85,400	3,400	10	5			

Accelerated Cost Recovery System (A.C.R.S.) Method

The Economic Recovery Act of 1981 included an incentive for business to invest in new equipment and other capital assets in order to improve the economy. This incentive was titled the **Accelerated Cost Recovery System (A.C.R.S.).** The A.C.R.S. method provides a shorter expected life for items placed in service after 1980. The salvage value is not considered in this method of computing depreciation. The shorter life and no scrap value combine to provide a larger depreciation amount, thereby reducing taxes for business. Items in service before 1981 must be depreciated by the methods explained earlier in the chapter. A firm may not switch to the A.C.R.S. method on older items. Depreciable items are classified by government regulation into four categories that indicate the term of depreciation.

Year	3-year	5-year	10-year	15-year*
1	25%	15%	8%	12%
2	38	22	14	10
3	37	21	12	9
4		21	10	8
5		21	10	7
6			10	6
7			9	6
8			9	6
9			9	6
10			9	5
11				5
12				5
13				5
14				5
15				5

Property Categories
- Three-year items include automobiles, light trucks, and some equipment.
- Five-year items include larger equipment but not real estate.
- Ten-year items include some real estate and some utility equipment.
- Fifteen-year items include the real estate not classified as ten-year items and some other equipment.

The calculation of the depreciation amount is done by multiplying the cost by the percent found in the information above.

To find the book value, the accumulated depreciation is subtracted from the cost.

---

*An eighteen-year category was established to go into effect beginning in 1984. This category will apply to some items previously classified as fifteen-year items. The I.R.S. will continue to adjust these categories/percentages to obtain the desired results in a changing economy.

Exercise G

Determine the missing values in the following exercises using the A.C.R.S. method.

	Cost	Category (Years)	Year	Depreciation	Accumulated Depreciation	Book Value
1.	$ 58,000	10	3	$ 6,960.00	$ 19,720.00	$38,280.00
2.	8,740	5	1			
3.	32,844	10	4			
4.	198,500	15	7			
5.	3,900	3	2			

Depletion

In the previous examples, the assets were in a usable state, such as machinery, buildings, and equipment. Other assets, such as natural resources, are not usually in a usable state. The conversion of these natural resources, termed "wasting" by the owner, is accounted for by a depletion allowance similar to depreciation.

These assets, such as coal, timber, oil, natural gas, and minerals, decline in value as they are pumped, mined, or cut. The amount of depletion is determined by estimating the percent of the asset that has been used or "wasted" at cost.

Example 10

An oil field was purchased for $650,000. The field has an estimated 320,000 barrels of oil production possible. If 60,000 barrels were pumped in a year, what would be the depletion for the oil field?

$$\frac{60,000 = \text{barrels pumped}}{320,000 = \text{barrels available}} = 18.75\%$$

$$\begin{array}{rl} \$650,000 = & \text{cost of oil field} \\ \underline{\times\ .1875} = & \text{percent of depletion} \\ \$121,875 = & \text{depletion amount} \end{array}$$

Exercise H   Determine the amount of depletion in the following exercises. Round off the factor to the nearest hundredth of a percent.

	Cost	Total Available	Wasted This Period	Depletion This Period
1.	$ 450,800	70,000 tons	15,000 tons	$ 96,606.44
2.	1,600,000	80,000,000 cubic feet	90,000 cubic feet	_____
3.	680,000	6,000,000 board feet	800,000 board feet	_____
4.	230,000	50,000 barrels	8,000 barrels	_____
5.	750,000	1,840,000 tons	450,000 tons	_____

Partial Year   Most firms will probably select the A.C.R.S. method of depreciation for tax purposes. A firm may elect to use one of the other methods of depreciation for their internal records, as it may be felt that another method more closely fits real values. When the A.C.R.S. method is used, the owner may use a full year's depreciation no matter when the asset was purchased during the year. The other systems require that an adjustment be made to the amount of depreciation for the period. Not all assets are purchased at the beginning or end of a fiscal year; this concerns all assets whose asset life overlaps the fiscal year. There is little problem when the straight-line method is used because the depreciation amount is the same each year. The S.O.Y.D. and declining-balance methods have a changing amount of depreciation per year and must be adjusted accordingly.

When an asset is purchased on or before the fifteenth of the month, the complete month is used to compute the amount of depreciation for the period. When it is purchased after the fifteenth, no depreciation is claimed for the month.

A **time line** is useful in determining the correct month and year in partial year depreciation problems. It will help visualize the relationship of the calendar to the fiscal year of the firm and the invoice date of the asset. This basic tool can be very beneficial in selecting the correct number of months of the correct year to use in solving the problem. It only takes a few moments to construct the time line and put the facts on it.

Example 11

Time Line

Asset Life _____

Fiscal Year

Example 12

A desk was purchased on August 1, 1984 for $870. The expected life is twelve years and the salvage value is $150. The firm has a fiscal year of June 1 to May 31. What is the depreciation amount for the first two fiscal years ending May 31, 1986?

	August 1984	August 1985	August 1986
Asset Life			
Fiscal Year			
	June 1984	June 1985	June 1986

There are ten months in the first fiscal year (from August 1984 to June 1985) and a full year in the second fiscal year (June 1985 to June 1986).

The full-year depreciation for any year is $\frac{\$720}{12} = \$60.$

The first fiscal year depreciation would be $\frac{10}{12} \times \$60 = \$50.$

The depreciation for the first two fiscal years would total $110 ($50 + $60).

Years of Expected Life	Year Number
12 ←	→ 1
11 ←	→ 2
10	3
9	4
8	5
+ 1	
78	

Example 12 *Continued*

	August 1984	August 1985	August 1986
Asset Life	Year #1	Year #2	Year #3
Fiscal Year	Year #1	Year #2	Year #3
	June 1984	June 1985	June 1986

The first fiscal year (ending June 1985) would be computed as shown below.

$$\$720 \times \frac{12}{78} \times \frac{10}{12} = \$92.31$$

The second fiscal year (ending June 1986) would be computed as shown below.

$$\$720 \times \frac{12}{78} \times \frac{2}{12} = \$18.46 \text{ plus } \$720 \times \frac{11}{78} \times \frac{10}{12} = \$84.62$$

The depreciation for the first two full fiscal years would be $92.31 + $18.46 + $84.62 = $195.39

Notice that the partial year of the first year is carried over into the computations of the second year. This process would be continued if the question were to ask for the depreciation for the third year, etc. In that case, the portion of the second year would be carried over into the computations of the third year.

Declining-balance method

The declining-balance method requires that the ten months of the first fiscal year be used to adjust the balance for the next year. After the first partial year, the succeeding years are computed as full years (without any adjustment for ten months/two months, etc.).

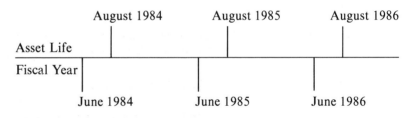

	August 1984	August 1985	August 1986
Asset Life			
Fiscal Year			
	June 1984	June 1985	June 1986

$870 Total Cost $\times \frac{2}{12} = \$145$ (full-year depreciation)

$145 $\times \frac{10}{12} = \$120.83$ for the fiscal year ending June 1985

The depreciation for the second year would be computed using the declined balance and a full-year factor of $\frac{2}{12}$.

$870 − $120.83 = $749.17 (book value June 1985)

$749.17 $\times \frac{2}{12} = \$124.86$ for the year ending June 1986

Example 13

A sign was purchased on July 10, 1983 for $7,100. The expected life is ten years with a $1,200 salvage value. What is the depreciation for the fiscal year ending March 31, 1986 if the firm uses the S.O.Y.D. method?

	July 1983	July 1984	July 1985	July 1986
Asset Life	Year #1	Year #2	Year #3	Year #4
Fiscal Year		April 1984	April 1985	April 1986

Years of Expected Life	*Year Number*	
10	1	$7,100 Total Cost
9 ←	2	− 1,200 Salvage Value
8 ←	3	$5,900 Total Depreciation
7	4	
6	5	
5	6	
4	7	
3	8	
2	9	
+ 1	10	
55		

$$\$5,900 \times \frac{9}{55} \times \frac{3}{12} = \$241.36 \text{ (from April 1985 to July 1985)}$$

$$\$5,900 \times \frac{8}{55} \times \frac{9}{12} = \underline{\$643.64} \text{ (from July 1985 to April 1986)}$$

$885.00 Depreciation for the fiscal year ending March 31, 1986

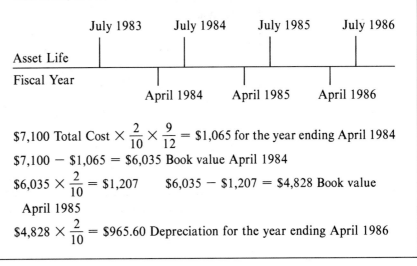

Example 14

If the firm in Example 13 had used the declining-balance method, what would be the amount of depreciation for the fiscal year ending March 31, 1986?

$7,100 Total Cost $\times \frac{2}{10} \times \frac{9}{12} = $1,065$ for the year ending April 1984

$7,100 - $1,065 = $6,035$ Book value April 1984

$6,035 \times \frac{2}{10} = $1,207 \qquad $6,035 - $1,207 = $4,828$ Book value April 1985

$4,828 \times \frac{2}{10} = 965.60 Depreciation for the year ending April 1986

Exercise I   Determine the depreciation amount in the exercises below. Use the depreciation method indicated.

	Total Cost	Expected Life (Years)	Salvage Value	Purchase Date	Fiscal Year Ended	Depreciation Method	Depreciation Amount
1.	$ 650	4	$ 50	August 15, 1985	January 15, 1987	S.O.Y.D.	$215.00
2.	1,300	8	100	June 1, 1982	January 1, 1985	Declining-Balance	
3.	900	4	300	September 9, 1986	January 1, 1987	S.O.Y.D.	
4.	700	5	100	May 1, 1984	August 1, 1988	S.O.Y.D.	
5.	630	4	0	June 1, 1985	March 1, 1987	Declining-Balance	

Skill Problems   Complete the problems below. Use the method indicated.

	Total Cost	Salvage Value	Expected Life (Years)	Year Number	Depreciation	Accumulated Depreciation	Book Value	Method
1.	$ 7,000	$ 500	20	8	_____	_____	_____	Straight-Line
2.	8,600	600	8	4	_____	_____	_____	S.O.Y.D.
3.	35,700	1,000	15	10	_____	_____	_____	Straight-Line
4.	1,250	50	20	3	_____	_____	_____	Declining-Balance
5.	9,800	500	15	2	_____	_____	_____	S.O.Y.D.
6.	950	150	10	3	_____	_____	_____	Straight-Line
7.	5,600	0	10	4	_____	_____	_____	Declining-Balance
8.	695	95	12	7	_____	_____	_____	Straight-Line
9.	1,350	350	5	2	_____	_____	_____	S.O.Y.D.
10.	856	56	15	3	_____	_____	_____	S.O.Y.D.

	Total Cost	Salvage Value	Expected Life	Units this Period	Depreciation this Period	Method
11.	$ 1,950	$ 50	1,400	60	_____	Units-of-Production
12.	1,650	350	90,000	4,000	_____	Units-of-Production
13.	5,300	300	19,500	900	_____	Units-of-Production
14.	800	200	80,000	650	_____	Units-of-Production
15.	41,600	0	156,000	3,500	_____	Units-of-Production

	Cost	Category (Years)	Year	Depreciation (A.C.R.S.)	Accumulated Depreciation	Book Value
16.	$ 9,000	3	2	_____	_____	_____
17.	15,900	5	3	_____	_____	_____
18.	85,000	10	4	_____	_____	_____

		Expected	Salvage		Fiscal Year		Depreciation
	Total Cost	Life	Value	Purchase Date	Ended	Method	Amount
19.	$2,000	5 years	$250	May 1, 1984	July 1, 1986	S.O.Y.D.	_____
20.	1,680	4	300	Sept. 23, 1985	March 1, 1987	Declining-Balance	_____

Business Application Problems

Blecher and Associates purchased a building for $139,000 for their office and storage space. The building is expected to have a useful life of twenty years. The salvage value at the end of that period is estimated to be $20,000. The owner of the firm has asked that a comparison be made at the end of the tenth year using three methods of depreciation. What is the depreciation for the tenth year?

1. Straight-line method: _____

2. S.O.Y.D. method: _____

3. Declining-balance method: _____

4. Demmer Manufacturing uses a shear to cut thick metal pieces. The press cost $129,000 when it was new fifteen years ago. The press is expected to have a useful life of 35,000 hours. It was used 1,500 hours this year. If the scrap value is expected to be $5,000, what is the depreciation amount for this year?

5. A heating system was purchased by the Fossum Import Company of New York. The system cost $89,000 installed when it was purchased twelve years ago. What is the difference in the amount of depreciation for this year if the system will have a scrap value of only $3,000 at the end of fifteen years? Compare the straight-line and S.O.Y.D. methods.

6. If an item is depreciated at the rate of 5 percent per year using the straight-line method, what was the original cost if the depreciation amount per year is $265 and the salvage value is $800?

7. The Felder Co. purchased an office building on March 1, 1976 for $60,000. The building is expected to last for 20 years. On March 1, 1987 a real estate appraiser stated the building's value was probably $46,000. Mr. Felder, company president, has asked that the appraisal be compared to the book value. Which method of depreciation would come closest to the appraisal?

8. A truck body for cold product delivery costs $6,000. The life of the body is stated to be fifteen years. The body will be scrapped for $200. When the body was nine years old, it was totally destroyed by fire. The accountant found that it had been depreciated using the S.O.Y.D. method. What was its book value?

9. The Morrison Company has a dispute with the I.R.S. over the classification of a piece of property. Morrison feels that the item should be categorized as a five-year item and the I.R.S. indiciates that it should be ten years. The dispute has been going on for two full years. The item cost $8,900 and will scrap out at $1,000 at the end of the expected life. What is the difference in the book values using the five- and ten-year categories?

10. The Forsythe Interdynamics Corporation purchased a computer printer for $5,800 two years ago. The printer is in the five-year category. The firm is now interested in trading in the printer for a laser graphics unit that cost $10,000. The firm will receive a $3,000 allowance for the trade-in. What is the difference in the trade-in value and the book value of the printer?

11. Doctor Monroe purchased a new light-signaling system for the series of patient exam rooms in her new office building. The system will cost $14,780. The expected life of the system will be ten years. The system will be junked at the end of its expected life. The doctor is unsure of which depreciation system to use. What is the difference in the book value at the end of $3 \frac{1}{2}$ years between the straight-line and S.O.Y.D. methods?

12. The accountant determined that the amount of depreciation expense for the year was $560 on a piece of equipment that has now been used for the second full year. The item is to be depreciated over a five-year period and have a salvage value of $3,000. The item is depreciated using the S.O.Y.D. method. What is the original price of the item?

13. If the item in problem 12 were depreciated over a ten-year period using the straight-line method, what would be the accumulated depreciation at the end of the second year?

Challenge Problem

The Bayer Corp. purchased a hydraulic press for $76,587 F.O.B. Cincinnati. Bayer Corp. is located in Wattona, South Carolina. The transportation charges were $942. The press was purchased on terms of 2/10,n/30 on July 16, 1984. It was delivered on July 23 and the invoice was paid on July 24. Trade discounts of 10 percent and 5 percent were granted by the selling firm, Gray Iron, Inc. Installation costs were $15,321. The salvage value is estimated to be $5,000 at the end of its expected life of twenty-five years.

Bayer uses the declining-balance method to determine the depreciation expense. The first full (fiscal) year ended on April 15, 1986.

You are asked to determine the book value of the press on April 15, 1986.

Match the following terms and explanations.

_____ 1. Depletion

_____ 2. S.O.Y.D. Method

_____ 3. Straight-Line Method

_____ 4. Declining-Balance Method

_____ 5. Book Value

_____ 6. Salvage Value

_____ 7. A.C.R.S. Method

_____ 8. Accumulated Depreciation

A. An equal amount of depreciation per year
B. Made up of all costs incurred to make the item operable
C. All properties are categorized to set the percent
D. Depreciation per year $\times$ the number of years to date (straight line)
E. Total cost less total depreciation; the residual value
F. Allowance for a used portion of natural resource
G. This method uses $\frac{2}{15}$ as a fraction to multiply by salvage value
H. This method considers the amount of operations performed. The fraction is multiplied by total cost to find book value.
I. This method uses total cost or book value multiplied by a rate to accelerate the depreciation amount in the early years
J. This method totals the years of expected life. This number becomes the denominator in a fraction.
K. Total cost less the depreciation to date

Calculate the missing values in each of the following problems. Use the depreciation method indicated.

	Total Cost	Salvage Value	Expected Life (Years)	Year Number	Depreciation Amount	Accumulated Depreciation	Book Value	Method
9.	$21,000	$1,000	10	4	_____	_____	_____	S.O.Y.D.
10.	35,900	1,900	8	2	_____	_____	_____	Declining-Balance
11.	12,600	50	20	17	_____	_____	_____	Straight-Line

	Total Cost	Salvage Value	Expected Life (Units)	Units this Period	Depreciation Amount	Method
12.	$42,000	$2,000	100,000	20,000	_____	Units-of-Production

13. Market Services Company purchased a new copier one year ago. The machine cost $5,800 and will be able to command a trade-in value of $500 when sold. The machine is categorized for a five-year life. What is the book value at the end of the first year?

14. Hoffman Associates purchased a piece of land for $150,000 with an estimated 50,000 barrels of oil that could be produced from it. The firm pumped 2,000 barrels of oil in the third year of ownership. What is the depletion allowance for the third year?

15. A building was purchased for $260,000 ten years ago. The expected life was established at thirty years. The firm decided to use a straight-line method to depreciate the property. The salvage value of the property will be $30,000. What is the book value of the property?

16. Flash Movers, Inc. purchased an airplane for $74,000 on October 17, 1983. The plane will have a salvage value of $3,000. The firm has decided to depreciate the property over a period of twenty years using the declining-balance method. Gwen Kimberlin, company accountant, must determine the amount of depreciation for the fiscal year ended March 31, 1986. What is the amount of depreciation for the period?

18 Taxes

After mastering the material in this chapter, you will be able to:

1. Calculate annual property taxes.
2. Calculate a property tax rate.
3. Calculate the customs duties on imported merchandise.
4. Calculate the income tax at the end of the year.
5. Describe the calculation of sales tax.
6. Understand and use the following terms and concepts:

Assessed Valuation	Taxable Income
Mills	Dependents
Customs Duty	Exemptions
Ad Valorem	Deductions
Specific	Zero Bracket Amount
Compound Rate	

Property Taxes

Property taxes are collected by local units of government, such as cities and townships, for the operations of such services as fire protection, schools, local government, and road maintenance. This tax is levied on property owners. Church and government property are not taxed.

Tax Amount

Assessed valuation

Mills

The tax amount is calculated by multiplying the taxable base by a tax rate. The taxable amount is termed the **assessed valuation.** This amount is set by a tax assessor, a representative of the taxing governmental unit. The assessed valuation is established from the apparent market value of the property.

The tax rate is often expressed in terms of **mills** or thousandths of a dollar. A one mill tax rate on $1 of assessed valuation would result in a tax of $.001. A tax rate of 23.6 mills would be a tax of $23.60 on each $1,000 of assessed valuation. The tax rate may also be expressed in hundredths. A tax rate of one hundredth would mean $1 tax on each $100 of assessed valuation. A property taxed at 2.36 hundredths would be taxed $2.36 for each $100 of assessed valuation or $23.60 on each $1,000.

Example 1

The office building of the Par-Tee Corp. has an assessed valuation of $42,600. The tax rate in the community is 31.85 mills. The current market value is $75,000. What is the amount of property taxes on the office building?

$$42.6 = \text{thousands of dollars of assessed valuation}$$
$$\underline{\times\ \$31.85} = \text{tax per thousand dollars of assessed valuation (31.85 mills)}$$
$$\$1,356.81 = \text{property taxes}$$

Example 2

Trizella Longoria owns a home that has a market value of $83,000 in San Benito. The assessed valuation is set at $40,000. The tax rate is $2.84 per hundred. What is the amount of the tax on her home?

$$400 = \text{hundreds of dollars of assessed valuation}$$
$$\underline{\times\$2.84} = \text{tax per hundred dollars of assessed valuation}$$
$$\$1,136 = \text{property taxes}$$

Exercise A Complete the exercise below by determining the missing value. Round off your answer to the nearest cent or hundredth of a mill.

	Market Value	Assessed Valuation	Tax Rate (in Mills)	Property Taxes
1.	$ 36,500	$22,000	13.07	$ 287.54
2.	169,800	90,000	25.4	_____
3.	47,000	36,800	_____	791.20
4	19,300	_____	23.5	211.50
5.	65,200	56,000	23.80	_____
			(In Hundredths)	
6.	23,000	15,600	3.15	_____
7.	48,000	30,000	2.91	_____
8.	36,800	18,200	_____	258.60
9.	125,900	52,000	3.67	_____
10.	72,800	_____	4.21	2,105.00

Determining the Tax Rate

The tax rate is set by the taxing unit of government. Costs for local government services are totaled and divided by the total assessed valuation within the taxing unit, that is,

$$\frac{\text{Taxes to be raised}}{\text{Total assessed valuation}} = \text{tax rate}$$

Example 3

The Township of Kimball has established an annual budget of $746,380. The budget amount must be raised by taxing the property in the township. The total assessed valuation is $43,904,706. What is the tax rate in mills?

$$\frac{\$746,380 = \text{taxes to be raised}}{\$43,904,706 = \text{total assessed valuation}} = .0169999 = 17 \text{ mills}$$

Example 4

The City Council of Teaneck established a budget of $1,650,000 for the next fiscal year. The assessed valuation for the city is $95,000,000. What is the tax rate per hundred?

$$\frac{\$1,650,000 = \text{taxes to be raised}}{\$95,000,000 = \text{total assessed valuation}} = .01833333 = \$1.83 \text{ tax}$$

Exercise B

Determine the tax rate in mills for each community below. Round off your answer to the nearest hundredth of a mill or cent.

Community	Total Assessed Valuation	Budget	Tax Rate (in Mills—nearest hundredth)
1. Jasper	$72,685,360	$1,368,419	18.83
2. Dandby Township	14,926,000	238,300	
3. Carson City	60,398,000	827,300	
4. Big Horn	37,567,000	721,100	
5. Portland	1,630,000	42,600	
			$\left(\begin{array}{c}In\\Hundredths\end{array}\right)$
6. Marine City	7,000,000	90,000	
7. Lake Worth	30,800,000	540,000	
8. Redwood	30,960,000	532,000	
9. Refugio	6,900,000	92,000	
10. Irving	45,600,000	1,230,000	

Customs Duty

The federal government taxes some imported goods. The tax is termed a **customs duty.** The purposes of customs duties are many, but are centered around the concepts of protecting American jobs and new domestic industries and international trade agreements. For the importing firm, customs duties represent an increase in the cost of the merchandise.

The amount of customs duties for each type of product is indicated in a tariff schedule. (See pages 399 and 400.) This document, prepared by the federal government, contains the amount of tax and type of tax. There are two types of customs duties: Ad valorem and specific.

Ad Valorem

An **ad valorem** customs duty is a percent of the market value of the imported item. The percent is indicated in the tariff schedule and the market value is indicated on the sales invoice or government estimation of the actual value.

Example 5

An importer purchased forty-two bolts of cloth material priced at $31 a bolt. The tariff schedule indicated that the ad valorem customs duty will be 12 percent. What will the customs duty amount be for the importer?

$$
\begin{array}{rl}
42 & \text{bolts} \\
\times\ \$31 & \text{per bolt} \\
\hline
\$1,302 & = \text{market value of purchase} \\
\times\quad .12 & = \text{ad valorem rate} \\
\hline
\$156.24 & = \text{customs duty}
\end{array}
$$

Specific

The tariff schedule may not indicate a percent of ad valorem customs duty but instead a specific customs duty. The **specific** tax is a set amount per unit, measure, or weight.

Example 6

The International House imported 350 art figures for $15 each. The specific duty was $3 per unit. What is the amount of specific customs duty?

$$
\begin{array}{rl}
350 & = \text{units} \\
\times\ \$3 & = \text{per unit specific tax} \\
\hline
\$1,050 & = \text{specific tax}
\end{array}
$$

SCHEDULE 3. - TEXTILE FIBERS AND TEXTILE PRODUCTS
Part 6. - Wearing Apparel and Accessories

Item	Stat. Suf- fix	Articles	Units of Quantity	Rates of Duty		
				1	Special	2
		Other handkerchiefs, not ornamented (con.):				
		Of vegetable fibers, except cotton:				
370.72	00	Not hemmed..................................	Doz.....	2.6% ad val.	Free (E*) 1.8% ad val.(I)	35% ad val.
		Hemmed or hemstitched, or not finished and having drawn yarns:				
		Made with hand-rolled or handmade				
370.76	00	hems....................................	Doz.....	0.1¢ each + 12.3% ad val.	Free (E*) 0.1¢ each + 8.6% ad val. (I)	51.5% ad val.
370.80	00	Other.....................................	Doz.....	6.1% ad val.	Free (E*) 4.3% ad val.(I)	50% ad val.
370.84		Of silk.....................................	....	8.9% ad val.	Free (E*) 6.2% ad val.(I)	60% ad val.
	20	Hemmed...........................	Doz. v Lb.			
	40	Not hemmed.......................	Doz. v Lb.			
370.88		Of man-made fibers............................	....	4¢ per lb. + 16% ad val.	2.8¢ per lb. + 11.2% ad val. (I)	68.5% ad val.
	20	Hemmed...............................(630)	Doz. v Lb.			
	40	Not hemmed...........................(630)	Doz. v Lb.			
370.92	00	Other...	Doz.....	6.5% ad val.	Free (E*) 4.6% ad val.(I)	40% ad val.
		Subpart B. - Mufflers, Scarves, Shawls and Veils; Men's and Boys Neckties				
		Mufflers, scarves, shawls, and veils, all the foregoing of textile materials:				
		Lace or net articles, whether or not ornamented, and other articles, ornamented:				
		Veils:				
372.04	00	Of cotton.........................(369)	Doz....v Lb.	13.3% ad val.	9.3% ad val. (I)	90% ad val.
372.06	00	Of man-made fibers.................(669)	Doz....v Lb.	14% ad val.	9.8% ad val. (I)	90% ad val.
372.08	00	Other...................................	Doz....v Lb.	12.2% ad val.	Free (E*) 8.5% ad val.(I)	90% ad val.
372.10		Other......................................	....	15% ad val.	Free (E*) 10.5% ad val.(I)	90% ad val.
		Knit:				
	10	Of cotton.....................(359)	Doz. v Lb.			
	20	Of wool.......................(459)	Doz. v Lb.			
	30	Of man-made fibers............(659)	Doz. v Lb.			
	36	Other.........................(359)	Doz. v Lb.			
		Not knit:				
	40	Of cotton.....................(359)	Doz. v Lb.			
	50	Of wool.......................(459)	Doz. v Lb.			
	60	Of man-made fibers............(659)	Doz. v Lb.			
	70	Other.........................	Doz. v Lb.			

SCHEDULE 3. - TEXTILE FIBERS AND TEXTILE PRODUCTS
Part 6. - Wearing Apparel and Accessories

Item	Stat. Suf- fix	Articles	Units of Quantity	Rates of Duty		
				1	Special	2
		Mufflers, scarves, shawls, etc. (con.):				
		Other articles, not ornamented (con.):				
372.15		Of cotton....................................	....	12.8% ad val.	9% ad val.(I)	37.5% ad val.
	20	Knit................................(359)	Doz. v Lb.			
		Not knit:				
	40	Hemmed.......................(359)	Doz. v Lb.			
	60	Not hemmed...................(359)	Doz. v Lb.			
372.20	00	Of vegetable fibers, except cotton...........	Doz....v Lb.	5.3% ad val.	Free (E*) 3.7% ad val.(I)	35% ad val.
		Of wool:				
		Knit:				
372.25	00	For infants' wear.............(459)	Doz....v Lb.	6¢ per lb. + 18.7% ad val.	4.2¢ per lb. + 13.1% ad val.(I)	83.5% ad val.
		Other:				
372.30	00	Valued not over $5 per pound.....................(459)	Doz....v Lb.	10¢ per lb. + 20% ad val.	7¢ per lb. + 14% ad val. (I)	63.5% ad val.
372.35	00	Valued over $5 per pound..(459)	Doz....v Lb.	6¢ per lb. + 10.8% ad val.	4.2¢ per lb. + 7.6% ad val. (I)	54% ad val.
		Not knit:				
372.40	00	Valued not over $4 per pound...(459)	Doz....v Lb.	4¢ per lb. + 16.8% ad val.	2.8¢ per lb. + 11.8% ad val. (I)	65.5% ad val.
372.45	00	Valued over $4 per pound.......(459)	Doz....v Lb.	6¢ per lb. + 16.8% ad val.	4.2¢ per lb. + 11.8% ad val. (I)	55% ad val.
		Of silk:				
372.50	00	Knit....................................	Doz....v Lb.	6.5% ad val.	Free (E*) 4.6% ad val.(I)	60% ad val.
		Not knit:				
		Weighing over 1 ounce per square yard and rectangular in shape:				
372.55	00	Valued not over $5 per dozen...	Doz....v Lb.	10% ad val.	Free (E*) 7% ad val.(I)	60% ad val.
372.60		Valued over $5 per dozen.......	....	8% ad val.	Free (A,E*) 5.6% ad val.(I)	60% ad val.
	20	Hemmed....................	Doz. v Lb.			
	40	Not hemmed...............	Doz. v Lb.			
372.65		Other............................	....	9.3% ad val.	Free (A,E*) 6.5% ad val.(I)	65% ad val.
	20	Hemmed.......................	Doz. v Lb.			
	40	Not hemmed..................	Doz. v Lb.			
		Of man-made fibers:				
372.70	00	Knit................................(659)	Doz....v Lb.	7¢ per lb. + 20% ad val.	4.9¢ per lb. + 14% ad val.(I)	68.5% ad val.
372.75		Not knit............................	....	4¢ per lb. + 10.7% ad val.	2.8¢ per lb. + 7.5% ad val.(I)	73% ad val.
	20	Hemmed.......................(659)	Doz. v Lb.			
	40	Not hemmed...................(659)	Doz. v Lb.			
372.80	00	Other.......................................	Lb......	6.5% ad val.	Free (E*) 4.6% ad val.(I)	40% ad val.

Compound Rate

When the tariff schedule specifies both an ad valorem and specific duty, it is termed a **compound rate**.

Example 7

The Far East Importers purchased seventy-five pieces of furniture valued at $37.50 each. The tariff schedule indicated an ad valorem duty of 43 percent and a specific duty of $4. What is the total cost of the purchase for Far East Importers?

75	= units	75	= units
× $37.50	= price per unit	× $4	= specific duty per unit
$2,812.50	= total market value	$300	= total specific duty
× .43	= ad valorem rate		
$1,209.38	= ad valorem duty		

$2,812.50 = total market value
1,209.38 = ad valorem duty
+ 300.00 = total specific duty
$4,321.88 = total cost to Far East Importers

Exercise C

Determine the amount of customs duties in the exercises below.

	Units Purchased	Value Per Unit	Ad Valorem Rate (%)	Specific Rate/Unit	Total Customs Duties
1.	1,500	$ 3.78	10	$ 1.20	$2,367.00
2.	144	9.20	$7\frac{3}{4}$	.70	
3.	35	46.30	. . .	11.25	
4.	100	27.00	3	.38	
5.	75	32.40	$2\frac{1}{2}$	. . .	
6.	20	846.00	8	.87	
7.	50	93.20	3	. . .	
8.	100	12.00	$\frac{1}{2}$	3.00	
9.	150	8.00	$4\frac{1}{4}$	16.50	
10.	10	23.00	9	. . .	

Sales Tax

Some cities and at least forty-five states have a sales tax. The tax is usually a specified percent of the total value of the merchandise sold. Often the state furnishes retailers with a table to place on the cash register. This table shows the clerk how much sales tax to add to the price of the merchandise. This eliminates the necessity of calculating the sales tax for each sale. A 4 percent sales tax table is shown below.

Amount of Sale	Tax	Amount of Sale	Tax	Amount of Sale	Tax	Amount of Sale	Tax
.01– .12	.00	9.38– 9.62	.38	18.88–19.12	.76	28.38–28.62	1.14
.13– .31	.01	9.63– 9.87	.39	19.13–19.37	.77	28.63–28.87	1.15
.32– .54	.02	9.88–10.12	.40	19.38–19.62	.78	28.88–29.12	1.16
.55– .81	.03	10.13–10.37	.41	19.63–19.87	.79	29.13–29.37	1.17
.82–1.08	.04	10.38–10.62	.42	19.88–20.12	.80	29.38–29.62	1.18
1.09–1.35	.05	10.63–10.87	.43	20.13–20.37	.81	29.63–29.87	1.19
1.36–1.62	.06	10.88–11.12	.44	20.38–20.62	.82	29.88–30.12	1.20
1.63–1.87	.07	11.13–11.37	.45	20.63–20.87	.83	30.13–30.37	1.21
1.88–2.12	.08	11.38–11.62	.46	20.88–21.12	.84	30.38–30.62	1.22
2.13–2.37	.09	11.63–11.87	.47	21.13–21.37	.85	30.63–30.87	1.23
2.38–2.62	.10	11.88–12.12	.48	21.38–21.62	.86	30.88–31.12	1.24
2.63–2.87	.11	12.13–12.37	.49	21.63–21.87	.87	31.13–31.37	1.25
2.88–3.12	.12	12.38–12.62	.50	21.88–22.12	.88	31.38–31.62	1.26
3.13–3.37	.13	12.63–12.87	.51	22.13–22.37	.89	31.63–31.87	1.27
3.38–3.62	.14	12.88–13.12	.52	22.38–22.62	.90	31.88–32.12	1.28
3.63–3.87	.15	13.13–13.37	.53	22.63–22.87	.91	32.13–32.37	1.29
3.88–4.12	.16	13.38–13.62	.54	22.88–23.12	.92	32.38–32.62	1.30
4.13–4.37	.17	13.63–13.87	.55	23.13–23.37	.93	32.63–32.87	1.31
4.38–4.62	.18	13.88–14.12	.56	23.38–23.62	.94	32.88–33.12	1.32
4.63–4.87	.19	14.13–14.37	.57	23.63–23.87	.95	33.13–33.37	1.33
4.88–5.12	.20	14.38–14.62	.58	23.88–24.12	.96	33.38–33.62	1.34
5.13–5.37	.21	14.63–14.87	.59	24.13–24.37	.97	33.63–33.87	1.35
5.38–5.62	.22	14.88–15.12	.60	24.38–24.62	.98	33.88–34.12	1.36
5.63–5.87	.23	15.13–15.37	.61	24.63–24.87	.99	34.13–34.37	1.37
5.88–6.12	.24	15.38–15.62	.62	24.88–25.12	1.00	34.38–34.62	1.38
6.13–6.37	.25	15.63–15.87	.63	25.13–25.37	1.01	34.63–34.87	1.39
6.38–6.62	.26	15.88–16.12	.64	25.38–25.62	1.02	34.88–35.12	1.40
6.63–6.87	.27	16.13–16.37	.65	25.63–25.87	1.03	35.13–35.37	1.41
6.88–7.12	.28	16.38–16.62	.66	25.88–26.12	1.04	35.38–35.62	1.42
7.13–7.37	.29	16.63–16.87	.67	26.13–26.37	1.05	35.63–35.87	1.43
7.38–7.62	.30	16.88–17.12	.68	26.38–26.62	1.06	35.88–36.12	1.44
7.63–7.87	.31	17.13–17.37	.69	26.63–26.87	1.07	36.13–36.37	1.45
7.88–8.12	.32	17.38–17.62	.70	26.88–27.12	1.08	36.38–36.62	1.46
8.13–8.37	.33	17.63–17.87	.71	27.13–27.37	1.09	36.63–36.87	1.47
8.38–8.62	.34	17.88–18.12	.72	27.38–27.62	1.10	36.88–37.12	1.48
8.63–8.87	.35	18.13–18.37	.73	27.63–27.87	1.11	37.13–37.37	1.49
8.88–9.12	.36	18.38–18.62	.74	27.88–28.12	1.12	37.38–37.62	1.50
9.13–9.37	.37	18.63–18.87	.75	28.13–28.37	1.13		

The sales tax is found by finding the appropriate bracket of "amount of sale" and then reading the tax to the right. For example, the total amount of sale ($34) is found in the bracket $33.88 — $34.12. The sales tax is $1.36.

Federal Income Tax

Federal, state, and city income taxes are designed to tax wages, salaries, commissions, dividends, royalties, tips, and other incomes of individual wage earners. The profits of business and industry are also taxed under a similar set of laws.

At the end of a calendar year wage earners and firms must file a report or income tax return with the Internal Revenue Service (I.R.S.). The income tax return determines the amount of income taxes for the year. Wage earners will have paid income taxes through payroll withholdings during the year. The amount of taxes paid and gross earnings are reported to employees on a W-2 form provided by the I.R.S. The income tax for the year and the final settlement amount is worked out on the income tax return and sent to the I.R.S. The form used is known as Form 1040 or Form 1040A.

1 Control number		OMB No. 1545-0008		
2 Employer's name, address, and ZIP code			3 Employer's identification number	4 Employer's State number
			5 Statutory employee / Deceased / Legal rep / 942 emp / Subtotal / Void	
			6 Allocated tips	7 Advance EIC payment
8 Employee's social security number	9 Federal income tax withheld		10 Wages, tips, other compensation	11 Social security tax withheld
12 Employee's name, address, and ZIP code			13 Social security wages	14 Social security tips
			16	
			17 State income tax	18 State wages, tips, etc	19 Name of State
			20 Local income tax	21 Local wages, tips, etc	22 Name of locality

Form **W-2 Wage and Tax Statement** **1985**   Copy A For Social Security Administration   Department of the Treasury Internal Revenue Service
* See Instructions for Forms W-2 and W-2P

Department of the Treasury—Internal Revenue Service.

Taxable income

Income tax is based on the wage earner's ability to pay. The greater the taxable income, the higher the income tax rate. **Taxable income** is the gross earnings of an individual less the amount of allowable expenses. The allowable expenses fall into two categories, dependents and deductions.

Dependents

Dependents are those persons living in the household of the wage earner and who are at least half supported by the wage earner during the year. The wage earner's spouse, children, relatives, or any person living in that household can be claimed as dependents.* For each dependent and for the wage earner, $1,040 of gross

Exemption

earnings are exempt from taxation. The $1,040 amount is known as an **exemption.** This amount is set aside, tax free, to cover basic needs.

Note: The figures used in this section are current as of the writing of this text.

*The reader should realize that the courts have established exceptions to the above explanation, but the exceptions are beyond the scope of this text.

> **Example 8**
>
> A family earns $14,680 for the year. The family is made up of a father, mother, and three dependent children. What is the amount of tax exempt income for the family?
>
> 1 exemption—father
> 1 exemption—mother
> 3 exemptions—children
> ‾‾‾‾‾‾‾‾‾‾‾‾‾‾‾‾‾‾‾‾‾
> 5 exemptions $\times$ \$1,040 = \$5,200

If a wage earner or wage earner's spouse is sixty-five years of age or older or if either is blind, an additional exemption is allowed for each case.

> **Example 9**
>
> Gus Ebson is sixty-eight. His wife Millie is sixty-six and blind. How many exemptions can they claim on their income tax return?
>
> 2—Gus (an extra exemption for age)
> 3—Millie (an extra exemption for age and an extra exemption for
> _   being blind)
> 5 exemptions

Households with lower incomes or a large number of exemptions may not need to pay income tax. In these cases, low gross earnings are balanced or overcome by the total exemption amount.

Deductions

Deductions are other allowable expenses beyond the exemption level needs. They are also subtracted from gross earnings in order to determine taxable earnings. Deductions include state and city income taxes; property taxes; sales taxes; interest; contributions to nonprofit organizations, such as churches or political parties; dental and medical expenses over a certain amount not covered by insurance; property losses not covered by insurance; and other items that will not be covered in this text.

Zero bracket amount

The wage earner may list or itemize all deductions on Form 1040 or use the **zero bracket amount.** The itemized deductions must be verifiable. The zero bracket amount is $3,540 for a couple filing jointly or $2,390 for a single person. The zero bracket amounts are already built into the tax tables and tax rate schedules. Hence, a taxpayer who elects to use the zero bracket amount need not deduct this amount from gross earnings to determine taxable income. The wage earner may select whichever method offers the greater benefits by reducing taxable income as much as possible. If the taxpayer intends to itemize deductions, Form 1040 will be used. Form 1040A will be used if the taxpayer does not plan to itemize deductions.

Gross earnings of a wage earner are adjusted by subtracting the dependent exemptions and deductions to find taxable income.

The coverage of federal income tax in this chapter is by no means complete. Students should realize that this topic is in itself a program of study and for some, a career. The material included here on this topic is designed to give you a basic understanding of this topic that is vital to business and individuals.

Form **1040** Department of the Treasury—Internal Revenue Service

U.S. Individual Income Tax Return 1985 (O)

For the year January 1-December 31, 1985, or other tax year beginning   , 1985, ending   , 19 | OMB No. 1545-0074

Use IRS label. Other- wise, please print or type.	Your first name and initial (if joint return, also give spouse's name and initial)	Last name	Your social security number
	Present home address (number and street, including apartment number, or rural route)		Spouse's social security number
	City, town or post office, state, and ZIP code	Your occupation	
		Spouse's occupation	

Presidential Election Campaign ▶ Do you want $1 to go to this fund? . . . . | Yes | No | **Note:** *Checking "Yes" will not change your tax or reduce your refund.*
If joint return, does your spouse want $1 to go to this fund? . | Yes | No

For Privacy Act and Paperwork Reduction Act Notice, see Instructions.

Filing Status

Check only one box.

1 ☐ Single
2 ☐ Married filing joint return (even if only one had income)
3 ☐ Married filing separate return. Enter spouse's social security no. above and full name here. _____
4 ☐ Head of household (with qualifying person). (See page 5 of Instructions.) If the qualifying person is your unmarried child but not your dependent, write child's name here. _____
5 ☐ Qualifying widow(er) with dependent child (year spouse died ▶ 19   ). (See page 6 of Instructions.)

Exemptions

Always check the box labeled Yourself. Check other boxes if they apply.

6a ☐ Yourself ☐ 65 or over ☐ Blind | } Enter number of boxes checked on 6a and b ▶ ☐
b ☐ Spouse ☐ 65 or over ☐ Blind

c First names of your dependent children who lived with you _____ | } Enter number of children listed on 6c ▶ ☐

d First names of your dependent children who did not live with you (see page 6). _____
(If pre-1985 agreement, check here ▶ ☐ .) | } Enter number of children listed on 6d ▶ ☐

e Other dependents:

(1) Name	(2) Relationship	(3) Number of months lived in your home	(4) Did dependent have income of $1,040 or more?	(5) Did you provide more than one-half of dependent's support?

} Enter number of other dependents ▶ ☐

f Total number of exemptions claimed (also complete line 36). . . . . | Add numbers entered in boxes above ▶ ☐

Income

Please attach Copy B of your Forms W-2, W-2G, and W-2P here.

If you do not have a W-2, see page 4 of Instructions.

7 Wages, salaries, tips, etc. (Attach Form(s) W-2.) . . . . | 7 |
8 Interest income (also attach Schedule B if over $400) . . . . . . | 8 |
9a Dividends (also attach Schedule B if over $400) _____ , 9b Exclusion _____
c Subtract line 9b from line 9a and enter the result . . . . | 9c |
10 Taxable refunds of state and local income taxes, if any, from the worksheet on page 9 of Instructions. | 10 |
11 Alimony received . . . . | 11 |
12 Business income or (loss) (attach Schedule C) . . . . | 12 |
13 Capital gain or (loss) (attach Schedule D) . . . . | 13 |
14 40% of capital gain distributions not reported on line 13 (see page 9 of Instructions) . . . . | 14 |
15 Other gains or (losses) (attach Form 4797) . . . . | 15 |
16 Fully taxable pensions, IRA distributions, and annuities not reported on line 17 (see page 9). | 16 |
17a Other pensions and annuities, including rollovers. Total received | 17a |
b Taxable amount, if any, from the worksheet on page 10 of Instructions . . . . . | 17b |
18 Rents, royalties, partnerships, estates, trusts, etc. (attach Schedule E) . . . . . | 18 |
19 Farm income or (loss) (attach Schedule F) . . . . | 19 |
20a Unemployment compensation (insurance). Total received | 20a |
b Taxable amount, if any, from the worksheet on page 10 of Instructions . . . . . | 20b |
21a Social security benefits (see page 10). Total received . . . | 21a |
b Taxable amount, if any, from worksheet on page 11. { Tax-exempt interest _____ } | 21b |
22 Other income (list type and amount—see page 11 of Instructions) _____ | 22 |

Please attach check or money order here.

23 Add lines 7 through 22. This is your **total income** . . . . ▶ | 23 |

Adjustments to Income

(See Instructions on page 11.)

24 Moving expense (attach Form 3903 or 3903F) . . . . . | 24 |
25 Employee business expenses (attach Form 2106) . . . . | 25 |
26 IRA deduction, from the worksheet on page 12 . . . . | 26 |
27 Keogh retirement plan deduction . . . . | 27 |
28 Penalty on early withdrawal of savings . . . . . . | 28 |
29 Alimony paid (recipient's last name _____ and social security no. _____) | 29 |
30 Deduction for a married couple when both work (attach Schedule W) | 30 |
31 Add lines 24 through 30. These are your **total adjustments** . . . . . . ▶ | 31 |

Adjusted Gross Income

32 Subtract line 31 from line 23. This is your **adjusted gross income.** *If this line is less than $11,000 and a child lived with you, see "Earned Income Credit" (line 59) on page 16 of Instructions. If you want IRS to figure your tax, see page 13 of Instructions* . . . . ▶ | 32 |

Department of the Treasury—Internal Revenue Service.

Tax Compu-tation (See Instructions on page 13.)	**33** Amount from line 32 (adjusted gross income) .		**33**
	34a If you itemize, attach Schedule A (Form 1040) and enter the amount from Schedule A, line 26 .		**34a**
	Caution: If you have unearned income and can be claimed as a dependent on your parents' return, check here ▶ ☐ and see page 13 of Instructions. Also see page 13 if you are married filing a separate return and your spouse itemizes deductions, or you are a dual-status alien.		
	b If you do not itemize but you made charitable contributions, enter your cash contributions here. (If you gave $3,000 or more to any one organization, see page 14.) .	**34b**	
	c Enter your noncash contributions (you must attach Form 8283 if over $500)	**34c**	
	d Add lines 34b and 34c. Enter the total .	**34d**	
	e Divide the amount on line 34d by 2. Enter the result here .		**34e**
	35 Subtract line 34a or line 34e, whichever applies, from line 33 .		**35**
	36 Multiply $1,040 by the total number of exemptions claimed on line 6f (see page 14) .		**36**
	37 **Taxable income.** Subtract line 36 from line 35. Enter the result (but not less than zero) .		**37**
	38 Enter tax here. Check if from ☐ Tax Table, ☐ Tax Rate Schedule X, Y, or Z, or ☐ Schedule G		**38**
	39 Additional taxes. (See page 14 of Instructions.) Enter here and check if from ☐ Form 4970, ☐ Form 4972, or ☐ Form 5544 .		**39**
	40 Add lines 38 and 39. Enter the total . ▶		**40**
Credits (See Instructions on page 14.)	**41** Credit for child and dependent care expenses (attach Form 2441)	**41**	
	42 Credit for the elderly and the permanently and totally disabled (attach Schedule R) .	**42**	
	43 Residential energy credit (attach Form 5695) .	**43**	
	44 Partial credit for political contributions for which you have receipts	**44**	
	45 Add lines 41 through 44. These are your total personal credits .		**45**
	46 Subtract line 45 from line 40. Enter the result (but not less than zero) .		**46**
	47 Foreign tax credit (attach Form 1116) .	**47**	
	48 General business credit. Check if from ☐ Form 3800, ☐ Form 3468, ☐ Form 5884, ☐ Form 6478 .	**48**	
	49 Add lines 47 and 48. These are your total business and other credits .		**49**
	50 Subtract line 49 from line 46. Enter the result (but not less than zero) . ▶		**50**
Other Taxes (Including Advance EIC Payments)	**51** Self-employment tax (attach Schedule SE) .		**51**
	52 Alternative minimum tax (attach Form 6251) .		**52**
	53 Tax from recapture of investment credit (attach Form 4255) .		**53**
	54 Social security tax on tip income not reported to employer (attach Form 4137) .		**54**
	55 Tax on an IRA (attach Form 5329) .		**55**
	56 Add lines 50 through 55. This is your **total tax** . ▶		**56**
Payments Attach Forms W-2, W-2G, and W-2P to front.	**57** Federal income tax withheld .	**57**	
	58 1985 estimated tax payments and amount applied from 1984 return	**58**	
	59 Earned income credit (see page 16) .	**59**	
	60 Amount paid with Form 4868 .	**60**	
	61 Excess social security tax and RRTA tax withheld (two or more employers) .	**61**	
	62 Credit for Federal tax on gasoline and special fuels (attach Form 4136)	**62**	
	63 Regulated Investment Company credit (attach Form 2439) .	**63**	
	64 Add lines 57 through 63. These are your **total payments** . ▶		**64**
Refund or Amount You Owe	**65** If line 64 is larger than line 56, enter amount **OVERPAID** . ▶		**65**
	66 Amount of line 65 to be **REFUNDED TO YOU** . ▶		**66**
	67 Amount of line 65 to be applied to your 1986 estimated tax . ▶	**67**	
	68 If line 56 is larger than line 64, enter **AMOUNT YOU OWE.** Attach check or money order for full amount payable to "Internal Revenue Service." Write your social security number and "1985 Form 1040" on it . ▶		**68**
	Check ▶ ☐ if Form 2210 (2210F) is attached. See page 17. **Penalty: $**		

Please Sign Here

Under penalties of perjury, I declare that I have examined this return and accompanying schedules and statements, and to the best of my knowledge and belief, they are true, correct, and complete. Declaration of preparer (other than taxpayer) is based on all information of which preparer has any knowledge.

▶ _____   _____   ▶ _____
Your signature   Date   Spouse's signature (if filing jointly, BOTH must sign)

Paid Preparer's Use Only

Preparer's signature ▶	Date	Check if self-employed ☐	Preparer's social security no.
Firm's name (or yours, if self-employed) and address ▶		E.I. No.	
		ZIP code	

U.S. GOVERNMENT PRINTING OFFICE: 1985—0-463-073 58-040-1110

Department of the Treasury—Internal Revenue Service.

Department of the Treasury—Internal Revenue Service.

1985

Schedule 1 (Form 1040A)

Name(s) as shown on Form 1040A.

OMB No. 1545-0085

Your social security number

You MUST complete and attach Schedule 1 to Form 1040A if you:

- Claim the deduction for a working married couple (complete Part I)
- Claim the credit for child and dependent care expenses (complete Part II)
- Have over $400 of interest income (complete Part III)
- Have over $400 of dividend income (complete Part IV)

Part I **Deduction for a married couple (filing a joint return) when both work** (see page 20)

Complete this part to figure the amount you can deduct on Form 1040A, line 12. Attach Schedule 1 to Form 1040A.

		(a) You	(b) Your spouse
1	Wages, salaries, tips, etc., from Form 1040A, line 6.	1	
2	IRA deduction, if any, from Form 1040A, line 11.	2	
3	Subtract line 2 from line 1. Write the result.	3	=
4	Write the amount from line 3, column (a) or (b) above, whichever is smaller.	4	
5	Percentage used to figure the deduction (10%).	5	× .10
6	Multiply the amount on line 4 by the percentage on line 5. Write your answer here and on Form 1040A, line 12.	6 =	

Part II **Credit for child and dependent care expenses** (see page 23)

Complete this part to figure the amount of credit you can take on Form 1040A, line 21a. Attach Schedule 1 to Form 1040A.

1 Write the number of qualifying persons who were cared for in 1985. (See the instructions for the definition of a qualifying person.) 1

2 Write the amount of **qualified** expenses you incurred and actually paid in 1985 for the care of the qualifying person, but DO NOT write more than $2,400 ($4,800 if you paid for the care of two or more qualifying persons). 2

3 • If **unmarried** at the end of 1985, write your earned income on line 3c, OR
• If **married**, filing a joint return for 1985, you must complete lines 3a and 3b.
  a. Write your earned income 3a
  b. Write your spouse's earned income 3b
  c. Compare the amounts on lines 3a and 3b, and write the **smaller** of the two amounts on line 3c. 3c

4 Compare the amounts on lines 2 and 3c. Write the **smaller** of the two amounts here. 4

5 Write the percentage from the table below that applies to the amount on Form 1040A, line 15.

If line 15 is:		Percentage is:	If line 15 is:		Percentage is:
Over—	But not over—		Over—	But not over—	
$0	10,000	30% (.30)	$20,000	22,000	24% (.24)
10,000	12,000	29% (.29)	22,000	24,000	23% (.23)
12,000	14,000	28% (.28)	24,000	26,000	22% (.22)
14,000	16,000	27% (.27)	26,000	28,000	21% (.21)
16,000	18,000	26% (.26)	28,000		20% (.20)
18,000	20,000	25% (.25)			

5

6 Multiply the amount on line 4 by the percentage on line 5. Write the result here and on Form 1040A, line 21a. ..... 6 = ×

⑮

Department of the Treasury—Internal Revenue Service.

Form 1040A

Department of the Treasury—Internal Revenue Service

US Individual Income Tax Return (B) **1985**

OMB No. 1545-0085

Step 1 **Name and address**

Use the IRS mailing label. If you don't have one, print or type:

Your first name and initial (if joint return, also give spouse's name and initial) — Last name

Your social security number

Present home address (number and street)

Spouse's social security no.

City, town or post office, state, and ZIP code

Presidential Election Campaign Fund

Do you want $1 to go to this fund? ☐ Yes ☐ No

If joint return, does your spouse want $1 to go to this fund? ☐ Yes ☐ No

Step 2 **Check your filing status** (Check only one)

1 ☐ Single (See if you can use Form 1040EZ.)
2 ☐ Married filing joint return (even if only one had income)
3 ☐ Married filing separate return. Enter spouse's social security number above and spouse's full name here.
4 ☐ Head of household (with qualifying person). If the qualifying person is your unmarried child but not your dependent, write this child's name here.

Step 3 **Figure your exemptions**

Always check the exemption box labeled Yourself. Check other boxes if they apply.

5a ☐ Yourself ☐ 65 or over ☐ Blind
b ☐ Spouse ☐ 65 or over ☐ Blind

Write number of boxes checked on 5a and b

c First names of your dependent children who lived with you

Write number of children listed on 5c

d First names of your dependent children who did not live with you (see page 11). (If pre-1985 agreement, check here ☐ .)

Write number of children listed on 5d

e Other dependents:

1 Name	2 Relationship	3 Number of months lived in your home	4 Did dependent have income of $1,040 or more?	5 Did you provide more than one-half of dependent's support?

Write number of other dependents listed on 5e

f Total number of exemptions claimed. (Also complete line 18.)

Add numbers entered on lines above

Step 4 **Figure your total income**

Attach Copy B of Forms W-2 here

6 Total wages, salaries, tips, etc. This should be shown in Box 10 of your W-2 form(s). (Attach Form(s) W-2.) 6

7 Interest income. (If the total is over $400, also attach Schedule 1, Part III.) 7

8a Dividends. (If the total is over $400, also attach Schedule 1, Part IV.) Total. 8a 8b Exclusion (see page 16). 8b

Attach check or money order here

c Subtract line 8b from line 8a. Write the result on line 8c. 8c

9a Unemployment compensation (insurance), from Form(s) 1099-G. Total received. 9a

b Taxable amount, if any, from the worksheet on page 17 of the instructions. This is your **total income**. ..... ▲ 9b

10 Add lines 6, 7, 8c, and 9b. Write the total. This is your **total income**. ..... ▲ 10

Step 5 **Figure your adjusted gross income**

11 Individual retirement arrangement (IRA) deduction, from the worksheet on page 19. 11

12 Deduction for a married couple when both work. Complete and attach Schedule 1, Part I. 12

13 Add lines 11 and 12. Write the total. These are your **total adjustments**. 13

14 Subtract line 13 from line 10. Write the result. This is your **adjusted gross income**. ..... ▲ 14

For Privacy Act and Paperwork Reduction Act Notice, see page 41.

Form **1040A** (1985)

⑬

1985 Tax Table

Your zero bracket amount has been built into the Tax Table.

Based on Taxable Income

For persons with taxable incomes of less than $50,000.

Example: Mr. and Mrs. Brown are filing a joint return. Their taxable income on line 37 of Form 1040 is $25,325. First, they find the $25,300-25,350 income line. Next, they find the column for married filing jointly and read down the column. The amount shown where the income line and filing status column meet is $3,545. This is the tax amount they must write on line 38 of their return.

At least	But less than	Single	Married filing jointly *	Married filing separately	Head of a household
			Your tax is—		
25,200	25,250	4,513	3,523	5,614	4,177
25,250	25,300	4,528	3,534	5,633	4,191
25,300	25,350	4,543	(3,545)	5,652	4,205
25,350	25,400	4,558	3,556	5,671	4,219

1985 Tax Table—*Continued*

24,000

At least	But less than	Single	Married filing jointly *	Married filing separately	Head of a household
24,000	24,050	4,171	3,259	5,158	3,858
24,050	24,100	4,184	3,270	5,177	3,870
24,100	24,150	4,197	3,281	5,196	3,882
24,150	24,200	4,210	3,292	5,215	3,894
24,200	24,250	4,223	3,303	5,234	3,906
24,250	24,300	4,236	3,314	5,253	3,918
24,300	24,350	4,249	3,325	5,272	3,930
24,350	24,400	4,262	3,336	5,291	3,942
24,400	24,450	4,275	3,347	5,310	3,954
24,450	24,500	4,288	3,358	5,329	3,967
24,500	24,550	4,303	3,369	5,348	3,981
24,550	24,600	4,318	3,380	5,367	3,995
24,600	24,650	4,333	3,391	5,386	4,009
24,650	24,700	4,348	3,402	5,405	4,023
24,700	24,750	4,363	3,413	5,424	4,037
24,750	24,800	4,378	3,424	5,443	4,051
24,800	24,850	4,393	3,435	5,462	4,065
24,850	24,900	4,408	3,446	5,481	4,079
24,900	24,950	4,423	3,457	5,500	4,093
24,950	25,000	4,438	3,468	5,519	4,107

25,000

At least	But less than	Single	Married filing jointly *	Married filing separately	Head of a household
25,000	25,050	4,453	3,479	5,538	4,121
25,050	25,100	4,468	3,490	5,557	4,135
25,100	25,150	4,483	3,501	5,576	4,149
25,150	25,200	4,498	3,512	5,595	4,163
25,200	25,250	4,513	3,523	5,614	4,177
25,250	25,300	4,528	3,534	5,633	4,191
25,300	25,350	4,543	3,545	5,652	4,205
25,350	25,400	4,558	3,556	5,671	4,219
25,400	25,450	4,573	3,567	5,690	4,233
25,450	25,500	4,588	3,578	5,709	4,247
25,500	25,550	4,603	3,589	5,728	4,261
25,550	25,600	4,618	3,600	5,747	4,275
25,600	25,650	4,633	3,612	5,766	4,289
25,650	25,700	4,648	3,624	5,785	4,303
25,700	25,750	4,663	3,637	5,804	4,317
25,750	25,800	4,678	3,649	5,823	4,331
25,800	25,850	4,693	3,662	5,842	4,345
25,850	25,900	4,708	3,674	5,861	4,359
25,900	25,950	4,723	3,687	5,880	4,373
25,950	26,000	4,738	3,699	5,899	4,387

26,000

At least	But less than	Single	Married filing jointly *	Married filing separately	Head of a household
26,000	26,050	4,753	3,712	5,918	4,401
26,050	26,100	4,768	3,724	5,937	4,415
26,100	26,150	4,783	3,737	5,956	4,429
26,150	26,200	4,798	3,749	5,975	4,443
26,200	26,250	4,813	3,762	5,994	4,457
26,250	26,300	4,828	3,774	6,013	4,471
26,300	26,350	4,843	3,787	6,032	4,485
26,350	26,400	4,858	3,799	6,051	4,499
26,400	26,450	4,873	3,812	6,070	4,513
26,450	26,500	4,888	3,824	6,089	4,527
26,500	26,550	4,903	3,837	6,108	4,541
26,550	26,600	4,918	3,849	6,127	4,555
26,600	26,650	4,933	3,862	6,146	4,569
26,650	26,700	4,948	3,874	6,165	4,583
26,700	26,750	4,963	3,887	6,184	4,597
26,750	26,800	4,978	3,899	6,203	4,611
26,800	26,850	4,993	3,912	6,222	4,625
26,850	26,900	5,008	3,924	6,241	4,639
26,900	26,950	5,023	3,937	6,260	4,653
26,950	27,000	5,038	3,949	6,279	4,667

27,000

At least	But less than	Single	Married filing jointly *	Married filing separately	Head of a household
27,000	27,050	5,053	3,962	6,298	4,681
27,050	27,100	5,068	3,974	6,317	4,695
27,100	27,150	5,083	3,987	6,336	4,709
27,150	27,200	5,098	3,999	6,355	4,723
27,200	27,250	5,113	4,012	6,374	4,737
27,250	27,300	5,128	4,024	6,393	4,751
27,300	27,350	5,143	4,037	6,412	4,765
27,350	27,400	5,158	4,049	6,431	4,779
27,400	27,450	5,173	4,062	6,450	4,793
27,450	27,500	5,188	4,074	6,469	4,807
27,500	27,550	5,203	4,087	6,488	4,821
27,550	27,600	5,218	4,099	6,507	4,835
27,600	27,650	5,233	4,112	6,526	4,849
27,650	27,700	5,248	4,124	6,545	4,863
27,700	27,750	5,263	4,137	6,564	4,877
27,750	27,800	5,278	4,149	6,583	4,891
27,800	27,850	5,293	4,162	6,602	4,905
27,850	27,900	5,308	4,174	6,621	4,919
27,900	27,950	5,323	4,187	6,640	4,933
27,950	28,000	5,338	4,199	6,659	4,947

28,000

At least	But less than	Single	Married filing jointly *	Married filing separately	Head of a household
28,000	28,050	5,353	4,212	6,678	4,961
28,050	28,100	5,368	4,224	6,697	4,975
28,100	28,150	5,383	4,237	6,716	4,989
28,150	28,200	5,398	4,249	6,735	5,003
28,200	28,250	5,413	4,262	6,754	5,017
28,250	28,300	5,428	4,274	6,773	5,031
28,300	28,350	5,443	4,287	6,792	5,045
28,350	28,400	5,458	4,299	6,811	5,059
28,400	28,450	5,473	4,312	6,830	5,073
28,450	28,500	5,488	4,324	6,849	5,087
28,500	28,550	5,503	4,337	6,868	5,101
28,550	28,600	5,518	4,349	6,887	5,115
28,600	28,650	5,533	4,362	6,906	5,129
28,650	28,700	5,548	4,374	6,925	5,143
28,700	28,750	5,563	4,387	6,944	5,157
28,750	28,800	5,578	4,399	6,963	5,171
28,800	28,850	5,593	4,412	6,982	5,185
28,850	28,900	5,608	4,424	7,001	5,199
28,900	28,950	5,623	4,437	7,020	5,213
28,950	29,000	5,638	4,449	7,039	5,227

29,000

At least	But less than	Single	Married filing jointly *	Married filing separately	Head of a household
29,000	29,050	5,653	4,462	7,058	5,241
29,050	29,100	5,668	4,474	7,077	5,255
29,100	29,150	5,683	4,487	7,096	5,269
29,150	29,200	5,698	4,499	7,115	5,283
29,200	29,250	5,713	4,512	7,134	5,297
29,250	29,300	5,728	4,524	7,153	5,311
29,300	29,350	5,743	4,537	7,172	5,325
29,350	29,400	5,758	4,549	7,191	5,339
29,400	29,450	5,773	4,562	7,210	5,353
29,450	29,500	5,788	4,574	7,229	5,367
29,500	29,550	5,803	4,587	7,248	5,381
29,550	29,600	5,818	4,599	7,267	5,395
29,600	29,650	5,833	4,612	7,286	5,409
29,650	29,700	5,848	4,624	7,305	5,423
29,700	29,750	5,863	4,637	7,324	5,437
29,750	29,800	5,878	4,649	7,343	5,451
29,800	29,850	5,893	4,662	7,362	5,465
29,850	29,900	5,908	4,674	7,381	5,479
29,900	29,950	5,923	4,687	7,400	5,493
29,950	30,000	5,938	4,699	7,419	5,507

Department of the Treasury—Internal Revenue Service.

Example 10

The Paret family had gross earnings of $13,685 for the year. The family consisted of the parents and two dependent children. During the year $1,786.40 was paid in interest, $1,862 for taxes, and $527 for contributions. What was the family's taxable income?

Gross Earnings for the year		$13,685	
− Dependent exemptions		− 4,160 (4 × $1,040)	
− Excess itemized deductions:			
Total itemized deductions	$4,175.40		
Less: Zero bracket amount	−3,540.00		
	$ 635.40	− 635.40	
Taxable Income		$ 8,889.60	

The taxable income is used to determine the amount of income tax for the year.

Determining the Tax

The amount of income tax is determined by using one of several tables provided by the I.R.S. The amount of taxable earnings is used to find the correct bracket on the table. The tax is determined by following the instructions on the tax table. See the tables on page 408.

Example 11

The Bierston family had a taxable income of $25,332 for the year. They will file a joint tax return. What is the income tax?

$25,332 is found in the bracket $25,300 to $25,350. The tax for a married couple filing jointly is $3,545.

Exercise D

Determine the income tax from the information below. Use the tax table indicated.

	Gross Earnings	Exemptions	Excess Itemized Deductions	Taxable Earnings	Tax Table	Income Tax
1.	$31,850	5	$ 2,160	$24,490	Married-Joint	$3,358
2.	28,690	2	1,410		Married-Joint	
3.	32,610	1	2,821		Head of Household	

	Gross Earnings	Exemptions	Excess Itemized Deductions	Taxable Earnings	Tax Table	Income Tax
4.	$32,386	2	$ 4,956	_____	Married-Joint	_____
5.	36,650	4	3,660	_____	Married-Separate	_____
6.	43,853	6	9,647	_____	Married-Joint	_____
7.	35,281	3	3,893	_____	Married-Separate	_____
8.	37,453	1	10,420	_____	Single	_____
9.	28,820	2	2,491	_____	Married-Separate	_____
10.	31,325	4	1,490	_____	Married-Joint	_____

Assignment

Chapter Eighteen

Name _____ Date _____ Score _____

Skill Problems

Determine the tax rate in mills for each community below. Round off your answers to the nearest hundredth of a mill or cent.

	Community	Total Assessed	Budget	Tax Rate (in Mills)
1.	Corpus Christi	$92,000,000	$4,580,000	_____
2.	Ubly	8,963,800	193,000	_____

				(In Hundredths)
3.	Wheaton	70,000,500	1,506,000	_____
4.	Port Huron	72,923,244	2,151,000	_____
5.	Lunenburg	1,504,600	78,000	_____

Determine the property taxes for problems 6 through 10.

	Assessed Valuation	Tax Rate (in Mills)	Property Taxes
6.	$47,000	23	_____
7.	62,500	31.06	_____
8.	17,000	17.3	_____
		(In Hundredths)	
9.	37,900	$ 3.21	_____
10.	19,300	26	_____

Determine the total cost of the merchandise purchased, including customs duties, in problems 11 through 15.

	Quantity Purchased	Market Value/Unit	Duties Ad Valorem	Specific	Total Cost
11.	500	$ 6.90	10%	. . .	_____
12.	144	46.00	. . .	$1.00	_____
13.	50	2.00	10	.60	_____
14.	93	8.50	17	1.23	_____
15.	12	1,350.00	21	. . .	_____

Determine the income tax from the information below.

	Gross Earnings	Exemptions	Excess Itemized Deductions	Taxable Earnings	Tax Table	Income Tax
16.	$32,089	3	$3,785	_____	Married-Joint	_____
17.	31,880	2	4,921	_____	Married-Separate	_____
18.	27,954	1	2,910	_____	Single	_____
19.	36,821	5	6,182	_____	Married-Separate	_____
20.	36,540	4	4,985	_____	Married-Joint	_____

Business Application Problems

1. Cindy imported 300 synthetic fiber-filled comforters from Norway at a cost of $26 each. The import duty on each unit is $4 specific and 15 percent ad valorem. What will the total cost be on each comforter to Cindy?

2. You have been appointed tax clerk for your township. Your first assignment is to determine the tax rate on property. The total budget amount is $3,680,000. The market value of all of the business and residential property is $137,000,000. The assessed valuation of the property in the township is $61,330,000. What is the tax rate in mills?

3. The tax rate in your community is 59 mills. Your property tax is $920.40. What is the assessed valuation of your property?

4. Jeremy is single. He earned $26,850 during the year. His total itemized deductions are $826 for the year. His W-2 form stated that he had paid a total of $3,126.80 in federal income tax for the year. What is the amount that he still owes the I.R.S.?

5. Tom and Nancy Grubbs are interested in estimating the property taxes on their new home. The home will cost $42,680. The city is assessing property at approximately 46 percent of market value. The tax rate in the community is 36.6 mills. What is the estimated property tax?

6. Christina Ferrara purchased a car that cost $9,800. She found that the car was subject to a 5 percent state sales tax and a 1 percent city sales tax. She plans to put $3,000 down on the purchase and ask the credit union for a loan on the balance. What will be the amount of her loan request?

7. The Pear Tree Gift Shop of Alta must make a choice between the purchase of two items to fill their open-to-buy budget. The first item is a locally woven evening shawl priced at $40 each. The other item is an Irish woolen jacket priced at $30. The Irish jacket must be imported from Dublin. An ad valorem duty of 20 percent and a specific duty of $5 must be added to the price of the imported jacket. There is a state sales tax of 5 percent on merchandise in Alta. What is the price to the customer, after taxes, of the lowest priced item?

8. The Harington Hotel has added onto its structure by increasing the total space available by 20 percent. Last year's property taxes were $4,860.66 at 42.6 mills. This year the tax rate is 43.8 mills. Estimate the property taxes for the year.

9. Jim and Rose earned $32,900 in the last year. They recently had a baby girl. They will claim a contribution of $1,230 to charities in the $3,890 excess deductions on this year's income tax return. If they file a joint return, what is the tax amount?

10. Buelah Swarts paid $6,080 income tax for the year. Her gross earnings were $25,508. What was the income tax rate on the gross earnings?

11. The tax on property in the community of Mahosic Notch is 32¢ per $100 of assessed valuation. The taxable property within the community has an assessed valuation of $82,970,570. The treasurer has found that the delinquency rate is usually 2 percent of the total tax revenue. What is the amount of the delinquency for the community of Mahosic Notch for the year?

12. When Jonny received the invoice for the crate of Chinese baskets, there was a total due of $390. The invoice price included a $70 amount for customs duties. The specific duties totaled $2.80. The remainder were ad valorem duties. What was the percent of ad valorem duties?

13. Carl noted that if he bought a car in his home state he would have to pay a sales tax of 7 percent. He could travel to the adjoining state and purchase the same car. The sales tax in the adjoining state is 5 percent. The cost of the trip would be $65. He would also need to purchase a temporary tag at a price of $5. The car that he is interested in will cost $14,800. How much will he save by making the trip?

Challenge Problem

The Yankee Trader, an import shop, purchased 100 figurines from a dealer in London for $18 each list price. Due to the large purchase they were sold by the London dealer at a 10 percent discount, F.O.B. destination. The duty on the purchase was 25 percent ad valorem and $3 specific. The items will be sold at a markup of 40 percent on cost. A 3 percent sales tax will be added to the selling price. What is the amount that a consumer will have to pay for a pair of figurines?

Name _____ Date _____ Score _____

Match the following terms and concepts.

_____	1.	Ad Valorem Duty	A. City- and/or state-imposed tax on retail sales
_____	2.	Taxable Income	B. The wage earner and all dependents are allowed one each
_____	3.	Mills	C. Both a percent of the market value and a set amount
_____	4.	Exemption	D. Thousandths of assessed valuation
_____	5.	Specific Duty	E. Gross income less dependent exemptions and deductions
_____	6.	Deductions	F. 16 percent of gross income or itemize allowable expenses
_____	7.	Sales Tax	G. A set amount per unit, weight, or measure
			H. Market value of imported item ✕ percent
			I. A maximum of 6 percent

Determine the amount of property tax in the problems below.

	Assessed Valuation	Tax Rate (in Mills)	Property Taxes
8.	$42,800	38.05	_____

(In Hundredths)

9.	28,900	4.05	_____

Determine the cost of the purchases to the retailer in the problems below.

	Quantity Purchased	Market Value/ Unit	Duties	Total Cost
10.	144	$16.00	15% Ad Valorem, $1.70 specific	_____
11.	50	17.58	10% Ad Valorem	_____

Determine the income tax from the information below.

	Gross Earnings	Exemptions	Excess Itemized Deductions	Tax Table	Income Tax
12.	$31,280	1	$4,953	Married-Joint	_____
13.	29,300	3	1,640	Married-Separate	_____

14. Ureel Township has established a $2,680,500 budget for the year. The total assessed valuation is $92,426,000. The township is expecting a 1 percent default on tax payments. The 1 percent amount must be added to the budget. What will be the property taxes on a home with an assessed valuation of $41,600? Compute the tax rate to the nearest hundredth of a mill.

19 Investments

Performance Objectives

After mastering the material in this chapter, you will be able to:

1. Calculate the rate of return on various types of investments.
2. Calculate the dividend rate on common stock when the firm has preferred stock outstanding.
3. Understand and use the following terms and concepts:

Risk	Participating
Liquidity	Cumulative
Cost of Investment	Secured Bonds
Rate of Return	Debentured Bonds
Inflation	Registered Bonds
Common Stock	Bearer Bonds
Preferred Stock	Government Bonds
Dividends	

Risk, Liquidity, and Cost of Investment

Risk

Liquidity

Cost of investment

Investors consist of individuals as well as firms. The investor expects to increase the initial value of the investment and thereby earn a profit. The **risk** or chance of no profit or even a loss must also be considered. When the profit potential is high, the risk of loss is frequently equally high. When the profit potential is low, the risk of loss is usually also low.

Another consideration for the investor is that of liquidity. **Liquidity** measures the ease with which an investment can be exchanged for cash. Stocks and bonds can easily be sold, usually the same day, for cash payment five days later. They, therefore, have high liquidity. Real estate or equipment may take several days or even months before it is sold and therefore is considered to have lower liquidity. If an investor wishes to move from one investment into another, liquidity may be a very important factor.

Most investments have a fee or service charge that covers the cost of investing. The **cost of investment** may range from no cost for savings accounts in banks or credit unions up to 10 percent for real estate. The fee or service charge may be levied when the investment is bought, when the investment is sold, or both.

Rate of Return　　　　Profit earned on the investment compared to the amount invested determines the rate of return. The **rate of return** is expressed as a percent. Savings accounts that have a 4 percent annual interest rate have a 4 percent rate of return if there is no service charge for investing. The service charges for investing must be subtracted from the profit in order to calculate the rate of return.

The Effect of Inflation　　　　**Inflation** is a general increase in the cost or price of goods or services. In times of inflation, prices rise. The purchasing power of the dollar goes down as compared to earlier time periods. Unless the investor's rate of return is keeping up with the inflation rate, money (purchasing power) will actually be lost. The loss would be greater if the money was simply held and therefore at the mercy of the inflation rate. The investment's rate of return reduces the effect of inflation on the buying power of individuals and firms.

Stocks　　　　The ownership or equity of a corporation is held by stockholders. Stockholders are individuals or other firms who have bought a portion of a corporation by purchasing shares of stock in the corporation. There are basically two types of stock: common and preferred. See appendix E, page 517*, Reading Market Quotations.

Stock owners rights will consist of variations in the basic rights listed below. The variations, if any, will be spelled out on the stock certificate.

1. The right to vote.
2. The right to share in the distribution of the corporation's earnings.
3. The right to maintain an equal share of ownership of the corporation if the firm decides to issue additional stock (termed Preemptive Right).
4. The right to share in distribution of the assets of the corporation upon its dissolution.

There are two classes of stock: Common and Preferred. Their rights differ in principle, and in many cases, by corporation.

Common Stock　　　　**Common stock** owners have a vote in the corporate stockholders meetings, which are held annually. They may have a return on investment in the form of an increase in the stock price or in the form of a dividend.

Preferred Stock　　　　**Preferred stock** owners may not have a vote in the corporate stockholders meeting. The term "preferred," indicates that the holder of preferred stock has preferred rights to dividends and to the assets of the corporation if it dissolves. They are paid before common stockholders are paid. If there is a limited amount of assets or earnings to be distributed to stockholders, the preferred stockholders are paid first. Any amount left over after the preferred stockholders are paid can be distributed to common stockholders.

Dividends　　　　Earnings of a corporation are usually split between the owners and stockholders, in the form of **dividends,** or they are held for future expansion of the firm. The manner in which the split is made is dependent on a variety of factors. Most of the factors are listed as follows:

* For more information write the Consumer Information Center, Pueblo, Colorado 81009, for a free pamphlet titled "Investigate Before You Invest."

1. The amount of liquid assets that the firm can use to make the dividend payment.
2. The specific rights of the preferred stockholders.
3. The amount of preferred stock outstanding.
4. The amount of the preferred stock dividend.
5. The amount of common stock outstanding.

The decision to pay a dividend rests with the board of directors. The decision can be made quarterly, semi-annually, or annually. The common method is quarterly. The decision may be announced at the stockholder's meeting or simply announced through the media. When the board decides to declare a dividend, the date is termed the Declaration Date. The dividend is to be paid in the future, on the Date of Record. This date is used to determine who actually owns the stock. Those who own stock in the corporation as of the date of record will receive a dividend on the Payment Date. The corporation must compile a list of names and addresses of the owners of the stock as of the date of record.

Dividends are usually paid as cash dividends. The corporation distributes the cash dividend in the form of a check to the stockholders of record.

Stock dividends are distributed in the form of an additional stock certificate. This type of dividend has an advantage in that the dividend is not subject to income tax until the stock is sold.

Example 1

The Eltron Corporation has the following stock outstanding as of August 31.

$5 Preferred stock	160,000 shares
Common stock	800,000 shares

Earnings for the year ended August 31 were $1,280,000. Determine the amount of the dividend per share on the common stock if the board decides to distribute all of the earnings.

Income for the year	$1,280,000
160,000 preferred shares at $5 dividend per share	− 800,000
Amount to be paid to common stock shareholders	$ 480,000

$$\frac{\$.60 \text{ dividend per share—common stock}}{800,000 \text{ shares })\$480,000 \text{ for common stockholders}}$$

Example 2

Three years ago, Marta and John Billson bought 400 shares of Eltron Corporation for $24 per share. What rate of return are they earning if a $3 dividend is paid annually?

$$\frac{\$ 3 = \text{return}}{\$24 = \text{cost of investment}} = 12 \frac{1}{2} \% \text{ rate of return}$$

Exercise A

Determine the dividend per share on common stock and the rate of return in each of the exercises below. (The price per share represents an average.) Round off your answer to the nearest cent or tenth of a percent.

Earnings To Be Distributed	Number of Preferred Shares	Preferred Dividend	Number of Common Shares	Dividend Per Share— Common	Price Per Share	Rate of Return— Common
1. $2,008,000	463,500	$3.50	860,000	$ .45	$ 9.60	4.7%
2. 1,268,420	120,300	5.00	1,000,000	$ .67	10.00	6.7%
3. 1,100,000	9,870	4.00	500,000	$2.12	30.50	7%
4. 4,200,000	758,900	5.00	3,600,000	.11	9.75	1.1%
5. 865,390	160,000	2.00	750,000	.73	8.00	9.1%

(handwritten calculations: 601500; 39 480; 3 794 500; 320000)

Participating

Preferred stockholders may have rights in addition to those shown in the previous examples or exercise. The preferred stockholders may have the right to share in the earnings above the stated dividend rate. The stockholder would have a right of participation. Each firm or issue of stock can specify the terms of the participation when the stock is sold. The degree of the rights will therefore differ with each issue. **Participating** preferred stock will have two chances at earnings.

When the stock does not participate in earnings beyond the stated rate it is termed Non-Participating.

Example 3

The Kreger Corporation has two classes of stock. A $5 preferred issue with 10,000 shares outstanding and a common issue with 40,000 shares outstanding. The preferred stock certificate states that the stock is participating after the common receives a dollar of dividends. The two classes will split the remaining earnings on an equal share for share basis. The corporation decided to retain 40 percent of the $260,000 earnings for future expansion. The remainder will be distributed in the form of cash dividends. What is the amount of dividends per share for each share of preferred stock?

$260,000
× .60
$156,000 = earnings to be distributed
− 50,000 = preferred dividends ($5 per share × 10,000 shares)
$106,000
− 40,000 = common dividends ($1 per share × 40,000 shares)
$66,000 = dividends to be split between preferred and common

$66,000 = $1.32 per share
50,000   (preferred and common) shares

$5 + $1.32 = $6.32 dividend per share of preferred stock

Cumulative   If a corporation does poorly during a period, the dividend that the preferred stockholders would have received may be passed, that is, not paid. In a later period, the firm may do very well and be able to pay preferred stockholders the dividend that was passed in the earlier period. The firm is not obligated to pay the passed dividend unless the preferred stock certificate states that the stock class has **cumulative** rights. This right states that preferred stockholders have the right to receive all dividends in arrears (unpaid) before the common stockholders receive any dividend. This right allows the preferred stockholder to receive the dividends over a period of time though they may be interrupted due to erratic earnings.

Preferred stock without this right is termed noncumulative.

Example 4

The earnings of the Watson Corporation have been poor for the past two years. The corporation has had a loss for the past two years and has not paid a dividend on the 5,000 shares of $3 preferred or the 30,000 shares of common. The preferred stock certificate states that the preferred shares will have the right to cumulative dividends. The earnings this year were $310,000. The firm decided to distribute 80 percent to stockholders. What will be the amount of the preferred stock dividend? What will be the amount of the common stock dividend?

$$\begin{aligned}
\$310,000 & \\
\underline{\times\ .80} & \\
\$248,000 &= \text{earnings to be distributed} \\
\underline{-\quad 45,000} &= \text{preferred dividends (\$3 per share} \times \text{5,000 shares} \times \text{3} \\
& \qquad\qquad\qquad\qquad\qquad \text{years)} \\
\$203,000 &= \text{earnings for common stock}
\end{aligned}$$

$$\frac{\$203,000}{30,000} = \$6.77 \text{ common dividend per share}$$

Preferred stock can be both Participating and Cumulative. If that were the case in Example 4, the preferred stockholders would first receive the dividends that have been passed, and then be eligible to receive an additional dividend to the extent of the stipulation on the certificate.

> **Example 5**
>
> If the preferred stock certificate stated that the class is to receive cumulative rights and participation to the extent of sharing dividends above $5 per share after the dividends in arrear were paid, what would be the dividend per share preferred? The additional dividend is to be determined on a share-for-share basis.
>
> $203,000 Earnings after the dividends were made up to the
>   preferred stockholders.
> − 150,000 Common dividends ($5 per share × 30,000 shares)
> $ 53,000 Dividends to be split between Preferred and Common
>
> $$\frac{\$53,000}{35,000} = \$1.51 \text{ per share (full cent)}$$
> (Preferred and Common) shares
>
> $3 × 3 years = $9 $9 + $1.51 = $10.51 total preferred dividend

Exercise B   Determine the dividend per share on preferred stock from the information below. Participation to be based on the number of shares of stock in both classes.

	Earnings To Be Distributed	Number of Preferred Shares	Preferred Dividend	Number of Common Shares	Cumulative (Years Passed)	Participating (After/ Common)	Dividend Per Share Preferred (Full Cent)
1.	$ 200,000	4,000	$ 2.00	10,000	No	Yes/$2	$14.28
2.	360,000	10,000	7.50	10,000	One	No	
3.	80,000	5,000	5.00	20,000	One	Yes/$3	
4.	450,000	10,000	8.00	50,000	No	Yes/$5	
5.	120,000	3,000	10.00	20,000	Two	Yes/$6	
6.	75,000	1,000	5.00	30,000	No	Yes/$1	
7.	100,000	3,000	6.00	40,000	One	No	
8.	1,500,000	50,000	5.00	65,000	Two	Yes/$4	

Bonds   Whereas stock represents ownership in a corporation, **bonds** represent debt. A firm that wishes to increase working capital may choose to sell bonds in place of selling stock. Bondholders have no vote in the organization but have preference over common and preferred stockholders when the income is divided. Bond interest must be paid before any dividends are paid.

Bonds are issued in denominations of $1,000. There are occasions when they are issued for $2,000, $3,000, $5,000, or even $100. Bond prices are quoted on the basis of 100. A price quote of 98 would mean that the $1,000 bond is now being sold for $980. A quote of $105\frac{1}{2}$ would mean a $1,055 current market price. See appendix E, page 517, Reading Market Quotations.

The current rate of interest in the marketplace will determine the selling price of the bonds. If the current interest rate is lower than the interest rate at the time that the bonds were originally sold, the price of the bonds will be higher than the face value. If the current interest rate is higher than the interest rate at the time that the bonds were originally sold, the price will be lower than the face value.

Example 6

The Hubble Corporation's bonds are quoted on the exchange as selling at 98. The bonds have a stated rate of interest of 5 percent. What is the current effective rate of interest on the bonds?

$$\frac{5\% \text{ of } \$1,000 = \$50}{98\% \times \$1,000 = \$980} = 5.1\% \text{ current effective rate}$$

Example 7

If the same bonds were to be quoted at 110, what would be the effective rate of interest on the bonds?

$$\frac{5\% \text{ of } \$1,000 = \$50}{110\% \times \$1,000 = \$1,100} = 4.5\% \text{ current effective rate}$$

Commercial Bonds

Bonds are sold by corporations for many reasons. The firm may be interested in expanding operations through an addition to their existing physical plant or need additional working capital. The reasons for selling bonds are varied. Bonds are usually sold to provide long-term financing. The term of the bonds will usually run from five to fifty years. The quality of the bonds will depend on the ability of the corporation to repay the bonds as well as the annual interest on the bonds. The bonds will also be measured in terms of quality by their type.

Secured

Secured bonds provide the bondholder with a claim to real property. If the corporation is unable to meet the obligation to repay, the bondholder has claim to specified properties.

Debentured

Debentured bonds do not provide the bondholder with a claim to any particular property. The bonds are issued on the general credit of the corporation.

Bonds may also be classified by the way in which the interest is paid. A **registered** bond must be endorsed upon delivery to the new owner. The corporation is notified and the interest is sent to the bondholder.

Registered

Bearer

Bearer or coupon bonds have a piece of the bond certificate predated with the amount of the interest stated on the face. The holder of the bearer bond removes the coupon and presents it at the bank for payment on the payment date. These bonds do not require the owner to notify the corporation when the bond is sold. The new bond owner simply removes the interest coupon when the interest is due.

Government and Municipal Bonds

The federal government has issued bonds to finance expenditures for many years. The Series E savings bonds are the most familiar type. They may be purchased through a payroll deduction and come in denominations of $25 or more. Unlike other bonds, the interest is paid at maturity. A $25 bond is bought for $18.75. In approximately seven years the bond is worth $25.

Municipal bonds are sold for the purpose of building schools, streets, sidewalks, municipal-owned utilities, etc. The interest rate on municipal bonds is often much less due to their tax-free status. The rate of return is therefore less. An individual in a high income tax bracket may choose municipal bonds as an investment.

Exercise C

Determine the rate of return on the following $1,000 denomination bonds. Round off your answer to the nearest tenth of a percent.

Current Price Quotation	Stated Interest Rate	Rate of Return
1. $101\frac{1}{4}$	$8\frac{1}{4}\%$	8.1%
2. 98	7	7.1.
3. $96\frac{1}{2}$	$9\frac{1}{2}$	9.8
4. 108	$7\frac{1}{4}$	6.7%
5. $102\frac{1}{4}$	$8\frac{3}{4}$	8.6

(handwritten work in right margin:)
$\frac{82.50}{101250}$
$\frac{70}{98000} = \times 1000$
$\frac{95}{965} =$
$\frac{72.5}{1080} =$
$\frac{87.50}{1022.5}$

There are many other investment possibilities beyond stocks and bonds. For example, the investor who wishes to maintain the same amount of liquidity can invest in commodity futures. This investment opportunity is very volatile and can make the investor great sums or lose the same amount in a very short period of time. The volatility is due to the fact that the investor need only place a 5 or 10 percent margin down on the investment position. A slight movement is multiplied by ten or twenty times. This type of investment is risky.

Real property, such as real estate, provides a much less volatile investment opportunity but, at the same time, a lower chance of a high return. The cost of investment is also a consideration beyond the rate of return. Liquidity is also often a negative. Property, unlike stocks and bonds, is not liquidated in the same day.

The cost of investing must be considered, no matter what the investment. Real estate brokers charge rates that reflect the difficulty of liquidating the asset. The standard rate for home property is usually 7 percent. The rate may vary to 10 percent for commercial property. The seller pays the real estate brokers commission, which is, in effect, paid by the buyer through the purchase price of the property.

Example 8

An investor buys a piece of property for $30,000 in July, 1987. The investor sells the same property for $38,000 in July, 1988. The investor must pay the broker a 7 percent commission rate on the selling price of the property. What is the amount of profit on the year-long investment? What is the rate of return?

$$\begin{array}{r} \$38,000 \\ \times\ .07 \\ \hline \$\ 2,660 \end{array} \text{ Commission to the real estate broker}$$

$$\begin{array}{r} \$38,000 \\ -\ 2,660 \\ \hline \$35,340 \end{array} \text{ Net proceeds from sale} \qquad \begin{array}{r} \$35,340 \\ -\ 30,000 \\ \hline \$\ 5,340 \end{array} \text{ Profit}$$

$$\text{Rate of return} = \frac{\$5,340}{\$30,000} = 17.8\%$$

Example 9

Kirk purchased three uncirculated coins at a cost of $590 three years ago. These coins were placed in a safe deposit box for three years. When Kirk sold them he had to pay a 5 percent dealer fee on the sale price of $950. What was the annual rate of return using a simple interest approach?

$$\begin{array}{r} \$950.00 \\ \times\quad .05 \\ \hline \$\ 47.50 \end{array} \text{ sale price} \qquad\qquad \begin{array}{r} \$950.00 \\ -\quad 47.50 \\ \hline \$902.50 \end{array} \text{ from sale}$$

dealer fee

$$\begin{array}{r} \$902.50 \\ -\ 590.00 \\ \hline \$312.50 \end{array} \text{ return} \div 3 \text{ years} = \$104.17 \text{ return per year}$$

$$\frac{\$104.17 \text{ return}}{\$590.00 \text{ cost}} = \underline{17.7\% \text{ return}}$$

Assignment

Chapter Nineteen

Name _____ Date _____ Score _____

Skill Problems Determine the rate of return in the following problems. The preferred stock is Nonparticipating and Noncumulative. Round off your answer to the nearest tenth of a percent.

	Earnings To Be Distributed	Number of Preferred Shares	Preferred Dividend	Number of Common Shares	Price Per Share	Rate of Return-Common
1.	$ 8,600,000	300,000	$ 5.00	1,500,000	$ 47.00	_____
2.	10,385,700	850,000	7.50	6,563,000	8.50	_____
3.	23,700,000	900,000	7.00	1,500,000	91.00	_____
4.	3,680,000	250,000	6.00	800,000	16.75	_____
5.	9,000,500	600,000	8.00	1,200,000	30.00	_____
6.	19,900,000	1,900,000	4.00	2,500,000	65.25	_____
7.	1,820,000	16,500	8.00	53,000	227.00	_____
8.	4,500,700	400,000	7.50	750,000	21.75	_____
9.	2,000,000	135,000	10.00	400,000	32.00	_____
10.	7,363,590	600,000	8.50	1,260,000	27.75	_____

	Bond Denomination	Current Price Quotation	Stated Interest Rate	Rate of Return
11.	$1,000	102	6%	_____
12.	1,000	99	$8\frac{3}{4}$	_____
13.	1,000	$105\frac{1}{2}$	8	_____
14.	1,000	$103\frac{1}{2}$	$8\frac{1}{4}$	_____
15.	5,000	96	$5\frac{3}{4}$	_____
16.	1,000	$97\frac{1}{4}$	$7\frac{3}{4}$	_____
17.	1,000	101	$7\frac{1}{2}$	_____

		Bond Denomination	Current Price Quotation	Stated Interest Rate	Rate of Return
$1000 \times 1.0015 = \dfrac{95}{100.15 \times 10} \times 1000$	18.	$1,000	$100\frac{1}{2}$	$9\frac{1}{2}\%$	9.4 %
$3000 \times 92 = \dfrac{845}{2760} = \times 3000 = 8.9$	19.	3,000	92	$8\frac{1}{4}$	9.0 %
$100 \times 9\% = 9 \rightarrow \dfrac{9}{88.75}$	20.	100	$88\frac{3}{4}$	9	10 %

Determine the dividend per share of common stock in the following problems. Participation is to be based on the number of shares of stock in both classes.

	Earnings To Be Distributed	Number of Preferred Shares	Preferred Dividend	Number of Common Shares	Cumulative (Years Passed)	Participating (After/ Common)	Dividend Per Share Common
21.	$4,500,000	600,000	$ 5.00	1,300,000	No	$10	_____
22.	985,000	50,000	7.00	80,000	Two	No	_____
23.	860,000	35,000	3.50	75,000	One	5	_____
24.	5,260,000	400,000	7.50	650,000	No	2	_____
25.	1,865,350	85,000	10.00	100,000	One	4	_____
26.	4,360,500	350,000	8.50	500,000	No	7	_____
27.	17,390,550	985,000	6.00	1,500,000	One	No	_____
28.	4,185,300	200,000	9.00	350,000	Two	2	_____
29.	47,359,680	1,600,000	7.50	2,500,000	No	10	_____
30.	285,600	3,580	6.50	70,000	One	5	_____

Business Application Problems

1. Becky Bush purchased a set of collector's stamps for $450 and sold them a year later for $560. She paid a 2 percent commission on each transaction. What was the rate of return on her investment? Round off your answer to the nearest tenth of a percent.

2. John Cooper bought a new car twenty years ago. The car cost $3,800. Though he drove the car for the first three years, he decided to store the vehicle as an investment. The car is now worth $14,000 as a collector's item. On a simple interest basis, what is the rate of return per year on John's investment? Round off your answer to the nearest tenth of a percent.

3. An investor is considering two investments. One alternative is a preferred stock quoted at $39.50 paying a $3.50 annual dividend. The other alternative is a commercial bond quoted at $92 \frac{1}{4}$ and paying a stated $8 \frac{3}{4}$ percent interest rate. Which is the best return?

4. A bond is quoted at $93 \frac{5}{8}$ in the financial section of the newspaper. The bond pays a stated interest rate of 8 percent. To the nearest tenth of a percent, what is the effective rate of return?

5. Steve is considering the purchase of a jewelry business for $128,000. The markup rate is an average 18 percent on sales, of which one-half is overhead and one-half profit. The company does $142,300 of business a year. He currently has the $128,000 invested in commercial bonds quoted at $97 \frac{3}{4}$ and paying a stated $9 \frac{1}{4}$ percent interest. Which investment would provide the greatest rate of return?

6. The Berman Company purchased a future position in wheat for $3,200 on a margin of 10 percent. The price of wheat went up by $.30 on each of the 10,000 bushels purchased for the total amount of $3,200. The brokers fee was $50 to purchase and the same to sell. What was the rate of return on the investment over the period of one year?

7. John bought a home for $42,000 in the spring of 1986. The home required some repairs that cost a total of $3,500. The home was sold a year later for $50,000. The brokerage firm charged a commission rate of 8 percent on the sale of the property. What was the rate of return on the investment?

8. The Kirbison Corporation purchased 100 shares of stock of the Deweuke Corporation at $54 $\frac{3}{8}$ per share. The brokerage firm charges a flat 1 percent per transaction. The Kirbison Corporation held the stock for twelve months. There were four $.80 dividends paid during the time that the stock was held. The stock was sold at a price of $62 $\frac{1}{8}$. What was the rate of return on the investment?

9. Alvin Person is considering the purchase of a large amount of grain as an investment. The price per bushel is $3.60. The commission rate is 1 $\frac{1}{2}$ percent on the purchase and on the sale. The storage will cost Alvin 1 cent per bushel per month. Alvin feels that the price will rise to $3.90 per bushel in six months. What will be the net profit on 6,000 bushels?

10. A stock was quoted at $42.50 on the local exchange. The stock pays a dividend after the preferred stock of the same corporation is paid a $7.50 dividend per year. There are 5,000 shares of preferred stock outstanding at this point. How much would the company have to earn in order to pay each common stockholder a dividend of $4 a share if they distribute 40 percent of their earnings over the 5,000 shares of preferred and the 10,000 shares of common?

11. Kirk purchased a sheet of 5¢ postage stamps for $63 six months ago. He sold them for $75. What is the annualized rate of return on the investment?

12. A piece of land that was purchased for $120,000 was resold for $160,000 eighteen months later. There were transfer costs of $690 on the sale as well as a realtor's commission of $11,200. What was the annualized rate of return on the investment?

13. Alvin Perkins invested his extra $20,000 in a certificate of deposit that paid $11\frac{3}{4}$ percent interest. The "C.D." was held for a period of one year. Alvin could have purchased 100 shares of a stock for the same amount of money. The stock has paid a quarterly dividend of $1.25 per share. The price of the stock has risen from $19\frac{7}{8}$ to $21\frac{1}{4}$. Alvin would need to pay a broker's fee of 1 percent of the sale. Would he have been better off to buy the stock and sell it a year later? What amount of money would he have earned on the best investment?

Challenge Problem   Rochelle Way purchased 400 shares of Piad Corporation common stock on June 1 for $33 per share. There are 1,680,000 shares of common stock outstanding and 500,000 shares of $5 preferred stock outstanding. The firm reported annual earnings of $7.6 million on November 1. The earnings were paid out in dividends on November 7. Rochelle sold her stock on December 1 for $40 per share. She paid a commission rate of 1 percent on the purchase and on the sale. What was the rate of return?

True or False

T F 1. Cumulative preferred stock has the right to "catch up" on dividends that have not been paid in the past.

T F 2. Selling fees reduce the return on the investment to the investor.

T F 3. Municipal bonds carry a lower rate of interest but have a greater risk.

T F 4. In a period of inflation, the investor is better off to hold cash so as not to lose to the rate of inflation.

T F 5. Common stockholders have the right to vote on corporate issues brought before the annual stockholders' meeting.

Determine the rate of return in the following problem. The preferred stock is nonparticipating and noncumulative. Round off your answer to the nearest tenth of a percent.

Earnings To Be Distributed	Number of Preferred Shares	Preferred Dividend	Number of Common Shares	Price per Share	Rate of Return
6. $6,500,000	250,000	$4	2,000,000	$38	_____

Determine the rate of return in the following problem.

Bond Denomination	Current Price Quotation	Stated Interest Rate	Rate of Return
7. $1,000	102	7%	_____

Determine the dividend per share of common stock in the following problems. Participation is to be based on the number of shares of stock in both classes.

Earnings To Be Distributed	Number of Preferred Shares	Preferred Dividend	Number of Common Shares	Cumulative (Years Passed)	Participating (After Common)	Dividend per Share (Common)
8. $1,020,000	60,000	$ 8	120,000	None	$8	_____
9. 3,400,000	240,000	12	600,000	Two	7	_____

10. Bill Dominy purchased a piece of land for $52,000 one year ago. The land was sold to an investor for $75,000. The commission fee was 10 percent on the sale. What was the rate of return on the investment?

6 Measuring Business Performance

20 Financial Statement Analysis
21 Statistics
22 Charts and Graphs

20 Financial Statement Analysis

After mastering the material in this chapter, you will be able to:

1. Use the basic accounting equation in balance sheet problems.
2. Complete a balance sheet and income statement when key values are missing.
3. Complete a comparative balance sheet and income statement.
4. Complete a horizontal analysis on a balance sheet or income statement.
5. Calculate the following ratios:
   a. current ratio
   b. acid-test ratio
   c. net income to net sales ratio
   d. accounts receivable to net sales ratio
   e. accounts payable to net purchases ratio
6. Use and understand the following terms and concepts:

Balance Sheet	Income Statement
Assets	Revenue
Liabilities	Expenses
Proprietorship	Ratio
Horizontal Analysis	
Comparative Balance Sheet	

Managers and owners of business firms need financial reports on which they can base decisions. The reports are termed financial statements. There are many types of financial statements. The most frequently used are the balance sheet and the income statement.

Balance Sheet

Assets
Liabilities
Proprietorship

The **balance sheet** is a "financial photograph" of a firm. If time could be stopped and if values could be expressed in dollars on a "financial film" report, we would develop a balance sheet. The balance sheet is dated and, therefore, only valid for the date that the financial photograph is taken. It shows the amount of **assets** (those things owned by the firm), the **liabilities** (that which is owed by the firm), and the **proprietorship** (the amount invested in the firm by the owners) of the firm at the date of the balance sheet.

The assets must equal the liabilities plus proprietorship on a balance sheet. This is known as the basic accounting formula: A = L + P.

Assets are divided into two classifications. Current assets are those assets that will be turned into cash within one year, and fixed assets are those assets that will last for a year or more without being turned into cash. Examples of current assets are cash, accounts receivable, merchandise inventory, and prepaid expenses. Examples of fixed assets are land, buildings, and various types of equipment.

Liabilities are classified on the same basis as assets. Current liabilities are those due in a year or less, and long-term liabilities are those due in a year or more. Examples of current liabilities are accounts payable, notes payable, and salaries payable. Examples of long-term liabilities are mortgages payable and long-term notes payable.

Proprietorship is termed capital in a corporation.

Example 1

National Travel Service
Balance Sheet
December 31, 1986

Assets		Liabilities	
Current Assets		Current Liabilities	
Cash	$ 3,000	Accounts Payable	$ 2,400
Accounts Receivable	10,400	Notes Payable	10,000
Notes Receivable	5,000	Total Current Liabilities	$ 12,400
Total Current Assets	$ 18,400	Long-Term Liabilities	
Fixed Assets		Mortgage, Building	$ 84,000
Office Equipment	$ 28,000	Total Liabilities	$ 96,400
Buildings	130,000		
Land	42,000	Owner's Equity	
Total Fixed Assets	$200,000	T. Bailey, Owner	$122,000
Total Assets	$218,400	Total Liabilities & Owner's Equity	
			$218,400

Just as it is interesting to compare photographs of past times with the present, it is also interesting to compare a balance sheet from last year to this year. This is termed a **comparative balance sheet.** Notice that the information is horizontally compared (i.e., cash of 1987 is compared to cash of 1986, a **horizontal analysis**). The comparison is always made to the earlier period or date (1986 in the following example). Decreases are always shown in parentheses.

Comparative balance sheet
Horizontal analysis

Example 2

James Williard Co.
Comparative Balance Sheet
December 31, 1986 and 1987

Assets	*1987*	*1986*	*Amount of Increase (Decrease)*	*% Increase (Decrease)*
Current Assets				
Cash	$ 6,840	$ 7,500	($660)	(8.8)
Accounts Receivable	10,085	9,360	725	7.7
Prepaid Insurance	2,580	1,620	960	59.3
Total Current Assets	$19,505	$18,480	1,025	5.5
Fixed Assets				
Office Building	$24,000	$24,000	$ 0	. . .
Office Furniture	1,570	1,695	(125)	(7.4)
Total Fixed Assets	$25,570	$25,695	(125)	(.5)
Total Assets	$45,075	$44,175	900	2
Liabilities and Proprietorship				
Current Liabilities				
Accounts Payable	$ 7,300	$ 5,625	$1,675	29.8
Taxes Payable	1,580	1,580	0	. . .
Total Liabilities	$ 8,880	$ 7,205	1,675	23.2
Proprietorship				
James Williard, Capital	36,195	36,970	(775)	(2.1)
Total Liabilities and Proprietorship	$45,075	$44,175	900	2

To find the 8.8% decrease in cash:

$7,500
− 6,840
$ 660 = difference

$$\frac{\$ 660}{\$7,500} = \frac{\text{difference}}{\text{base year (1986)}} = 8.8\% \text{ decrease}$$

Exercise A   Determine the missing values and the percent of increase or decrease on the comparative balance sheet below.

Gordon and Associates
Comparative Balance Sheet
July 1, 1986 and 1987

Assets	1987	1986	Amount of Increase (or Decrease)	% Increase (or Decrease)
Current Assets				
Cash	$ 7,840	$ 5,890	$1,950	33.1
Accounts Receivable	1,270	6,200		
Merchandise on Hand	9,250	3,600		
Total Current Assets	$18,360	$15,690		
Fixed Assets				
Delivery Trucks	$44,260	$44,260		
Total Assets				
Liabilities and Proprietorship				
Current Liabilities				
Accounts Payable	$ 4,360	$ 5,680		
Long-Term Liabilities				
Mortgage Loan Payable	26,500			
Total Liabilities		$38,180		
Proprietorship				
J. T. Sorm, Capital				
Total Liabilities and Proprietorship				

Determine the missing values and the percent of increase or decrease on the current assets portion of the comparative balance sheet below.

Metro Cleaning Service
Comparative Balance Sheet
March 31, 1986 and 1987

Assets	1987	1986	Amount of Increase (or Decrease)	% Increase (or Decrease)
Current Assets				
Cash	$12,750	$15,360	($2,610)	(17)
Notes Receivable	2,500	500		
Accounts Receivable	13,368	7,920		
Cleaning Supplies	820	1,685		
Office Supplies	60	380		
Prepaid Rent	1,200	1,200		
Prepaid Insurance	380	1,898		
Total Current Assets				

Income Statement

Revenue
Expenses

An **income statement** is a portion of a business firm's financial history. Whereas a balance sheet shows what exists at a point in time, an income statement shows what took place during a period of time. The heading must indicate the period covered by the statement (usually a year, six months, or a quarter), not simply a date.

The income statement shows **revenue** (the result of selling goods or services) and **expenses** (used up or expired assets). The difference between revenue and expenses is termed net income or net loss. An income is earned when revenue is larger than expenses. A loss is incurred when expenses are larger than the revenue.

```
                    Dafford Accounting, Inc.
                       Income Statement
                    Year Ended July 31, 1987


    Revenue
       Accounting Fees              $147,300
       Consulting Fees                 9,500
       Interest Earned                 1,250
          Total Revenue                              $158,050

    Expenses
       Salaries Expense            $ 82,600
       Rent Expense                  12,000
       Utilities Expense              4,600
       License Fees                     400
       Telephone Expense              1,360
       Computer Rental Expense        4,800
       Transportation Expense           980
          Total Expenses                             $106,740
    Net Income                                       $ 51,310
```

Service Firm

A service firm sells only time in its operation, not merchandise. The income statement for a service firm includes sales of service time; expenses, such as wages, supplies, expired rent; and expired insurance.

```
    Example 3
                       Watman Business Service
                          Income Statement
                       Year Ended June 30, 1986

    Revenue
       Sales of Accounting Service    $135,600
       Sales of Computer Service       117,350
          Total Revenue                              $252,950
    Expenses
       Wages Expense                  $ 63,480
       Computer Rental Fees              5,800
       Utilities Expense                 3,865
       Rent Expense                      4,800
       Expired Insurance                   720
       Supplies Used                       985
          Total Expenses                                79,650
    Net Income, year ended June 30, 1986                $173,300
```

Comparisons within the income statement are always made to total revenue or net sales in the case of a merchandising firm. In the previous example, "Wages Expense" was 25.1 percent of total revenue, that is,

$$\frac{\$\ 63,480}{\$252,950} = 25.1 \text{ percent.}$$

A comparative income statement is similar to a comparative balance sheet. An item-by-item horizontal analysis is made comparing the difference to the earlier time period.

Exercise C   Determine the missing values, the percent of total revenue, and the percent of increase or decrease in the comparative income statement below.

Andres Perez Delivery Company
Comparative Income Statement
Year ended September 30, 1985 and 1986

Revenue	1986	% (1986)	1985	% of Increase (or Decrease)
Revenue from Deliveries	$142,360	59.2	$148,980	(4.4)
Special Revenue	98,000		36,000	
Total Revenue				
Expenses				
Gasoline Expense	$ 17,300		$ 17,000	
Wages Expense	84,780		82,900	
Repair Expense	15,800		2,600	
Utilities Expense	2,300		2,200	
Office Supplies Used	700		840	
Miscellaneous Expense	21,400		31,380	
Total Expenses				
Net Income for the Year				

Merchandising Firm

The revenue of a merchandising firm is mainly a result of buying and reselling merchandise at a markup. The income statement for a merchandising firm has a special category of expenses termed cost of goods sold. Cost of goods sold represents the cost price of purchases that were resold. This category of expenses is important to a retailer or wholesaler. A measure of business performance is found by subtracting cost of goods sold from net sales. The result is termed gross margin or gross profit.

A merchandising firm must deal with customer returns or after-sale allowances. These are subtracted from revenue on the income statement to find net sales.

Exercise D   Determine the missing values, the percent of net sales, and percent of increase or decrease in the partial comparative income statement below.

James Goodbody—Wholesalers
Comparative Income Statement
Quarter ended June 30, 1987 and June 30, 1986

	Quarter 1987	% (1987)	Quarter 1986	% Increase (or Decrease)
Revenue				
Sales	$487,360	100.7%	$487,480	(0)
Less: Sales Return	3,120		485	
Sales Allowances	85		226	
Net Sales	$484,155	100%	$486,769	
Cost of Goods Sold				
Merchandise Inventory April 1, 1987	$107,085		$ 79,350	
Merchandise Purchases	262,400		307,850	
Freight In	5,800		4,200	
Goods Available for Sale			$391,400	
Less: Merchandise	98,465		107,085	
Inventory June 30, 1987 Cost of Goods Sold			$284,315	
Gross Profit			$202,454	

Ratios

Though the balance sheet shows "what is" and the income statement shows "what took place," other specific measures of business performance are also used. These measures are termed ratios and are taken from parts of the balance sheet or income statement. A **ratio** compares one item to another.

Example 4

The Brodman Co. has forty-two sales representatives who are meeting their sales quotas. Another twelve sales representatives have fallen short of their quotas. What is the ratio of success to failure?

$$\frac{42}{12} = \frac{\text{success}}{\text{failure}} = 3.5 \text{ to } 1 \text{ ratio}$$

There are 3.5 successful sales representatives to each unsuccessful sales representative.

Ratios are useful when comparing one time period to another time period.

Current Ratio

The current ratio compares current assets to current liabilities. This is a measure of the ability of a firm to pay off its liabilities over a time period.

Example 5

A firm has total current assets of $4,386 and total current liabilities of $1,762. What is the current ratio?

$$\frac{\$4,386 = \text{current assets}}{\$1,762 = \text{current liabilities}} = 2.5 \text{ to } 1 \text{ current ratio}$$

Acid-Test Ratio

The acid-test ratio measures the ability of a firm to pay off its liabilities in a brief time period. The acid-test ratio differs from the current ratio by considering only cash, receivables, and marketable securities to use to compare to current liabilities. This ratio then measures the ability of a firm to pay off its liabilities without making further sales.

Example 6

The current liabilities of the Rierdon Co. are $19,960. The firm has $14,000 cash, $11,365 in receivables, and a bond that has a face value of $1,000. What is the acid-test ratio?

$$\frac{\$14,000 + \$11,365 + \$1,000}{\$19,960} =$$

$$\frac{\text{Assets} + \text{Receivables} + \text{Securities}}{\text{Total Current Liabilities}} = 1.3 \text{ to } 1$$

Net Income to Net Sales Ratio

An increase in net sales doesn't necessarily mean an increase in net income. Nor does it mean a higher income percent on sales. As sales increase, expenses also tend to rise. The key is to increase sales while holding down expenses. From the income statement we can determine net sales as well as net income. To find the net income to net sales ratio divide net income by net sales for the period.

Example 7

What is the net income to net sales ratio for the Watman Business Service (Example 3)?

$$\frac{\$173,300 = \text{net income}}{\$252,950 = \text{net sales}} = .7 \text{ to } 1$$

Accounts Receivable to Net Sales Ratio

Extending credit to customers may increase sales, but it may also increase the amount of credit extended if customers delay payment. Though accounts receivable is an asset, it is not cash. A cash shortage and accounts receivable abundance can place a firm in financial difficulty. Cash is required to pay the debts of the selling firm. The accounts receivable to net sales ratio measures how well credit extension is being managed. The accounts receivable to net sales ratio is found by dividing accounts receivable at the end of a period by net sales for the period.

Example 8

The Teller and Bodine Corp. had net sales of $1,386,450 in 1987. Accounts receivable at the end of 1987 were $263,850. What is the accounts receivable to net sales ratio?

$$\frac{\$\ 263,850}{\$1,386,450} = \frac{\text{accounts receivable}}{\text{net sales}} = .19 \text{ to } 1$$

Accounts Payable to Net Purchases Ratio

This ratio is very similar to the accounts receivable to net sales ratio. This ratio indicates how well credit is being managed in the buying firm instead of the selling firm. It is found by dividing accounts payable at the end of a period by net purchases during that period.

Example 9

Stark and Associates have $13,600 of accounts payable on the balance sheet dated June 1, 1988. Net purchases for the year ended June 1, 1988 are shown on the income statement at $87,365. What is the accounts payable to net purchases ratio?

$$\frac{\$13,600}{\$87,365} = \frac{\text{accounts payable}}{\text{net purchases}} = .16 \text{ to } 1$$

Exercise E   Kay Miller, owner of the Solid Sound Studio, has the financial statements for the year ended September 30, 1986 as shown below. Ms. Miller plans to make comparisons to last year's financial performance. Determine the ratios requested.

Solid Sound Studio
Balance Sheet
September 30, 1986

Assets

Current Assets		
Cash	$13,120	
Accounts Receivable	4,265	
Merchandise on Hand	10,050	
Total Current Assets		$27,435
Fixed Assets		
Building		30,000
Total Assets		$57,435

Liabilities and Proprietorship

Current Liabilities		
Accounts Payable	$ 3,420	
Notes Payable	15,000	
Total Liabilities		$18,420
Proprietorship		
K. Miller, Capital		39,015
Total Liabilities and Proprietorship		$57,435

Solid Sound Studio
Income Statement
Year Ended September 30, 1986

Revenue		
Sales of Merchandise	$86,420	
Less: Sales Returns	763	
Net Sales		$85,657
Cost of Goods Sold		
Merchandise Inventory		
September 30, 1985	$ 7,300	
Merchandise Purchases	41,680	
Goods Available for Sale	48,980	
Less: Merchandise Inventory,		
September 30, 1986	10,050	
Cost of Goods Sold		38,930
Gross Profit		$46,727
Operating Expenses		
Rent Expense	$ 4,300	
Advertising Expense	1,200	
Salaries Expense	8,900	
Payroll Tax Expense	534	
Utilities Expense	2,620	
Total Operating Expenses		17,554
Net income, year ended September 30, 1986		$29,173

1. Current Ratio = _____1.5 to 1_____

2. Acid-Test Ratio = _____

3. Net Income to Net Sales Ratio = _____

4. Accounts Receivable to Net Sales Ratio = _____

5. Accounts Payable to Net Purchases Ratio = _____

Name _____   Date _____   Score _____

Skill Problems   Use the comparative balance sheet and comparative income statement below to determine the answers to the skill problems.

Albrecht's
Comparative Balance Sheet
June 1, 1987 and 1986

Assets	1987	1986	% of Increase (or Decrease)
Current Assets			
Cash	$ 8,000	$ 9,300	_____
Accounts Receivable	2,800	2,960	_____
Merchandise on Hand	_____	15,300	_____
Total Current Assets	$28,000	_____	_____
Fixed Assets			
Store Display Equipment	$15,800	$15,950	_____
Automobile	3,000	_____	_____
Total Fixed Assets	_____	19,550	_____
Total Assets	════	════	_____
Liabilities and Proprietorship			
Current liabilities			
Accounts Payable	$ 4,900	$ 4,200	_____
Notes Payable—Bank	10,000	12,000	_____
Total Current Liabilities	_____	_____	_____
Long-Term Liabilities			
Mortgage Payable	$ 1,000	0	_____
Total Liabilities	_____	_____	_____
Proprietorship			
L. K. Worthy, Capital	_____	_____	_____
Total Liabilities and Proprietorship	════	════	_____

Albrecht's
Comparative Income Statement
Year ended June 1, 1987 and 1986

	1987	1986
Revenue		
Sales	$183,975	$167,385
Less: Sales Returns	3,920	3,680
Net Sales		
Cost of Goods Sold		
Merchandise Inventory	$ 15,300	$ 16,380
June 1, 1986		
Merchandise Purchases	127,100	120,850
Goods Available for Sale		
Less: Merchandise Inventory June 1, 1987	17,360	15,300
Cost of Goods Sold		
Gross Profit		
Operating Expenses		
Wages Expense	$ 12,300	$ 13,600
Rent Expense	6,000	6,000
Legal Fees	3,500	2,000
Payroll Tax Expense	700	750
Miscellaneous Expense	3,000	900
Total Expenses		
Net Income, year ended June 1		

1. Determine the net sales increase from 1986 to 1987 _____ %

2. Determine the acid-test ratio for 1987 = _____

3. Determine the percent of increase of L. K. Worthy, Capital from 1986 to 1987 _____ %

4. Determine the percent of sales returns for 1987 = _____ %

5. Determine the percent of cost of goods sold for 1987 = _____ %

6. Determine the total Liabilities and Proprietorship for 1987 = _____

7. Determine the accounts payable to net purchases ratio for 1987

= _____

8. Determine the percent of increase of operating expenses from 1986 to 1987 = _____ %

9. Determine the current ratio for 1987 = _____

10. Determine the percent of increase in net income from 1986 to 1987 = _____ %

11. Determine the accounts receivable to net sales ratio for 1987 = _____

12. Determine the net income to net sales ratio for 1987 = _____

13. Determine the percent of increase in cost of goods sold from 1986 to 1987 = _____ %

14. Determine the percent of gross profit for 1986 = _____ %

15. Determine the current ratio for 1986 = _____ to 1

16. Determine the percent of sales returns for 1986 = _____ %

17. Determine the acid-test ratio for 1986 = _____ to 1

18. Determine the percent of net income to net sales for 1986 = _____ %

19. Determine the accounts receivable to net sales ratio for 1986 = _____

20. Determine the net income to net sales ratio for 1986 = _____

Business Application Problems

1. Sun State, Inc. had a current ratio at the end of the year of 1.3 to 1. The current ratio for the same date was 1.9 to 1. The firm had $138,000 in current liabilities. What is the value of merchandise on hand if the firm does not have any prepaid assets?

2. The total assets of the Moloton Corporation are $968,100. The total liabilities are equal to proprietorship. What are the total liabilities of the Moloton Corporation?

3. The comparative balance sheet for LaPage and Co. shows that there was a decrease in accounts payable from last year by 10.4 percent. Accounts payable were $65,000 this year. What were accounts payable last year?

4. The accounts receivable to net sales ratio is .04 to 1. Accounts receivable are $3,640. What are net sales?

5. The total assets of the Levy Corporation were three times the amount of the liabilities. The proprietorship consisted of $450,000 of capital stock. What was the amount of the firm's assets?

6. Bilby and Son, Inc. had an acid-test ratio of 2.1 to 1. The current liabilities total $421,860. The current ratio is 3.1 to 1. What is the value of merchandise on hand?

7. Salane Interiors has $24,900 in cash, $22,300 in receivables, and $38,500 in liabilities. What is the acid test ratio for the firm?

8. Hollen and Cartwright had an accounts payable to net purchases ratio of 2 to 1. Their purchases for the period were $43,800 less $2,650 in purchase returns and allowances. What is the amount of the accounts payable?

Challenge Problem   A comparative balance sheet shows a decrease in current liabilities from 1986 to 1987 by 14.3 percent. The current ratio in 1987 is 1.7 to 1. The acid-test ratio in 1987 is 1.5 to 1. What were current liabilities in 1986? Merchandise inventory and prepaid assets were $32,000 in 1987.

1. The purpose of a comparative balance sheet or comparative income statement is to compare _____ to _____

2. Assets = _____ + Proprietorship

3. The report that gives the recent financial history of a firm is the _____ _____

4. When the revenue of a firm is less than the expenses for the same period, the firm has incurred a ____

5. Dividing the current assets—less merchandise inventory—by current liabilities will determine the _____ ratio.

6. The report that shows a firm's current financial status is termed the _____

7. The ratio that indicates how well the firm is managing the credit extended as a buyer is the _____

8. The ratio that measures how well our firm is collecting from our customers is the _____ ratio.

9. The two factors that are shown on an income statement are _____ and _____

10. There are two general types of income statements. They are for _____ firms and _____ firms.

The following information was taken from the 1987 comparative financial statements of the Owens Art Co. Use this information to solve the problems below. Round off your answers to the nearest tenth of a percent or tenth.

	1987	1986
Net Sales	$240,000	$220,000
Cost of Goods Sold	180,000	178,000
Merchandise Inventory	12,500	13,800
Cash	5,400	5,400
Income for the year	34,800	29,350
Accounts Payable	6,000	6,000
Accounts Receivable	7,900	8,500
Net Purchases	178,600	177,000

11. Determine the percent of increase of net sales. _____ %

12. Determine the current ratio of 1987 = _____

13. Determine the acid-test ratio for 1987 = _____

14. Determine the percent of cost of goods sold to net sales in 1987

    = _____ %

15. Determine the accounts receivable to net sales ratio in 1987 = _____

16. Determine the accounts payable to net purchases ratio in 1987 = _____

17. Determine the current ratio for 1986 = _____

18. Determine the percent of change in cash from 1986 to 1987 = _____ %

19. Determine the net income to net sales ratio for 1987 = _____

20. Determine the percent of increase of net purchases = _____ %

21

Statistics

After mastering the material in this chapter, you will be able to:

1. Calculate the mean value of a data set.
2. Calculate the median value of a data set.
3. Calculate the mode value of a data set.
4. Use and understand the following terms:
   Data set   Median
   Mean   Mode

Statistics are used in business to aid in the selection of the best alternative to solve a problem. A manager faced with a problem in market analysis, pay rates for employees, quality control, or population effects, can use statistics as a tool with which to solve the problem. Statistics are becoming more important as our population grows and as we move into a service-oriented economy. Sophisticated information gathering systems are being developed to deal with these changes.

Data set

Statistics deal with understanding a data set. The **data set** is a series of values, grouped by year, employee classification, sales by product, scrapped material by finished product, etc.

Quality Paint Co. Sales by Product

Year	Hightone A	Percent Increase*	Glass Cover	Percent Increase	Flat Cover	Percent Increase
1980	$185,687	. . .	$ 63,470	. . .	$39,450	. . .
1981	192,562	3.7	82,357	29.8	41,680	5.7
1982	192,800	3.8	96,119	51.4	40,350	2.3
1983	195,362	5.2	101,350	59.7	41,600	5.4
1984	195,020	5.0	103,280	62.7	42,965	8.9
1985	197,790	6.5	104,050	63.9	45,307	14.8

* 1980 is used as a base year for comparison.

The source for such data is either primary or secondary.

Primary data is gathered by the firm from its own records or as a result of its own survey.

Secondary data is gathered by the government, trade associations, or public agencies. This information is published and is readily available.

A thorough study of statistical analysis includes a great deal of advanced math and is beyond the scope of this text. A basic understanding, however, requires very little arithmetic.

Each value in a data set has meaning and is of importance to a decision-maker. There are also some useful generalizations that can be made about the data. These generalizations are termed mean, median, and mode.

Finding the Mean

The **mean** is the arithmetic average of a data set. The mean is found by dividing the sum of the values by the number of values in the data set.

Example 1

In the chart for Quality Paint Company, the mean for the sales of Hightone A is $193,203.50.

$$\frac{\$1,159,221}{6} = \frac{\text{sum of values (1980 to 1985)}}{\text{number of values (years)}} = \$193,203.50 = \text{mean}$$

In this example the actual value $193,203.50 is not found in the data set. The mean is only a representative value.

Example 2

Find the mean in the following data set.
Hourly rates—Shipping Department

$4.60	$6.90	$4.75	$7.20	$6.80
$4.78	$5.20	$7.25	$5.00	$6.30

$$\frac{\$58.78}{10} = \frac{\text{sum of values (hourly rates)}}{\text{number of values (employees)}} = \$5.88/\text{hr.} = \text{mean}$$

Finding the Median

The **median** is the middle ranked value in a data set. The values must be ordered or ranked from high to low or low to high. The middle value is then selected as the median.

Example 3

Find the median in the data set below.

147 92 46 35 81 72 65 63 81 19 64 96 163
ranked data set:
163 147 96 92 81 81 72 65 64 63 46 35 19

There are thirteen values. The middle value must be number 7. Count in seven from either end of the ranked data set; the median will be 72.

If there is an even number of values in the data set, there cannot be a middle value. In such cases, the two middle values are averaged to determine the median.

Example 4

Find the median in the following data set.

$27.50	$72.50	$57.80	$63.00	$30.00	$12.00
$26.35	$9.30	$86.80	$31.75	$130.20	$47.50

ranked data set:

$130.20	$86.80	$72.50	$63.00	$57.80	$47.50

— middle ranked values —

$31.75	$30.00	$27.50	$26.35	$12.00	$9.30

There are twelve values. The middle two values are $47.50 and $31.75. The median is $39.63.

$$\$47.50 + \$31.75 = \frac{\$79.25}{2} = \$39.63 = \text{median}$$

Finding the Mode

The **mode** is the value of greatest frequency. Some data sets have values that appear more than once. The repetition is a fact that a decision maker should notice. An f is used to indicate frequency.

The mode is easily found by ranking a data set as in finding the median.

Example 5

Find the mode in the following data set.

47	91	63	81	82	52	63	37	44	64
27	63	82	88	93	59	51	37		

ranked data set:

93	91	88	82	82	81	64	63	63	63

$f = 2 \qquad f = 2 \qquad f = 3$

59	52	51	47	44	37	37	27

The mode is 63. Sixty-three has the greatest frequency ($f = 3$).

Occasionally, two or more values will have the greatest frequency. When two values have the greatest frequency, the data set is said to have a bimodal distribution. If a data set has no values with frequency greater than one, there is no mode.

Example 6

Find the mode in the following data set.

12	13	27	31	51	36	24	62	36	18
		18		12		18	12		15

ranked data set:

62	51	36	36	31	27	24	18	18	18

$f = 2$ $f = 3$ $f = 3$

| 15 | 13 | 12 | 12 | 12 |

There are two modes, 18 and 12. Each has a frequency of 3.

Example 7

Find the mean, median, and mode of the following data set.

Rejected parts—
  Poly-Ormin

Date		Rejects	Ranked Data Set
June	1 =	7	23
	2 =	1	18
	3 =	6	16
	4 =	14	14
	5 =	8	13
	6 =	7	13 } 2
	7 =	6	12
	8 =	5	11
	9 =	18	11 } 3
	10 =	9	11
	11 =	4	10
	12 =	6	10 } 2
	13 =	13	9
	14 =	8	9 } 2
	15 =	12	8
	16 =	6	8 } 3
	17 =	5	8
	18 =	13	7
	19 =	3	7 } 2
	20 =	5	6
	21 =	10	6
	22 =	11	6 } 4
	23 =	11	6
	24 =	23	5
	25 =	16	5
	26 =	9	5 } 4
	27 =	11	5
	28 =	10	4
	29 =	8	3
	30 =	5	1
			270 = Sum

Example 7 *Continued*

$$\text{mean} = \frac{270}{30} = \frac{\text{sum of values}}{\text{number of values}} = 9$$

$$\text{median} = \frac{8 + 8}{2} = 8$$

$$\text{mode} = 6 \text{ and } 5$$

Exercise A Find the mean, median, and mode in the following data sets. Round off your answers to the nearest tenth of a unit or cent.

Exercise	*1*	*2*	*3*	*4*	*5*	*6*	*7*
	173	65	120	15	42	$4.20	$3.93
	47	23	280	29	48	6.80	4.12
	62	44	216	13	62	7.20	3.08
	49	26	381	18	57	7.20	3.63
	39	83	90	16	39	4.90	3.90
	87	53	261	21	42	7.35	3.47
	55	19	142	26	50	8.20	4.01
	23	22	288	18	51	6.57	4.20
	89	26	120	32	83	6.80	3.91
	62	30	138	36	41	6.50	3.87
	44	18	164	29	60	9.00	4.28
	162	25	93	13	86	4.75	4.60
	12	15	287	16	39		4.07
	93	82	306	28	42		4.30
	55	23	291	29	48		3.90
	62	47	222	13	56		3.98
		36	427	30			4.22
		23	230				3.68
		5					
		24					

mean   = 69.6 ____ ____ ____ ____ ____ ____

median = 58.5 ____ ____ ____ ____ ____ ____

mode   = 62 ____ ____ ____ ____ ____

____

____

Exercise	8	9	10	11	12	13
	$11.20	$6.57	$4.60	$10.62	$7.00	$ 7
	17.95	7.02	4.58	9.88	6.50	3
	8.76	8.08	4.40	8.62	7.75	4
	13.70	7.01	4.61	8.68	6.00	7
	10.30	7.75	4.60	6.84	6.25	8
	8.50	6.83	4.91	9.30	5.50	9
	13.80	8.10	4.56	8.61	6.75	10
	17.00	8.51	4.23	8.60	7.25	8
	13.80	7.70	4.60	8.48	7.00	6
	6.90	9.00	5.01	9.32	6.75	5
	10.00	6.70	4.71	8.91	6.25	6
		6.90	4.68	10.00	5.75	9
		8.08	4.62	16.40	6.00	2
		9.23	4.60	9.30	5.25	8
		8.53	4.41			1
						4

mean = ____ ____ ____ ____ ____ ____

median = ____ ____ ____ ____ ____ ____

mode = ____ ____ ____ ____ ____

____

Data is often grouped by categories of value. In a large data set the data may be grouped by intervals of 100 or $10 or by years. This grouping allows a frequency to be stated for each category.

Example 8

Group the data in the data set below into $10 categories. Provide an indication of frequency in each category.

$477	$462	$392	$459	$460	$419	$446	$410
$427	$437	$432	$436	$429	$431	$436	$423
$448	$453	$386	$419	$399	$448	$407	$427

Categories by $10 intervals	Frequency
$381 to $390	1
391 to 400	2
401 to 410	2
411 to 420	2
421 to 430	4
431 to 440	5
441 to 450	3
451 to 460	3
461 to 470	1
471 to 480	1

Assignment

Chapter Twenty-One

Name _____ Date _____ Score _____

Skill Problems

Determine the mean, median, and mode in the following data sets. Round off your answer to the nearest tenth or cent.

Problem	1	2	3	4	5	6	7	8	9	10
	14	386	27	9	3	48	13	62	51	$1.47
	18	412	29	12	8	62	28	38	46	1.51
	23	302	31	16	6	37	17	47	43	1.48
	16	219	31	10	12	41	26	61	49	1.50
	20	309	28	13	14	36	15	53	46	1.48
	18	427	27	18	5	40	21	46	54	1.48
	28	403	31	13	10	38	32	42	62	1.60
	22	386	30	16	11	32	27	47		1.46
		392	27	15	7	44	16	45		1.47
		472	32	20	12	37	24			1.48
			30	11	10	47	26			1.50
			26			50				1.52
			31							1.61

mean   = ___ ___ ___ ___ ___ ___ ___ ___ ___ ___

median = ___ ___ ___ ___ ___ ___ ___ ___ ___ ___

mode   = ___ ___ ___   ___ ___ ___ ___ ___

___

___

Business Application Problems

1. Charlie's Chili Restaurant recorded the following sales for the first ten days of the month.

June   Find the mean _____ median _____

1 $230
2 345
3 330
4 410
5 280
6 200
7 340
8 340
9 260
10 380

2. The Suburban Transit Authority logged the following mileage during the month of August. What was the mean, median, and mode for the month?

Date	Mileage	Date	Mileage
August 1 =	17,460	August 16 =	28,356
2 =	20,300	17 =	29,041
3 =	28,356	18 =	28,386
4 =	27,462	19 =	28,572
5 =	28,360	20 =	28,674
6 =	26,391	21 =	18,330
7 =	18,492	22 =	19,437
8 =	21,005	23 =	26,990
9 =	28,431	24 =	27,385
10 =	27,300	25 =	28,104
11 =	28,106	26 =	28,671
12 =	27,998	27 =	18,200
13 =	28,304	28 =	18,200
14 =	18,620	29 =	20,465
15 =	19,962	30 =	28,465
		31 =	29,231

mean = _____

median = _____

mode = _____

3. The daily output from the keypunch section of the Deliss Company was as follows for the week of March 16. What is the mean, median, and mode for the week's AM shift and PM shift?

Shift	Operator	Mon.	Tues.	Wed.	Thur.	Fri.
AM	1	862	683	731	790	836
	2	768	840	780	831	802
	3	823	847	835	890	862
	4	795	685	735	768	775
	5	820	836	840	898	839
PM	1	685	646	705	690	730
	2	790	830	810	805	768
	3	830	860	865	855	806
	4	855	830	848	820	890

AM *Shift*   PM *Shift*

mean = _____   mean = _____

median = _____   median = _____

mode = _____   mode = _____

4. The operators for Oliver Express, an independent trucking firm, had the following 40 pound box loads of fruit for the week of September 3. What was the mean, median, and mode of their loads?

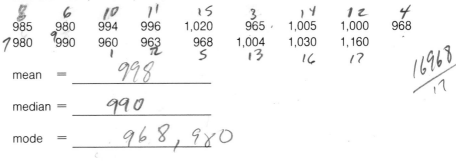

8	6	10	11	15	3	14	12	4
985	980	994	996	1,020	965	1,005	1,000	968
7 980	9 990	960	963	968	1,004	1,030	1,160	
		1	72	5	13	16	17	

16968 / 17

mean   =   998

median =   990

mode   =   968, 980

5. The Courier recorded the following results of a circulation drive on total sales. The amount of circulation for the first ten-day period is shown below.

May	Circulation
6	42,300
7	42,360
8	43,000
9	43,050
10	43,630
11	43,700
12	43,900
13	43,900
14	43,980
15	44,250

What is the mean   = _____

median   = _____

mode   = _____

6. Determine the mean, median, and mode for your mastery tests to date.

   mean   = _____

   median = _____

   mode   = _____

7. Find the difference between the mean and the median in the following data set.

461	352	403	189	381	429	223

8. The number of months that each of the cars in the fleet of taxi cabs went without a breakdown is shown below. What is the median number of months?

20	31	18	24	19	27	31	30	12	25
31	22	8	26	29	23	16	23	20	26
26	30	20	21	26	32	18	31		

9. The Personnel Department has maintained records of all retired employees for the past ten years. The years of service have been averaged and are shown below. What is the mean of the ten-year period?

1986	1985	1984	1983	1982	1981	1980	1979	1978	1977
21	23	26	21	24	25	28	28	30	29

10. In the week of July 17, the Office Manager noted the following absences.

Monday	Tuesday	Wednesday	Thursday	Friday
8	6	5	7	12

    Find the median for the week.

Challenge Problem

Find the mean and median for the information below.

43	16	18	67	9	48	68	37	23	84	35	57	127
75	78	107	47	68	32	38	126	26	60	90	28	
93	10	93	85	27	53	56	53	46	26	13		

True or False

T F 1. The middle-ranked value in a data set is termed the mode.

T F 2. The mean is the value that occurs most often in the data set.

T F 3. There may be more than one mode in a data set.

T F 4. The data set is a group of related numbers.

T F 5. The mean may not actually be in the data set as a number.

T F 6. The median is the value that is in the middle of a data set after the values have been placed in a numerical order.

T F 7. The mean, median, and mode are values that allow certain generalizations to be made about the data set.

8. The Stanley Ambulance Service Company recorded the following calls over the past two weeks. Determine the mean, median, and mode for the period. Round off your answer to the nearest tenth.

July	Calls	July	Calls
6	5	13	10
7	14	14	6
8	8	15	7
9	13	16	13
10	6	17	2
11	7	18	14
12	12	19	13

Mean _____

Median _____

Mode _____

9. Spectrum Views had a sale on video cassettes for home use. The sales are recorded below. Determine the mean sale amount for the period.

$ 230
   290
   260
   200
   325
   290
   285
   300

Mean _____

10. The output of two employees doing word processing is shown below. Which employee had the best output as measured by the mean?

	Nancy	Gwen
Mon.	35	34
Tues.	32	35
Wed.	28	26
Thur.	32	35
Fri.	32	32

_____

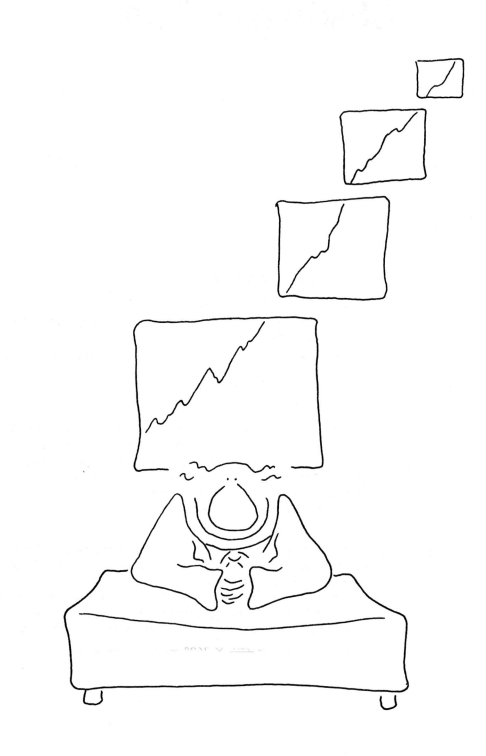

22 Charts and Graphs

Performance Objectives

After mastering the material in this chapter, you will be able to:

1. Draw a circle graph, bar graph, and line graph.
2. Describe information on a bar or line graph using a base period or a direct comparison.
3. Describe two or more sets of information on one bar or line graph.
4. Use and understand the following terms:
   Circle Graph   Bar Graph   Line Graph

A graph is used when a business manager wishes to show the relationship of two or more facts to each other. Though the exact figures are usually not available at a glance, the graph does give a quick comparison of the information. The saying "One picture is worth a thousand words" is true of a graph as well. Graphs are often used to supplement actual statistics.

There are three types of graphs: circle, bar, and line.

Circle Graph

The **circle graph** shows the whole or base as a complete circle. The parts that make up the whole are shown as pie-shaped slices of the circle. The bigger the part is to the whole, the bigger the pie slice.

A circle is made up of 360°, a half circle equals 180°, one quarter circle equals 90°, etc. A protractor may be used to measure the degrees.

To determine the size of the pie slice, compare the part to the whole and then multiply by 360°, that is $\frac{\text{part}}{\text{whole}} \times 360° =$ degrees in pie slice.

Example 1

The Buton Company has three departments. Sales has fourteen employees, manufacturing has thirty-five employees, and there are ten employees in the office staff. Draw a circle graph showing a comparison of each department to the total number of employees.

14 = Sales
35 = Manufacturing
10 = Office
59 = Total Employees

$$\frac{14}{59} = \frac{\text{Sales}}{\text{Total}} \times 360° = 85°$$

$$\frac{35}{59} = \frac{\text{Manufacturing}}{\text{Total}} \times 360° = 214°$$

$$\frac{10}{59} = \frac{\text{Office}}{\text{Total}} \times 360° = 61°$$

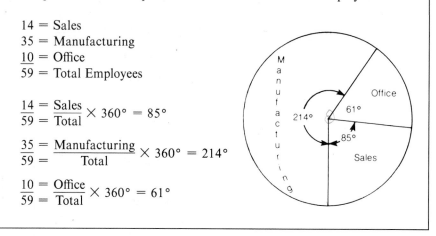

Circle graphs can be used to show a comparison of a variety of factors. The comparison is always made to the whole, the entire circle.

Example 2

The Valmer Candy Shoppe sells their one-pound box of soft chocolates for $1.80. The cost of the ingredients is $1.05. Overhead is an estimated 32¢ per box. Draw a graph to show the profit, overhead, and cost per box.

$1.80 = selling price
− 1.05 = cost price
− .32 = overhead
$ .43 = profit

$$\frac{\$1.05}{\$1.80} = \frac{\text{cost price}}{\text{selling price}} \times 360° = 210°$$

$$\frac{\$ .32}{\$1.80} = \frac{\text{overhead}}{\text{selling price}} \times 360° = 64°$$

$$\frac{\$ .43}{\$1.80} = \frac{\text{profit}}{\text{selling price}} \times 360° = 86°$$

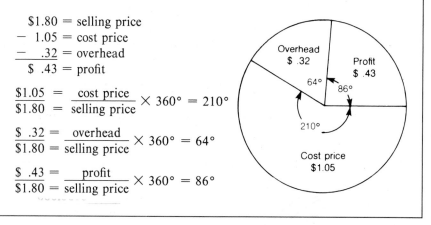

Bar Graph   A **bar graph** is used to show increases or decreases in an item over a period of time. There are two factors shown on a bar graph, usually time and the measurable item, such as sales, number of employees, rejected parts, costs, etc.

Each column or bar represents one time period. By comparing the height of each bar, a manager can see the changes.

The bar graph can be used to show only the increase or decrease from a base time period or the total amount.

The bar graph is best used to show changes or trends.

Example 3

The sales for Campbell and Associates were as follows:

1981 = $136,000	1983 = 126,000	1985 = 360,000
1982 = 240,000	1984 = 259,000	1986 = 370,000

Draw a bar graph to show the sales for years 1981–1986.

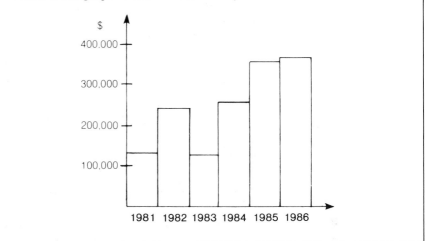

(handwritten in left margin: BAR Graph →)

Example 4

Using the sales for Campbell and Associates (from example 3), draw a bar graph showing increases and decreases in sales. Use 1981 as a base year.

1981 sales = $136,000 = base year

$$1982 \text{ sales} = \frac{\$240,000 - \$136,000}{\$136,000} = 76\% \text{ increase}$$

$$1983 \text{ sales} = \frac{\$126,000 - \$136,000}{\$136,000} = 7\% \text{ decrease}$$

$$1984 \text{ sales} = \frac{\$259,000 - \$136,000}{\$136,000} = 90\% \text{ increase}$$

$$1985 \text{ sales} = \frac{\$360,000 - \$136,000}{\$136,000} = 165\% \text{ increase}$$

$$1986 \text{ sales} = \frac{\$370,000 - \$136,000}{\$136,000} = 172\% \text{ increase}$$

By using colors or shading techniques, more than one item can be shown on a bar graph.

Care must be taken to select a representative year as a base or the results will not accurately reflect the comparison of periods.

Example 5

The Portland Meat Company packages beef, pork, and poultry. The output over the past five months is shown below.

	Beef (lbs.)	*Pork (lbs.)*	*Poultry (lbs.)*	*Total (lbs.)*
February	4,600	2,650	2,280	9,530
March	4,960	2,400	2,600	9,960
April	4,850	2,500	2,480	9,830
May	5,280	2,600	3,250	11,130
June	5,800	2,300	4,160	12,260

From the information above, draw a single bar graph that will show (1) total output, (2) beef output, (3) pork output, and (4) poultry output.

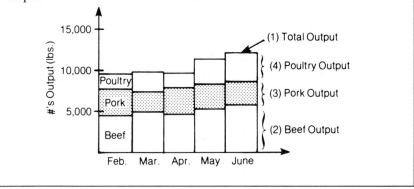

Line Graph

A **line graph** is very similar to a bar graph. The two factors are shown as on a bar graph. The bars are not shown, but instead a point is established at the top of where the bar would have been shown. The points are then connected with straight lines. The lines show the relationship from one period to another. The line graph is best used to show changes and trends.

Example 6

Draw a line graph to show the number of rejected parts in the Tube Inspection Department over the past eight weeks.

Week of October	Rejected Parts
3	48
10	216
17	57
24	63
31	81
November	
7	54
14	37
21	61

Example 6 *Continued*

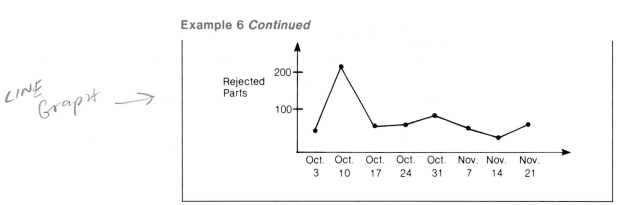

LINE Graph →

Bar graphs and line graphs can be used to show several items on a single graph.

Example 7

Draw a line graph to show selling price and cost price per unit for the Watts Corporation over the past six years.

Year	Selling Price	Cost Price
1980	$4.63	$2.80
1981	4.82	3.35
1982	5.20	3.80
1983	5.20	3.65
1984	5.35	4.30
1985	5.38	4.30

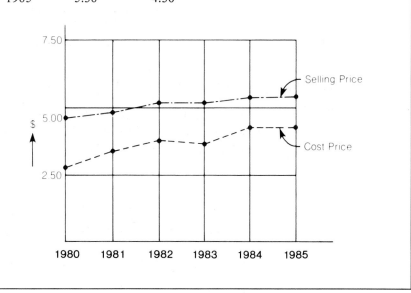

Draw a circle graph for each of the exercises below. Round off to the nearest degree.

1. The Plum Tree Shop has five departments. The sales of each department are shown below:

Junior Misses	$47,360
Sports Wear	39,400
Young Misses	53,980
Ladies Fashions	72,480
Accessories	19,200

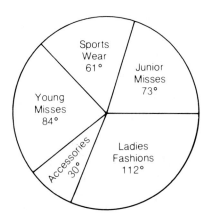

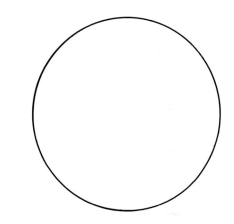

2. Davis Personnel found that there was a significant amount of new positions in the area of technical jobs.

Administrative	430
Sales	270
Computer	310
Technical	360
Labor	120

3. The township of Delray noted the following new housing units being built in the month of May.

Single family   108
Apartment   230
Multi-unit   420

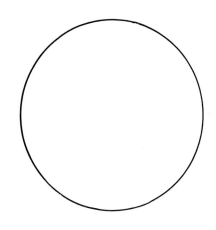

4. The Metro Sports Shop determined sales for the month to be as follows:

Hiking and Camping $42,600
    Equipment
Hunting and Fishing   31,850
    Equipment
Baseball, Football, and   12,600
    Soccer
Miscellaneous   8,980

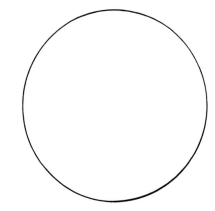

Exercise B   Draw a bar graph for each of the exercises below.

1. Yearly sales for the TASCO Company were as follows:

1981 $4,300,000
1982   6,059,300
1983   7,300,500
1984   4,800,000
1985   5,693,000
1986   8,360,000

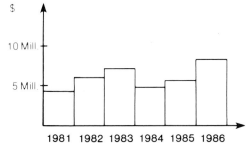

2. A traffic count at the corner of Weber and Staples indicated the following volume for the week of January 23.

Monday	2,380
Tuesday	3,200
Wednesday	1,780
Thursday	2,900
Friday	3,450

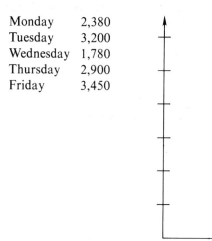

3. The number of employees at year-end for the Pilson & Weber Company are shown below. Show the change per year, using 1981 as a base year.

1981	4,680
1982	4,935
1983	4,320
1984	4,163
1985	4,528

4. The total number of employees and number of male employees are shown below for the Scott Company. Draw a bar graph to show total employees, male employees, and female employees.

Year	Total Employees	Male Employees
1980	60	39
1981	56	38
1982	84	56
1983	85	52
1984	90	63

Exercise C   Draw a line graph for each of the exercises below.

1. The costs of the Engineering Department over five months are shown below.

March	$4,360
April	4,823
May	4,230
June	3,986
July	5,852

2. Employee turnover has been as follows for the months of July through November.

July	3
August	7
September	8
October	0
November	5

3. The sales of the Apersond Company have been steadily increasing over the six-month period of March through August. Much of the success in increased sales is due to the introduction of their quick-release valve. Draw a line graph to show both total sales and the sales of the quick-release valve.

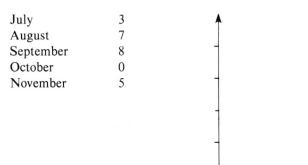

Month	Total Sales	Quick-Release Valve
March	$32,680	$14,230
April	32,800	16,050
May	33,560	16,400
June	34,700	16,362
July	34,890	16,800
August	35,620	17,950

Name _____   Date _____   Score _____

Skill Problems

1. Draw a circle graph to show the following information.

    Total Sales
    (A, B, C, and D)   = $62,580
                Product A = $ 4,350
                Product B = $30,600
                Product C = $ 4,860
                Product D = $22,770

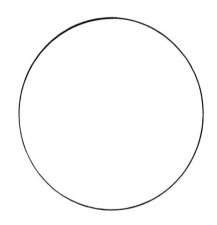

2. Draw a circle graph to show the portion of student representation at a
    college.

    Freshmen   20,362
    Sophomores   16,490
    Juniors   17,105
    Seniors   16,230

3. Draw a bar graph to show the changes in sales for the years reported
    below. Use 1981 as a base year.

    1981 = $61,190
    1982 = $48,650
    1983 = $56,890
    1984 = $69,400
    1985 = $72,350
    1986 = $68,870

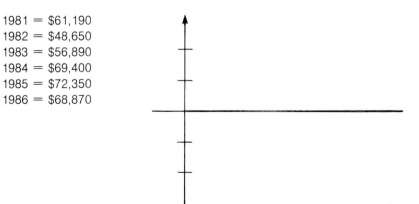

4. Draw a line graph to show your mastery test scores.

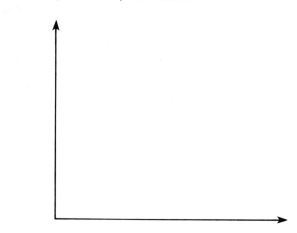

5. Draw a line graph to show the passenger miles flown by Freedom Airlines.

4,390 = June
8,620 = July
8,890 = August
9,450 = September
4,600 = October
6,450 = November
7,900 = December

1. Draw a graph that will show the units produced and scrapped parts from the information below.

August	Units Produced	Units Scrapped
2	6,005	312
9	5,656	362
16	5,820	341
23	4,362	340
30	5,885	322

2. Draw a graph that will show the following information. Of the forty-two new employees hired last month, twelve were fired, eighteen were transferred, and the remainder were retained in their positions.

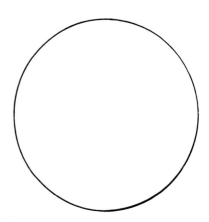

3. Draw a graph to show the different wage levels in the departments shown below.

Office	$5.10 to $5.90
Manufacturing	4.01 to 4.95
Inspection	4.31 to 5.10
Engineering	4.80 to 6.00
Processing	4.60 to 5.50

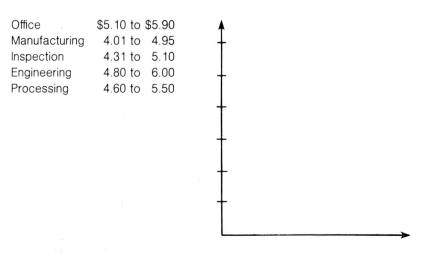

4. Draw a graph to show the following temperature changes at a motel outdoor pool.

	Air		Water	
	High	Low	High	Low
Monday	78	63	72	68
Tuesday	72	64	70	67
Wednesday	75	68	72	65
Thursday	74	62	70	67
Friday	81	68	71	68
Saturday	80	69	72	68
Sunday	76	67	70	69

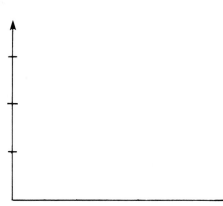

5. The number of employees that have resigned are shown below by age group. What is the percent of the total that are below forty years old?

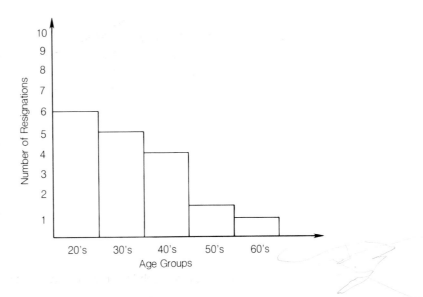

6. If the number of employees regularly employed by the firm above is 210, what is the percent of resignations for the firm?

7. The price of a condominium has risen by 4 percent last year and by 8 percent the previous year. Show the effect of the price increase on a condominium unit that sold for $38,000 two years ago.

8. What would the chart in problem 7 look like if the price is projected to drop by 2 percent next year?

Challenge Problem   Chart the mean, median, and mode of the following grouped data sets.

Group A				Group B				Group C			
37	62	61	31	25	53	49	61	57	49	38	18
83	49	49	19	35	18	68	53	18	81	19	31
46	19	26	35	19	26	53	27	16	26	25	27
19	38	33	27	26	42	20	30	32	53	30	62

Name _____   Date _____   Score _____

1. Draw a circle graph to show the following information.

Total Revenue   = $4,500,000
Revenue from
  Credit Sales   = $ 800,000

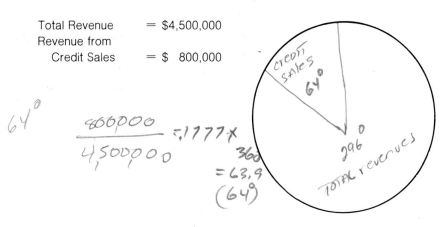

64^0

$$\frac{800,000}{4,500,000} = .1777 \times$$

360

$= 63.9$

(64)

2. Draw a bar graph to show the following information for the Marlin Bank.

Year	Total Savings	Certificates of Deposit
1981	$2,600,000	$1,100,000
1982	3,000,000	1,080,000
1983	3,700,000	1,430,000
1984	3,800,000	1,500,000
1985	4,200,000	1,450,000
1986	4,580,000	1,700,000

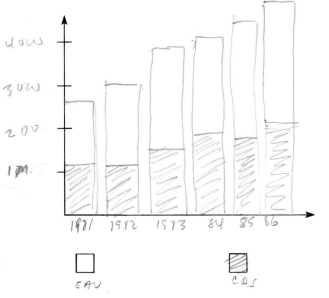

3. Draw a line graph to show the changes in the number of employees from 1982 to 1987. Use 1982 as a base year.

Year	Employees
1982	380
1983	390
1984	430
1985	360
1986	400
1987	420

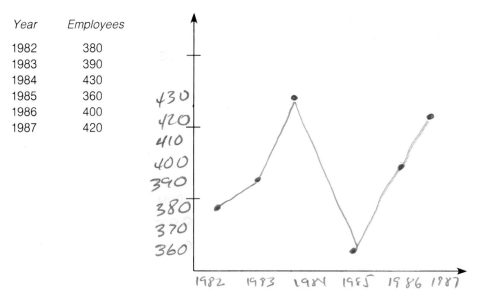

4. The result of the Green Greens Open are shown below. Prepare a graph that will show the players scores by those who hit in the 30s, 40s, and 50s.

Scores

36	56
34	41
42	37
38	40
41	45
51	33
39	49
43	38

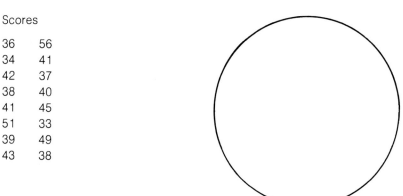

5. A graph must be prepared to be used as a visual aid at a departmental meeting. The graph must show the number of man-hours worked and lost last year due to illness or accidents over the six-month period January 1 to June 30. Prepare a graph based on the information below.

Month	Hours Worked	Hours Lost
January	8,900	600
February	9,100	550
March	8,750	700
April	9,400	290
May	8,050	350
June	9,400	450

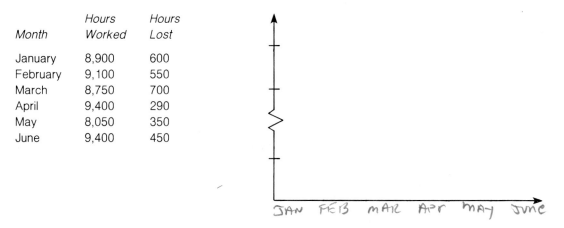

23 Review

23 Review

The purpose of this chapter is to review the material that you have mastered in the book's twenty-two chapters. This chapter may be useful in preparation for a final exam. Each problem is referenced to a chapter portion for quick review if necessary.

A review of your mastery test scores will further pinpoint areas that need extra review.

1. $92 + 8.003 + 16 + 9.627 + 8 =$
   (Reference: chapter 3, page 62.)

2. $6\frac{3}{4} - 4\frac{7}{8} =$
   (Reference: chapter 2, page 36.)

3. $21 \div \frac{3}{5} =$
   (Reference: chapter 2, page 41.)

4. $2\frac{3}{5} \times 1\frac{2}{3} =$
   (Reference: chapter 2, page 42.)

5. $6 - 1.306 =$
   (Reference: chapter 2, page 64.)

6. $89 \times 3.2 =$
   (Reference: chapter 3, page 64.)

7. $16 \div .005 =$
   (Reference: chapter 3, page 65.)

8. The footing for an addition along one side of an existing tool shed is 40' long. The footing will be 42″ deep and 18″ wide. Cement to fill the hole costs $33 a cubic yard. Using the nearest cubic yard, what will be the cost for the cement? (Reference: chapter 6, page 115.)

9. The front yard of a new home is to be sodded. The yard measures 80′ by 60′. Sod costs $8 a square yard. How much will it cost to buy the sod for the front yard? Use the nearest full yard. (Reference: chapter 6, page 118.)

10. Base = $800
    Rate = 30%
    Percentage = _____
    (Reference: chapter 7, page 136.)

11. Eight percent of the new store will be set aside for customer service and checkout. The new store will have 72,000 square feet of space. How much of the store will be used for customer service and checkout? (Reference: chapter 7, page 136.)

12. How many square meters in problem 11? (Reference: chapter 6, page 123.)

13. Sixty percent of the books sold at The Shelf were fiction. Fiction sales amounted to $45,000 for the period. What were total sales for The Shelf for the period? (Reference: chapter 7, page 136.)

14. Anglebrandt & Company purchase on account. Their policy is to take advantage of all discounts available. A purchase of $700 worth of merchandise from Stubbs, Inc., on terms of 2/10,n/60 was made on July 16. Payment is made on July 24. How much was remitted? (Reference: chapter 13, page 282.)

15. M. Gayeski & Sons purchased $1,700 worth of goods from Arnott Associates on August 9. Ten percent and 5 percent discounts were offered. Terms were 2/10,n/30. How much was remitted if payment was made within the discount period? (Reference: chapter 13, page 282.)

16. What was the latest date that M. Gayeski & Sons could have received a cash discount in problem 15? (Reference: chapter 13, page 281.)

17. Dick Brennan sells products on a commission formula plan. He earns a salary of $500 a month. His commission rate is 1 percent on sales above $60,000 and an additional $\frac{1}{2}$ percent on sales above $100,000. His sales this month were $117,000. What was his income? (Reference: chapter 14, page 306.)

18. Cost Price = $300
    Markup = 40% on cost
    Selling Price = _____
    (Reference: chapter 15, page 320.)

19. Cost Price = $300
    Markup = 40% on sales
    Selling Price = _____
    (Reference: chapter 15, page 321.)

20. Markup on cost = 25%
    Markup on retail = _____ %
    (Reference: chapter 15, page 327.)

21. Cost Price = _____
    Markup = 30% on cost
    Selling Price = _____
    Discount = 10%
    List Price = $100
    (Reference: chapter 15, page 329.)

22. Dave Yost bought a truck for $9,700. It cost $85 to have it delivered and another $7,215 to have a custom body installed. The unit should last five years at which time the salvage value is expected to be $4,000. What is the book value at the end of the second year using the declining-balance method? (Reference: chapter 17, page 375.)

23. What is the depreciation for year three of Yost's truck using the A.C.R.S. method if the property is categorized as a three-year item. (Reference: chapter 17, page 377.)

24. What is the accumulated depreciation for year four for Yost's truck using the sum-of-the-years'-digits method? (Reference: chapter 17, page 372.)

25. Ms. Jurk signed a promissory note on December 17, 1986 for $3,000 for ninety days at 9 percent interest. What date will the note come due? (Reference: chapter 9, page 174.)

26. How much will Ms. Jurk have to pay when the $3,000 note comes due? Use ordinary interest. (Reference: chapter 10, page 192.)

27. Ken Beach made a deposit of $6,000 in his local bank that pays 4 percent compounded semiannually. The deposit was made six years ago today. How much is the deposit worth today? (Reference: chapter 12, page 249.)

28. Martin Franke would like to make a deposit in his bank that pays 5 percent compounded annually in order that he may have $8,492 two years from now. How much must he deposit today? (Reference: chapter 12, page 252.)

29. Interest = $9
    Principal = $600
    Rate = 12%
    Time = _____
    (Reference: chapter 10, page 197.)

30. Note face value on January 16, 1987 = $1,000
    Interest on Note = 8%, term of 90 days
    Discount Date = February 2, 1987
    Discount Rate = 10%
    Proceeds = $ _____
    (Reference: chapter 10, page 193.)

31. A piece of land was purchased on July 1 for $46,000. A down payment of $10,000 was made and the balance was financed at 14 percent. The monthly payment was determined to be $700. What is the principal balance after the second monthly payment? (Reference: chapter 11, page 225.)

32. A. J. Corporation received its monthly bank statement with a balance of $1,072.21. The chief accountant found that the balance in the cash account of the firm is $942.17. He also noted that the bank had not recorded two deposits of $40 each made yesterday. Also missing from the bank statement was a check for $217.62. The statement noted a service charge, but it was so blurred that it was illegible. What was the service charge? (Reference: chapter 4, page 80.)

33. The purchase records of the Ureel Company for an item called "Soil Rich" are presented below:

Date of Purchase	Quantity	Cost/unit
July 16, 1984	100	$1.20
June 4, 1985	600	$1.15
January 15, 1986	400	$1.60
September 4, 1986	250	$2.00

What is the value of ending inventory of 300 units using the L.I.F.O. method? (Reference: chapter 16, page 345.)

34. Use the F.I.F.O. method to determine ending inventory in problem 33. (Reference: chapter 16, page 349.)

35. Use the average cost method to determine ending inventory in problem 33. (Reference: chapter 16, page 352.)

36. **T   F**   As income increases, the amount of income tax increases with a given number of claimed exemptions. (Reference: chapter 5, page 97.)

37. Eric earns $6 per hour. He is paid overtime (time and one half) for all hours in excess of forty per week. He worked forty-six hours last week. What were his gross earnings? (Reference: chapter 5, page 95.)

38. Two weeks ago Eric earned $270. Income tax was $63.20. F.I.C.A. is 7.15 percent of $42,000. Eric's accumulated earnings for the year before this check totaled $32,200. Eric has one other deduction of a city income tax of $\frac{1}{2}$ percent. What was Eric's take-home pay? (Reference: chapter 5, page 97.)

39. The selling price of the merchandise is $870. How much must be paid if there is a 4 percent sales tax on the merchandise? (Reference: chapter 18, page 402.)

40. Sandy Baxendale imported a shipment of foreign china subject to an ad valorem tax of 10% and a specific tax of $2. The customs agent determined the market value of each of the eleven items to be $70. How much must Sandy pay for the merchandise including customs duties? (Reference: chapter 18, page 398.)

41. Meharg, a small community in Ohio, has a tax base of $1,600,000 (assessed valuation). The community must raise $147,000 in taxes. To the nearest tenth of a mill, what will be the tax rate? (Reference: chapter 18, page 395.)

42. Beauvais' $47,000 house is assessed at $25,000. The tax rate in his community is 21.3 mills. How much are the property taxes? (Reference: chapter 18, page 395.)

43. 7, 17, 3, 1, 8, 6, 5, 3, 10.
    What is the mean in the above data? (Reference: chapter 21, page 462.)

44. What is the mode in the above data? (Reference: chapter 21, page 463.)

45. What is the median in the above data? (Reference: chapter 21, page 462.)

46. Calculate the amount of payoff on a loss of $26,000 when the coinsurance clause specification is 80 percent and the amount of coverage is $30,000 on a $39,000 building. (Reference: chapter 8, page 154.)

47. Goods listed at $8,360 are shipped to a buyer in Texas F.O.B. shipping point, terms 2/10,n/35. The cost of freight is $462. What is the amount of payment sent to the seller if paid within the discount period? (Reference: chapter 13, page 287.)

48. Shari Krzysiak purchased a bond at $103 \frac{1}{2}$ with a stated rate of $10 \frac{1}{4}$ percent interest. To the nearest tenth of a percent, what is the actual rate of return? (Reference: chapter 19, page 422.)

49. Determine the missing figures in the partial income statement below. (Reference: chapter 20, page 445.)

	1985	1986
Cost of Goods Sold		
Merchandise Inventory, January 1	$ 42,690	$ 44,620
Purchases	61,456	
Freight In	+ 2,341	+ 1,780
Goods Available for Sale	$106,487	$117,610
Merchandise Inventory, March 31	− 83,420	− 81,485
Cost of Goods Sold	$ 23,067	

50. Prepare a circle graph to show the following sales. (Reference: chapter 22, page 475.)

Products priced from $ 18 to $ 25 $= f = 10$
25 to 50 $= f = 7$
50 to 80 $= f = 18$
80 to 150 $= f = 13$
150 and up $= f = 18$

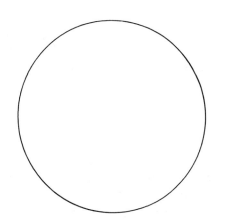

The Ristau Company imported sixty upholstery machines for use in their furniture factory. The machines were listed at $800 each in the catalogue of the Kreger Company. Kreger Company shipped the merchandise F.O.B. shipping point. They also offered the Ristau Company a 10 percent trade discount because of the size of the order. Terms of 2/10,n/30 EOM were also extended by the Kreger Company for early payment. The purchase was made on July 26, 1986. The delivery was made to the location of Ristau's home office on August 10 with an invoice date of August 8. The Ristau Company made the payment for the sixty machines on September 6, 1986.

When the machines entered the country, a $100 specific duty and a 5 percent ad valorem duty was imposed on the invoice amount.

The Kreger Company paid their sales representative a 7 percent commission on the sale of the machines. It was the largest single order they had ever received.

The machines were installed on August 23. This date will be used to depreciate the machines.

Each machine cost $50 to install.

The machines are estimated to have an expected life of ten years. They are also expected to have a salvage value of $100 each at the end of their expected life.

The firm uses the S.O.Y.D. method to compute depreciation. The fiscal year ends on December 1.

Determine the total depreciation on the sixty machines for the second fiscal year ending December 1, 1987.

A Mini Calculator Selection and Operation

Ten years ago most students and businesspeople solved business math problems by using the skills they had learned and by putting their problems on paper. The only other option was an expensive, large, semiportable desk-model calculator. Today, the mini calculator, a small, highly portable battery-operated device, usually priced under $25, is available. This offers the student and businessperson a much better means to solve business math problems. Through the advances of technology, the student is able to take a large amount of the long and tedious efforts out of the "arithmetic" aspect of business math. More effort can be placed on understanding the "why" of business math.

The mini calculator has earned a place in the business world and is being used more as an aid to learning in the classroom. Some cautions should be stated, however. This device should not be used in the first three chapters of this book— Rebuilding the Fundamentals. These skill areas are necessary for an understanding of the operation of the mini calculator and for working problems out when the calculator is not available.

Selection

When selecting a mini calculator for business math, the student should look for a model that has: (1) the four mathematical functions, (2) a floating decimal, and (3) an eight-place readout. Other features that may interest the student are the constant and the accumulating memory. This device can be purchased for $25 or less.

Operation

The fundamental operations on the calculator are performed just as you would state the problem. Press the keys on the calculator as you say the problem.

3 plus 9 equals 12

84 divided by 2 equals 42

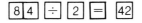

With the floating decimal feature, the decimal point is automatically placed by the machine.

42.07 times .36 equals 15.1452

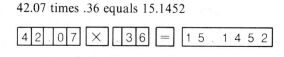

54.06 minus 18.561 equals 35.499

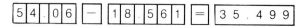

Fractions can be added and subtracted by finding the decimal equivalent of each fraction and then performing the addition or subtraction.

$\frac{3}{4}$ minus $\frac{5}{8}$ equals

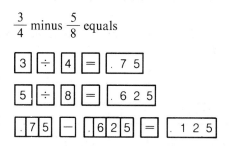

Fractions in problems with whole numbers can be done by using the following example.

$$147 \times \frac{3}{8} = 147 \times 3 = 441 \div 8 = 55.125$$

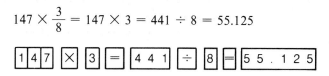

Multiple function problems are also done as they are read.

$$\frac{(3.18 \times \frac{1}{4}) + 27}{1.6} =$$

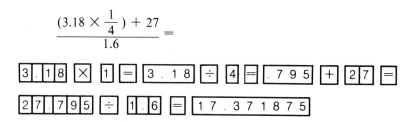

Memory

A memory feature can allow the operator to do a part of a problem, store the answer, and then retrieve the stored answer later. This is helpful when solved information is needed in conjunction with another part of the problem. The memory portion of the mini calculator usually has four keys: an M+ key for adding a value to memory, an M− key for subtracting a value from memory, an RM key for memory recall, and a CM key for clearing the memory. The problems below will show the advantages of the memory feature.

$$\frac{47 \times 16.5}{8.3 + 9.6} =$$

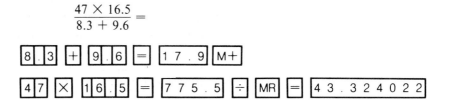

The memory function saves writing down partial answers, errors in copying, and time!

$$(75.67 - 8.06) - (85 \times .1687)$$

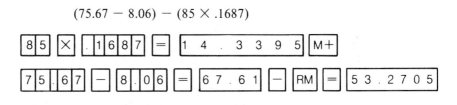

The operation of mini calculators differs slightly from one to another. You should consult the instruction pamphlet accompanying your unit or the instructions on the back panel of the unit.

Use the problems above to check the operation of your own mini calculator.

B Math Shortcuts

Interest-Time Shortcuts

When the interest rate and the time factor are considered together, a shortcut method for computing interest can be used. This method is often termed the 6 percent/sixty-day or 4 percent/ninety-day method. It is especially useful when a mini calculator is not available.

If a promissory note is negotiated for $1,868 at 6 percent for sixty days, the rate and time factors $\left(.06 \times \frac{60}{360}\right)$ can be reduced to .01 $\Big($i.e.,

$$\frac{\overset{.01}{\cancel{.06}}}{1} \times \frac{\overset{1}{\cancel{60}}}{\underset{\underset{1}{\cancel{6}}}{\cancel{360}}} = .01\Big).$$ This factor multiplied by the principal will yield the interest

amount. In this problem the interest amount would be $18.68. By moving the decimal point in the principal amount two places to the left, we have determined the interest amount.

The same approach is used with a problem using 4 percent and ninety days.

$$I = P \times R \times T$$

$$I = \$16,520 \times \overset{.01}{\cancel{.04}} \times \frac{\overset{1}{\cancel{90}}}{\underset{4}{\cancel{360}}} = \$165.20 \text{ interest}$$

Not all promissory notes are at the stated rates or time periods as those in the problems above. The shortcut can still be used with some adjustments.

Problem: $I = P \times R \times T$

$$I = \$1,568 \times .06 \times \frac{90}{360}$$

$$\left(.06 \times \frac{60}{360}\right) = .01 \quad
\begin{aligned}
60 \text{ days} &= \$15.68\text{—interest} \\
30 \text{ days} &= \underline{7.84}\text{—interest one half the time pe-} \\
& \text{riod} = \text{one half the interest} \\
90 \text{ days} &= \$23.52\text{—total interest}
\end{aligned}$$

The same type of thinking can be applied to similar problems.

Problem: I = P × R × T

$$I = \$450 \times .08 \times \frac{90}{360}$$

$$\left(.04 \times \frac{90}{360}\right) = .01$$

(4%/90 days) = \$4.50—interest
+ (4%/90 days) =   4.50—interest
Interest (8%/90 days) = \$9.00

The application can become even more interesting as well as a challenge to the problem solver.

Problem: I = P × R × T

$$I = \$4,840 \times .075 \times \frac{90}{360}$$

(6%/60 days) interest	\$48.40
(6%/30 days) interest	+ 24.20
(6%/90 days) interest	\$72.60
$\left(1\frac{1}{2}\%/90 \text{ days} = \frac{1}{4} \text{ of } 6\%/90 \text{ days}\right)$	+ 18.15
interest	
Interest $\left(7\frac{1}{2}\%/90 \text{ days}\right)$	\$90.75

Problem: I = P × R × T

$$I = \$1,570 \times .08 \times \frac{135}{360}$$

(4%/90 days) interest	\$15.70
(4%/90 days) interest	+ 15.70
(8%/90 days) interest	\$31.40
$\left(8\%/45 \text{ days} = \frac{1}{2} \text{ of } 8\%/90 \text{ days}\right)$ interest	+ 15.70
Interest (8%/135 days)	\$47.10

Aliquot Parts

Another shortcut method used in business problems is termed aliquot parts. This method makes use of the fractional parts of 100. Knowledge of fractions and their decimal equivalents is very useful here. The table below may serve as a refresher.

Common Fraction	Decimal Equivalent	Common Fraction	Decimal Equivalent
$\frac{1}{25}$	.04	$\frac{1}{6}$	.166
$\frac{1}{20}$	.05	$\frac{1}{5}$	.2
$\frac{1}{12}$	.0833	$\frac{1}{4}$	.25
$\frac{1}{11}$	.099	$\frac{1}{2}$	.5
$\frac{1}{10}$	.1	$\frac{5}{6}$	.833
$\frac{1}{9}$	.111	$\frac{3}{8}$	.375
$\frac{1}{8}$	.125	$\frac{5}{8}$	.625
$\frac{1}{7}$	.14285	$\frac{7}{8}$	.875

The clear advantage of aliquot parts becomes evident when the student can visualize the shortcut's use and then do the problem in his or her head.

Problem: What is the total price of 680 units of a product to be sold at 25¢ each?

25¢ is equal to $\frac{1}{4}$ of $1.00; $\frac{1}{4}$ of 680 = 170 or $170

Problem: What is the cost per unit of 750 units produced at a total cost of $1,860?

750 units equals $\frac{3}{4}$ of 1,000; $\frac{3}{4}$ of $1,860 = $\frac{\$1,395}{1,000}$ or $1.395 each

Problem: A product is priced at $28. Twenty percent of the product price is packaging cost. What is the packaging cost?

$20\% = \frac{1}{5}$ of $28 = $5.60

C Math of Computers

Throughout this text we have been using a numbering system termed the decimal system. This system has a base of 10. It uses the digits 0 through 9. Once ten units have been counted, the decimal system records that ten by placing a one in the column to the left. Each place value counts ten units of the position to the right. This system works well for most quantitative problem-solving methods, but not in the computer. The computer operates using only two digits, 0 and 1, because it has only "on-off" or "yes-no" capability. Hence, there is the need for only two digits. This number system is termed the binary system because of the use of two (bi) digits.

Below is a conversion table of decimal numbers to binary numbers.

Decimal Numbers (Base 10)	Binary Numbers (Base 2)
0	0
1	1 (2^0 power $= 1$)
2	10 (2^1 power $= 2$)
3	11 (2^1 power $+ 2^1$ power $= 3$)
4	100 (2^2 power $= 4$)
5	101 (2^2 power $+ 2^0$ power $= 5$)
6	110
7	111
8	1000
9	1001
10	1010
11	1011
12	1100
13	1101
14	1110
15	1111
16	10000
17	10001
18	10010
19	10011
20	10100

Notice that each one is a power of two. Each position to the right increases the power by one.

Converting binary to decimal

Problem: $100000 = 2^5$ power $= 32$

Problem: $10100 = 2^4$ power $(16) + 2^2$ power $(4) = 20$

Problem: $1011000 = 2^6$ power $(64) + 2^4$ power $(16) + 2^3$ power $(8) = 88$

Converting decimal to binary

Problem: $23 = 10111$ binary   That is, 2^4 power $(16) + 2^2$ power $(4) + 2^1$ power $(2) + 2^0$ power (1)

Problem: $17 = 10001$ binary   That is, 2^4 power $(16) + 2^0$ power (1)

Problem: $67 = 1000011$ binary   That is, 2^6 power $(64) + 2^1$ power $(2) + 2^0$ power (1)

Decimal numbers can be converted to binary by dividing the decimal number by two until the dividend is zero. The remainder, placed in reverse order, is the binary number.

Problem: Convert 259 decimal into binary

```
2) 259          Remainder
2) 129            1
2) 64             1
2) 32             0
2) 16             0
2) 8              0
2) 4              0
2) 2              0
2) 1              0
   0              1
```

259 decimal equals 100000011 binary

Problem: Convert 123 decimal into binary

```
2) 123          Remainder
2) 61             1
2) 30             1
2) 15             0
2) 7              1
2) 3              1
2) 1              1
   0              1
```

123 decimal equals 1111011 binary

D Employment Math Test

Often business firms use a mathematics test as a screening device in personnel selection. The skill of mathematics as well as logic ability is measured in a mathematics test. Some of the types of problems used on employment tests are shown below.

Arithmetic Progression

This type of problem tests logic more than mathematical skills. The applicant is tested on his or her ability to see an arithmetic pattern and extend that pattern to the blank space.

Problem: 2, 4, 8, 16, 32, _____
The pattern in this problem is to double the previous number. The blank would be filled with a 64.

Problem: 5, 10, 50, 100, 500, 1,000, _____
The pattern in this problem is to multiply the first value by 2, the next value by 5, and then repeat this pattern. The blank should be filled with 5,000.

Problem: 60, 30, 15, 20, 10, 5, 10, _____
The pattern is ÷ by 2, ÷ by 2, add 5. The blank should be filled with a 5 (÷ by 2).

Problems:
 1. 72, 70, 66, 64, 60, 58, 54, 52, _____
 2. 80, 70, 61, 53, 46, 40, _____
 3. 360, 180, 60, 30, _____
 4. 4,000, 800, 200, 40, 10, _____
 5. 6,720, 840, 120, 20, 4, _____
 6. 68, 61, 63, 56, 58, 51, 53, _____
 7. 600, 300, 100, 25, _____
 8. 72, 76, 73, 75, 79, 76, 78, 82, 79, _____
 9. 8, 40, 10, 30, 15, _____
10. 3, 9, 27, 108, 432, _____

Find the answers below.

1.	48	6.	46
2.	35	7.	5
3.	10	8.	81
4.	2	9.	15
5.	1	10.	1,296

A Sample Employment Math Test

An employer may ask you to take a test to determine your math skills. This is legal if math will be part of your actual job performance (bona fide occupational skill). The problems below are a sampling of the type that you may encounter on such a test. Test your skill. (See your instructor for answers to these problems.)

1. Add $\frac{1}{7}$, $\frac{1}{8}$, $\frac{1}{21}$, $\frac{1}{14}$

   (a) $\frac{57}{83}$ (b) $\frac{65}{168}$ (c) $\frac{15}{32}$ (d) $1\frac{13}{97}$

2. A photocopy machine can run 390 copies in one half hour. How many copies can be run in $3\frac{1}{4}$ hours?

   (a) 2,535   (b) 1,268   (c) 1,860   (d) 2,350

3. To drive from Billerston to Dillworth takes $15\frac{1}{2}$ hours. The same trip by bus takes $27\frac{3}{4}$ hours. How much time is saved by driving?

   (a) $3\frac{3}{4}$ (b) $43\frac{1}{4}$ (c) $12\frac{3}{4}$ (d) $12\frac{1}{4}$

4. Sarah plans to save 10 percent of her salary each week. When she has saved enough she will buy a bond for $375. Her salary is $130 weekly. How many weeks will she need to work before she can buy her first bond?
   (a) 27   (b) 4,875   (c) 26   (d) 29

5. A women's apparel shop has 4,368 units in stock. Half of the stock is slacks, $\frac{1}{8}$ is sweaters, $\frac{1}{16}$ is belts and scarves. How many units are not included above?
   (a) 3,003   (b) 1,365   (c) 1,638   (d) 2,965

6. The receiving department uses forty-three inspection forms each day. How many days will a six-gross inventory last?
   (a) 20   (b) 18   (c) 0   (d) 36

7. $\frac{1}{2}$ of $\frac{3}{8}$ of a stock of pens have been used in the past ten days. The total inventory was 862. What is the daily usage rate?
   (a) 162   (b) 32   (c) 46   (d) 16

8. $3\frac{5}{8} \times 17\frac{1}{4} =$

   (a) $62\frac{17}{32}$ (b) $13\frac{5}{8}$ (c) $50\frac{11}{32}$ (d) $73\frac{7}{16}$

9. 280 of the employees are in the painting department. They represent 40 percent of the total labor force. How many are in the labor force?
(a) 112   (b) 11,200   (c) 700   (d) 168

10. 140 percent of x is 1,344. What is x?
(a) 1,882   (b) 538   (c) 188   (d) 960

11. The Wilkum Company bought $630 of merchandise. They were able to deduct a 10 percent discount. What was the net amount due?
(a) $693   (b) $63   (c) $567   (d) $630

12. A train averages sixty-three miles per hour. The departure time was 9:20 P.M. How far had it gone by midnight?
(a) 168 miles   (b) 924 miles   (c) 147 miles   (d) 146 miles

13. A merchant purchased a lamp at $17 and marked it up by 30 percent over the cost. What was the amount of the markup?
(a) $11.90   (b) $22.10   (c) $5.10   (d) $10.20

14. An employee, Jack Terril, earns a commission of $3 \frac{1}{4}$ percent on sales. His sales were $43,680. What was the commission?
(a) $1,419.60   (b) $1,310.40   (c) $1,683   (d) $15,387.68

15. If the interest on a promissory note for $500 is $6.67 for thirty days, what was the interest rate?
(a) 10.3%   (b) 5.8%   (c) 16%   (d) 12%

16. Bill earned a commission of $463 this week. This was a 30 percent increase over last week. What was last week's earnings?
(a) $601.90   (b) $356.15   (c) $324.10   (d) $138.90

17. Janis typed fourteen more letters today than did Karen. This represented a 20 percent increase over Karen's output. What was Karen's output?
(a) 56   (b) 70   (c) 84   (d) 280

18. A farmer plowed a field at the rate of $2 \frac{1}{4}$ acres per hour. How many acres will he plow in $3 \frac{1}{2}$ hours?
(a) $5 \frac{3}{4}$ (b) $7 \frac{7}{8}$ (c) $8 \frac{3}{4}$ (d) $9 \frac{1}{8}$

19. Of the 465 students enrolled in a school, ninety-three were ill with the flu. What percent were ill?
(a) 20%   (b) 93%   (c) 50%   (d) 30%

20. If a 20 percent discount on an invoice saved a firm $79, what was the original amount of the invoice?
(a) $158   (b) $15.80   (c) $395   (d) $98.75

21. One hundred sixteen people registered for a workshop on energy conservation. One fourth were late registrants. The early registrants showed a two-to-one male to female relationship. How many of the early registrants were males?
(a) 15   (b) 47   (c) 58   (d) 37

22. An $8.95 gallon of paint will cover 500 square feet. How much will it cost to cover the side walls of a room that measures 15 feet by 10 feet by 7 feet 6 inches high?
(a) $17.90   (b) $8.95   (c) $26.85   (d) $89.50

23. Multiply and round off to the nearest tenth: 8.63 × 5.0473
(a) 43.6   (b) 43.5   (c) 13.7   (d) 37.8

24. A pool measuring 20 feet by 40 feet by 5 feet deep must be filled with water. How many hours will be required if it will fill at the rate of 900 gallons an hour? There are $7\frac{1}{2}$ gallons in a cubic foot.
(a) 33   (b) 4   (c) 23   (d) 31

25. Jim processes forty reports a day, which is 25 percent more than Tom's output. How many does Tom process?
(a) 65   (b) 50   (c) 32   (d) 30

26. Mark had $3,957 in his savings account. He bought a new motorcycle for $1,680. What percent of his savings was left after the purchase?
(a) 58%   (b) 47%   (c) 42%   (d) 43%

27. If wheat sold for $3.60 a year ago and sells for $4.25 today, what is the percent of increase?
(a) 118%   (b) 18%   (c) 85%   (d) 15%

Complete the following using arithmetic progression.

28. 60, 30, 15, 20, 10, 5, 10, _____
(a) 10   (b) 0   (c) 5   (d) 15

29. 5, 10, 30, 120, _____
(a) 600   (b) 240   (c) 60   (d) 480

30. 72, 76, 73, 75, 79, 76, 78, 82, 79, _____
(a) 76   (b) 83   (c) 81   (d) 77

Appendix **E**

Reading Market Quotations

The price of stocks and bonds are printed in the business section of most newspapers. The price as well as its activity in the market are of interest to investors. A sample of a stock exchange report found in a newspaper is shown below.

52 Weeks				Yld	P-E	Sales				Net
High	Low	Stock	Div.	%	Ratio	100s	High	Low	Close	Chg.
35⅞	25⅛	Goodyr	1.60	4.6	9	2914	35⅞	34¾	34¾	− ¾
18⅝	15⅛	GordnJ	.52	2.8	25	6	18⅜	18⅛	18⅜	.....
37¾	19⅝	Gould	.68	2.4	..	1871	28⅞	28⅜	28⅝	+ ¼
57¼	35½	Grace	2.80	5.6	18	5162	51	49	49⅞	+ ⅞
42¾	28⅞	Grangr	s.68	1.6	17	326	41¾	40½	41⅜	− ⅜
29	13⅛	GtAFst	.48	1.7	8	193	28⅝	28⅛	28⅛	− ⅜
22⅞	15¼	GtAtPc	.10e	.4	10	680	u23⅛	22½	23	+ ⅛
22⅛	15	GNIrn	3.25e	14.	..	36	u22½	21⅞	22½	+ ⅜

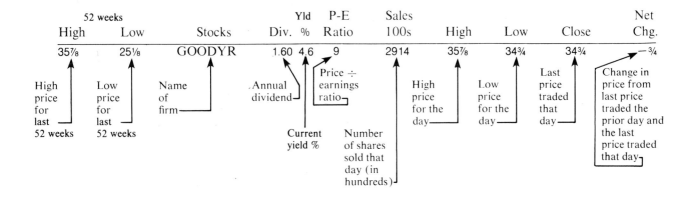

Bond prices are quoted in a similar fashion in the newspaper each business day. A sample of a **bond** exchange report is shown below.

Bonds		Cur Yld	Vol	High	Low	Close	Net Chg.
Dow	6.70s98	8.0	3	84⅛	84⅛	84⅛	− ⅜
Dow	7.75s99	8.6	3	90⅛	90⅛	90⅛	+ ⅛
Dow	8⅞2000	9.2	5	96½	96½	96½	.....
Dow	8.92000	9.2	6	96¾	96⅝	96⅝	− ⅛
Dow	7⅝s03	8.9	10	86	86	86	−1⅝
Dow	11¼10	10.	23	107½	107½	107½	.....
duPnt	8.45s04	8.9	10	95	94⅝	95	+ ½
duPnt	8½06	8.9	5	96½	95	95	+ ½
duPnt	14s91	12.	17	112½	111⅝	112½	+ ⅞
duPnt	d6s01	7.8	79	77¼	76⅜	76½	+ ⅛
duPnt	12⅞s92	12.	31	111¾	110½	110½	− ⅛
DukeP	7¾02	8.9	3	87½	87½	87½	+ ½
DukeP	8⅛03	9.0	27	91	90⅛	90⅛	+ ⅛
DukeP	9¾04	9.8	17	100⅛	99¾	99¾	−2¼
DukeP	9½05	9.5	6	99½	99½	99½	−1½
DukeP	8⅜06	9.1	61	93⅛	92⅛	92⅛	− ⅜
DukeP	8⅛07	9.1	25	89¼	89¼	89¼	− ¾
DukeP	10⅛09	9.8	5	103	103	103	−1¾
DukeP	12s90	12.	-45	103½	103	103½	.....
DuqL	5s2010	9.3	47	54	52	54	+4¼
DuqL	8¾00	9.6	5	91	91	91	+1
DuqL	9s06	9.6	36	94⅛	92½	93¾	+1½
DuqL	8⅜s07	9.7	2	86½	86½	86½	.....
DuqL	10⅛09	10.	10	100½	100½	100½	+ ½
DuqL	16s11	14.	2	111⅝	111⅝	111⅝	+ ⅜
ECL	9s89f	..	x12	59⅞	57⅝	59⅞	+3⅜
EasAir	5s92	cv	74	59	59	59	.....
EasAir	4¾93	cv	32	59	59	59	+ ½
EasAir	11½99	cv	1066	84	82⅛	83⅞	+2⅜
EasAir	11¾05	cv	307	88	87	87½	+1¼
EasAir	17½97	15.	69	114	112	113	+2

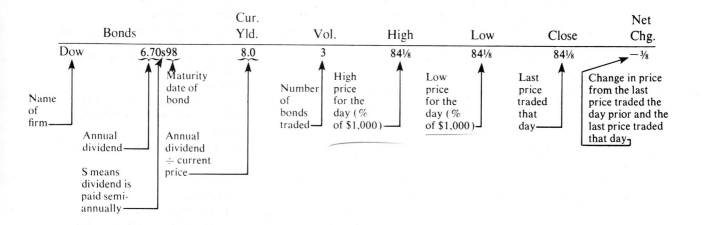

		Cur.					Net
Bonds		Yld.	Vol.	High	Low	Close	Chg.
Dow	6.70s98	8.0	3	84⅛	84⅛	84⅛	− ⅜

Name of firm

Annual dividend

S means dividend is paid semi-annually

Maturity date of bond

Annual dividend ÷ current price

Number of bonds traded

High price for the day (% of $1,000)

Low price for the day (% of $1,000)

Last price traded that day

Change in price from the last price traded the day prior and the last price traded that day

Glossary

A

Accumulated Depreciation

The amount that the asset has depreciated to date.

Accelerated Cost Recovery System (A.C.R.S.)

A depreciation method established for use beginning 1981. For tax use.

Adjusted Balance

The actual amount available in the checking account at a point in time.

Ad Valorem

A type of customs duty that is a percent of the market value.

Amortizing

Paying off a loan by making monthly payments.

Assessed Valuation

The base on which property taxes are computed.

Assets

Items that are owned by a firm.

B

Balance Sheet

A summary of the financial condition of a firm at a point in time.

Balloon Payment

A single payment due on a home mortgage at the end of one to five years, although payments are based on a longer term.

Base

The basis of comparison; the number of which so many hundredths is taken.

Beneficiary

The person or organization that will receive the financial benefits of a life insurance policy.

Book Value

The total cost of an asset less the accumulated depreciation.

C

C.O.D. (Cash on Delivery)

The merchandise delivered by this method must be paid for when it is received.

Cash Discount

A reduction of the price of the merchandise offered to the buyer for early payment.

Check

A demand by a depositor on his or her bank to pay the payee the amount specified.

Closing

The meeting when buyer, seller, and lender meet to sign documents and exchange monies due.

Coinsurance

The policy holder and the insurance company share in the financial loss of property damage.

Common Carrier

A transportation firm that is authorized to carry freight over routes on established schedules and at approved rates. The federal government is the authorizing agent.

Common Fraction

A type of fraction in which the numerator is smaller than the denominator.

Compound Interest

The interest earned in one period is added to the principal. Interest for the next period is calculated on both interest and principal from the previous period.

Contract Carrier

An independent transportation firm that has negotiable rates, schedules, and routes.

Cost Price

The price that the retailer pays for goods.

D

Deductions

Amounts subtracted from gross pay for such items as taxes, contributions, and savings.

Denominator

The number on the bottom of a fraction.

Deposit

A sum of money that adds to the balance of a checking and savings account.

Depreciation

An adjustment in the value of an asset due to its decline in market value. An estimate.

Dividends

Profits distributed to shareholder owners of a corporation.

E

E.O.M. (End of Month)

A portion of terms of trade for a cash discount.

Endorsement

The signature of the payee on the back of the check. There are several types of endorsements.

Escrow Account

An account kept by the lending institution that the borrower pays into in order to accumulate enough money to pay property taxes and property insurance when they come due.

Exemptions

Legal dependents and the employee; can be claimed by the employee in order to reduce the amount of income tax withheld.

Expenses

Used up or expired assets.

F

F.I.F.O. (First In-First Out)

A method of determining the value of ending inventory or cost of goods sold.

Fixed Payment

Payment amount on a home mortgage is a set or fixed amount for the term of the loan.

Fixed Rate

Rate remains the same, fixed, over the term of the loan. Usually home mortgage.

F.O.B. (Free on Board)

The merchandise will be placed on the transportation vehicle free.

Face Value

The amount stated on a promissory note. The amount borrowed.

G

Goods Available for Sale

Beginning inventory plus net purchases. The cost of goods sold comes from this category.

Gross Earning

The amount earned by the employee in a pay period.

Gross Sales

All the sales of a firm for a time period.

H

Home Mortgage

An installment loan on a home. Loan may carry a fixed or variable rate, fixed or variable payment, or a balloon payment.

I

Income Statement

A report that shows the financial activity of a firm over a period of time.

Inflation

An increase in the price of most goods and services.

Interest

A financial return to the lender for the risks undertaken during the term of the loan.

L

L.I.F.O. (Last in-First out)

A method of determining the value of ending inventory or cost of goods sold.

Liabilities

Amounts due others; financed obligations.

List Price

The price shown in a catalog. This price is often subject to trade discounts.

M

Markup

An amount added to the cost price of merchandise in order to cover overhead and profit. Can be based on cost or selling price.

Markdown

An amount or percent subtracted from the selling price.

Mean

The average of a data set.

Median

The middle ranked value of a data set.

Mills

A means of expressing one thousandths.

Mixed Number

A type of a fraction consisting of a whole number and a common fraction.

Mode

The value of greatest frequency in a data set.

N

Net Pay

The amount due a person after deductions are subtracted from gross pay.

Net Sales

The dollar value of sales after sales returns and sales allowances are subtracted from gross sales.

Numerator

The number on top in a fraction.

P

Payroll Record

A form showing gross earnings, deductions, and net pay for all employees.

Percent

A means of expressing some part of 100.

Percentage

The result of taking so many hundredths of the base.

Points

A percent of the face value of the loan. Usually paid by the buyer at closing.

Policy

A contractual document explaining the financial commitment of an insurance company to the policy holder.

Premium

A payment amount for insurance protection.

Present Value

The current value of an investment due some date in the future. The present value is found by discounting back the future value at prevailing interest rates.

Principal

The amount borrowed.

Proceeds

The amount due the payee when the note is discounted.

Product

The result of multiplication/the answer.

R

Rate

A percent.

Rate of Return

The amount earned on an investment expressed as a percent of the amount invested.

R.O.G. (Receipt of Goods)

A portion of terms of trade for a cash discount.

Repayment Schedule

A record of payments made, interest amounts, and the principal balance.

Revenue

The result of selling goods or sevices.

S

Sales Allowances

Adjustments made in the price of the merchandise in order to compensate the buyer for keeping damaged or wrong merchandise.

Sales Returns

Merchandise returned to the seller due to damage, errors in ordering, etc.

Selling Price

The price that the buyer (consumer) pays for the goods.

Service Charges

Expenses charged to the depositor by the bank for use of the account, imprinting of checks, etc.

Sinking Fund

The accumulation of payments into an interest-paying investment in order to provide a desired amount to the firm at a future date.

Specific Duty

A type of customs duty. A flat amount per unit.

Sum

The amount resulting from the addition of two or more numbers.

T

Term of Note

The number of days between the date of the note and the due date.

Time

Used to compute interest or discounts. Usually a fraction of 360 days (ordinary interest) or 365 (exact interest).

Total Depreciation

The amount that the asset will depreciate over its expected life.

Trade Discount

A reduction of the list price to the buyer based on large quantity purchases or the assumption of marketing functions by the buyer.

Turnover

The number of times that the average inventory is sold. A measure of success for the retailer.

V

Variable Payment Amount

Payment on a home mortgage begins low and increases in time. May cause loan balance to increase in early years.

Variable Rate

Interest rate changes based on an index of interest indicators—usually government securities.

Z

Zero Bracket Amount

A non-taxable amount used in computing federal income tax.

Answers to the Student Edition

Chapter One
(Pages 3–24)

Exercise A

1. 8   4. 0
2. 2   5. 1
3. 3

Exercise B

1. Thousands
2. Hundred thousands
3. Tens
4. Hundreds
5. Ten thousands

Exercise C

1. One thousand, six hundred ninety-seven and no/100
2. Five thousand, eight hundred forty-three and no/100
3. One hundred sixty-five and no/100

Exercise D

1. 98,000
2. 2,640
3. 278,900

Exercise E

1. $1,900,000
2. $630,000
3. $320,000,000

Exercise F

A. 1. 124
    2. 53
    3. 112
    4. 219
    5. 90
    6. 106
    7. 99
B. 1. 4,344
    2. 115,459
    3. 75,681
    4. 91,427
    5. 18,253
C. 1. $8,116
    2. $92,131
    3. $16,417
    4. $76,901
    5. $89,140
D. 1. $114,635
    2. $11,565
    3. $84,744
    4. $27,935
    5. $23,980

Exercise G

Patterson 2,576
Atkins 384
Larson 572
Willis 3,254
Swix 1,732
Smith 365
Bowersox 2,831
Johnson 2,468
Sommers 1,779
Kreger 3,510

Monday 4,111
Tuesday 4,122
Wednesday 3,531
Thursday 3,984
Friday 3,723
Week 19,471

Exercise H

A. 1. 19
    2. 68
    3. 24
    4. 42
    5. 28
    6. 16
    7. 62
B. 1. $17
    2. $36
    3. $160
    4. $138
    5. $86
    6. $47
C. 1. $174
    2. $98
    3. $437
    4. $155
    5. $64
    6. $544

Exercise I

1278—$906, $286
1279—$286, $186
1280—$186, $117
1281—$117, $70
1282—$590, $526

Exercise J

A. 1. 67,300
   2. 89,200
   3. 5,460
   4. 891,000
   5. 8,940
B. 1. 8,190
   2. 96,100
   3. 5,700
   4. 46,900
   5. 162,000
C. 1. $1,860,408
   2. $4,250,224
   3. $4,907,034
   4. $1,622,534
D. 1. $2,339,865
   2. $2,937,725
   3. $2,012,799
   4. $138,678

Exercise K

$94
$279
$534
$46
$108
$27
$102
$120
$144
$192
$82
$104
$42
$100
$70
$60
$64
$126
$50
$20
$12
$48
$36
$68
$2,528

Exercise L

1. 157
2. 1,334
3. 118
4. 3,489 R32

5. 421
6. 2,033 R33
7. 224 R364
8. 19 R11

Exercise M

1. 7,930
2. 80,006,300
3. 906
4. 891
5. 537,205

Assignment

Skill Problems

1. 9,999
3. $26,628
5. 17 R23
7. $4,729
9. $141,982 R10
11. 19,400
13. 47,280
15. $60,991,140
17. $32,571
19. Four hundred eighty-three thousand, three hundred twenty dollars

Business Application Problems

1. $16,498
3. $243
5. 1,071
7. College
9. $900
11. $157,509
13. 5
15. 48,028
17. 327
19. $2,921

Mastery Test

1. 54,400
2. $10,873
3. $830,079
4. 4,214 R7
5. $10,773
6. 102,663
7. 19 R8
8. $6,249,488
9. 680
10. $326,723
11. $197,217

12. Forty-three thousand, six hundred seventy-nine dollars
13. $370,000
14. $11,760
15. 685,200

Chapter Two
(Pages 27-54)

Exercise A

1. common
2. improper
3. improper
4. improper
5. mixed
6. common
7. improper
8. common
9. common
10. common
11. mixed
12. mixed

Exercise B

1. $1\frac{5}{8}$
2. $5\frac{7}{12}$
3. $2\frac{4}{5}$
4. $3\frac{5}{14}$
5. $3\frac{1}{6}$
6. $2\frac{1}{2}$
7. $2\frac{1}{9}$
8. $9\frac{3}{10}$
9. $4\frac{3}{10}$
10. $1\frac{1}{8}$
11. 4
12. $7\frac{1}{8}$

Exercise C

1. $\dfrac{27}{4}$
2. $\dfrac{59}{6}$
3. $\dfrac{39}{5}$
4. $\dfrac{15}{8}$
5. $\dfrac{551}{5}$
6. $\dfrac{7}{2}$
7. $\dfrac{147}{8}$
8. $\dfrac{20}{3}$
9. $\dfrac{19}{4}$
10. $\dfrac{3}{2}$
11. $\dfrac{87}{16}$
12. $\dfrac{21}{2}$

Exercise D

1. $\dfrac{1}{2}$
2. $\dfrac{3}{4}$
3. $\dfrac{7}{10}$
4. $\dfrac{2}{5}$
5. $\dfrac{1}{2}$
6. $\dfrac{7}{8}$
7. $\dfrac{11}{25}$
8. $\dfrac{1}{2}$
9. $\dfrac{3}{4}$
10. $\dfrac{3}{5}$
11. $\dfrac{8}{11}$
12. $\dfrac{3}{8}$

Exercise E

1. 15
2. 33
3. 90
4. 28
5. 15
6. 27
7. 16
8. 5
9. 410
10. 12
11. 15
12. 5

Exercise F

1. $1\dfrac{1}{12}$
2. $2\dfrac{1}{8}$
3. $1\dfrac{16}{105}$
4. $2\dfrac{3}{8}$
5. $1\dfrac{1}{35}$
6. $1\dfrac{11}{40}$
7. $1\dfrac{11}{60}$
8. $1\dfrac{37}{80}$
9. $1\dfrac{1}{16}$
10. $1\dfrac{13}{14}$

Exercise G

1. $\dfrac{5}{8}$
2. $\dfrac{3}{8}$
3. $\dfrac{7}{30}$
4. $\dfrac{1}{20}$
5. $\dfrac{113}{180}$
6. $\dfrac{11}{24}$
7. $\dfrac{7}{36}$

8. $\dfrac{5}{12}$
9. $\dfrac{51}{80}$
10. $\dfrac{5}{16}$

Exercise H

1. $15\dfrac{1}{4}$
2. $14\dfrac{7}{24}$
3. $5\dfrac{1}{16}$
4. $10\dfrac{23}{24}$
5. $11\dfrac{4}{5}$
6. $8\dfrac{67}{72}$
7. $24\dfrac{81}{100}$
8. $8\dfrac{17}{24}$
9. $15\dfrac{11}{12}$
10. $17\dfrac{19}{24}$

Exercise I

1. $7\dfrac{1}{3}$
2. $2\dfrac{1}{4}$
3. $5\dfrac{11}{40}$
4. $52\dfrac{23}{24}$
5. $2\dfrac{11}{30}$
6. $5\dfrac{1}{40}$
7. $6\dfrac{7}{12}$
8. $173\dfrac{1}{6}$
9. $3\dfrac{1}{12}$
10. $6\dfrac{11}{18}$

Exercise J

1. $\frac{1}{6}$

2. $\frac{77}{80}$

3. $\frac{5}{8}$

4. $\frac{5}{42}$

5. $\frac{1}{2}$

6. $\frac{7}{18}$

7. $3\frac{1}{4}$

8. $19\frac{19}{24}$

9. $\frac{25}{84}$

10. $\frac{13}{224}$

Exercise K

1. $1\frac{5}{7}$

2. $1\frac{1}{2}$

3. $1\frac{5}{7}$

4. $2\frac{1}{2}$

5. $1\frac{11}{16}$

6. $1\frac{2}{7}$

7. $3\frac{1}{2}$

8. 6

9. $4\frac{2}{7}$

10. $1\frac{1}{4}$

Exercise L

1. $106\frac{47}{256}$

2. $4\frac{5}{7}$

3. $4\frac{2}{13}$

4. 4

5. $1\frac{71}{84}$

6. $2\frac{53}{76}$

7. $10\frac{19}{35}$

8. $1\frac{83}{162}$

Exercise M

1. 3:2
2. 1:10
3. 4:1
4. 5:3
5. 5:2
6. 1:4

Assignment

Skill Problems

1. $1\frac{5}{8}$

3. $\frac{1}{2}$

5. $\frac{1}{30}$

7. $2\frac{9}{40}$

9. $6\frac{3}{8}$

11. $6\frac{7}{8}$

13. $\frac{7}{24}$

15. $7\frac{1}{2}$

17. $\frac{3}{14}$

19. $2\frac{1}{4}$

21. $\frac{8}{75}$

23. $1\frac{1}{8}$

Business Application
Problems

1. $210
3. 2
5. 5:1
7. $271,835
9. 4:1
11. $6

13. $\frac{1}{16}$

15. 30,488

17. $227\frac{7}{10}$

19. 130

Mastery Test

1. Whole number (8), numerator (4), denominator (7).
2. 1. B
   2. A
   3. C
   4. A
   5. B
   6. C

3. $1\frac{11}{20}$

4. $\frac{5}{6}$

5. 50

6. $4\frac{3}{8}$

7. $5\frac{1}{3}$

8. $147,720

9. 9:1

10. $5\frac{2}{5}$

11. $28,980
12. $78
13. 270

Chapter Three
(Pages 57-74)

Exercise A

1. 7
2. 8
3. 5
4. 3
5. 2
6. 9

Exercise B

1. hundred thousandths
2. hundredths
3. millionths
4. ten thousandths
5. tenths
6. thousandths

Exercise C

Reading

Exercise D

Reading

Exercise E
1. Eight hundred twenty-three dollars and sixty-seven cents
2. Two thousand, one hundred five dollars and forty-six cents
3. Eight hundred sixty-seven dollars and twenty-eight cents
4. Two hundred thirty-four dollars and eighty-seven cents
5. Three thousand, eight hundred sixty-nine dollars and sixty-one cents

Exercise F
1. $935.49
2. $63.26
3. $572.21
4. $3,018.07
5. $51,307.36

Exercise G
1. .6
2. .47
3. .0
4. .546
5. 1

Exercise H
1. $605.84
2. $5,867.95
3. $486.94
4. $68,640.27
5. $375.97

Exercise I
1. 607.80
2. 800
3. 759.9
4. 550,000
5. 64,983.99

Exercise J
1. 15,576.1975
2. 889.1357
3. 745.22646
4. 1,165.7941
5. 55,864.261

Exercise K
1. 612,026.0913
2. 346.2974
3. 79.8762
4. 502.2
5. 158,463.0286

Exercise L
1. 7.530
2. 16.433
3. .4383
4. 56.043
5. 41.863

Exercise M
1. $835.49
2. $530.05
3. $48.17
4. $596.99
5. $278.92

Exercise N
1. 8,445.2
2. .5696
3. 49.53
4. .07035
5. 2.754

Exercise O
1. 35.7
2. .4
3. 308.7
4. 1.7
5. 0

Exercise P
1. .375
2. .6
3. .3125
4. 2.4
5. 2.1875

Assignment

Skill Problems
1. 2
3. 1,458.6557
5. .885
7. 48.8
9. 72.1589
11. 6.27
13. 29,470.143
15. 1,462.6193

Business Application Problems

1. $28.70
3. $32.66
5. $39.09
7. 14
9. $66,783.94
11. $125,819.25
13. $4.90
15. $96.89
17. $12,286.30
19. $2,227.50

Mastery Test

1. a. 10
   b. .1
   c. 600
   d. 64.097
   e. 43.9
2. Three hundred eighty-five dollars and seventy cents.
3. 755.167
4. 47.674
5. 1
6. $.47
7. a. .625 b. .3 c. 4.2
8. 19¢
9. $844,875.20
10. 10,835
11. $817.86

Chapter Four
(Pages 77-92)

Exercise A
1. restrictive
2. special
3. blank
4. blank

5. restrictive
6. restrictive
7. blank
8. special
9. blank
10. blank

Exercise B

1. $775.44
2. $159.80
3. $3,895.07
4. $1,563

Assignment

Skill Problems
1. $1,349.80
3. $790.22

Business Application Problems

1. $1,936.20
3. $142.30
5. $7
7. $331.28
9. $1,341.32
11. $2,706.63
13. $67.98
15. $338

Mastery Test

1. a. For deposit only, G.S. Student
   b. Gerry S. Student
   c. Payable to B. Instructor, G.S. Student
2. $1,197.55
3. $10.98
4. $7.40
5. $754.54

Chapter Five
(Pages 95-112)

Exercise A

1. $303.20, $0, $303.20
2. $288, $21.60, $309.60
3. $320, $12, $332
4. $424, $31.80, $455.80

5. $168, $0, $168
6. $148.20, $0, $148.20
7. $276, $10.35, $286.35

Exercise B

1. $226.20, $182.70, $408.90
2. $201.60, $0, $201.60
3. $228, $243, $471
4. $195, $15, $210
5. $144, $12, $156
6. $235.60, $195.30, $430.90
7. $273, $189, $462
8. $175.50, $74.25, $249.75

Exercise C

1. $42.90, $404.40
2. $90.33, $822.34
3. $64.21, $491.51
4. $54.11, $537.96
5. $49.64, $461.43

Exercise D

1. $16, $19.16, $232.84
2. $28, $21.95, $257.05
3. $30, $0, $266.40
4. $19, $21.64, $261.96
5. $32, $14.30, $237.48
6. $35, $0, $287
7. $25, $20.02, $234.98
8. $29, $4.29, $249.01
9. $32, $23.24, $269.76
10. $28, $24.31, $287.69

Assignment

Skill Problems
1. $228.87
3. $187.63
5. $194.61
7. $53.70, $588.83
9. $25.03, $346.98

Business Application Problems

1. $243.83
3. $96.32
5. $3,003
7. $20.72
9. $366.61
11. $269.23

13. $180.26
15. $18
17. $2,749.70

Mastery Test

1. F
2. T
3. F
4. F
5. F
6. T
7. $453.10
8. $64
9. $1,823.14
10. $244.96
11. $396
12. $208.73

Chapter Six
(Pages 115-130)

Exercise A

1. 55 yds., 1 ft., 4 ins.
2. 1 lb., $6\frac{1}{3}$ ozs.
3. 33 mins., 5 secs.
4. 424 lbs., 13 ozs.
5. 1 hr., 26 mins., 47 secs.

Exercise B

1. 27 sq. yds., 1 sq. ft., 7 sq. ins.
2. 23 sq. yds., 6 sq. ft.
3. 6 sq. yds., $7\frac{3}{4}$ sq. ft.
4. 21.76 sq. miles
5. 1 sq. yd., 7 sq. ft.

Exercise C

1. 5 cu. yds.
2. 3 cu. yds., 9 cu. ft.
3. 10 cu. yds., 24 cu. ft.
4. 20 cu. yds., 4 cu. ft.
5. 4,000 cu. ft.

Exercise D

1. 9.632
2. 8.56
3. .806329
4. 76
5. 473,570

Exercise E
1. 3.8354
2. 4.4196
3. 39.47896
4. 15.1408
5. 8.4539
6. 18.123
7. 3.1096
8. .1135749
9. 1.7577
10. 8.37748

Exercise F
1. 8.31136
2. 6.449118
3. 2.39382
4. 736.3364
5. 595.608
6. .0610312
7. 58.96464
8. 4.56
9. 5.467
10. 4.38

Assignment

Skill Problems
1. 7 yds., 2ft., 4 in.
3. 10 hrs., 8 min., 40 sec.
5. 55 cu. yds., 11 cu. ft.
7. 6.278 m.
9. 4.445 m.

Business Application
Problems

1. 4 hrs., 14 min.
3. 48
5. 200 sq. yds.
7. $133 \frac{1}{3}$ hrs.
9. $267,596

Mastery Test

1. 1 mile, 885 yds.
2. 486
3. 3
4. 56
5. 33.558352
6. 5.81096

7. 583.2
8. 3 yds., 10 in.
9. 14,300
10. $35.96
11. no
12. 11.5¢

Chapter Seven
(Pages 133-150)

Exercise A
1. .17
2. .56
3. .11
4. .09
5. 1.56

Exercise B
1. 41, .41
2. 62, 62
3. 127, 127
4. 10, 10
5. 21, .21

Exercise C
1. 8.2, .082
2. 1.375, .01375
3. .6, .006
4. 52.9, .529
5. 29.5, 29.5

Exercise D
1. 100
2. 86%
3. 26
4. 69
5. 11%
6. 500

Exercise E
1. $7.14
2. $180
3. 512%
4. $23.20
5. $7.08
6. 43%

Exercise F
1. 25
2. 10
3. 14

4. 3
5. 11
6. 935
7. $400,000
8. $115,384.61
9. 20
10. 9

Assignment

Skill Problems
1. 62
3. 64
5. .07
7. 175.9
9. 4.58
11. 7
13. 91
15. $64.80

Business Application
Problems

1. 301
3. 53%
5. 61.2
7. $24,000
9. 13%
11. $786.36
13. 2%
15. 3,600,000
17. 30%
19. $325,000

Mastery Test

1. .09
2. 87.5
3. 21
4. 9.5
5. T
6. F
7. F
8. $150
9. 2%
10. $1.88
11. $240
12. 595,000
13. 8.9%
14. $27,200,000
15. 1.2%

Chapter Eight
(Pages 153-170)

Exercise A

1. $111.60
2. $95.04
3. $194.04
4. $169.32
5. $66.83
6. $250.60
7. $132.30
8. $159
9. $138.13
10. $73.27

Exercise B

1. $11,739.13
2. $20,000
3. $5,783.13
4. $33,333.33
5. $3,000
6. $10,000
7. $80,000
8. $15,000
9. $22,500
10. $26,000

Exercise C

1. $299.60
2. $249.15
3. $2,202
4. $96
5. $1,219.80
6. $178.10
7. $538.40
8. $774.75
9. $93.40
10. $4,414.80

Exercise D

1. $78
2. $75.70
3. $69
4. $29.30
5. $108.30
6. $69
7. $55.20
8. $61.60
9. $87.20
10. $69

Assignment

Skill Problems

1. $123.60
3. $172.32
5. $219.95
7. $1,010.40
9. $406.60
11. $110.14
13. $69
15. $78
17. $35,600
19. $86,400

Business Application Problems

1. $1,923.75
3. $35,000
5. $75,000
7. $38,000
9. $29,000
11. $39,375
13. $480,000
15. $87.20

Mastery Test

1. T
2. T
3. F
4. F
5. T
6. T
7. T
8. F
9. T
10. F
11. $136.80
12. $169,000
13. $104.37
14. $27,200
15. $77.20

Chapter Nine
(Pages 173-188)

Exercise A

1. 35
2. 44
3. 83
4. 78
5. 42

Exercise B

1. March 8
2. November 26
3. August 2
4. December 28
5. March 23

Exercise C

1. $5.60
2. $9.72
3. $245
4. $13.57
5. $9.71
6. $93.33

Exercise D

1. $5.92
2. $181.23
3. $7.80
4. $11.32
5. $9.86
6. $12.95

Assignment

Skill Problems

1. 73
3. 78
5. 96
7. October 1
9. April 15
11. $500
13. $826.67
15. $1,496.25

Business Application Problems

1. $100
3. $241.64
5. Mr. Severance
7. $5,553.37
9. $4,318
11. $184.38
13. $3.77
15. $308.50

Mastery Test

1. c
2. 148
3. April 20
4. $66.67
5. $65.75
6. June 26
7. $13.44
8. $1,013.44
9. $11.63
10. $5,290.27
11. $5,037.26
12. $21.30

Chapter Ten
(Pages 191-208)

Exercise A

1. $6,662.50
2. $4,080
3. $13,785.33
4. $25,746.53
5. $9,110
6. $7,303.33
7. $8,623.96
8. $5,000
9. $61,703.33
10. $3,540

Exercise B

1. 23
2. 23
3. 69
4. 21
5. 26
6. 75
7. 22
8. 30

Exercise C

1. $453.60
2. $5,048.63
3. $1,126.58
4. $6,086.85
5. $1,849.20
6. $170.90
7. $807.81
8. $1,017.06
9. $1,020.90
10. $3,533.95

Exercise D

1. $720
2. $30.56
3. 14%
4. 27
5. $750
6. 12%
7. $212.50
8. $1,080
9. 7
10. 13%
11. $4,132.09
12. $6,000.02
13. 24
14. 12%
15. 251
16. $1,155
17. 10%
18. $4,615.38
19. 59
20. $1,757.15

Assignment

Skill Problems

1. $4,054.09
3. $753.12
5. $3,531.66
7. $6,996.09
9. $413.92
11. $7,000
13. 90
15. 23

Business Application Problems

1. $1,482.50
3. $725.28
5. $183.78
7. 7%
9. $1,221.10
11. $1,198.63
13. $2,380

Mastery Test

1. b
2. e
3. d
4. k

5. c
6. a
7. 62
8. $95.72
9. $3,609.58
10. $3,705.30
11. $54.17
12. $680
13. 10
14. 15%
15. $3,650
16. $893

Chapter Eleven
(Pages 211-244)

Exercise A

1. $38.68
   $64.07
   $77.31
2. $171.87
   $153.59
   $175.13
3. $16.87
   $53.14
   $55.47
   $46.02
4. $53
   $109.03
   $100.12
5. $36.66
   $208.53
   $212.12
   $184.24

Exercise B

1. 15.5
2. 23.0
3. $35.87
4. 14.25
5. 21.0

Exercise C

1. $209.99
2. $430.44
3. $444.50
4. $442.13
5. $437.74
6. $1,348.90
7. $549.04
8. $408.27

Exercise D
1. $381.98
2. $696.32
3. $344.82
4. $680.01
5. $929.96
6. $108.75
7. $339.31

Assignment

Skill Problems
1. $213.82
3. $232.47
5. $312.19
7. $63.55
9. $348.20
11. $18 \frac{1}{2}$ %
13. 8%
15. $33.19

Business Application
Problems

1. $304.29
3. $318.67
5. $17.04
7. $444.30
9. $126.74
11. $74,651.40
13. $66.67
15. $827.78

Mastery Test

1. True
2. False
3. True
4. $30.03
5. $482.75
6. $27,706.85
7. $156.34
8. $44.13
9. 17.5%
10. $4,997.31

Chapter Twelve
(Pages 247-273)

Exercise A
1. $1,792.12
2. $7,234.90
3. $7,550.32
4. $10,494.58
5. $43,822.46
6. $8,704.06
7. $27,057.50
8. $6,348.67
9. $12,033.10
10. $12,854.22

Exercise B
1. $1,365.58
2. $1,672.77
3. $3,905.99
4. $1,531.70
5. $624.60
6. $9,970.67
7. $5,435.70
8. $6,015.68
9. $6,736.25
10. $10,053.29

Exercise C
1. $42,576.09
2. $6,603.39
3. $15,449.34
4. $22,337.43
5. $7,423.10
6. $9,702.61
7. $11,687.27
8. $73,088.95
9. $9,581.01
10. $24,984.23

Exercise D
1. $2,046.15
2. $1,439.30
3. $7,664.70
4. $3,168.78
5. $2,419.02
6. $8,088.26
7. $8,795.56
8. $4,695.14
9. $14,384.73
10. $1,670.23

Assignment

Skill Problems
1. $7,147.51
3. $29,049.26
5. $7,139.84
7. $32,200.32
9. $4,841.60
11. $5,031.16
13. $2,970.33
15. $2,865.26
17. $7,096.01
19. $10,083.60

Business Application
Problems

1. $5,994.28
3. $4,975.53
5. $2,867.25
7. $5,811.69
9. $6,340.11
11. $384,483.96
13. $1,936,725

Mastery Test

1. $2,745.57
2. $2,981.34
3. $37,618.70
4. $7,490.68
5. $4,011.39
6. $2,498.73
7. $6,267.37
8. $24,271.84
9. $374.66
10. $8,233.49

Chapter Thirteen
(Pages 277-300)

Exercise A
1. $5,120
2. $57,562
3. $585.23
4. $4,320
5. $253.80
6. $432
7. $15,552
8. $684
9. $449.55
10. $1,796.40

Exercise B
1. $7,866
2. $4,590
3. $522.50
4. $54,432
5. $59,280
6. $6,361.20
7. $13,608
8. $1,988.35
9. $1,923.75
10. $431.11

Exercise C
1. $654.75
2. $882
3. $200
4. $51.48
5. $175
6. $1,400
7. $841.50
8. $490
9. $118.80
10. $38.12

Exercise D
1. $190
2. $150
3. $59.40
4. $735
5. $600
6. $252.20
7. $550
8. $1,514.70
9. $31.20
10. $693

Exercise E
1. $601.40
2. $83.30
3. $120
4. $450
5. $323.73
6. $693
7. $171.50
8. $76.44
9. $321.75
10. $802

Exercise F
1. $492.63
2. $1,339.20
3. $233.77

4. $704.95
5. $2,245.32

Exercise G
1. $2,067.41
2. $8.50
3. $2,619
4. $180
5. 30

Exercise H
1. $2,257.70
2. $3,559
3. $23,659.51
4. 150
5. $76

Assignment

Skill Problems
1. $450
3. $2,968.75
5. $6,156
7. $881.11
9. $117.60
11. $1,026
13. $444.72
15. $1,681.02

Business Application Problems

1. $3,910
3. $850
5. $1,453.50
7. $86
9. $1,764
11. $4,888.80
13. $700
15. $739.83

Mastery Test

1. L
2. J
3. E
4. H
5. B
6. C
7. D
8. M

9. N
10. G
11. I
12. A
13. K
14. F
15. $492
16. $640.80
17. $891
18. $733.04
19. $564.48
20. $812.25
21. $501.06
22. $739.31
23. $470.45

Chapter Fourteen
(Pages 303-317)

Exercise A
1. $57,048
2. $1,052.04
3. $19,994.96
4. $396,541.50
5. $14,875
6. $13,629
7. $92,890
8. $344,233.76
9. $56,232.90
10. $2,437,678

Exercise B
1. $2,504.70
2. $3,358.75
3. $5,509.60
4. $3,818
5. $2,943.50
6. $879.60
7. $3,532
8. $4,037.75
9. $2,901.31
10. $4,037.40

Exercise C
1. $1,380
2. $1,170
3. $1,870.50
4. $1,255
5. $274.50
6. $959
7. $815
8. $880
9. $2,212.75
10. $2,440

Assignment

Skill Problems
1. $8,485.40
3. $12,355
5. $47,088.99
7. $3,388.40
9. $3,354
11. $1,046
13. 0
15. $970

Business Application Problems

1. $64
3. $61.20
5. $5,070.12
7. $11,935
9. $5,200
11. $4,500
13. $7,203

Mastery Test

1. T
2. T
3. T
4. F
5. F
6. $23,600
7. $507.20
8. $677.20
9. $32,000
10. $2,250
11. $3,499.20
12. $2,719.04
13. $87.80

Chapter Fifteen
(Pages 319-339)

Exercise A
1. $20, $60
2. $12, $72
3. $35, $135
4. $50, $175
5. $11.16, $59.66

Exercise B
1. $37.50, $187.50
2. $134.62, $384.62
3. $53.33, $133.33
4. $48, $96
5. $10.64, $23.64

Exercise C
1. $99
2. $42
3. $200
4. $365
5. $24
6. $20.30
7. $20
8. $1,131
9. $25.33
10. $153.33

Exercise D
1. $128, $32
2. $35, $15
3. $133.33, $93.33
4. $111.60, $18.60
5. $34.07, $11.93
6. $33.25, $14.25
7. 82, $17.95
8. 31, $20.50
9. $171, $228
10. $228.57, $308.57
11. 140, $28
12. 25, $12
13. 59, $74.50
14. $44.80, $11.20
15. $189, $147

Exercise E
1. $59.50
2. $10.20
3. $30
4. $14.36
5. 41%
6. 43%
7. 38%
8. 31%

Exercise F
1. 29%
2. 33%
3. 43%
4. 100%
5. 44%
6. 23%
7. 67%
8. 17%
9. 31%
10. 25%

Exercise G
1. $117.65
2. $42.74
3. $298.30
4. $95.19
5. $149.40
6. $102.78
7. $120.28
8. $10,000
9. $119.47
10. $180.72

Exercise H
1. $166.01, 6%
2. $720.56, 16%
3. $522.88, 16%
4. $142.48, 20%
5. $339.23, 6%

Assignment

Skill Problems
1. $189, $49
3. 29%, $25
5. $90, $150
7. $115.20, $43.20
9. $57.14, $17.14
11. $50, $58.82
13. $59.80, $63.62
15. $38.40, $48
17. $44.58, 7%

Business Application Problems

1. 56%
3. 11%
5. $10,061.86
7. 89
9. $128.57
11. $96
13. $168,000
15. $1,094,846.10

Mastery Test

1. $65
2. $95
3. $142.86
4. $23.50
5. 140%
6. 43%
7. 67%
8. 33%
9. $746.67
10. $345
11. $258.06
12. $188.96
13. $392
14. $1.91
15. 15%

Chapter Sixteen
(Pages 343-364)

Exercise A
1. 1,728
   1,428
   $383.62
   $1,855.14
2. 1,150
   800
   $1,743.75
   $3,882.25
3. 370
   190
   $6,992
   $6,732.50
4. 2,005
   1,273
   $7,456.60
   $14,245.65

Exercise B
1. $6,720.45
   $11,415.55
2. $264.25
   $22,196.75
3. $1,597.12
   $8,784.13
4. $7,528.51
   $36,701.49

Exercise C
1. $8,608, $17,669
   $1,820.41, $3,738
2. $46,018, $54,351
   $15,910.05, $18,784
3. $80,683, $117,595
   $9,394.77, $13,695
4. $136,062, $221,256
   $122,891.76, $199,824

Exercise D
1. $346,650.41
   $52,117.25
   6.7
2. $90,330.77
   $49,925
   1.8
3. $103,488
   $45,650
   2.3
4. $17,777.78
   $3,616.67
   4.9
5. $15,840
   $5,042
   3.1

Assignment

Skill Problems
1. $46,518.52, $14,431.48
3. $52,656.55, $89,963.45
5. $1,492.60
   $412.80
   $1,509.52
   $395.88
   $1,498.10
   $407.30
7. $1,311.70, $2,341.80
   $112.11, $200.20
9. $95,080, $235,510
   $21,990.84, $54,840
11. 5.1

Business Application Problems

1. $31,928.57
3. $98,678.45
5. $16,153.30
7. $800
9. 1.8

Mastery Test

1. F
2. F
3. T
4. T
5. $185,000
6. $158,455
7. $17,800
8. $39,786
9. $40,189
10. $39,979.77
11. 2.1
12. $192,250, $385,830
    $62,215.14, $124,930
13. 1.0
14. $230,885

Chapter Seventeen
(Pages 367-392)

Exercise A
1. $2,318.33
   $9,273.32
   $21,756.68
2. $650
   $4,550
   $16,207
3. $100
   $300
   $600
4. $3,000
   $6,000
   $46,980
5. $100
   $300
   $825

Exercise B
1. $55,000
2. 7
3. 10
4. $5,000
5. $20,000

Exercise C
1. $586.93, $32,351.40
2. $227.50, $393.25
3. $2,625, $8,980
4. $456, $7,273.20
5. $30.50, $592.60

Exercise D

1. 105, $\frac{12}{105}$

2. 210, $\frac{19}{210}$

3. 91, $\frac{10}{91}$

4. 120, $\frac{10}{120}$

5. 55, $\frac{1}{55}$

Exercise E
1. $2,330.95
   $32,845.24
   $15,654.76
2. $2,137.14
   $9,714.29
   $11,285.71
3. $1,318.75
   $9,890.63
   $5,984.37
4. $287.27
   $7,756.36
   $1,143.64
5. $211.43
   $6,871.43
   $728.57

Exercise F
1. $950
   $2,850
   $950
2. $10,800
   $28,800
   $16,200
3. $2,376.56
   $9,770.31
   $7,129.69
4. $988.15
   $8,020.74
   $1,979.26
5. $6,995.97
   $57,416.13
   $27,983.87

Exercise G
1. $6,960
   $19,720
   $38,280

2. $1,311
   $1,311
   $7,429
3. $3,284.40
   $14,451.36
   $18,392.64
4. $11,910
   $115,130
   $83,370
5. $1,482
   $2,457
   $1,443

Exercise H
1. $96,606.44
2. $1,760
3. $90,644
4. $36,800
5. $183,450

Exercise I
1. $215
2. $208.20
3. $80
4. $70
5. $196.88

Assignment

Skill Problems
1. $325
   $2,600
   $4,400
3. $2,313.33
   $23,133.30
   $12,566.70
5. $1,085
   $2,247.50
   $7,552.50
7. $573.44
   $3,306.24
   $2,293.76
9. $266.67
   $600
   $750
11. $81.43
13. $230.77
15. $933.33
17. $3,339, $9,222, $6,678
19. $447.22

Business Application Problems

1. $5,950
3. $5,385.14
5. $2,866.66
7. $27,000
9. $1,335
11. $3,023.18
13. $420

Mastery Test

1. F
2. J
3. A
4. I
5. K
6. E
7. C
8. D
9. $2,545.45
   $12,363.64
   $8,636.36
10. $6,731.25
    $15,706.25
    $20,193.75
11. $627.50
    $10,667.50
    $1,932.50
12. $8,000
13. $4,930
14. $6,000
15. $183,333.33
16. $6,382.50

Chapter Eighteen
(Pages 395–418)

Exercise A
1. $287.54
2. $2,286
3. 21.5
4. $9,000
5. $1,332.80
6. $491.40
7. $873
8. 1.42
9. $1,908.40
10. $50,000

Exercise B
1. 18.83
2. 15.97
3. 13.70
4. 19.20
5. 26.13
6. 1.29
7. 1.75
8. 1.72
9. 1.33
10. 2.70

Exercise C
1. $2,367
2. $203.47
3. $393.75
4. $119
5. $60.75
6. $1,371
7. $139.80
8. $306
9. $2,526
10. $20.70

Exercise D
1. $24,490, $3,358
2. $25,200, $3,523
3. $28,749, $5,157
4. $25,350, $3,556
5. $28,830, $6,982
6. $27,966, $4,199
7. $28,268, $6,773
8. $25,993, $4,738
9. $24,249, $5,234
10. $25,675, $3,624

Assignment

Skill Problems
1. 49.78
3. 2.15
5. 5.18
7. $1,941.25
9. $1,216.59
11. $3,795
13. $140
15. $19,602
17. $24,879, $5,481
19. $25,439, $5,690

Business Application
Problems

1. $33.90
3. $15,600
5. $718.56
7. Shawl—$42
9. $3,674
11. $5,310.12
13. $226

Mastery Test

1. H
2. E
3. D
4. B
5. G
6. F
7. A
8. $1,628.54
9. $1,170.45
10. $2,894.40
11. $966.90
12. $3,534
13. $5,348
14. $1,218.46

Chapter Nineteen
(Pages 421–437)

Exercise A
1. 45¢, 4.7%
2. 67¢, 6.7%
3. $2.12, 7.0%
4. 11¢, 1.1%
5. 73¢, 9.1%

Exercise B
1. $14.28
2. $15
3. $10
4. $10
5. $30
6. $6.29
7. $12
8. $19.26

Exercise C
1. 8.1%
2. 7.1%
3. 9.8%
4. 6.7%
5. 8.6%

Assignment

Skill Problems
1. 10.1
3. 12.7
5. 11.7
7. 14.0
9. 5.1
11. 5.9
13. 7.6
15. 6.0
17. 7.4
19. 9.0
21. $1.15
23. $7.18
25. $1.65
27. $3.71
29. $12.53

Business Application
Problems

1. 22%
3. Bond return 9.5%
5. Jewelry Business
7. 1.1%
9. $765
11. 38%
13. $2,350

Mastery Test

1. T
2. T
3. F
4. F
5. T
6. 7.2
7. 6.9
8. $4.50
9. 0
10. 29.8%

Chapter Twenty
(Pages 441–458)

Exercise A
Accounts Receivable
($4,930, 79.5%)

Exercise B
Notes Receivable
$2,000, 400%
Accounts Receivable
$5,448, 68.8%

Exercise C
Special Revenue
40.8%, 172.2%

Exercise D
Net Sales
(.5%)

Exercise E
1. 1.5 to 1
2. .94 to 1
3. .34 to 1
4. .05 to 1
5. .08 to 1

Assignment

Skill Problems
1. 10.0%
3. 0%
5. 69.4%
7. .04 to 1
9. 1.88 to 1
11. .02 to 1
13. 2.6%
15. 1.70 to 1
17. .76 to 1
19. .02 to 1

Business Application Problems
1. $82,800
3. $72,544.64
5. $675,000
7. 1.2 to 1

Mastery Test
1. this year, last year
2. Liabilities
3. Income Statement
4. loss
5. acid test
6. Balance Sheet
7. Accounts Payable to Net Purchases Ratio
8. Accounts Receivable to Net Sales Ratio
9. Revenue, Expenses
10. Service, Merchandising
11. 9.1
12. 4.3
13. 2.2
14. 75
15. .03 or 0
16. .03 or 0
17. 4.6
18. 0
19. .1
20. .1

Chapter Twenty-One
(Pages 461–472)

Exercise A
1. 69.6, 58.5, 62
2. 34.5, 25.5, 23
3. 225.3, 226, 120
4. 22.5, 21, 13 & 29
5. 52.9, 49, 42
6. $6.62, $6.80, $6.80 & $7.20
7. $3.95, $3.96, $3.90
8. $11.99, $11.20, $13.80
9. $7.73, $7.75, $8.08
10. $4.61, $4.60, $4.60
11. $9.54, $9.11, $9.30
12. $6.43, $6.38, $7.00 & $6.75 & $6.25 & $6.00
13. $6.06, $6.50, $8.00

Assignment

Skill Problems
1. 19.9, 19, 18
3. 29.2, 30, 31
5. 8.9, 10, 10 & 12
7. 22.3, 24, 26
9. 50.1, 49, 46

Business Application Problems
1. $311.50, $335
3. 806.8, 823, ---, 795.9, 815, 830
5. 43,407, 43,665, 43,900
7. 32.7
9. 25.2

Mastery Test
1. F
2. F
3. T
4. T
5. T
6. T
7. T
8. 9.3, 9, 13
9. $272.50
10. Gwen

Chapter Twenty-Two
(Pages 475–492)

Exercise A
1. Junior Misses 73°
2. Administrative 104°
3. Single family 51°
4. Hiking and Camping Equipment 160°

Assignment

Skill Problems
1. Product A 25°
2. Freshmen 104°

Business Application Problems
2. Transferred 154°
5. 61%

Mastery Test
1. Credit Sales 64°
4. 30's = 158°

**Chapter
Twenty-Three**
(Pages 495–504)

1. 133.63
2. $1\frac{7}{8}$
3. 35
4. $4\frac{1}{3}$
5. 4.694
6. 284.8
7. 3,200
8. $264
9. $4,264
10. $240
11. 5,760 sq. ft.
12. 535.104 sq. meters

13. $75,000
14. $686
15. $1,424.43
16. August 19
17. $1,155
18. $420
19. $500
20. 20%
21. $69.23, $90
22. $6,120
23. $6,290
24. $12,133.33
25. March 16, 1986
26. $3,067.50
27. $7,609.45
28. $7,702.49
29. 45
30. $999.32
31. $35,436.73
32. $7.58

33. $350
34. $580
35. $433.33
36. T
37. $294
38. $186.14
39. $904.80
40. $869
41. 91.9
42. $532.50
43. 6.7
44. 3
45. 6
46. $25,000
47. $8,192.80
48. 9.9%
49. $71,210, $36,125
50. f = 10, 55°

Index

a

Accelerated cost recovery system (A.C.R.S.) method, depreciation, 377–378, 379
Accounts payable to net purchases ratio, 450
Accounts receivable to net sales ratio, 450
Accumulated depreciation, 368
Acid-test ratio, 449
Addition
  decimal numbers, 62
  fractions, 32–33
  horizontal, 8
  whole numbers, 8
Additional trade discounts, 331–332
Adjusted balance, 81
Ad valorem customs duty, 398
Aliquot parts, 510
Amortizing, installment loans, 217
Annual Percentage Rate, 217
  tables, 218–222
Annuities
  annuity date, 256
  annuity due, 260–261
  growth of, 257
  ordinary annuity, 256–257
  tables, 258–259
Assets, balance sheet, 441–442
Auto insurance, 158–159
Average cost method, 352

b

Balance sheet, 441–445
  assets, 441–442
  horizontal analysis, 443
  liabilities, 441–442
  proprietorship, 441, 442
Balloon payment, home mortgages, 229
Banking records
  deposits, 78
  endorsements, 79
    blank endorsement, 79
    restrictive endorsement, 79
    special endorsement, 79
  payments, 79
  reconciliation of bank statement, 80–81
Bar graph, 476–478
Base, percentage, 136
Bearer bonds, 427
Beginning inventory, 343
Beneficiaries, 156
Blank endorsement, 79
Bonds
  bearer bonds, 427
  bond exchange report, 518
  commercial bonds, 427
  debentured bonds, 427
  government bonds, 428
  municipal bonds, 428
  registered bonds, 427
  secured bonds, 427
Book value, 368
Borrowing, 9

c

C.O.D. (cash on delivery), 291
Calculator, operation of, 505–507
Calendar, simple interest, 174
Cash discounts, 281–283, 286
Catalog pricing, 329
  list price, 329
Checks, 79
  outstanding, 80
Circle graph, 475–476
Closing costs, home mortgages, 230
Coinsurance clause, 154
Collision insurance, 159
Commercial bonds, 427
Commission sales, 95
  commission formula, 306
  gross earnings, determining, 305
  gross sales, 303
  net sales, determining, 303–304
  sales allowances, 303
  sales returns, 303
  straight commission, 305
Commodity futures, 428
Common carriers, 287
Common denominators, 33
Common fraction, 28, 38
Common stock, 422
Compound interest
  compounded amount, 248
  savings accounts, 249
  tables, 249–252

Compound rate, customs duty, 401
Comprehensive insurance, 158
Computers, decimal to binary conversion, 511–512
Contract carriers, 287
Cost of goods sold, 343
Cost of Investment, 421
Cost price, 319
Credit cards
    bank cards, 213
    gasoline cards, 212
    minimum payment amount, 213
    monthly statement, 213
    service charges, 216
    store cards, 212
    travel/entertainment cards, 213
Cumulative rights, stocks, 425
Current ratio, 449
Customs duty, 398–401
    ad valorem customs duty, 398
    compound rate, 401
    specific customs duty, 398
    tariff schedules, 399–400

d

Data set, 461, 466
Debentured bonds, 427
Decimal numbers
    addition, 62
    decimal point placement rule, 64
    decimal to a fraction, 134
    decimal to a percent, 134
    division, 65
    fractions changed to, 66
    multiplication, 64
    place values, 57–58
    rounding off, 60–61
    subtraction, 64
Declining-balance method, depreciation, 375–376, 381
Deductions
    federal income tax, 404
    net pay, 97–102
        mandatory, 98–102
        voluntary, 102

Denominator, 28
Dependents, federal income tax, 403
Depletion, 378
Depositor, 77
Deposits, 78
    in transit, 80
Depreciation
    accelerated cost recovery system (A.C.R.S.) method, 377–378, 379
    accumulated depreciation, 368
    book value, 368
    declining-balance method, 375–376, 381
    depletion, 378
    expected life, 367
    market value, 368
    partial year depreciation, 379–383
    salvage value, 368
    straight-line method, 368–371, 380
    sum-of-years'-digits, (S.O.Y.D) method, 372–375, 379, 380
    time line, use of, 380
    total cost, 368
    total depreciation, 368
    units-of-production method, 371–372
Difference, 9
Direct method, trade discounts, 279
Discounts
    cash discounts, 281–283, 286
        net price, 282
        terms of trade, 281
    cash/trade combination, 286
    E.O.M. (end of month) stipulation, 284
    R.O.G. (receipt of goods), 285
    trade discounts, 277–279, 286
        direct method, 279
        equivalent trade discount, 280
        selling price, finding, 277
    transportation charges, 287, 289, 291
        C.O.D. (cash on delivery), 291
        F.O.B. (free on board), 287, 289
Dividend
    in division, 13
    stocks, 422–424
Division
    checking, 15–16
    decimal numbers, 65
    fractions, 41
    long division, 14
    remainder, 14
    whole numbers, 13–14
Divisor, 13
Down payments, 223

e

E.O.M. (end of month) stipulation, discounts, 284
Early payment penalties, home mortgages, 231
Employment math test, 513–516
Ending inventory, 343
Endorsements, 79
Endowment life, 157
Equivalent trade discount, 280
Escrow account, home mortgages, 230
Exact interest, 178
Exemption, federal income tax, 403–404
Expected life, 367

f

F.I.F.O. method, 349–351
F.O.B. (free on board), 287, 289
    F.O.B. destination, 287, 289
    F.O.B. shipping point, 289
Face Value, promissory notes, 191
Federal income tax, 403–410
    deductions, 404
    dependents, 403
    determination of, 409
    exemption, 403–404
    taxable income, 403
    zero bracket amount, 404
Financial statement analysis
    balance sheet, 441–445
    income statement, 445–448
    ratios, 449–451
    See also specific statements.
Fire insurance, 154
Fixed payment amount, 229
Fixed rate, 229
Form W-4, 98
Four-step process, percentage, 138
Fractional percent, 135
Fractions
    addition, 32–33
    changed to decimal numbers, 66
    common denominators, 33
    common fraction, 28, 38
    decimal to a fraction, 134
    denominator, 28
    division, 41
    improper fraction, 28, 29
    interchanging fraction types, 29
    lowest common denominator (LCD), 33
    mixed numbers, 28, 36, 42
    multiplication, 38–40
    numerator, 28
    percent to a fraction, 134
    reducing fractions, 31
    subtraction, 35

g

Goods available for sale, 343
Government bonds, 428
Graphs
    bar graph, 476–478
    circle graph, 475–476
    line graph, 478
Gross earnings, 95–97
    determining, 305
Gross sales, 303

h

Home mortgages
    balloon payment, 229
    closing costs, 230
    early payment penalties, 231
    escrow account, 230
    interest rates, 227, 229
        fixed payment amount, 229
        fixed rate, 229
        variable payment amount, 229
        variable rate, 229
    maximum monthly cost, 227
    points, 229
    Rule of 78s, 232
Horizontal analysis, balance sheet, 443
Hourly rate, 96

i

Imprinting checks, 77
Improper fraction, 28, 29
Income statement, 445–448
    expenses, 445
    for merchandising firm, 448
    revenue, 445
    for service firm, 446–447
Installment loans
    amortizing, 217
    Annual Percentage Rate, 217
        tables, 218–222
    down payments, 223
    monthly payment tables, 224
    payment amount, 225
    principal balance, computing, 225
    Regulation Z, 217
    repayment schedule, 225
    total interest on loan, computing, 233
    See also Home mortgages.
Insurance
    auto insurance
        collision insurance, 159
        comprehensive insurance, 158
        property damage insurance,
            158–159

life insurance
    beneficiaries, 156
    endowment life, 157
    limited pay life, 156
    straight life, 156
    term life, 156
    policy, 154
    premiums, 154
    property insurance, 154
    fire insurance, 154
Interest
    interest-bearing rate, 192
    interest rates, 227, 229
    See also Compound interest; Simple
        interest.
Inventory
    beginning inventory, 343
    cost of goods sold, 343
    ending inventory, 343
    goods available for sale, 343
    purchases, 343
    valuation of
        average cost method, 352
        F.I.F.O. method, 349–351
        L.I.F.O. method, 345–349
        retail inventory estimating method,
        354
        specific identification method, 355
        turnover, 356
Investments
    bonds, 426–429
    commodity futures, 428
    cost of investment, 421
    inflation, effect of, 422
    liquidity, 421
    rate of return, 422
    real estate, 428
    risk, 421
    stocks, 422–426
    See also Bonds; Stocks.

jk

l

L.I.F.O. method, 345–349
Leap year, simple interest, 174
Liabilities, balance sheet, 441–442
Life insurance, 156–157
Limited pay life, 156
Linear measure, 116, 122
Line graph, 478
Liquidity, investments, 421
List price, 329
Lowest common denominator (LCD), 33

m

Maker, promissory notes, 191
Markdown, 322, 326–327
Market value, 368
Markup
    additional trade discounts, 331–332
    catalog pricing, 329
    on cost, 320
    cost, sales, markup, markdown,
        calculating, 322
    cost price, 319
    list price, 329
    markdown, 322, 326–327
    markup rate, conversion of, 327
    on sales, 321
    selling price, 319
Maturity value, promissory notes, 192
Mean, 462
Measurements
    conversion tables, 122–123
    linear measure, 116, 122
    measurements table, 116
    metric system, 120–121
    surface measure, 118
    volume measure, 119
Median, 462–463
Metric system, 120–121
Minuend, 9
Mixed numbers, 28, 36, 42
Mode, 463
Monthly payment tables, installment loans,
    224
Multiplicand, 11
Multiplication
    checking, 15–16
    decimal numbers, 64
    fractions, 38–40
    by (ten) 10, 100, 1000 etc., 12
    whole numbers, 11–12
Multiplier, 11
Municipal bonds, 428

n

Net income to net sales ratio, 450
Net pay
    deductions, 97–102
        exemptions, 98
        mandatory, 98–102
        voluntary, 102
Net price, cash discounts, 282
Net sales, determining, 303–304
Noninterest-bearing rate, 192
Numerator, 28

o

Ordinary annuity, 256–257
  tables, 258–259
Ordinary interest, 178
Outstanding checks, 80
Overtime, 96

p

Partial year depreciation, 379–383
Participating, stocks, 424
Payee, promissory notes, 191
Payment amount, installment loans, 225
Payroll
  employers' payroll taxes, 104
  gross earnings, determining, 95–97
  net pay, determining, 97–103
  overtime, 96
  pay systems
    commissions, 95
    hourly rate, 96
    piece-rate, 95
    salary, 95
Percent
  decimal to a fraction, 134
  decimal to a percent, 134
  percent to a decimal, 134
  percent to a fraction, 134
Percentage
  base, 136
  definition of, 136
  four-step process, 138
  fractional percent, 135
  increases/decreases, 139
  rate, 136
Piece-rate, 95
Place values, 3, 57–58
Points, home mortgages, 229
Policy, insurance, 154
Preferred stock, 422
Premiums, insurance, 154
Present value, 252–255
  tables, 253–254
Prime numbers, as divisors, 31
Principal balance, computing, 225
Principal, computing, 198
Proceeds, computing, discounting, 193
Product, 11

Promissory notes
  discounts, 193
    computing discount, 193
    computing proceeds, 193
    discount amount, 193
    discount rate, 193
    term of discount, 193
  face value, 191
  interest, computations, 198
  interest-bearing rate, 192
  maker, 191
  maturity value, 192
  noninterest-bearing rate, 192
  payee, 191
  term of note, 191
Property insurance, 154–155
  damage insurance, 158–159
Property taxes, 395–397
  assessed valuation, 395
  tax rate
    determining, 397
    mills, 395
Proprietorship, balance sheet, 441, 442
Purchases, 343

q

Quotient, 13

r

R.O.G. (receipt of goods), discounts, 285
Rate
  computing, 198
  percentage, 136
Ratios, 44, 449–451
  accounts payable to net purchases
    ratio, 450
  accounts receivable to net sales ratio,
    450
  acid-test ratio, 449
  current ratio, 449
  fractions, 44
  net income to net sales ratio, 450
Real estate, 428
Reconciliation of bank statement, 80–81
Reducing fractions, 31
Registered bonds, 427
Regulation Z, 217
Remainder, division, 14
Repayment schedule, installment loans, 225
Restrictive endorsement, 79
Retail inventory estimating method, 354

Risk, investments, 421
Rounding off, 6–7
  decimal numbers, 60–61
  whole numbers, 6–7
Rule of 78s, home mortgages, 232

s

Salary, 95
Sales. See Commission sales
Sales allowances, 303
Sales returns, 303
Sales tax, 402
  tax table, 402
Salvage value, 368
Secured bonds, 427
Selling price, 319
Service charges, 80
Simple interest
  calendar, 174
  exact interest, 178
  formula for computing, 178
  leap year, 174
  ordinary interest, 178
  principal, 173, 178
    computing, 198
  rate, 173, 178
    computing, 198
  short cut in computation, 508–509
  time, 173
    computing, 198
  time table, 175
Sinking funds
  compared to annuity, 262
  payment amount, computing, 263
  tables, 264–265
Social Security tax, 100–101
Special endorsement, 79
Specific customs duty, 398
Specific identification method, 355
Statistics
  data set, 461, 466
  mean, 462
  median, 462–463
  mode, 463
Stocks, 422–426
  common stock, 422
  cumulative rights, 425
  dividends, 422–424
  market quotations, reading, 517
  participating, 424
    preferred stock, 422

Straight commission, 305
Straight life, 156
Straight-line method, depreciation,
     368–371, 380
Subtraction
    borrowing, 9
    checking, 10
    decimal numbers, 64
    fractions, 35
    whole numbers, 8–9
Subtrahend, 9
Sum-of-years'-digits (S.O.Y.D.) method,
     depreciation, 372–375, 379, 380
Surface measure, 118

t

Tariff schedules, 399–400
Taxable base, 100
Taxable income, 403
Taxes
    customs duty, 398–401
    employers' payroll taxes, 104
    federal income tax, 403–410
    from net pay, 97–102
    property taxes, 395–397
    sales tax, 402
    See also specific taxes.
Term life, 156
Term of note, promissory notes, 191
Terms of trade, cash discounts, 281
Time, computing, 198
Time card, 96
Time line, use of, 380
Time table, simple interest, 175
Total cost, depreciation, 368
Total depreciation, 368
Trade discounts, 277–279, 286
    additional trade discounts, 331–332
    catalog pricing, 329
Transportation charges, discounts, 287,
     289, 291
Transportation firms
    common carriers, 287
    contract carriers, 287
Turnover, 356

u

Units-of-production method, depreciation,
    371–372

v

Valuation. *See* Inventory valuation
Variable payment amount, 229
Variable rate, 229
Volume measure, 119

w

Whole numbers, 3
    addition, 8
    division, 13–14
    multiplication, 11–12
    place values, 3
    rounding off, 6–7
    subtraction, 8–9

xy

z

Zero bracket amount, 404